EB

INDIAN EMBERS
LADY LAWRENCE

T0204554

By the same author (Rosamond Napier)

Bitter-Sweet

The Heart of a Gypsy

Tamsy

Letters to Patty

Release

Conversations in Heaven

Alpine Episode

INDIAN EMBERS

LADY LAWRENCE

Introduction by
Kenneth Wimmel

"Only stay quiet while my mind remembers
The beauty of fire from the beauty of embers."

JOHN MASEFIELD

Trackless Sands Press
Palo Alto

Published in the United States by
Trackless Sands Press
Palo Alto, California

Printed on acid-free paper
Manufactured in the United States of America

Library of Congress Cataloging-in-Publication Data

Lawrence, Lady, 1878–1976
Indian Embers / by Lady Lawrence
p. cm.
Reprint. Originally published: Oxford: George Ronald, 1949.
ISBN 1-879434-03-2 : $22.95 — ISBN 1-879434-02-4 (pbk.): $13.95
1. British—India—Social life and customs. 2. India—Description and travel—1901–1946. 3. Civil service—India.
DS428.L3 1991
954.03'5—dc20 91–18463
CIP

TO

HENRY

"I shall go to him, but he shall not return to me."

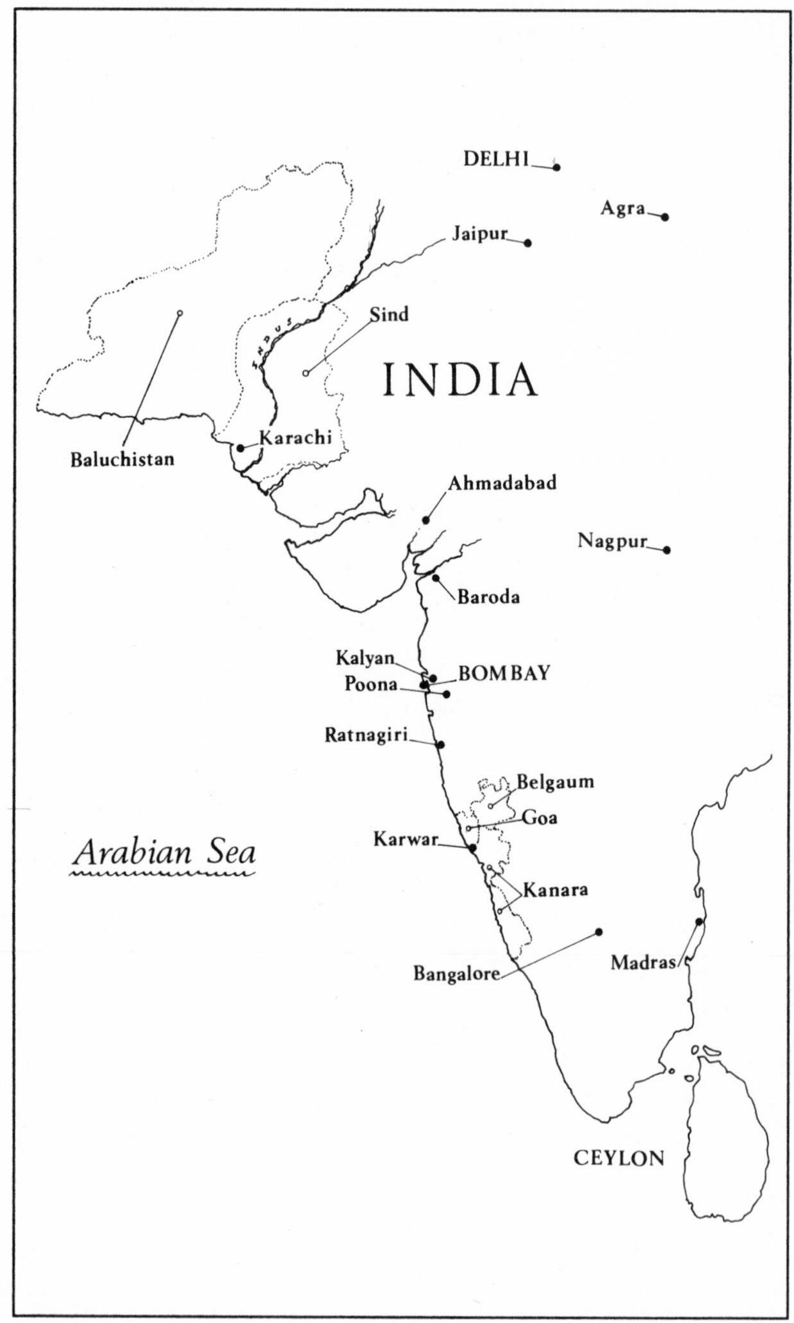
DELHI
Agra
Jaipur
Sind
INDUS
INDIA
Karachi
Baluchistan
Ahmadabad
Nagpur
Baroda
Kalyan
BOMBAY
Poona
Ratnagiri
Belgaum
Goa
Karwar
Arabian Sea
Kanara
Bangalore
Madras
CEYLON

CONTENTS

INTRODUCTION

Kenneth Wimmel

THE British Raj in India produced, among other things, a plethora of published memoirs, diaries, and collections of letters. During the 190 years of British ascendancy in the subcontinent between, roughly, 1757 and 1947, the British population resident in India at any given time was a tiny fraction of the total population, but many of those few empire builders wrote about their experiences. Published accounts of personal experiences began to appear soon after the British became established—Warren Hastings, the first governor-general, wrote his memoirs aboard ship on his way home in 1785—and they proliferated in the late nineteenth and early twentieth centuries. They continued to appear for years after the Raj officially ended.

Most of those books have been long out of print and have sunk into deserved obscurity, because not all of the writers lived lives of adventure on the northwest frontier or of romance in exotic locales. Many lived humdrum lives as merchants or engineers or clerks in cities or small towns. Even the soldiers often led lives marked mainly by long spells of boredom and discomfort, as Winston Churchill describes in *My Early Life.* Moreover, few of those people had the literary skill of a Winston Churchill to make their experiences come alive for a reader. Their accounts may be useful for the scholar or historian, but they make dull fare for the general reader.

A few published memoirs and diaries have survived to be reprinted and read years after their initial publication by those of us interested in learning about ways of life far removed in time and place from our own. They have survived because they are well written and give firsthand accounts of exciting or significant events. For example, Emily Eden's letters, written during the governor-generalship of her brother, Lord Auckland, in the 1830s and 1840s have been published as *Up the Country* and portray a period of British confidence and expansion. They include a riveting eyewitness account of a visit to the court of Ranjit Singh, the larger-than-life ruler of Punjab. Lord Roberts's memoirs, *Forty-One Years in India,* which gives gripping firsthand accounts of major events during two times of battle, the Great Mutiny of 1857–58 and the second Afghan War in 1879, is deservedly considered a classic. Of more recent origin is Philip Mason's *A Shaft of Sunlight,* an account of life as a member of the Indian Civil Service during the last twenty years of the Raj. Novelist John Masters's *Bugles and a Tiger* tells what life was like on the north-west frontier for a young British officer in the Indian army during the years just prior to World War II. Among others still worth reading are John Beame's *Memoirs of a Bengal Civilian,* Francis Yeats-Brown's *The Lives of a Bengal Lancer,* and E. M. Forster's *The Hill of Devi.*

Lady Lawrence's *Indian Embers,* long out of print, deserves to be lifted from its unmerited obscurity and placed on the shelf beside these other still-popular accounts. Part diary and part memoir, it bears the mark of an accomplished writer who knew how to winnow out the telling scene or revealing anecdote from a mass of material and bring it to life. The book was published in 1949, long after the events it describes took place. Despite its artistic excellence, it apparently attracted little attention at the time, probably because the timing of its publication was unfortunate. Indian independence had been granted only two years earlier, and there was little interest in reading about life during the Raj. The British wanted to put that behind them and get on with rebuilding a country shattered by World War II and with facing up to shedding an empire.

Twenty-five years later, with the empire gone, attitudes had changed. The British Broadcasting Corporation, realizing that the number of men and women with firsthand recollections of life during the Raj was inevitably dwindling, broadcast a series of oral history programs drawing upon the recorded recollections of men and women who had lived and worked in India before 1947. Lady Lawrence was one of them. Nostalgia for a bygone time and way of life had set in. The radio series became a best-selling book, *Plain Tales from the Raj,* that has gone through several printings since its publication in 1976. Now, Lady Lawrence's own full account of her life in India is, at long last, again available, more than forty years after its publication and seventy-five years after the events it depicts.

Jane Rosamond Napier was already a published author with several well-received books to her credit when she married Henry Lawrence in 1914 and set sail with him for India. She was his second wife and was probably more widely known than her husband. She was a mature woman of thirty-six, and her interest in India went beyond mere curiosity about the exotic East. She was proud of her family's long and distinguished connection with the country. She explains in her book the significance surrounding the marriage of a Lawrence with a Napier, two family names that resound through the history of nineteenth-century British India.

Although Lady Lawrence does not write primarily of large historical or political events—one is only intermittently reminded that World War I is occurring—the twelve years of her residence in India was a time of significant transition for the Raj, and the background lends increased interest to the account. When she arrived in India in 1914, British authority and confidence were still strong, although perhaps not quite so strong as they had been three years earlier when King George V, the only sitting British monarch to visit India before independence, was crowned King-Emperor at a great durbar in Delhi. By 1926, when her husband's career as a member of the Indian Civil Service (ICS) ended, it was obvious to everyone that the Raj's days were numbered. Philip Mason, who joined the ICS three years later, has explained that he did not expect to fulfill his father's ambition that he become a governor of an Indian province, even if he had the right combination of luck and ability to reach that exalted rank, because he did not expect the Raj to last long enough for him to do so.

By the time he retired, Sir Henry Lawrence had risen to senior levels in the ICS and had served as governor of Bombay, but Lady

Lawrence prefers to focus on their earlier life until 1919 when her husband was a district officer. British society in India was rigidly hierarchical. In a curious way it paralleled the Hindu caste system. At the top of the social pyramid were the members of the Indian Civil Service, often called the heaven-born or twice-born after the Brahmins, the highest Hindu caste. It was an elite service entered by competitive examination. The ICS was called the "steel frame" of the British administration. An ICS officer might serve for years on end in a particular district or region, so he became intimately acquainted with it and the people who lived in it. He spoke the local language fluently (he had to, in order to carry out his duties, which he took very seriously). With a small staff of mixed Indians and British, he represented the government to millions of people within his district. The Indian Civil Service was accurately described as the best civil service in the world. Indians had been admitted to the service through the examination since shortly after the Great Mutiny in the nineteenth century, but the number grew as independence loomed ever closer. Between 1920 and 1925, the number of Indian officers doubled.

The life of an ICS officer in a district, as seen through the eyes of Rosamond Lawrence circa 1914, had not changed in its general outline in fifty years or more, and in the more remote districts it would remain pretty much as she describes it until independence, as Philip Mason's memoirs attest. The high point of the year was the cold-weather tour, when the officer traveled throughout his district to hold court, render judgments, supervise the construction of public works, inspect institutions of education and public health, consult with forestry officers about conservation of wildlife and protection of the environment (yes, those were concerns of ICS officers that long ago), and carry out a host of other official duties. It was a time of long days crammed with intense activity that put the officer in close, direct touch with the people he governed. It was lived on horseback during the day and under canvas at night, and was later remembered with intense pleasure by those who experienced it. The hot weather, by contrast, was a time of tedium and discomfort and perhaps of family separation; many wives and children retreated to cool hill stations and left their husbands and fathers to swelter in the plains. Rosamond Lawrence accompanied her husband on many of his tours and stuck out the hot weather with him.

Henry Lawrence is always in the background of his wife's account, but seldom comes to the forefront, because the book describes her life in India, her observations and experience, not his. The changes she observes over the course of the five years covered by the book, 1914 to 1919, reflect in microcosm the larger changes that occurred in Britain's relations with India during that period. When she arrived in 1914, relations between Britons and Indians were cordial, and the onset of the war that was about to erupt made them even more so. "The outbreak of the war in August 1914," wrote Sir Percival Spear, "called forth an outburst of loyal sentiment among both the political classes and the princes ... in this atmosphere of goodwill, 1,200,000 men, 800,000 of whom were combatants, were recruited, 100 million pounds were given outright to Britain for the prosecution of the war, and 20–30 million contributed annually" (*Oxford History of Modern India, 1740–1947* [Oxford: Oxford University Press, 1965], 335).

By the time the book ends, and the Lawrences depart on home leave, the protracted war had produced sharp changes. "By the end of the war," Spear wrote, "India was as war-weary, restless, and irritable as Britain itself" (ibid., 336). Mohandas Gandhi had arrived from South Africa to mobilize the masses for independence. The Jallianwalla Bagh massacre in Amritsar in April 1919 had poisoned relations between rulers and ruled, and unrest, fueled by resentment against British colonial rule, had spread among the rural masses. The Lawrences had taken to sleeping with revolvers beside their beds, in fear for their lives. Though the Indian National Congress would not embrace total independence as an official goal until 1929, the independence movement had actually begun in earnest when *Indian Embers* ends.

After his retirement, Sir Henry Lawrence remained involved in Indian affairs, notably the discussions that led up the landmark 1935 India Government Act. He died in 1949 just as *Indian Embers* was going to press. Lady Lawrence died in 1976, at the advanced age of ninety-seven. She thus lived to witness changes in both Britain and India that must have been unimaginable when she arrived in Belgaum on the eve of World War I.

I first arrived in India in 1963 as a junior American foreign service officer. Jawaharlal Nehru was the prime minister, a link with preindependent India. New Delhi had only just begun the expansion that today has spread housing developments to areas that were remote paddy fields and scrub hills then. One drove out from the city to the Kutub Minar in the great tower of medieval Delhi, the Kutab Minra, through several miles of farmland and rural villages; now, the road is lined on both sides by blocks of concrete flats that extend right up to the grounds of the monument. Living links with preindependent India and the Raj were fast disappearing, but some still existed. One could still encounter sophisticated, well-read old gentlemen here and there who were proud to explain that they had been members of the "old" ICS of preindependent India (which most of them compared with the postindependence civil service to the latter's disadvantage).

I recall visiting Benares soon after I arrived and being invited by the maharajah to witness the traditional activities associated with the Hindu festival of Dussehra. We departed the city at dusk and crossed the Ganges in country boats. We were met on the opposite shore by a torchlight procession. We climbed the bank to the accompaniment of gongs and drums and cymbals to a spot where three elephants stood waiting. In a magnificent howdah on the back of the largest elephant, a shadowy figure sat in an attitude of prayer. We boarded the other elephants and set off down a country lane in flickering torchlight with chanting throngs accompanying us on both sides of the road. We asked the old mahout if the man on the lead elephant was the maharajah. "Yes," he replied, "that is maharajah. Poor maharajah down to last three elephants." Of course, the maharajah or his descendant is presumably even poorer now, his traditional privileges and government subsidy having been cut off during the 1970s.

I remember visiting Meerut for a few days, where I stayed at the officers' club in the military cantonment. The officers drifted into the bar in the evening for a drink before dinner. They divided into two distinct groups at opposite ends of the bar, with the more senior majors and colonels at one end and the younger lieutenants and captains at the other. I came to realize that the division was not caused by rank alone. The older, more senior officers had begun their careers in the old preindependence Indian army, so they shared an experience their younger colleagues had not had. I heard snatches of conversation at their end of the bar about a visit to England for a reunion with some of their former, now retired, British colleagues, and apparently plans were being made to welcome a group of former British officers who were planning a visit to India to see their old comrades. I imagine the atmosphere in the club is rather different now, and the conversation around the bar has changed over the intervening twenty-five years.

Those living links with the Raj in India have all but disappeared completely. What remains of it is confined to museums like the Victoria Memorial in Calcutta, where one can see busts of such legendary figures as Robert Clive, Arthur Wellesley, and Henry Lawrence (he of mutiny fame, not Rosamond's husband) and where statues of Queen Victoria, James Outram, Lord Curzon, and King Edward VII still grace the memorial's grounds. The many statues of other heroes of the Raj that used to be found all over the city were pulled down years ago and now lie stored in dusty ignominy in Barrackpore. Traces of the Raj can also be found in a few churches like St. John's in Calcutta, where marble memorial plaques to departed friends and loved ones, some two hundred years old, dot the walls. In the churchyard stands the tomb of Job Charnock, the seventeenth-century founder of Calcutta, and, according to tradition, of his Indian wife, whom he married after rescuing her from a widow's funeral pyre.

The passing of the last generation in Britain and India who knew the Raj firsthand has loosened the strong bonds of mutual affection and respect that were forged between so many Britons and Indians of that and earlier generations. But its passing has also had its beneficial aspect. New generations who have known only independent India do not feel the enmities and resentments that were also an inevitable product of colonial rule. The British period of Indian history can now be examined dispassionately in both countries by people whose judgment is not clouded by personal and partisan animosities and prejudices. Those who would seek better relations between the developed and the developing worlds during the years and decades that lie ahead could do worse than examine the lessons of the British period in India. That period is now being reexamined and reevaluated, and the lessons it holds for both sides are being sought.

Books like *Indian Embers* are valuable sources to be mined in this process. The battles and historical movements of peoples that defined the creation of the Raj and the political negotiations about independence that marked its last years must, of course, be studied. But the myriad daily interactions of people of different backgrounds and cultures in their everyday lives, as depicted by Lady Lawrence and other memoirists of the Raj, may hold even more important lessons for us today. One need not, however, have such a utilitarian purpose in mind to read *Indian Embers* with profit and pleasure. Anyone interested in a gracefully written account of how some interesting people once lived in a fascinating corner of the world—a portrait of a way of life now long past—will find it absorbing and entertaining.

Washington, D.C.
December, 1990

NAPIERS AND LAWRENCES

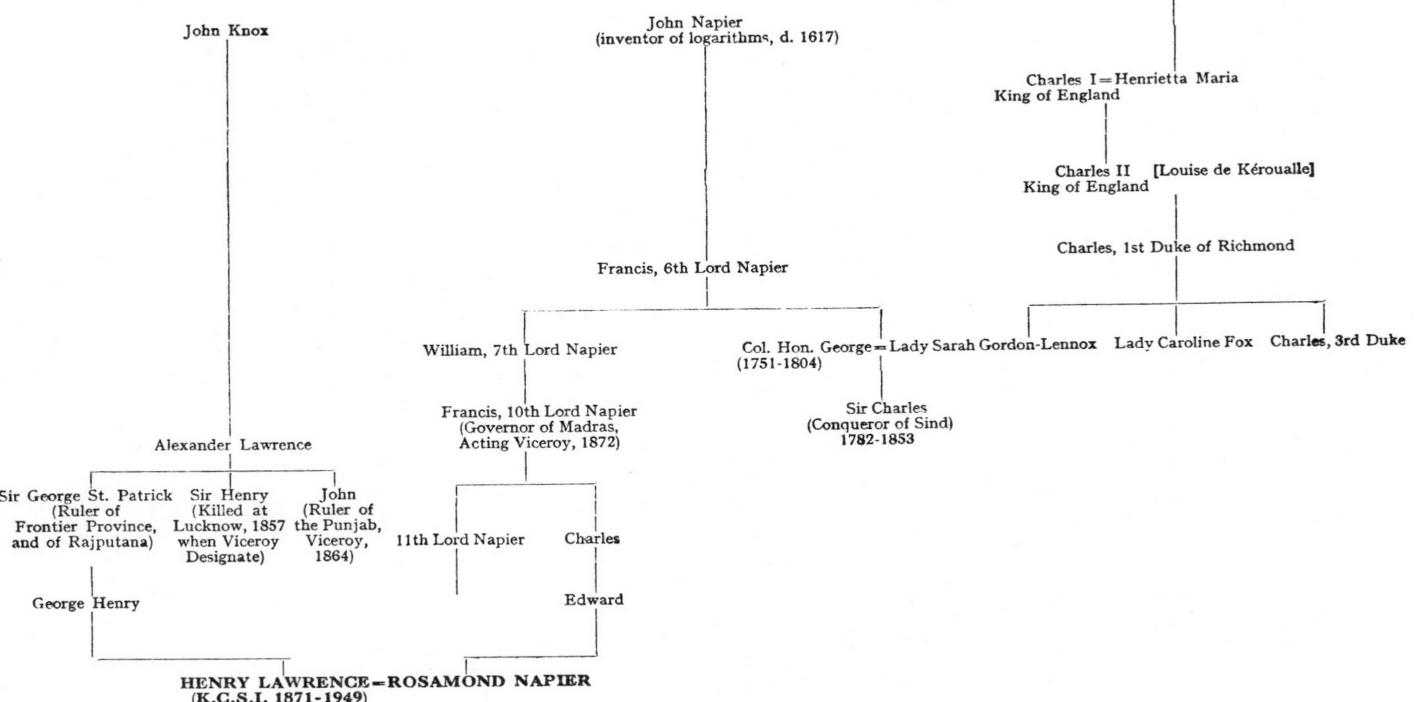

NAPIERS AND LAWRENCES.

NOW that the British have left India these pages may be of interest for the picture they give, not of political strife, but of those equally true days when the District Officer was regarded by millions of Indians as his "Ma-Bap", his Mother-Father.

When in 1914 I first went out it did not seem going to a strange country, for the forbears of both my husband and myself had been servants of India—Ma-Bap—for close on one hundred and twenty years in military, political or forest spheres.

In the mutiny of 1857 at the siege of Lucknow, my husband's father was wounded by a fragment of the shell which killed his uncle Sir Henry Lawrence. Sir Henry's elder brother George had been a hostage with Akbar Khan in the first Afghan war, and John the youngest brother but one was to be known as the Saviour of India, and become Viceroy. The father of these three brothers, Alexander, had gone to serve in India in the King's Regiment in 1792, and had been left for dead at the storming of Seringapatam in 1799. *His* three elder brothers had migrated from Ireland to America in the early seventies to escape the commercial policy of London which provoked the American War of Independence.

My own relations with India reach back to Sir Charles Napier, Conqueror of Sind.

Lord Napier (Francis) was Governor of Madras in 1866-72 and after acted as Viceroy for some months.

My first station was Belgaum, in the Province of Bombay. My father had been there as a young cavalry officer shortly after the Mutiny, and one of my brothers followed him as Forest Officer fifty years later. In 1916 my husband and myself left Belgaum to take up life at Government House, Karachi, which had been built by Sir Charles Napier, and bears a plaque upon its walls to say so.

Lawrence and Napier. Such was our common background.

Sir Charles was the eldest son of that bewitching Lady Sarah Lennox, talk and toast of London. After her father, the second Duke of Richmond died, she left Dublin to live with her sister, Lady Caroline Fox, at Holland House, where Charles James Fox was her close companion. The two sisters, Caroline and Sarah, were the great-grand-daughters of Charles II, and through Henrietta Maria, wife of Charles I, could trace their ancestry back to Henry IV of France. Sarah, in particular, was provokingly attractive and beautiful. As a little girl she was petted and teased by George II, and later George III fell passionately in love with her and proposed marriage. But it was not till after sundry matrimonial adventures that Lady Sarah settled down to the love of her life, the impecunious Colonel George Napier, who however was of no mean birth himself, being descended from the sister of the great Montrose. It was of three of the sons of this most devoted couple, Lady Sarah and Colonel the Honourable George Napier, that the Duke of Wellington found time in the midst of the arduous campaign of the Peninsula War to write at different times long descriptions of their bravery and wounds:

> "Your ladyship has so often read accounts of the same description with which I am now writing to you, and your feelings on the subject are so just and proper that it is needless to trouble you further. Your sons are brave fellows, and an honour to the Army, and I hope that God will preserve them to you and their country."

This is an extract from March 16th, 1811. On January 20th, 1812 comes another long letter in which the Duke writes:

> "Having such sons I am aware you expect to hear of these misfortunes which I have more than once had to communicate to you . . . Under such circumstances I perform the task which I have taken upon myself with less reluctance hoping at the same time that this will be the last occasion on which I shall have to address you on such a subject, and that your brave sons will be spared to you . . . I have the honour to remain, Yours, etc., Wellington."

Again it is of these three sons that Sir John Fortescue wrote:

> "It is not common in the British Army or I should imagine in any other Army for three brothers to enter a military career practically together, to distinguish themselves by signal valour as regimental officers, not without severe and grievous wounds, to

rise to general's rank, to hold one and all administrative offices of greater or lesser importance, and to leave two of them a mark upon English history, the one as a military reformer, and successful commander in the field, Sir Charles, and the other as a writer of genius, whose best work has earned a permanent place in English literature . . . yet this is the record of the three brothers Napier, Charles, George and Sir William, historian."

So much for my family.

Now the brothers Lawrence living at the same time were no less remarkable, and are far better known to the public.

When I first became engaged many were the remarks, "How suitable! The two famous Indian families. A Napier marrying a Lawrence". I said nothing, for my father had frequently told me how the families disagreed. What he had said in the forcible language of his day was, "Lawrences and Napiers quarrelled like hell. The Lawrences were always a d— psalm-singing lot . . . "

It is true that Sir Charles did admit "Colonel George Lawrence is a right good fellow, and a right good soldier" but of Henry he said acidly, "The knowledge of his profession appears to be much lower than his rank".

Yes. I said nothing. Just hoped for the best. For in both families there had been wonderful lovers. Sir Henry had waited nine years for his Honoria, and their absorbed devotion never faltered. John, the harder and more practical of the brothers wrote at the end of his Viceroyalty: "In August, 1841 I took, perhaps, the most important, and certainly the happiest step in my life—in getting married. My wife has been to me everything that a man could wish or hope for". And one day when looking up from his book he enquired "Where's Mother?" His daughter replied she had gone upstairs. A few minutes later he asked her again, and a little later yet again. Whereupon his sister Letitia broke in "Why really John it would seem as though you could not get on for five minutes without your wife". "That's why I married her", said John.

These brothers had all come from Inishowen, in Northern Ireland, and so had their brides. My Henry came from the same spot, and in Inishowen we became engaged.

Then too on my side love matches were famous, beginning with Lord March, the grandson of Charles II. He was brought from college to be married to cancel a gambling debt. His wife to be, poor scrap, was brought down from the nursery in tears. "You are not going to marry me to that dowdy?" exclaimed the lad in disgust. But married he was, and then his tutor took him straight away to the continent to finish his education. After three years the boy returned, and that first night instead of joining his wife he hurried off to the theatre. There he sees an exquisite young creature, and eagerly enquiring her name is told "Why the reigning Toast. The beautiful Lady March".

This fairy-like tale ended as fairy tales should. How constantly Horace Walpole refers to the passionate and enduring love of these two! She was said to have been with child no less than twenty-seven times, and yet to the very end retained her beauty.

In her turn her daughter, Lady Sarah, idolised her impecunious Colonel Napier, as he his lovely wife.

Their eldest son Sir Charles, Conqueror of Sind, was another great lover. When Governor of Cephalonia in the Mediterranean he bestowed all the fire and tenderness in his nature on a beautiful Greek. She refused to marry him even after the birth of her two daughters, declaring that so perfect a love as theirs could only be spoiled by a formal bond, at least so goes the family tradition. Charles was to marry twice, women far older than himself whom he regarded with much affection and tenderness. On May 20th, 1847, when he was sixty-five, he writes in his journal:

> "My first wife's birthday. For years it was one of pleasure to me, and now that the dream of life, now that all life's dramatic scenes have passed away, and my own existence is fast ebbing, this day still brings brightness to my mind".

And four years later when he is sixty-nine:

> "This is my first wife's birthday. It never arrives without lowness for me, and deep reflections on the folly of ever being possible to be happy in this life, which fact is to me a proof that there is another life".

Sixty-one years after he wrote that, I myself met Cephalonia's great-grand daughters.[1] They had reached the gawky school girl age, but even so in those intelligent and intensely spiritual faces, those beaming almond eyes, I could guess at the charm which had captured Charles.

Yes. Napiers and Lawrences had snarled at each other in India and at home, but both families had bred grand lovers. Henry and I risked it . . . and now, after thirty-five years can say we have never regretted it.

It was after the Chillianwallah disaster that Sir Charles Napier, who had returned home after the conquest of Sind, was sent back to India by the Duke of Wellington. The Duke when asked which of three generals should go had replied:

1. Sir Charles Napier
2. Sir Charles Napier
3. Sir Charles Napier.

When Sir Charles demurred to the Duke at returning to India on account of his age, his wounds and many enemies, the Duke exclaimed: "Pooh, pooh, pooh. Enemies. Don't care for enemies. Pooh, pooh, pooh. If you don't go I must".

Just before that time Sir Henry Lawrence, my husband's great-uncle, had been ruling in the Punjab. No sooner had Sir Charles arrived in India as Commander-in-Chief than he hurried up, and after one short interview condemned the whole system devised and so successfully run by Sir Henry! It is hardly surprising therefore that when the time came for Sir Charles to hand in his resignation after a row with Lord Dalhousie, the Governor-General, that we find Sir Henry writing: "We shall be well rid of him. His natural arrogance has been so increased by the circumstances of his return to India that there is no holding him. To us in the Punjab he has become a greater hindrance than all the ex-chiefs and rebels".

And yet? These two families, Lawrence and Napier, quarrel though they did, were alike under their skins. Both George Lawrence and George Napier contented themselves to stand aside and let their brothers take the lime-light. Then Charles Napier and Henry

[1] Daughters of Charles Doughty, author of *Arabia Deserta*.

Lawrence were one in their zeal to help the under-dog in days when not so much attention was paid to him as now. They were alike too in their brilliant fighting qualities, their administrative abilities, their amazing capacity for work, their austere tastes, and above all in the worship they inspired in those who served under them.

We find a young officer serving under Sir Charles writing: "When I see that old man incessantly on his horse, how can I be idle who am young and strong? By God, I would go into a loaded cannon's mouth if he ordered me to."

And one of Sir Henry's young men wrote of him: "In times of difficulty and danger his confidence seemed almost an inspiration . . . it kindled a glow in all those who came within its influence", and when Sir Henry quarrelling in his turn with the Governor-General left the Punjab, "The Punjab is a watch with the main-spring broken".

In fact these two men, Lawrence and Napier, with their perpetual rows with authority, their grievances, their sense of frustration were strangely alike in that both were "dented all over with defeat and disapproval" though apparently so successful.

If I write more of my Sir Charles than of Henry's Sir Henry it is because he is less well known, and also because I myself find him more human. Sir Henry was much prone to religious sentiments and self-examination, whilst Sir Charles, though he too gives thought to Time, Death and Judgment, writes cheerfully of a certain general . . . "his nose full of grog and his heels full of Highland reels". Besides, most schoolboys know something of "Henry Lawrence who tried to do his duty" and they have heard John described as the "saviour of India"; but beyond the fact there was once somebody called Sir Charles Napier who made a pun "Peccavi I have Scinde", they know nothing of the witty truculent old fellow who could best be described like the Rajput warrior; "this scarred wounded old man, this fragment of a warrior". There are even doubts now whether Sir Charles ever did say "Peccavi I have Scinde", but doubters will not be amongst those who have read his journals for they are full of such felicitous racy sayings. When the Duke of Wellington asked to see them, Sir William said hastily "But there are many queer rough things". "So much the better. That's what I want", returned the Duke.

Even Dalhousie, the Governor-General later to condemn him so harshly, admitted, "He is full of anecdotes. Full of fun and cleverness".

Indeed one is tempted to make an anthology of some of his pithy remarks.

Of Dalhousie himself he writes: "He is weak as water. Vain as a pretty woman or an ugly man".

After he had received many flattering compliments from Marshal Soult he declares: "Depend upon it when a French soul is damned it puts on a great coat, and compliments the devil on his fine climate, 'Mais un peu froid' ".

Of Whigs: "I do not know why the good God afflicts this England with Whigs and bugs, but He does so".

In his General Orders he wrote: "Gentlemen as well as beggars may if they like ride to the devil on horseback, but neither gentlemen nor beggars have the right to send other people there, which will be the case if furious driving is allowed in camp or bazaar".

"If officers shoot peacocks, Baloochs will shoot officers".

"The enforcement of obedience is like physic, not agreeable but at times very necessary".

But he philosophises too. "Merciful God what are we? We have a part to perform in this drama. So has the bug that bites. Which has the more important part of the two? We both act by the direction of our nature, and who shall presume to decide? The bug may produce a sleepless night for the body and to the ingenious mind thus kept awake a great invention may occur. Who is the originator? The bug who sucks blood or the man who unwittingly lies awake under bug grazing? Yet the invention may turn the order of things, perhaps enable us to reach the moon".

I wonder if his mind had turned thus to invention because his forbear John Napier, the inventor of logarithms or Napier's Bones, who died in 1617, was said to have invented a means of destroying sheep on a hill hundreds of yards away? He determined not to make this discovery known fearing it might be put to improper use.

Then it was in 1844 that Charles wrote (though how well it might be at the present day): "One of our greatest evils is that every head of an office fancies himself a gentleman who is to amuse himself and sign papers presented by his clerk, and they gradually getting better coats on vote themselves gentlemen too! Of course more clerks are registered and large establishments are found without reason. When Pombal seized the Government of Lisbon he found twenty-two thousand clerks. He cut the twenty-two thousand down to two hundred".

Sir Charles Napier's despatches of the conquest of Sind are the very first in our military history to mention the names of the private soldiers. They were kept long from the public. . . At a complaint in the House of Lords at this delay Lord Ripon declared he had forgotten them! Sir Charles had written "There are boys in this camp who require and have more luxuries than I who am Governor of Scinde. The want of beer and wine is absolute misfortune to them . . . the private soldier cannot have luxuries and if he sees his officer despise them he does the same; but if his officer sacrifices every thing to enjoyment he is not a fool, and holds that officer in contempt".

In the violent quarrel between Dalhousie and Charles, resulting in the latter's resignation, it seemed to him that the Duke—if only outwardly—had sided with the Governor-General.

His emotions when he heard the Duke was dead are not recorded by himself, but William, his brother who was with him, wrote "A first momentary sense of recent injustice not in human nature to suppress was instantly overcome by a tumultuous rush of remembrance . . . ancient times and deeds and kindness came over him like a flood to wash away all but regret and reverence for the hero. He assisted as pall-bearer at the funeral. (Too gorgeous it was for death, and scarcely in harmony with the feeling of the aged warriors who, having in youth followed him through all dangers were then bending in grief over his bier. . . Pride and luxury rather than veneration and sorrow seemed to predominate). Many eyes were turned on Charles Napier, and low voices were heard to say 'the next in genius stood by the bier.' 'They saw' said the *Times*, 'that eagle face, that bold strong eye, and felt there was still a mighty man of battle before them' ".

These words are taken from Sir William's life of his brother, and serve to illustrate one way in which the Lawrence brothers did differ from the Napiers. For it has been said not without truth that Charles and William, great men as they were, dearly loved to scratch each others backs. Henry and John Lawrence scratched each other too, but they scratched to tear!

Charles settled down in Hampshire with "riches, house and lands of mine own. All my life have I longed for this".

His charity had always been unbounding. He had given a nephew five thousand pounds when he himself was still toiling to earn enough money to keep his own wife and children. I have in my hand a letter written in his quick clear writing. The ink is brown, the paper brittle, for the date is September 7th, 1840. It is to one Major Gordon, and is headed "Secret".

> "My dear Sir,
>
> Having seen by a letter of yours that a Mrs. Spurgeon, the widow of your quarter-master is in great distress, and that her husband was an old and deserving soldier, I take the liberty of enclosing a draft for five hundred rupees for her, and think as probably her wants are few this may assist in little comforts to her in her distress".

I am tempted to quote from another letter showing that his generosity was not confined to money.

> "My dear Murray,
>
> When the Commander-in-Chief sees a man distinguish himself, and sees this with his own eyes, the said C-in-C must be the son of a bitch if he cannot break rules and show his regard. You have 8 officers on the staff, but none of the 8 ever saved 2 or 3 sepoys lives! You have, and I have appointed you to be Adjutant of the 13th Irregular Cavalry . . . I wish I could do as much for the men that are with you. For with me officer and

private soldier are all alike, but want of power is an undeniable excuse.

Yours truly, C. NAPIER.

To Ensign Murray, March 12th, 1850".

Settled at Oaklands "To the aged and helpless he gave gently . . . to the young and able he furnished aid, not in humiliating gifts, but in remuneration. Finding much temporary unemployment and destitution he employed fifty labourers on full wages without having real need for five."

But his enemies pursued him in retirement.

There were lawsuits and recriminations and torturing ill-health not only from abcesses on the liver, but from his facial wounds from Peninsula days, which at times caused him to fear madness. Yet his diary keeps its humour.

In his journals from Sind there had been much passionate longing for the life beyond the grave where again he could have all he loved. "What is to happen to us? A very short time will now let me into the secret, and curiosity is strong within me as the time grows near", he had written. The time was growing very near now, but in his diary he is laughing at himself. "I am again unwell. I wish to be like the cockroaches kept by a man to prove insects have no feelings. He disembowels them, stuffs them with cotton wool and they run about happy as princes", or he recounts "speaking to a sergeant about B— of the 22nd Regt., I asked if it were true that B— had married 2 wives, both living. With great solemnity he replied 'Sir Charles, I am sorry to say he has done worse . . . he has committed not only bigamy but trigonometry'. 'A terrible fellow', said I".

And again when expecting the French to invade in 1852 he writes: "Our houses are much too near the coast. He (his cousin Black Charles) has therefore advertised his for sale. I shall not do that, but expecting an invasion, as I am too old to fight, I mean to put on a red nightcap and sit at my door with a flannel petticoat over my knees, and a black draught in my hand, and my feet in hot water awaiting the arrival of a French General of Brigade. 'Je suis un pauvre ancien militaire Monsieur. Ayez pitié de moi', and Oaklands shall be called Frogmore in compliment".

To the end his great love of horses persisted. He had Red Rover, the favourite charger of his battles, brought to his bedside; that same Red Rover of whom he had written: "Red Rover stands firm under fire", and "Our lives are on the simmer now and will soon boil; I have been obliged to take Red Rover into my tent where he lay down exhausted poor beast, and makes me very hot".

But now Red Rover, backing and snorting, would not approach his dying master, and sadly Sir Charles turned away begging he should be cared for after he was gone. But let Sir William describe the end of the old warrior.

"He expired like a soldier on a naked bedstead, the windows of the room open, and the fresh air of heaven blowing on his manly face. Surrounded by his family and some of his brothers, he died. All of his grieving servants were present, and at his feet stood two veterans of his regiment, gazing with terrible emotion at a countenance then settling in death which they had first seen beaming in the light of battle. Easy was the actual dissolution however, and as the last breath escaped, Montagu McMurdo with a sudden inspiration snatched the old colours of the 22nd Regt., the colours that had been borne at Meanee and Hyderabad, and waved them over the dying hero".

He was buried privately at Portsmouth, but every officer and man of the garrison attended his funeral, and the whole body of the naval officers also. His statue in Trafalgar Square relates how it was chiefly raised by private soldiers. He loved them, and they knew it.

"All my life the idea of making soldiers do what I did not do myself has been odious to me. With me private soldier and officer are the same".

And four years later Henry Lawrence, that old enemy of his, lay dying at Lucknow.

"I forgive everyone" . . . (so Sir Charles must be forgiven too!) "No surrender. No fuss. No nonsense. Here lies Henry Lawrence who tried to do his duty".

So passed these brilliant, violent, God-fearing forbears of Henry and myself, their aggressive spirits quiet at last under the soft drifting dust of years.

But this diary deals not with those fighting days, but with the everyday life of my husband and myself between the years 1914 and 1920. For my husband's achievements one must look elsewhere, though even as I write he receives this letter from a distinguished Governor.

> "It is very kind of you to speak so flatteringly of my career. May I say how I realise how much I owe to the strenuous but happy years which I spent as your *chela* (disciple), and to the way you inspired me to work hard and think clearly, and to have the courage of my convictions and to say what I thought. Speaking one's mind is a luxury, and like other luxuries must be paid for. I have paid fairly dearly for mine, but have never regretted the years I spent in the wilderness through taking the line I thought to be right. I believe you had the same experience, and I have always admired you for it. And one of my greatest satisfactions to-day is to know that there are one or two juniors of whom I have had the training who will certainly go ahead; and as far as I have mastered your methods I have made use of them with my youngsters".

Well—foolishly no doubt—I am at times assailed by the thought that the vividness of those days 1914—1920 now quitted for ever, when my husband and I moved through jungle, village, and desert, servants of the people, their Ma-Bap, may not be entirely subjective. Perhaps they exist outside Time, and still continue their measured way in the scheme of things.

BELGAUM.

April, 1914.

Our arrival in Belgaum was a public one. It was all so bewildering to me; I have asked Henry to help me with the particulars in writing this. Our train drew in about nine o'clock. The platform itself was packed with representatives of the Indian gentry who had come in from many miles around. Indian gentlemen with such ancient sounding titles as Deshpandi and Deshmal—Head of the Country, Protector of the Country. There were Parsees with their curious little grey felt, or shiny patent-leather looking hats, prosperous merchants, some of them in European dress with the exception of their brilliant turbans: others more orthodox in voluminous white dhotis, bare brown legs, curly-toed shoes, and caste marks on their foreheads. There were leaders of the Indian Bar buttoned to the throat in black frock coats, white and gold scarves swathed round them, and bright little turbans on their heads. There were members of the Municipality in every kind of dress, schoolmasters, magistrates, and of course the English officials. The Collector and his wife, the Judge and Assistant Judge, the Cantonment Magistrate, the Civil Surgeon, Forest officers, P.W.D.,[1] the Police and numbers of others, and their wives. As the train steamed slowly in I saw all these, collected and packed under the station roof. The crowds, the dark faces, the turbans pink, green, white, gold and deep rose, the sunshine, the dust, the heat—and now the door was open, and what I after learned to be pattawallas in stiff white, with scarlet belts and turbans, were salaaming deeply to Henry and myself as we climbed down onto a red carpet.

The Collector began introducing people to Henry, and he was shaking hands. He had told me I had better do what he did, so I began shaking hands all round too, to the deep confusion of those who were servants and pattawallas, but all the same to me. For the pattawallas in flawless white and scarlet looked grander far than some of the Indian gentlemen in dhotis, and shirts hanging below their

[1] Public Works Department.

black coats, with sock suspenders clasped over bare brown legs, or shirts worn without collars or ties, and buttoned with pink composition studs.

Then came garlanding. Pink roses heaped on a silver dish, Henry bending his head, and the great five-stranded rose garlands mazy with silver whiskers catching on his topi. It was all I could do not to laugh, but someone was garlanding me now, and presently I had five or six of them round my neck mounting to my ears, and the rose water with which they were drenched trickling down my neck. There were little stripey tinsel balls with winking mirrors and chains of silver beads in the garlands. What a pretty custom! Even the dreadful little bouquets with the heads of the roses mounted on canes, and stiff tinsel buttons amongst the petals have something fascinating about them. They make one think of Struwelpeter, and the page where the angels have red and blue wings on a black background.

You can picture Henry and me wreathed in roses, jasmine and marigolds down to the knee, hands full of bouquets, coming out on the station steps blinking there as the sun struck at us like a sword. Outside a body of fifty police with their smart Subadar in command, and the police band. Six mounted sowars on fidgety white Arabs, brandishing their long tails as Arabs do. Picturesque figures these sowars in blue tunics, canary breeches, and blue and white turbans with scarlet kulas. They were picked out sunbright with their white Arabs against the darkness of mango trees. There were red carpets, fluttering pennons of every colour, a little faded and draggled if you looked into them, but the scarlet "Welcome to our Commissioner", stretched right across the road was brand new.

After the police had been inspected, up thundered a whole crowd of bullock carts or dhamnies as they are called. Springless boxes on two wheels, which in the rains have rigid roofs clamped onto their sides.

The Commissioner's dhamny was a gorgeous affair. Freshly painted white, with ramping tigers, and charging elephants on its sides. It was lined with white leather, and the two huge bullocks who rattled it along were white too. Their immense spreading horns were dyed crimson, and crimson and magenta tassels swung from their tips. There were cowrie necklaces, and bells about their creasy white satin necks, and when we clambered in at the back, we started off at a great rate, the oxen galloping, the bells clashing, the dhamny-wallah shouting, as he leaned forward digging his bare toe into the rumps of the poor beasts, and twisting their tails, whilst the sowars on their white Arabs caracoled before and behind us in clouds of red dust.

We bumped and rattled along the red road salaaming to the brilliant crowds who lined it. (I felt exactly like Queen Alexandra whom I used to see bowing to the crowds as she drove through Hyde Park, when I was a schoolgirl).

Belgaum is alive with parrots and not unlike a parrot itself with its red soil and vivid grass and bamboos and other trees. We passed the cross road where in its shrine under a huge peepul tree there was a freshly daubed Ganpati with his elephant head, and wrinkled belly. A woman was laying a little bunch of marigolds before him. "Idols!" I thought, astonished, I don't know why.

The goats everywhere scrambling over walls, standing on their hind legs to pluck at a succulent shoot, delighted me. And the naked babies carrying their stomachs in front of them like pregnant women. They had silver anklets and painted eyes. "Oh I must have a tea party for them all", I cried with memories of school treats at home I suppose running in my head.

Henry looked a little astonished, but said nothing. I suppose there are about five thousand babies at least in Belgaum.

Hulme Park.

By a hedge of aloes, formidable blueish and ivory tusks pushing out of the ground, we turn into the park, rattling up a deeply shaded avenue with lion-coloured grass reaching away on either side, between the dark tree trunks. Jolt, jolt, jolt, behind the jerky trotting bullocks and then the dhamny emerges from the tunnel-like avenue into a world of sunlit greenery, of roses, and plumbago, and white creeper, and tall trees and ferns, and amongst all this our home. Long, low and friendly it looks, with its country tiles projecting out over the deep verandahs. Not in the least like "Hulme Park", much more like the "Commissioner's Bungalow", as indeed it is always called. The dhamny draws up under a high portico, and I have a confused impression of maiden-hair fern twinkling with water drops, and many salaaming servants, their hands and faces brown against spotless white. We go up steps into a red-tiled verandah through which you could drive two dog-carts abreast. Chairs, tables, magazines, and vases of flowers, and behind, lofty dim windowless rooms all leading, without doors, merely archways, sometimes with a bead curtain, more often without, into bedrooms beyond.

Henry and I explore through the echoing rooms. It's fun! He has handed his topi to a servant, and his garlands to another, but though mine have now become like warm poultices I still keep them on and they scatter rose petals on the floor as we pass out to the back. There is a courtyard here with leaning trees blazing with red gold blossom, and casting shadows almost purple on the red earth. (What sketching I shall do!). A wide verandah runs three sides of this courtyard. The bedrooms open onto it. They have half canvas doors, so that when we are inside we still see the turbaned heads above, and the bare feet below, of the servants as they pass along from the kitchen and their quarters to the dining room and drawing room. The bedrooms are very dim and lofty. I look up and see bare rafters. There is absolutely no furniture except the beds shrouded in mosquito net. Behind, more archways into the dressing rooms, and here are windows looking into the park. Henry takes me on into the bath rooms. White-washed walls, and a zinc tub already filled with water, and a tin pot beside it.

"You mustn't use a sponge because of scorpions", he explains. "You pour the water out of the pot over you".

There is a large earthenware pot containing more water, and the bath it seems, is just turned upside down, for the water to run away through a hole in the wall.

"Frogs come in through the hole", explains Henry, "and snakes after the frogs. So always keep your eyes skinned". A whole procession of thousands of ants is traversing the floor, and marching up one of the walls. One of the servants says he will fetch some boiling water to send them away.

Out of the bath room opens another apartment, containing a commode. It appears there is no drainage. Each bath room is furnished with its room and commode in the care of sweepers. A man for Henry, a woman for me. These belong to the Untouchables, familiar to readers of missionary magazines. Outcasts. Even as we stand there silently appears a woman in dark earthen-coloured draperies, and many glass bangles. On seeing us she is paralysed with fright, appearing to flatten herself against the wall, to obliterate herself in her embarrassment. She carries the basket of her trade.

The day is one surprise after another. We have a breakfast of soup, porridge, fish, fried mutton, eggs and fruit which I am too excited to eat. But at luncheon time no sign of anything! Henry does not appear even. It seems the next meal is tea at five when there will be eggs. In the meantime Henry is seeing visitors, and I am supposed to go to bed. Why? *Dastur;* custom. But if the men work all through the afternoon why should it be thought necessary for the women to sleep? I never can sleep in the daytime anyway. It's too dim to read with comfort, and I lie on my bed with a yawning hole in my protesting tummy till Henry appears, and tea.

We change to go to the Club which I feel should be called the Gymkhana, as in novels. Apparently it simply isn't done to wear a topi in the afternoon. The Club is nestling amongst tall feathery bamboos, and from it comes the surprising sound of bagpipes, but instead of the familiar kilted figures it is the band of the 110th Mahrattas. All Indians. How surprising. On the red earth by a see-saw and merry-go-round, ayahs are squatting, and their small charges, all in white playing around. We go into the Club. Crowds of people. Women in muslins, women in riding habits and tennis kit. Men everywhere. How am I ever to remember all these people? People sitting at tables eating chip potatoes, and dipping their fingers into parched gram, and drinking immense tumblers of very weak whisky and soda, or tiny glasses of milk punch. People playing badminton now it is too dark for tennis. Insects banging and flopping about everywhere. Faces, even the women's, glistening with perspiration which the flaring kitsen burners exaggerate. Talk. Noise. We walk home through the hot dark night, a servant carrying a lantern to guide our footsteps, and banging a stick to frighten away snakes. We each have a boiling bath in the bathroom lit only by the uncertain light of a hurricane lantern standing on the mud floor, and emerge hotter still. I wonder if a snake is coming through the hole in the wall. Dinner is at nine. Any amount of courses, beautifully cooked; lovely flowers. It has been cooked hours before Henry tells me, and has been sitting in a hot cupboard till we are ready for it. As we eat I jump out of my skin at a loud exclamation over my head. A lizard coming out from behind a picture frame. He sprawls motionless as though glued to the wall.

After dinner we go onto the verandah. The arms of the chairs are elongated into ends over which you put your legs. The chairs have a hole at one side in which you put your tumbler. It's very hot, and from the hot darkness hundreds and hundreds of crickets are shrilling. It is exciting somehow like the Venusberg music, and away down in the bazaar there is a constant tom-toming and squealing of native pipes. I feel very over-excited. There is such lots of everything. The garden is so full of plants and trees and ferns hidden in the darkness. The Club was so full of men and women and children and servants. Here in the Bungalow Henry and I never seem to be alone. Servants rising up unexpectedly. Pattawallas on the verandah sleeping or just sitting. I feel like a child with too many Christmas presents. I don't know what to play with. Thoughts turn restlessly from one thing to another.

Second Day.

Henry has his office at the end of the verandah. Here he sits in a tussore suit at an immense table piled with files. There are wire baskets on the floor, and as they are filled a pattawalla, one of those bare-footed men in white with scarlet sash and belt, comes forward and carries it swiftly away. All the morning there has been a ceaseless stream of visitors. Victorias and bullock carts drive up, and their occupants are received by the pattawallas, and wait in the verandah till Henry has done with his present visitor. I watch them out of the tail of my eye, for at the extreme opposite end of the verandah I have my writing table, and I am trying to write home, but there is too much to say. The voyage? Owing to the hot weather the boat had been very empty. Henry and I had overflowed into three double cabins. There was the scientist, leaning hour after hour over the rail staring through his field glasses at the white short arc of the flying fish, his mind on aeroplanes. And then at our table the "bad woman". I do not know why but I had assumed "bad women" drank brandy, and had dyed hair and rouged cheeks. But this girl, for she seemed little more, though she was constantly drinking, was fresh and attractive to look at, with a lovely figure. Hot as it was, she and the young subaltern danced endlessly to her small portable gramophone just outside the smoking room. Almost glued together there in the dimness they revolved on a threepenny bit, and when the boy went into the smoking room, the young woman scribbled a note and sent it in by a passing steward. Sheepishly he would emerge, and the dancing and drinking and whispering would begin all over again. I was distressed and fascinated. It was like watching a fly struggling in treacle. "Poor devil", said Henry. "A good thing he is getting off at Aden".

But when we got to Aden, in a drenching thunder-storm, with all the leaves of the cirrus trees turned up white and protesting, the young woman changed her plans and she got off too. No. I couldn't write home about the "bad woman".

Well, Bombay on arrival? The great harbour, the steamers with their bright funnels and sombre sirens, the misty heat, and the native boats looking with their queer rigging and sloping masts like ill-tempered horses with ears laid back. Perspiration standing out in beads on one's forehead and upper lip, prickling in the roots of one's hair under the unaccustomed topi. And there on the quay alongside, customs officials, friends, servants, scallywags of all kinds. I had never seen so many people; a mixture of brown faces, and dirty white garments and spotless uniforms, and helmets, mixed up with oxen, mangy dogs, crows, and beggars, and driving through narrow streets between tall colour-washed houses, with vivid trees jammed between them, jingling victorias and bullock carts round you, and parrots shooting across the road over your head, black crows squawking. People. People. People. And your frock stuck to your shoulders.

I was astonished at the shabbiness of the Taj, the best hotel in Bombay. The basin and jug were cracked in our room and did not match; there was a long strip of discoloured paper detached from the wall and it scratched backwards and forwards in the wind of the electric fan. The mosquito curtains were heavily darned, the floor was composed of broken bits of domestic china, forming a rough mosaic.

Henry had left me in this room to rest, while he went off to the Secretariat. A pattawalla lay on the floor outside my door. There was plenty to look at. Endless people in the street; a snake-charmer; the cotton stretching across the windows to prevent the bold crows coming thronging into one's room; the native craft in the harbour.

On his return Henry spoke sharply to me for hanging out of the window without my topi. I could see he was put out. After, I learned the reason. He had cut short his furlough, and accepted the post of Commissioner in Belgaum till such time as the Commissionership in Sind, the plum of the service—should fall vacant. This had been promised to him by the late Governor, Sir George Clark. Meanwhile Belgaum had a pleasant climate for me, and the work would be interesting to him in a part of the Presidency which was new to him. But at the Secretariat he had just learned that Sind had unexpectedly fallen vacant, and the colleagues of the new Governor, Lord Willingdon, disapproving of Henry's innovating policy of giving more power to Indians, had advised H.E. to send instead a Mr. A—. Now this was peculiarly galling to Henry as recently he had confidentially informed the Government that Mr. A's reactionary views on the fundamental problem of administration in Sind were unworthy of British history! Moreover it was proposed that Henry, instead of going to Belgaum, for which he had cut short his furlough, should instead be posted to A—'s former post at Ahmedabad—a notoriously bad climate. And we were arriving in the hot weather. He was afraid it would kill me. No wonder he was preoccupied, and in what seemed to me a very bad temper. It was not only the fact that a long cherished ambition was not to be realised, but that Mr. A— had recommended that the Hindus who number only 5 per cent. of the population of Sind should be in control of the Muslims.

Well I couldn't write of that either.

But to return to this morning. It has grown very still. Thunder booms in the distance. It is dark. The pale green walls have dulled to grey. I keep wiping my face and neck with my handkerchief. It is red with dust. I keep pushing away the tiny black eye-flies which crowd into the corners of my eyes. My hand won't slip over the paper, it's so sticky. It is growing darker and darker. The air seems solid, not breathable at all. I can't see to write. The thunder comes louder and louder, the lightning more incessant. From outside there arises a protesting rattle from myriads of dead leaves as a little wind searches through their multitudes. I'm frightened. I hate thunder storms. A brilliant flash. Shall I retreat into the windowless drawing room behind? Suddenly a delicious smell like a newly watered greenhouse . . . and then an uproar. A tremendous wind. Banging doors, pots of fern and crotons blowing over, vases crashing, curtains blowing out horizontally, pattawallas and servants running. It is pouring with rain . . . Oh! The most blinding lightning, and a hundred thousand sheets of corrugated iron seem to be falling over my head—Henry tearing down the verandah.

"Are you all right? . . . It's got us . . . "

It hadn't, but the Civil Hospital which was in our grounds only a few hundred yards away.

"Why didn't you come to me?" reproached Henry.

"But you told me I was never to disturb you in your office!". His answer to this was completely satisfactory. How characteristic of Henry. It appears he had never noticed the storm till he thought we were actually hit, so absorbed was he in his work.

We stood on the verandah and watched the rain beating down. It was coming through the roof, and the servants were running about putting little bowls and buckets to catch the water. The heat had shrunk the country tiles, so that you could see the sky through. These are just the mango showers I learned, and we shall get thunderstorms three and four times a day while they last. Anyway it was cool and lovely, and the scent delicious. I wasn't frightened with his arm round me. But by and by the wind dropped, and it was hotter than ever again. Not a dry thread on one. If you pushed your fingers through your hair, they were wet. Your very lungs seemed like sponges full to repletion, such was the humidity. Unbearable. Then another storm, wind, lightning . . . rumours of cattle killed near by.

After tea we walked to the Civil Hospital. In the tigerish light the great gold mohur trees seemed to give out a sort of radiance. They burned against slaty black, ice blue, and rose coloured mountainous clouds. These were quite motionless in spite of angry gusts of a rising wind. Lightning flickering, thunder grumbling.

A night nurse had been buried in her bed, but was rescued unhurt. There had been a strong smell of singeing. The lightning had then skipped two rooms completely, and finally gone to ground, leaving a black hole in the Matron's little office.

As we came back dark red dust was spinning up to the very blossoms of the gold mohurs. In the strange streaming horizontal sunshine the dust itself had brightened to the colour of the blossom. The wind blew more stormily. The hanging roots of the banyan trees swayed like dead men from gibbets. Overhead a vulture gleamed unnaturally buff against a steel-black cloud.

Everything seemed to me to be working up to some awful climax but Henry tells me the weather is normal for the end of April.

The Third Day.

Henry tells me he will be especially busy this morning. The former Commissioner from whom he has taken over, has camp kit to sell. Will I look it over therefore with Hyder Khan, and decide what we shall buy?

So Hyder Khan led me to the back verandah. He is a magnificent man with square cut black beard, and the bearing of a king. His hands are small, and well kept as a woman's. He is dressed in spotless white, the immensely full trousers gathered into a tight embroidered band at the ankle. His feet are bare. A scarlet and gold belt, ten inches deep, is round his waist, and his large white turban is wound round a scarlet kula. I accompany this august personage to the wide verandah at the back, where the two beautiful gold mohur trees are leaning towards each other in full blossom in the quadrangle. Hyder Khan gives me a chair, and respectfully indicates the whole of the late Commissioner Sahib's camp kit spread neatly before me. What does the Memsahib wish to buy?

There are folding teak wood tables, and chairs, and washstands, dingy little spotted mirrors, chipped enamel jugs, basins, and mugs, and soap dishes. There are charpoys for dogs, and several camp bedsteads lying unrecognisable in a forest of unvarnished mosquito poles. There are rolled up and rather uninviting looking mattresses, and a heap of darned mosquito curtains. There are commodes, and Hyder Khan says "many piss-parts". I don't know what "piss-parts" are, and am covered with confusion when I am shown.

"What does the Memsahib wish to buy?"

Stores are also needed. Stores not only for the bungalow, but stores for the "district". Hyder Khan has caused to be written out a list for me to sign, when it will be immediately posted and sent to Bombay. I look at it dumbfounded. There are two and a half foolscap sheets and everything is ordered by the dozen and marked "first class quality". Tinned sausages, tinned fruits, tinned peas, tinned mushrooms, tinned chocolates, bottles of vanilla, and almonds. All by the dozen. And hops. (Why hops?). Tinned asparagus. Two dozen tins of asparagus. Henry had said "I draw the line at tinned asparagus for our dinner-parties". Why? I had no idea, but anyway it was a relief to draw the pencil so beautifully sharpened for me, very firmly and blackly through one item. Hyder Khan saw me, but made no remark. His arms were crossed. He rested one bare foot on the other. There was a broad silver band round his big toe. Baking powder, tinned salmon, tinned butter, tinned milk . . .

I was utterly at sea. I could not appeal to Henry. He had said I ought to have come to him in the thunderstorm—but this was different.

I asked something in English. Hyder Khan professed not to understand. I stumbled into the little Hindustani Henry had taught me on the boat. Hyder Khan responded in an unintelligible flood.

My head began to ache.

Then Hyder Khan slipped a printed paper with an extraordinary name printed on top, before me. The three horses Henry had bought in Bombay were arriving that night with their syces. They must be fed. On what did the Memsahib desire they should be fed? How many pounds daily? Also they would require new jhools. (What on earth were jhools?). These must be got from Cawnpore. Thick ones and thin ones. Also many jharans. Jharans for the hamal, the masal, the second boy, Misteri and his mate, and the three syces.

I had no idea of Henry's income, nor his pay. He had never spoken as though he were a rich man. Looking at these lists, and the money they represented I felt distraught. I remember how he had impressed upon me that he absolutely refused to give champagne as a matter of course at every dinner party, contrary to the usual Indian custom. I had never done any housekeeping except at the rectory at Maperton, after my sister Diana died. There expenses had to be cut to the bone to educate the children. This prospect of dinner parties, garden parties, and buying food and furniture for months in camp stunned me. I was near to tears in my ignorance and perplexity. I hesitated, and now Hyder Khan slipped a long pale blue book before me with *Government Dairy* printed on it. I was to write therein the milk required for morning and evening, and whether it was to be pasteurised or not. How much cream . . . and to add to everything the quantities were in pounds instead of pints.

There was a slight sound. I looked up. Deeply salaaming was the head mali, the head gardener. A small monkey-like figure clothed only in a shirt reddened from the soil. His sleeves were rolled to the shoulder. His bare arms and skinny thighs gleamed like bronze. He handed me a type-written list of vegetable seeds to be bought. Brinjals. Knolkols. Ladies Fingers . . .

How am I ever to become a Bara Memsahib?

Added later. Hyder Khan enjoyed himself that morning, but very soon he became a tower of strength. I am devoted to him. I am positive he would unhesitatingly lay down his life for Henry and myself, just as he would have done for Louise, and George, Michael and Bim. In speaking of them he always adds "George Baba bahut gharib walla" (very gentle quiet) "but Michael Baba bahut ghussa-walla, and Missy Baba bahut *bahut* ghussa walla" (very, very angry, passionate).

I asked Henry this morning what exactly his work would be here in the Southern Division. This is what he said. "First to understand the people and then to find out what can be done to help them. I've only visited this part of the country before when I was Director of Agriculture, and then started various experimental farms for improving the crops. Now I've got to administer an area twice the size of Wales and many times more populous. A good bit of it is under State Forests, and there's often trouble between the villagers and the Forest officials.

"There is one big thing I have to do, and if I talk of it I shall fail, for it is rank mutiny against the present Bombay Government" and he gave me a little mischievous wink.

I never ask questions on these occasions, and was now rewarded by Henry telling me he had a special enemy at Headquarters, Mr. X— who had somehow persuaded the Government to issue an order confiscating certain hereditary rights in most villages. Henry considered this order not only unjust but impolitic. He explained to me that these government village officials had hereditary right existing before British Rule, and to sweep them all away just because some were tyrannical would have shaken confidence in British justice. By masterly inactivity Henry was determined to withhold its enforcement throughout the Southern Division. If Mr. X— discovered this mutiny he could have us removed from Belgaum, and appoint someone more compliant.

I love Henry for his courage and determination to do the right things, no matter at what cost to himself. Right through his character like a seam of quartz running through stone, runs this singleminded purpose for things which really matter. Let the roof fall in! Come what may! Certainly it is upsetting at times to the routine of domestic life, the little things that can fret so much! But even in the most devastating moments I'm glad to think I don't regret it—am indeed proud of it. Worthy kinsman of John Knox, of Henry, George and John Lawrence. Often Henry has imitated to me his grandfather George singing robustly Sankey and Moody's hymn:

"Dare to be a Daniel
Dare to stand alone
Dare to have a purpose firm
Dare to make it known."

Did this influence the little boy? Who can tell?

Our servants:

Hyder Khan, our Major Domo, and two boys under him, one being Henry's "dressing boy".

Tulsi, my ayah, who looks after me, washes out my stockings and little things.

Misteri, the cook.

The hamal, the houseman.

The masal, the lampman.

Three malis. Gardeners.

The dhobi. Washerman.

The dirzi. Tailor.

The bhisti. Waterman.

The gauli. Cowman.

The three syces. Grooms.

The two sweepers, male and female.

In addition a number of pattawallas—official messengers—who however are ready to turn their hand to anything from pushing a baby's pram to cleaning brass or carrying golf clubs.

This seems an absurd number of individuals to look after Henry and myself, both people of simple tastes. But it must be remembered they take the place of social services in other countries.

Where there is no laundry someone must wash the household linen, and the frequent changes of clothes made necessary by the climate.

Where there is no light there must be someone to fill the innumerable oil lamps and hurricane lanterns not only over all the bungalow and in dark corners, but also to carry to and fro from club or servants' quarters, for protection from snakes. The very horses have hurricane lanterns in their stalls at night.

Where there is no water there must be a bhisti to bring it to you, and bullocks to draw it up from the well, and someone to attend to the bullocks.

Where there is no delivery you must have a young man to accompany the cook on his early morning visits to the market to carry back the meat, the fish, the ice, the soda water and fruit.

Where there is no sanitation there must be a male and female sweeper.

Where there are no shops you must have a dirzi who will make the shirts, pyjamas, and silk suits for the Sahib, and frocks for the Memsahib, and copy London tailor-mades so exactly that if there be a small patch, unless warned the dirzi will cut out a hole in the new material and make a corresponding patch.

The servants are paid very little according to our standards, but they know to the last anna their master's salary, and the day he gets promotion a rise is automatically asked for and given. Because they do know exactly the pay their master receives it is understandable that the cook adds a pice here, a pi there to every item on his book; the syces "ease" the horse shoes off to make more frequent visits to the nalband (blacksmith) and so on. What difference can a hundredth part of a penny make to Henry whose pay they know is £2,500? What they do not know is the cost of passages home, the cost of children at preparatory and public schools, and holidays, that he had to pay for a widow's pension for me, and so much is subtracted for his own pension also.

The I.C.S. are much more fortunate in their servants than the Army. For the servants of the former feel they belong to the Sircar.[1] The I.C.S. are their *Ma-Bap*. The I.C.S. belong to the country and are not merely passengers of a year or two. Our servants look down on what they call "soldier-log servants". When the civilian goes home

[1] Civil Government.

on furlough his servants take temporary places, and on his return are waiting on the Apollo Bunder with garlands of flowers to welcome their old master.

Much of Ayah's day was taken up by preventing the damp rotting, and cockroaches and white ants devouring my trousseau. Coming into our lofty dim bedroom you would find her lifting out dresses from tin-lined boxes, or filling up the saucers with water, in which the feet of the almirahs stood, to prevent the white ants climbing. Hyder Khan superintended the second boy's care of Henry's clothes. This was even more important. For a Commissioner's uniform costs anything from £200 to £300 with its coats and tunics of finest navy blue cloth and its gold lace, its cocked hat, its two swords, and above all its "kerseymeres". "Kerseymeres" are the softest white breeches worn with silk stockings and gold buckled shoes only on ceremonial affairs such as State quadrilles, or a royal visit. There is something sumptuous and regency-like about "kerseymeres". (How a cockroach would relish getting his tooth in). Henry had been considerably annoyed at the necessity of spending so much money and time at his London tailors on his uniform. I can see now his stubborn face as the three men bent reverently, smoothing or chalking or perhaps ripping a seam with the point of a pen knife! But now the thing was done he had dismissed the whole affair from his mind, confident that Hyder Khan would see his time and money did not provide cockroach fodder.

If I express a wish, or give an order Hyder Khan returns an imperturbable "Accha Memsahib",[1] keeping the difficulties, or impossibilities even, to himself. And somehow that order gets carried out.

It is no exaggeration to say that he presides over our destinies. He keeps Henry's money, engages and dismisses the servants, settles disputes and wife beating, gives orders in an authoritative voice, and without hesitation would yield his life to save Henry's or mine.

With all this he is a thing of beauty to look at. Proud, bearded, upright. Even in the month of Ramadan when no Mussulman can

[1] All will be done, Madam.

touch food or water between dawn and dark Hyder Khan waits on us at table just the same. He may be parched with thirst, faint with hunger. There is nothing to show. He moves round with the bearing of a king.

Station Life.

I feel absolutely at home. It is like a swan come home to roost on her own pool. She ruffles her plumage, she plunges her neck deep into green water, she paddles her leaf-like feet, shakes the drops off her wings, and draws her scarlet bill smoothly along each quill before gently shaking and settling down with all around her sky-reflecting water and the crowding beauty of trees. Henry must not see what he would call "one of your flights of fancy", but seriously that is how I do feel, so happy as to know I am happy.

No painted faces here! Nor boredom! Men work hard. Their wives share their interests. For instance Reg Maxwell and his young pretty wife with hair like yellow satin, are absorbed in their spare time in artistic photography, entomology and botany, to give one instance alone. Belgaum has its sketching club, and we meet after church to criticise each others' work. We are all interested in our bungalows, families, gardens, horses and dogs. We go to the Y.W.C.A. It is rather a patriarchal existence altogether, the women inspecting their kitchens and cooking pots, seeing that the milk is properly boiled, and the gutters free from mosquito larvae, doling out quinine to the servants with fever, finding work for the dirzi as he sits crosslegged on the verandah whirling his "Singer"; weighing out grain for the horses in case the syces eat it themselves, which they will not do if handled by a European. Then in the evening tennis, golf, badminton and bridge after dark, and the buzz and chatter at the Club, not of scandal, but of tiger, elephant or jungle doings especially now that the forest officers, police and district officers are beginning to trickle back from camp.

Yes. Life is full and fun. I ride Leviathan, the gigantic black Waler Henry gave me. He is seventeen hands, and all but thoroughbred. A most beautiful animal. Secretly I am a little scared of him at times, as he rears so high there is talk of him being handed over to the military to see if he can be cured by throwing him on to his back, but nothing comes of it, and I am so proud of the universal admiration he excites, any slight nervousness is forgotten.

At dinner parties it is quite astonishing what the Goanese cook can turn out on charcoal and a few bricks, one on top of each other. By the way there is always tinned iced asparagus, so now I understand why Henry had drawn the line at asparagus! Even junior officials give champagne at their dinners. Henry thinks this quite wrong as they cannot possibly afford to do it on their pay. He himself refuses to give it except at our very biggest dinners, hoping thereby to set an example, making it easier for the junior official to stand up against the custom.

Oddly enough Sir Charles Napier seventy or eighty years ago had written to Sir Colin Campbell as follows:

> "I am resolved on a great attempt. I expect to fail, still I will try to reduce the expense and drinking of messes. To begin with my self, and abolish all wine at my own table except sherry and claret . . . The damning sin of the magnificent armies in India, Queen's and Company's is an outrageous and vulgar luxury. We burst ourselves in trying to live like men of £20,000 a year . . . This I think is gross vulgarity, snobbish . . . If we can save a parcel of youngsters from ruin we shall not sleep the worst".

These are Henry's sentiments also.

There were not a few who regarded Sir Charles as altogether too austere. I have the feeling that there are those who regard Henry likewise in spite of the good company he can be, and the imp of mischief lurking near the surface. Certainly it had not taken me long to discover that Henry held views too advanced, in the eyes of the majority of his fellows. Certainly he advocates the ideals of Macaulay and others, and how often he quotes to me Sir Thomas Munro who had said in 1824 "that the natives in some future age become sufficiently enlightened to frame a regular government for themselves, and to conduct and preserve it".

To this end Henry maintains that the I.C.S. are steadily labouring, the majority perhaps only unconsciously by their example, but the few by precept. He declares that many of the I.C.S. as a matter of course preach doctrines out here which would be thought highly reprehensible at home! Such as Nationalisation of Land, State Ownership of Railways and Forests, Irrigation and Canals and so forth. Yet though his ideas are too advanced for many, that is not to say he minimises for one moment the benefit India has received from British Rule. He insists not so much on obvious benefits such as economic development and security from invasion, but the moral change of India. He has written:

> "Something intangible and subtle which cannot be measured in miles of iron and steel or tons of bricks and mortar", and this he claims is the "outstanding result of British Rule, and is derived from precepts of equal law and justice from the influence of Christianity . . . the example of good administration, the equal dealing between man and man, which are the chief glories of the British Empire . . . work of individuals, district officers, teachers, missionaries, doctors and their personal influence on the hearts and minds of the people".

But to return to our dinners. Before leaving England Henry had impressed on me the necessity of bringing out plenty of recipes for toast. Now I had imagined toast was either crisp or leathery, but I asked everyone, even penetrating a well-known restaurant, for recipes for toast. No one could help me. Now it appears "toast" is the Indian way of describing "savoury"!

The Commissioner dines only with the General, the Judge and the Collector, and just once in the season. But as ourselves we have three large dinner parties every week. Hyder Khan superintends. Misteri turns out wonderful dinners, and I write out menus in my best French.

Everything is new and strange to me, but Henry is never in the least disturbed by my mistakes, treats them as a joke, and makes me too.

I remember the first big dinner party I went to wearing my wedding dress. There were some thirty people there, all very senior. As the bride and the Commissioner's wife I, of course, had to be the first to leave. Somehow after shaking hands with my hostess, the

General's wife, I couldn't stop, and I went on as in a nightmare shaking hands with every single guest, aware all the time of the twinkle in Henry's eye, and the teasing I should get driving home.

But one solace was that as the wife of the Commissioner what I did was "right" equally with English and Indian society. To wear long wrinkly white kid gloves at dinner was not only hot but expensive. I wore none; so though perhaps shocked at first, all the women in the station thankfully left off wearing gloves too.

I said what I do is right equally with Indian as well as English society, for social relations are only just beginning to be established. The Hindu caste system forbids Hindus from eating or drinking with Europeans, and in the higher ranks secludes the women in purdah of course. Henry is very keen on breaking down these restrictions, and we have to our house Indian guests whenever they are willing to break down their own caste rules.

Before our marriage one of Henry's greatest friends, G. K. Gokhale, had defied outcasting by inviting Henry to dine in Poona, the very home of orthodoxy. Two other Brahmin rebels joined them. They were Mr. R. P. Paranjpe, senior Wrangler at Cambridge, and Mokshagundam Vishvesivaraya, later Premier of Mysore. They sat on the ground, ate with their fingers, and were served by the wife and daughters of the host. Henry considers this the greatest compliment he has ever received.

G. K. Gokhale was a talented statesman of the moderate school. It was he who founded the "Servants of India" which has done such wonderful work. It may not be generally known that when Gandhi returned from South Africa and proposed to join this society, Mr. Gokhale told his friends to accept his help, but never to put him in a place of authority, as he would be a danger to the movement.

I begin to recognise that though there is less than ten years between Henry and myself there are certain phases through which he has passed already, and done with, and that I yet have to find my way through. Photography for instance. I want to snap buffaloes submerged in the tank showing only noseholes and horn tips, or Henry in cocked hat, hand on sword about to present a police medal, or a naked capped baby astride its mother's hip—but years before Henry had passed that way. He tries to disguise impatience when I fiddle with stops. Indeed there are a whole series of passages through which I must pass before I arrive at the ultimate end of Henry's life out here . . . I mean the amelioration of the people's lot, schemes of reform and progress, and (without a hint of heroics) a determination to be a good citizen of the world.

Henry may—does indeed, get bursts of irritation with a pattawalla or the railway servant who serves up an atrocious dinner in the train, where I should not . . . but beneath this anger there is forever burning a steady flame of "duty", and beside it I feel like some frivolous gnat dancing over an evening pool.

Yet I am conscious that I help Henry . . . and not only because we are most happy in our married life. He tries his speeches on me. Moreover not infrequently adopts my suggestions. "You're right. I'll alter that". Then too though the speech itself is admirable, and full of meat, and would read well, yet secretly I find the delivery dull. No ups and downs, lights and shades. Grey. Flat. Now Henry loves my singing, and he accepts my shy criticism from *that* point of view.

(1945. Colour did not come into his speaking all at once, but come it did. He was once complimented by no one less than Winston Churchill himself, and for this I take a little credit remembering those early days in Belgaum when speeches were "tried on the dog").

We do all sorts of things together. If we are alone after dinner, which is rare, I sing. *Let Erin Remember* and *The West's Awake* must always be included. Sunday evening surprisingly enough we sing hymns! One Henry always wickedly insists upon,

From the awful place of doom
Where in rayless outer gloom
Dead souls lie as in a tomb
Save us Holy Jesu.

From the unknown agonies
Of the soul that helpless lies
From the worm that never dies
Save us Holy Jesu.

And he grasps my shoulder at "the worm that never dies" as he stands behind me at the piano.

Now Henry is descended from John Knox. Speaking to the ladies of the Court Knox had said:

> "O fair ladies how pleasing were this life if it should abide; and then in the end that we might pass to Heaven with all this gay gear! But fie upon that Knave Death that will come whether we will or not! And when he has laid on his arrest the foul worms will be busy with this flesh be it never so fair and so tender; and the silly Soul I fear shall be so feeble that it can neither carry with it gold, garnishing, targetting, pearl nor precious stones!".

Is old John Knox whispering down the centuries in Henry's ear? Is it he who gives at times a macabre twist to his usual robust enjoyment of life? His love of a joke? After all John Knox himself "has a vein of drollery in him which I much like in combination with his other qualities. He has a true eye for the ludicrous", wrote Thomas Carlyle. It is misplaced zeal on the part of the old man's bigoted followers which has concealed the fact that "he was a devoted husband, a loving father, a kind master, a genial host, a warm friend, a humane enemy".

Really this describes Henry himself not at all badly. To quote again: "Because he had a stern part to play, and played it appropriately and with success, it is inferred, with strange ignorance of human nature, that, as a man, Knox must have been stern, unbending, even cruel". That too is like Henry at times.

Henry loves Beethoven and Chopin . . . but he is tone deaf. As he stood behind me as I played, one hand resting on my shoulder, the most extraordinary sounds issued above my head. Deep, low and high. Rather like an angry bee that can't get out of a jam jar. Now I did not know Henry really very well, and I was not sure whether I was meant to laugh or not. Finally I decided to treat it like the drone to my bagpipe as it were . . . I need not have troubled. Henry cares no more for what people think about his doings or his appearance than a duck cares for the diamonds of water she shakes from her wings.

That was another thing. Henry was so utterly and entirely different to the men to whom I was accustomed.

I remember one day at Cheltenham, just before our marriage, Father asking where we had both been that morning.

"I took her to see the Sewage Farm", said Henry.

"God's truth!" ejaculated Father under his breath, and relapsed into silence for the rest of luncheon.

Yes. There are undoubtedly adjustments to be made . . . but we are both wonderfully happy together.

Coming to a new country, living an entirely different life, seeing not one living soul one has ever met before, and putting on each day new and unfamiliar clothes, I cannot somehow find myself.

But to-day there was heavy rain after a thunderstorm. I put on a thin coat and skirt I had worn at home, as the temperature had dropped appreciably. That coat and skirt enabled me to find myself. I slipped back into Rosamond Napier, and I began to walk feet on the ground instead of floating along. I even inadvertently signed a cheque Rosamond Napier. I should always advise a bride to include some of her old clothes in her trousseau.

The Sind-Worki.

A busy morning for Henry. Dhamnies and victorias rolling up incessantly. Pattawallas rising from their hunkers to escort Lingayat or Mahratta landholders to discuss with Henry their villages, their crops, their disputes. Occasionally an Indian pleader, or a Subedar of Police with sword and shining brown leather. Kanarese, Mahratta and Hindustani voices all very loud and echoing through the verandah.

But now from the dark shady tunnel of the drive advances a little procession on foot. First an Indian in a dress unfamiliar to me, followed by three coolies carrying on their heads corded battered yellow tin trunks. This will certainly be for *me*. Hastily I bend to the dirty bit of paper from which I am trying to decipher the dirzi's accounts. "Butons for Sahib's weskit, 5 pies. Blak thred for butons, broon thred, 1 anna nine pies".

Sure enough. Here comes Syed the lanky indeterminate pattawalla I like least. "Ramchand box-wallah for Memsahib".

I say I have no wish to buy anything this morning. That I am busy. But already I can feel without seeing that the yellow boxes have been brought up into the verandah, laid on the tiles, uncorded, and are already being opened. And here is Mr. Ramchand himself before me, all smiles, no longer the broad facade of ferns and crotons and coleus to separate us! He speaks some English. I assure him I am terribly occupied, and in any case I need nothing. I say "Salaam" and again study the dirzi's bit of paper earnestly, but all the while Mr. Ramchand is standing there, and the coolies are lifting out layers and layers of glowing silks and embroideries. It is as though a rainbow had penetrated into the dim verandah. I implore Mr. Ramchand not to let the coolies take out any more.

"It is only wasting your time. I need nothing".

"But Memsahib. I not wish to *sell.* If Memsahib only look at my beautiful sil-iks I go away happy".

Every chair, every charpoy, even the floor is piled with Benares saris stiff with gold, Kin Khob from Surat, shot silks from Bokhara, bolts of tussore silk, and China silk, and all the while more and more are being lifted out from those seemingly bottomless tin boxes. Even on my lap Mr. Ramchand has slipped "Chinese sil-ik drars. Ver-ree chee-ep".

If only Henry would come!

Sometimes on gruelling mornings he leaves his visitors for three minutes, and comes down to me for a breather . . . and thank goodness here he is; he will send this fellow packing.

Not at all! The two seem delighted to meet. They are talking in a language I do not recognise. I catch the words Hyderabad, and Shikapur, and Henry breaks off to explain this is a Sind-Worki, whose head, the Mukhi, lives at Hyderabad Sind; that he has shops in Aden and Malta and Gibraltar, London, Paris and Singapore . . . all over the world, and don't I remember going to see one of the Mukhis in their shop at Port Said, and drinking Turkish coffee there?

"Isn't there anything you'd like here", asks Henry looking at all the scattered brilliance around, overflowing even into the drawing room behind us.

My eyes have strayed to some gorgeous Bokhara silk glittering in green and blue like a peacock. I say "The dirzi says you want some new tussore suits", for after all my trousseau is only a month or two old.

A whole bolt of heavy tussore is put on one side, another for me. Then a lovely faded mulberry bit of silk takes Henry's fancy. It is a little tattered and worn but is covered with phalanxes of embroidered peacocks. Next some stiff rose and purple shot Bokhara silk for cushions, and half a dozen hand printed Sind cotton chadars for bed spreads. Bold black and Indian red designs on a white ground, and two others with blue and green Trees of Life, and clambering monkeys.

So at last the rest of the goods are miraculously fitted back into their tin trunks. Henry returns refreshed to his office, and Mr. Ramchand marches down the shady drive again followed by his three coolies, the tin trunks on their heads.

"But I not wish to *sell* Memsahib. If Memsahib just *look* at my beautiful sil-iks I go away happy".

At dawn when the magpie robins are beginning to sing from the roof, clear sweet-acid notes like a slate pencil dipped in honey, Misteri and his mate carrying a basket set out for the bazaar to buy food for the day. A chicken for six annas, mutton for four annas, vegetables, spices, "currystuff", fruit and all manner of things. These items are afterwards laboriously written down in a child's exercise book, and it is my duty when I go into the kitchen to see the table is scrubbed and the aluminium pots clean, to check these items. I can make out "Shukar" and "Curry-Stuff", but all the other items are indecipherable, and though their cost may be only the eighth or tenth part of a penny it is amazing the sum Misteri's book can mount up to. So though I can't make head or tail of it, I have to pretend to. It is a relief to escape from the greasy book to outside.

Under the trees just now there are quantities of very bright, very pink little begonias blooming. (I don't know why but they remind me of daffodils growing under the trees at home). It is so darkly shady here I need scarcely wear a topi, and further on where the sun strikes through a clearing it picks out the two white bullocks plodding up the ramp drawing our water from the well, to dazzling quicksilver.

Under the trees I came on what looked like an old fashioned stone sink. Imagining it to be used by the malis for filling their watering cans I found instead of water, it was quivering to the very brim with layers and layers of living spiders all touching each other, so closely packed were they. There must have been thousands upon thousands of them. A disgusting sight. Later I brought the frankly sceptical Henry to see them, half afraid they might have vanished meanwhile. But there they were still quivering! Horrible. We can find no one to explain it.

I can't get used to the pattawalla habit.

I pull a chair to a different part of the verandah.

"Why don't you call a pattawalla?" asks Henry.

I roll up a chick to let the level rays of the sun stream in through the hanging baskets of ferns and flowers.

"Why don't you call a pattawalla?" asks Henry.

There is always a pattawalla present. (His name means that). You never feel alone for a moment. The servants being barefoot, and the rooms having archways instead of doors you can't count on a moment's privacy—except in your bath room. And Ayah would like to come in there too.

It is delightful to have your long hair brushed smoothly and tirelessly three times a day. It is amusing—at first—to have your shoes arranged left foot to right and right to left for luck, but to have the dear old woman patiently holding out my chemise till I am ready for it, or expecting to draw on my stockings, is more than I can bear. I am resigned to having my hairpins arranged in a neat pattern and even handed to me, but now I have told her I prefer to be alone when dressing. Poor old Tulsi. Her seamed faithful old face is full of distress. Has she done anything wrong?

Other people don't seem to mind pattawallas and ayahs doing everything for them.

Henry tells me one must conserve one's energies in this climate, for the things that matter. Let others do those that don't.

The Munshi.

I have lessons in Urdu to enable me to speak to Indian ladies grammatically in the third person. Women out here usually content themselves with jabbering kitchen Hindustani.

My Munshi comes every afternoon. A quiet little Muhammadan with a shaven upper lip, sparse beard, tight black frock coat buttoned to the chin, a fez, and white cotton trousers. Depositing his curly-toed shoes under his chair, he sits cross-legged, and fiddles with his toes. He is patient with my slowness over the complicated alphabet. *Afsos*! he has no son—but a little daughter whom it is quite clear he adores—though of course she has no soul. I tell him to bring her to see me, and promise to photograph them both, and he shows his splendid teeth in a grateful smile.

He delights in telling tales of what he calls *Hikmat* (trick) and rolls on his chair with laughter as we read from my primer how one person does another down in some dirty way or other.

"But that was dishonest!" I exclaim ponderously.

"No! No! It is *hikmat*", he shrieks, laughing so much that I fear he will fall off his chair.

I like best a never-ending fairy tale he tells me of a Persian princess, Huss-naf-Ruz. I don't know how to spell it, but her name too is Rosamond, Rose-of-the-World.

To-day I stick in my lesson. I can't make out a letter, try as I may. Munshi bends forward on his chair playing desperately with his toes.

"But Memsahib knows it. Memsahib KNOWS it".

I don't, and say so.

"But it is *Alif*. The very first letter the Memsahib learnt".

"*Alif*? *Alif*? *Alif*? But what then is this, and this and this?" I cry indignantly pointing to endless curves and dots and flourishes.

Munshi smiles sweetly.

"They are for beauty's sake".

Munshi came late to-day. The lesson dragged. He seemed distrait. Presently it came out. The little girl I had photographed with him was ill, and he could not afford to send her to hospital.

"But you don't have to pay at all at the Civil Hospital!" I exclaimed.

But it seems though officially you don't pay, the native sub-assistant surgeons, and the servants of the hospital all demand their backsheesh, putting every manner of difficulty in the way of seeing the patient (whose food has to be brought by the relations) if that backsheesh is not forthcoming.

"I will speak to Colonel Houston," I told him.

"No difference Memsahib. The Colonel Doctor Sahib like other Wilayati sahibs do what they can—but it is *dastur*, the custom of the country", and Munshi made a little hopeless gesture with his hands.

Henry corroborated his story. I was horrified. Henry pointed out that we also have bribery at home though in an infinitesimal degree as compared with the East. The tip slipped into the manservant's hand at the consultant's door to get in earlier. The butcher, the baker in league with the cook.

May, 1914.

We are giving a dance. Excited, delighted bustle from servants and pattawallas. How they love a "tamasha"! Hyder Khan is giving orders like a Commander-in-Chief. Brass is rubbed till it almost blinds you. The parquet floor in the drawing room is polished to glass. *Kala Jagas* (black places) are prepared for sitting out. Delicacies, chocolates and printed programmes with their little blue and pink pencils and tangled silk cords have arrived from Bombay . . . and a little boy dies at Bognor.[1] A pebble thrown in, but the widening rings reach us out here. Our dance has to be called off for "Court Mourning".

[1] Prince John.

We send the piles of food to the Convent to distribute amongst native Christians, for no one else except our Goanese cook and his mate would touch it. Sadly the pattawallas take down the "Connaughts".

Disappointing. Never mind. Jumping rice bunds is better fun than dancing, and soon the time for it will be over. Miles of terraces have been prepared for the rice. The walls vary from two to four feet, or a little more. They are about thirty to forty feet apart. You put your horse to the walls . . . the cocked veined ears, the snatched bridle and snorts! . . . and away you go clearing jump after jump, your horse increasingly excited, till your arms are nearly pulled from their sockets.

Well, a "window can be opened" I think by such intoxicating exercise no less than by a poem, a symphony, or noble architecture.

Thunder-storms daily, and cattle killed. You get used to it. Every manner of insect. A beetle comes zooming in, ricochets off Henry's forehead, whacks on to the tiles, lying there helpless on his back furiously buzzing. No one pays any attention. Lizards are barking at you from the top of picture frames. Moths and flies in one's face, and flopping into the soup; and now Henry is delightedly watching a praying mantis motionless on the white cloth under the brass lamp with its hurricane top. There is something sinister to me about the long pale green stick with its disproportionately tiny head, its little hands clasped as though in prayer. It is some five inches long and no thicker than a twig. With black beady eyes it fixes the silvery little moth it intends to devour. Its half open blades tremble . . . I brace myself backwards in my chair. Henry shall not guess . . . but if it advances towards me I know I shall cry out.

But I get used to praying mantises too.

We wake one night. A hideous scream. By the light of the hurricane lantern standing on the floor we see the ceiling cloth which is stretched over the rafters bulge and quiver. A rat up there is being devoured by a damon, that snake harmless to humans. Harmless to humans yes, but it somehow disgusts me to see it threading its long length of eight or ten feet through the grass, or drawing itself over the split bamboos which cover the rafters of the verandah.

A cobra slipping into our bedroom is seen and despatched. It is almost yellow. Mr. Bell, the naturalist, says females often turn that colour when about to lay eggs. A pleasant bed-fellow.

Henry declares I attract snakes; that he has never seen so many in all the years he has been in India, as during the past three months. The answer being, of course, that this is a snake infested district. He goes on however to tell me when he first came to the country he went into his bathroom at night, and saw behind his bath the shadow on the white-washed wall of a cobra sitting on its coils swaying to and fro. He went to his room, fetched his revolver, fired—and with a hideous shriek a cat whose tail he had fired at darted out between his legs. That's all very well, but I tell him *Father had told me that same tale, when I was a child, about himself*!

But Henry did tell me something interesting. He was travelling down to Bombay and a Jesuit priest was in the compartment. He had a bundle of something on the seat beside him.

"Feel that", said the priest.

Henry did, and felt a writhing, squirming india-rubbery mass.

"Whatever is it?"

"Kraits" returned the priest. "It's all right. They don't strike through cloth!"

Yes. I'm getting used to insects, thunder-storms and snakes, but I can't get used to the absence of time-sense. A man comes with a message requiring an answer, the syces want to know if they can take the horses to be shod, the dirzi wants to try on the Sahib's coat, the brasswallah has some old brass he would like the Bara Sahib to see.

"Let them wait", says Henry at his office table.

So he or they join the little group of pattawallas sitting on their hunkers.

Presently I pass them. They are still there. They are certainly perfectly happy "sitting away" or "eating the air" as they call it, or playing cards, but I picture them consumed with the impatience that

I should be consumed with myself. I pass Henry's table, and say as unobtrusively as I can:

"Did you know that man is still waiting?"

"Let him wait. Which do you think is the more valuable. His time or mine?"

Henry has not raised his head from his writing.

Mother always feared a sarcastic tongue! I don't—at least not very often.

The man continues to wait.

Monsoon.

The heat grows fiercer, the gold mohur trees smoulder and blaze in their vanity through whirling clouds of crimson dust snatched up by a fitful wind. Through the long hours the coppersmith bird beats out his ceaseless "Tonk! Tonk! Tonk!" On Sundays the padre has changed the hour of the parade service to eight a.m. Henry and I drive down in the victoria in sun-topis, and wait there under the trees to watch the band and the troops come swinging down the road, the drum major twirling his staff round his head, the sweat rolling down his face, his tunic black with sweat between his shoulders.

It's a large church, and well filled. On the right side Henry and I and all the other civilians and their wives filling two or three long pews. On the left General Fry and the officers and their wives. Behind, all the troops and those few Eurasians and native Christians who are not Roman Catholic. Our Padre is very high church. To-day he opened his sermon "There is no such thing as a Protestant—who was Martin Luther? Just a monk who broke his vows and made a nun break hers". Now General Fry is an Ulster Protestant! Across the aisle I could almost hear him sizzling with fury! He contemplated marching the men out of church!

Skies blaze, spear-grass hooks itself into your stockings on the links, cattle become daily more emaciated. There is a feeling of expectancy abroad. In the cantonments coolies are covering the sides of the barracks and the officers quarters exposed to the south-west with matting. They are closing in the verandahs, they are swaddling all the gateways, and the low mud walls with matting too. Hyder Khan has caused our topis to be enamelled, which I do realise will make them waterproof, but also makes them terribly heavy! Talk is all of the hopes of a good monsoon.

In the Club new faces are appearing, as district officers and their wives and families trickle in from the district. Some of the Forest officers have been in camp for six or seven months. They look "apart", what they themselves would describe as "jungli". Lean, and ill-at-ease even in this unsophisticated society. They tend to keep together, and as you pass you hear snatches of "tiger", "devastation by kumri", "timber slides", and "emboisements". The young Butterworths belong to the Forest Service. I had heard that the previous year he had been attacked by a wounded tiger which not only tore, but literally chewed the flesh from his arm. "Feel", said he, when I asked him about it one day at dinner. I felt. There was just a bone seemingly lost in the sleeve of his coat.

The Monsoon is expected to arrive on June the sixth it seems. Strange. One day to move automatically from this brittle parched world into a dripping one! No one seems to think this wonderful but me. As the sixth approaches I feel an inward and rising excitement. It is like waiting for tremendous news, or an operation, or a baby.

June 5th.

No sign of the Monsoon.

June 6th.

We woke this morning feeling oddly chilly. The room seemed unusually dark; outside whirling grey mist. Everything clammy to the touch. The casuarina trees by the porch appear and disappear in rolling mist. The red tiles of the verandah are dulled to raspberry.

The Monsoon has arrived to the day.

July 15th

The Monsoon is very weak. Sagging purple clouds come driving over the golf links, and now and again the rampart of hills which divide us from the coast is blotted out in drizzle. It has been just sufficient to change the lion-coloured downs into sweeps of living green dotted all over with little white orchids. That's all. Rice is turning yellow. I hear from my brother that Government is already buying up grass for famine relief, and one dark and gloomy evening this week there is a great crying and tomtoming out past Musketry Hill where the Hindus have gathered, praying for rain.

The Little Shepherds.

We have had rain. With it it seemed as though the little shepherds came. The west wind blew straight from the sea eighty miles away, bringing a salt tang to your lips. Faraway hills were veiled in flying rain one moment, hardening to a lilac silhouette against the watery silver sky the next, and from everywhere you heard the piping of the little shepherds on their bamboo pipes. Very clear and melancholy came their sweet piping through the moist air. On the deserted uplands of the golf links they stood motionless watching their grazing flocks, looking through the drenching pelting rain like small black coffins set up on end. It was only as one drew close one saw that these small isolated coffins were little shepherds hooded and shrouded in their black country blankets.

I drew one. His thin arms crossed holding the blanket tightly over his chest, his spindle thighs glistening wet bronze, his eyes bright as raindrops looking out from his blanket. All round the goats fed, some pushing along on their knees, their angular hind quarters silhouetted against the sky, others strutting and jerking as they stepped, and others again fading into the mist, yet all feeding in such a desperate greedy hurry to make up for months of hunger, that from every side rose the sound of tearing and nibbling and snatching as well as stamps and impatient snorts.

By and by the rain which had been descending in crystal rods lessened. Away to the west the grey rags tore apart, wild blue hills could be seen flung up against a white sky, and shining out of the purple and green distances of the Krishna valley miles of flood gleamed and glistened.

As the rain ceased to a few spitting silvery drops the little coffins broke open, and the goat herds with their red turbans, their scraps of shirts, and naked thighs began piping to each other through the moving airs like jolly storm-cocks.

Far away down in soft bright green of sugar-cane a black partridge called, and from the rice rose the fluty music of millions of frogs. The wind blew hollowly in one's ear. Sounds I shall always remember and treasure . . . and there far ahead straying into a sudden gleam of sunlight a little shepherd in his black blanket leading his black flock over the hills and far away.

We are living as though under a waterfall. The air seems solid with water, and the lungs like saturated sponges unable to draw in more. Breakfast is eaten by lamplight and Henry has a lamp on his office table throughout the day. We have to keep a sharp look-out for snakes. Insects of every conceivable kind invade the bungalow. We can hardly hear ourselves speak for the waters roar and gush and pour off the corners of the gutters swelling the sheets of red water surrounding the bungalow and under the dripping and swaying trees on whose branches sprays of white orchids have come into flower.

In the drawing room are bowls, basins and a saucer bath to catch the water streaming down between the tiles shrunk by the hot weather. Hyder Khan causes crumpled newspaper to be put in these basins lest the drumming noise disturbs us.

Last night I lay giggling, because Henry and I were forced to sleep under umbrellas. All day our bedding is spread over wicker cages enclosing a charcoal sigri, but even so my pillow smells fusty; there is mould on my white kid gloves kept in their glass bottles, and Ayah has to sandpaper the rust off my hair pins. One day we had 15 inches in the twenty-four hours. In most parts of England it is about 24 inches for the whole year.

Everywhere, in spite of that matting the coolies put up, the mud walls are subsiding. News comes of breaches on the line. Cattle drowned. Whole tracks of country are under water. The rice is saved, and from every side rises the million rejoicing voices of the frogs as though they were offering thanks to the gods on behalf of the people.

Owing to the line being breached, fish coming from Goa or Bombay is delayed, and so arrives tainted. Housewives have either to give tinned fish at their dinner parties or go without.

This week we dined at the Judge's. His wife is at home which no doubt explains why we had "fresh" fish for dinner.

It was preceded by a most powerful smell. Everyone looked up startled, but our host appeared to notice nothing, and we were all helped. Seated at my right hand was Colonel Houston the I.M.S. surgeon. "For God's sake don't touch it", he muttered laying down his own knife and fork.

But what could I do? On my left was my host eating his unconcernedly. How could I leave mine? Yet the smell was horrible. I played and pushed the stuff about on my plate, talking at random in my embarrassment. And then a new trouble arose.

Henry had been put at the bottom of the table facing our host. And now from that end came commotion and wild hilarity. One always takes one's own servants out to dinner, and Hyder Khan had been standing a majestic figure with folded arms behind my chair as usual. But Henry had beckoned to him, and now down there over the tops of the roses and silver candlesticks and pink shades I could see Hyder Khan filling up little glasses, and Henry and everyone laughing. Little Mrs. Houston whose merry eyes always disappeared when she laughed was convulsed. Colonel Houston was leaning forward to look at his wife. What on earth was happening? There was Hyder Khan bending forward gravely filling little glasses—Henry laughing—talking.

Like a blow it came to me Henry was drinking too much.

Though no teetotaler, indeed scornful of the breed, Father had an intense contempt for "drinking" or anyone who could not hold his liquor, and we had been brought up to share it. That Henry of all people should get "noisy"! It was incredible! And yet had he not said to me on Beachy Head that morning, "You know I shall be an entirely different person in India to the person you know here. Can you face it?" Here was I in a strange country married to a man who at the very beginning of a dinner party had evidently taken too much.

It had hitherto been such fun jolting home after dinner parties. The curtains of the dhamny (white leather they are), tightly buttoned down so that it is as intimate as being shut up in a box. The bullocks splashing through the puddles to the jangling of the bells and the cries of the dhamny wallah. The rain pelting down on the roof like bullets, and Henry and I dry and cosy laughing and talking over the dinner and the people. But tonight I was stiff in misery, and silent.

At last he got it out of me, but at my mumbled accusation, no penitence, only shouts of amused laughter.

"My dearest girl . . . "

It seems he and others at the end of the table had been aghast at the state of the fish. It must be remembered in India you may be well one day, buried the next. "You can't eat it. You mustn't. Its death", he had exclaimed to Mrs. Houston in much the same way Colonel Houston had warned me.

But it seems some of the women had already embarrassedly eaten some, and Henry declared to save their lives they must instantly take neat brandy. He had beckoned to Hyder Khan with that little oriental motion of the hand, to serve brandy all round. This was the cause of the merriment and laughter which had frightened me.

Astonishing my absurd mistake. Father and Henry, as dissimilar as two men could well be, yet on the subject of "drink" united. Abstemious themselves, not "amused" by jokes on drink, even going so far as to dislike it portrayed on the stage!

Oh well. Driving home in the dhamny with the rain pelting down on the roof like bullets was fun after all.

August 4th, 1914. *WAR!*

Incredible!

A frightened feeling. Some dark agency abroad, and adding somehow to the nervous tension, the heaviest monsoon for years thrashing down outside. Henry and I shout at each other to be heard over the roar of waterfalls thundering off the tiled roof at the corners of the verandah. It is dark at ten o'clock. Lamps lit. Pattawallas bunched together and whispering. Rumours spread. The bazaar is alive with them. The line is breached. No mail. Many cattle drowned. Mud bungalows and walls collapsing . . . and War. Stones loosening from the very foundation of existence.

I remember a few years past the laughing explanation of a hospital nurse who had taken all her life savings out of Consols to put them into something more paying. "It's absolutely safe. Mr. —" (he was Secretary to Queen Alexandra's Nursing Fund) "says the only possible danger would be a European War! ! "

Well the impossible had happened. Life disintegrating.

War.

It was impossible to stay doing nothing. Henry ordered out the victoria. We could go and see the damage done by floods. We should have kept dry in the dhamny but seen nothing. In Burberrys and the leather apron pulled up to our chins we set off down the flooded drive under the tempestuous trees, leaving the wild wet commotion of the casuarinas behind us.

The tank by the Fort was flooded to an enormous size, its waters thick Indian red. Herds of buffaloes had submerged themselves, only their noseholes, and the tips of their horns visible. We drove along the raised Poona road, the little ditches by the roadside where they find crayfish now flush with the road and spilling red water over it. We came to miles and miles of water on either side bouncing with rain. The Krishna and its tributaries had burst their banks and the red water was rippling briskly across the road from right to left, and Lot was splashing through it past his fetlocks. Sakharam turned, his face streaming with water beneath his sou-wester to say he thought we should turn back. But ahead the road climbed a hill clear of the floods, and Henry told him to drive on.

And then in seeming madness Sakaram turned Lot at right angles right off the raised road to plunge down into the sweeping floods.

Tearing back the apron Henry sprang up, snatched at the reins, forced Lot right round on his hind legs from that swaying rushing water . . .

It seemed that the sight of the waters on either side and pouring across the road had turned the old man suddenly giddy. We turned, Henry still driving standing up at the back of the victoria, till the water was less rushing.

But when we did get back, to remain in the bungalow was impossible. Wet through as we were we would go to the Club. Colonel Peebles of the Norfolks or Colonel Frazer of the 110th might be there. News might somehow be getting through. Sakharam had quite recovered, and insisted on driving us. We set off again. This dreadful feeling. This hole in one's chest where one's heart should be. This apprehension. Security vanishing. The air white with beating rain, ears numb with the roar of it . . .

And then suddenly Henry had burst up from his seat. And now he was actually wrestling with Sakharam. The old man was calling out. Henry shouting. He had wrenched the whip out of Sakharam's hands. He had jumped down into the road and was thrashing at something over and over again like a maniac.

"Khabardar! Khabardar! Aré, Aré", wailed Sakharam . . . and now I could see what was happening.

Henry had seen from his side a great cobra slipping across the road. Sakharam being a Hindu would not kill a cobra . . . yet when finally he saw it lying there, black, evil with broken back, he too seemed almost relieved as he had not done the deed himself.

I suppose for Henry it was some satisfaction, some relief to tense nerves to do something, but the cobra for me, like the rain, the subsiding walls and bungalows, the darkness, added to the atmosphere of apprehension and alarm.

WAR.

September, 1914.

We have meetings to interest the Indian ladies in the war. They are eager to help. They cannot sew, they cannot knit, but we hand out to them khaki shirts already cut out, and they employ dirzis from the bazaar to run them up. Then they themselves make Indian sweetmeats, and chutneys and spices, and collect bundles of the wooden sticks with which Indians clean their teeth. These women are very interested, and welcome anything to break the monotony of their lives.

To-day I went to meet some of them at the house of an old chief. His child wife is about to bear a child herself. She was dressed in a magnificent sari of scarlet and gold. Her eyes were dazed, but her skin looked livid and almost alive in its ghastly pallor over the brown. Her upper lip was constantly beaded with sweat which she patiently wiped away with the stiff corner of her red and gold sari. I could have wept. She appears to me to be terribly ill. There is something monstrous and atrocious in this little, little ill girl, married to an old, old man and about to bear his child. She garlands me with pink roses, and offers me limes and pan supari in chilly little hands like birds's claws. There is a song of welcome for me. None of the ladies can speak anything but Mahratti or Kanarese . . . and yet was not that an English word I caught in the song? Can it be? *Can* it be?

"SSSSund him victor . . . ious
Happ . . . eee King Georgius . . . "

A Music Party, August 25th, 1914.

To-day we went to an important and influential Lingayat. A little old man, whose laughter is as the crackling of thorns under the pot.

Marigold garlands, and coloured pennons over the gateway. Prancing elephants and tigers painted on the walls. Late gold mohur trees still flaming in the courtyard, and the red earth covered in their fallen petals seeming to radiate fire. Henry and I are garlanded, and shown rare old brasses, jewels, wonderful silk saris and embroideries, artificial wooden fruit and animals from Gokok and so on. After eating fruit and being photographed we are entertained by music.

The men were seated on the ground. The tom-tom man was truculent looking with round face, bolting eyes, and fierce moustache. He struck at his tom-toms as though he were striking an enemy.

Angry defiance breathed from him. The violinist poised the end of his instrument on his bare foot. With his bow he drew forth the weirdest music with terrific rapidity. So soft you could scarcely hear it, climbing painfully, dreadfully, with tortured steps as it were, all up the scale, his face corresponding with agony . . . then suddenly breaking into smiles and gaiety . . . and even as you smiled in relief, lo before you the tortured features again.

There was another man who had a little wooden book with wooden pages. He was Mephistopheles, leering, scowling murderously, head on one side, as though listening for the steps of an invisible enemy, he was yet threatening and mocking. He played with incredible speed, sudden snaps over his head, then delicate little flutterings and trillings of his wooden pages down by his toes.

A gentle old man was at a large droning instrument, and two others were singing, their heads flung back, their mouths wide, showing betel-nut-stained red tongues. The same tune went on and on and on in a thousand different patterns. Now sad, now bad, now gay . . . but always on and on and on with a dreadful restlessness. There was something dreadful too about the mechanical grins. Something frightening about the defiance . . . something hideous about the macabre crackling gaiety. Eyes starting, bare brown toes twitching, heads going . . .

I was exhausted.

The Bride.

There is a fine old Fort here surrounded by a moat, empty for the greater part of the year. Within its crumbling walls, shaggy with grasses, and with fig trees floating like banners from the crenellated bastions, are bungalows set down amongst great banyan trees, and tamarinds, sirrus palms and creepers. These bungalows are occupied by members of the different services, I.C.S., P.W.D., Forest and Police. They are comfortable roomy old bungalows with deep eaves of country tiles, and mud floors and walls. Their untidy compounds are a tangle of overgrown roses, dahlias, and cosmos, with too many snakes. Each bungalow has its own deep well going to below moat level. In the undergrowth, half-hidden, are Muhammadan graves, Jain temples, and relics of former occupations and dynasties.

The inhabitants of the Fort seem to form a little friendly coterie of their own apart from the cantonment. This is emphasised by the fact that as certain Government stores are still kept within the walls, there is a guard at the massive entrance, and dog carts and bullock carts returning late from the Club or dinners, have to shout to have the great gates opened. To this "happy family" an alien so to speak has lately arrived. A young bride who detests India and all things Indian. She is horrified at the huge pot-bellied figure of Ganpati with his elephant head at the gate, always kept freshly painted in pink gold and scarlet. "An idol", she exclaims. She is terrified at being alone in the bungalow, but equally terrified, and moreover repelled by her Indian servants. Her husband having something to do with Government distilleries is away in the *mofussil* (district) for hours each day. She is neglectful in seeing that the milk is boiled, the water filtered. She cannot drive, and will not learn to ride. Because it is the monsoon and raining, she refuses to believe one can get a sunstroke, and goes out without a topi. We do try to be kind, but she complains all the time. She is quite young, and should be good looking, but already in these few weeks her long narrow face has become haggard and sallow under its lovely crown of daffodil hair. It is clear she is eating her heart out for an English suburban villa with H and C laid on.

Day before yesterday Dr. Fisher told me she had dysentery.

Yesterday that she was dead.

To-day she is to be buried.

Hating and fearing India as she did it seems a pitiful thing she should be buried out here.

It is streaming and deluging with rain, but Henry and I feel we must go to the funeral. Too wet for anything but the dhamny. We button down all the white leather curtains. We can't see out, but at all events we are dry, as we jolt along as in a box, the bullocks splashing through the red water past the Club and the racecourse to the English Cemetery, lying within its foursquare walls. The rain is coming down in sheets bouncing up to one's knees. The wind is bending the casuarinas, and the bright dripping banners of the plantains are being torn into shreds as with heads bent beneath our streaming umbrellas we come straight up the gravel walk to the graveside. There is no-one there but ourselves . . . and we are too late. We must have mistaken the time. As we reach the grave the padre and the husband come away.

In silence Henry and I walk back to our dhamny where the bullocks wait with hanging heads, streaked and dark with rain. We left the bride all alone under the dripping and gesticulating branches of the trees.

Could one have been more understanding?

I wonder.

My brother Lloyd and Minnie his wife used to live in the Fort. In a corner of their compound was a tumbled down old bungalow still known as the *Bibi Khana,* the same age as the bungalow itself. Doubtless it was a relic of the days when English women were few and "officers took unto themselves wives of the daughters of the country."

One evening Lloyd's horse, who had been uneasy all day, grew worse, and Lloyd had him put in slings. Suddenly he smashed his slings and began screaming. His syce darted out from under the two bamboo poles and ropes at the entrance of the loose box, and the horse seizing the bamboos in his teeth smashed them like matches and hunted the terrified syce all down the stables. He just managed to get out slamming the door behind him, while the poor brute raved up and down the passage screaming most horribly. Lloyd fetched his gun, but before he could act he had to warn his friend Hutchinson in the next bungalow for Mrs. Hutchinson was in child-birth at the moment. Finally from outside he had to take snap shots at the horse as the wretched animal rushed at lamps held by syces at openings in the wall . . . There were many shots before he could drop him, and to add to the confusion the guard came hurrying up to see what it was all about. They never discovered what had sent the horse mad. Lloyd imagined rabies, but the native theory was the poor beast had swallowed one of those loathsome black six inch centipedes in his hay.

When I was telling Lloyd of the bride he said it put him in mind of a funeral he had attended some years before in that same cemetery. An officer had been shot by one of his own men as he was dressing for Mess, on account of some fancied grievance. The man was eventually hanged, but secretly buried in the cemetery. The curious thing was the Colonel received a petition from the men that they should be shown the site of the grave so that they might erect a memorial on it!

The murdered officer came from New Zealand. His epitaph was "He lies far from his New Zealand home". Not farther I feel than the poor bride from hers.

September 8th.

This evening the Norfolks were mobilised. It was dark and lowering with a chilly wind blowing a few drops of rain. The excited, anguished look on the faces of their smiling women! The regiment passed the Club, and there as though no such thing as War existed, under the immense banyan tree was the band. It was playing some dreadful tune which would never be forgotten. A piccolo solo. An evil dancing cruel little tune tripping quickly over the drums like some little devil tripping with spiked feet over women's hearts.

September 9th.

Early to-day we watched the Norfolks go. The sharp barked orders. The stamp. The march of boots. Colonel Peebles, the cheery fellow always called *Mr. Peebles* by his men. All those young officers one had ridden with, and eaten dinners with and laughed with, where were they all marching to, and how many would we see again?

The previous Sunday the padre leaning over the pulpit told the men that when they were lying on the battlefield they would regret not having come to him in confession as he had urged.

Incredible . . . yet I heard him with my own ears.

The End of the Rains.

Up to the racecourse we ride every morning in between the tremendous storms. Dripping, swaying trees and grass on either side of the road which itself is running red water. Men and boys shrouded in black country blankets with woven baskets over head and shoulders, like testudos, splash through carrying their country shoes. Mahratta women, their red and blue saris pulled between their thighs, follow, baskets on their heads supported by one up-lifted arm glittering with glass bangles. They step along like storks.

From the racecourse reaches miles of flooded country, showery lights on sugar cane and rice, and blue hills so close you could put your hand on them. When the storms come on we get the horses under the little umbrella trees . . . but even so by the time we get home to hot baths we are drenched.

But this morning the sun shines! Everything steams and sweats. Little visions of beauty are suddenly encountered. A spray of white orchids gesticulating from the darkness of a mango tree. Bulbuls are gushing into song, the wind has a voice of fluting sweetness as it shakes down twinkling drops from the casuarinas. In the night the garden has rushed into beauty. Dahlias, and such dahlias! Smoky brilliance of zinnias thrusting their heads through shining wet leaves. Cannas, balsam, a dripping hedge of monthly roses and blue plumbago, an unexpected flash of scarlet, too-early poinsettia, bridal creeper tossing its wreaths everywhere into the air. Butterflies flicking in and out . . .

The brilliance of the light, the purity of the skies, the whole gaiety of this scene of commingled scents and sounds and delights intoxicated me. *The Rains were over.*

It was such unexpected release from the sound of thrashing rain, fusty-smelling pillows, and gloves in air-tight glass bottles, a gloom, a thralldom whose very existence I had not even suspected till now, that I sang for joy, and called to Tulsi to fetch out my cotton habit. *The Rains are over.*

It is Henry's custom before mounting his horse, to go to his office table to see if any files have come in awaiting signature. As I come out on the verandah I see him, his long tailed red fly whisk across his knees, and Sadrudhin Pattawalla waiting to carry away the files.

Looking up he sees my khaki habit.

"You can't go out in that thing!"

"But why not? The sun is shining. It's *lovely*!"

"It'll rain presently".

"Oh no! I've been out. It's a wonderful morning".

"You'd better run along and change".

"But Henry I couldn't wear my Busvine to-day. If we get a shower we can shelter".

Henry raised his eyebrows and said no more.

As soon as we had got out of the park it was clouding over; before we got to the racecourse it was pelting.

I supposed we would turn into the Club nestling there amongst its feathery bamboos. Henry rode on. We came out on to the racecourse. The whole country was blotted out in the downpour. Leviathan hates the rain on his fine skin. He gave sudden and unexpected bucks in the middle of his stride almost unseating me, but after a few minutes he was soaked completely, and settled down to that wonderful gallop of his.

As we left the shelter of the cemetery where dripping bamboos and casuarinas swished over the poor little bride, a tremendous wind blowing direct from the sea, took us so suddenly, the horses were blown sideways and staggered. Jamming his topi, bending forward, Henry rode on without a word. Pink, with the rain streaming down his face, the burberry breeches and gaiters I call his "thrusters" black with moisture he galloped on. Larrikin, his bay waler, was spattered to the ears. Great phids of wet turf from his hoofs struck me in the face, as Leviathan thundered alongside. The wind shrieked through the hole in the top of one's topi, there was the sog of the horses's galloping hoofs, and just a momentary clatter as we passed over hidden rock. Long ago Henry had broken away from the racecourse. On we went over Treetop Hill, across the Vengurla Road. The horses were pulling like mad, covered in soap suds. The wet reins slipped through my fingers. My cotton habit was pasted to my thigh, my brown riding boots jet black, the breath pumping out of my body. I could scarcely keep my seat for fatigue, and on and on we galloped through the blinding rain, over those downs of brilliant green with their dripping, swaying bushes of lantana.

When finally we got home, my arms were trembling so I could not control them. I nearly fell as I slid from my saddle which was pulp.

The syces led away the steaming, streaming horses to their stable.

Henry said not one word. Neither did I.

We went to our baths!

This morning we were riding over the sunlit and undulating downs and had come scrambling down into a narrow little valley. The sun went in. We rode splashing down a little water way. The shadowed water was a cold blue, and bright bushes of burning scarlet and orange lantana brushed our horses flanks on either side, and the curranty smell was strong in our nostrils. Just as we emerged from the nalla the sun burst out again, and Henry looking back over his shoulder smiled at me with the sun in his eyes.

Why do some trifles like these stick in one's memory? It's the little things that make one happy.

October, 1914.

If anyone were to read these pages I suppose he would feel surprised that I write of birds, of riding and the servants and so on, making no mention of war. But when it occupies the whole background of life one does not think to mention it in a diary any more than speak of the air one breathes. These people I meet, mostly men, going about their daily business inspecting this and that, signing files, reading and writing reports, riding, shooting, what are they thinking about? Have they not all sent some such letter as Henry handed me one day in silence, a letter he had written to Du Boulay, the Viceroy's private secretary:

My dear Du Boulay,

I shall be obliged if you will place before His Excellency the Governor-in-Council my request for permission to join the army.

> Should it be urged that I am beyond the age limit for active service I would ask that an exception be made in my case. Surely a man who rides his twenty miles a day, and can follow up a wounded panther or tiger for hours through thick jungle, can shoulder his rifle as well as others.
>
> I do not wish to depreciate the importance of the post to which Government has appointed me, but during the period of the war, economy will have to be practised, and administrative activity be reduced to a minimum. There are many men available who could carry on most competently.
>
> If the Military Authorities prove obdurate over my age, cannot I go in some non-active capacity as interpreter or political officer?
>
> Most earnestly I beg that sympathetic consideration may be accorded to my request.

Yes. How many of the men I see daily have sent some such letter as this.

I've got a bull terrier.

The young subaltern to whom she belonged has gone to Mesopotamia. In the past few weeks she has changed hands many times. Finally she was left with native servants who starved and beat her. She is cowed and ill-tempered. Heart and spirit seemingly broken. Her complete indifference to our overtures is humiliating. We call her Lorraine, the War Dog.

Henry is sailing some three hundred miles down the Malabar Coast to inspect. He has borrowed a small revenue yacht. Everyone advises him not to take me. She is famous—infamous—for her exaggerated rolling, unless there is a very stiff breeze. Belonging to the Salt Department, she is known as Lot's Wife. There is a legend of some financial purist who questioned the propriety of expenditure on Lot's Wife!

So Lorraine and I are sent up to Mahableshwar to stay with Mildred Quin and the baby. Mahableshwar with its stupendous precipices, the azure emptiness of its valleys, the lake set like a blue eye in the jungle, its hot noon, and tart airs and wood fires at night. No bad place to be left in.

MAHABLESHWAR.

The Organ Note.

Mildred, Nanny and Baby Den and I take two tongas every afternoon and picnic at one or other of the Points. No carriages with fat sleek horses and spectacled Parsi ladies now as in May. The Club is shut. The place deserted. I confess it irks me that boiling a kettle and spreading a white cloth should be considered an end in itself in the majesty of these surroundings. There are drops of thousands of feet all about us, and the mountains, or hills as we call them, stand tranquil in the golden light, and down there in the valleys with their pathetic little patches of cultivation, sky blue rivers wind away to the sea. I don't want to talk. I want to be alone. I want to watch the kite suspended and gleaming in the sun at the level of my eyes. Suddenly he slants . . . down . . . down . . . down . . . and again down till one catches one's breath. I want to watch him, not Baby Den drinking his milk for the first time from a cup.

So to-day on pretext of sketching I took a tonga to Lodwick Point. Climbing cautiously over the slippery turf I stood on the top of the sphinx-like head, with all those tumbled wooded valleys dropped in purple shadow thousands of feet below the sole of my foot. Saddle-back to my left, the naked lunar-like range of Elphinstone Point to my right, the last "ku-tur ku-tur" of the green barbets rising up like incense from the woods below. The sun dipped in the sea at the level of my eyes. I caught the instantaneous emerald flash Henry had taught me to look for . . . and then poised there all alone up in that bright sky, the world foundering below me I felt an intense perception of the extraordinary and majestic beauty growing minute by minute, and then I heard a curious hum.

Was it in my own ears? No, it was increasing. Now it seemed to be throbbing even as the shining sky was throbbing all round me. And now it had swelled into a grave sustained note rather like the opening bars of the Rhinegold. Now it was the low note of some gigantic organ whose music was flooding the whole universe . . .

Perhaps a minute it lasted. Then complete silence shattered by the tonga ponies shaking their heads with a clash of bells, as they waited on the road below.

I could hardly wait to ask Mildred what it could be. She was incredulous. Twenty-three years had she spent in the country, and never had she heard such a thing. So the following evening Baby Den was left and she came with me to Lodwick Point. We stayed late and waited in silence till the last barbet was still, and the sun dipped in the sea. Silence.

Then the tiny hum. The throb. The deep loud organ note swelling up to us on our eyrie.

Mildred turned startled, her face dyed by the afterglow. Why had she never heard this? What could it be?

> *"The world is too much with us. Late and soon*
> *Getting and spending we lay waste our powers."*

Added later.

Camping in Kanara jungles Henry and I hear this same hum every night. Mr. Bell, the Chief Conservator, and a great naturalist, explains it is caused by the myriad wing cases of night insects stirring from their day-time sleep into flight.

COASTAL CRUISE.

Henry writes from the island of Janjira where an Abyssinian had once ruled, and threatened the foundation of the English settlement in Bombay. "I do wish you were here. You would delight in it all."

He was returning to Bombay to pick up a bull terrier he had just acquired. So off goes the telegram. "Coming".

We came. Ayah, a boy, a pattawallah and the depressed bull terrier Lorraine. It was desperately sticky and hot in Bombay. Henry awaited us. At once we went on board. Lot's Wife is delightful, all white and gold and spick and span with a crew of picturesque lascars. Windows, not port-holes, in Henry's office, the dining room and our cabin. Here in a corner lay an obese and motionless white mass. The bull terrier. My heart sank. Luther as we call him reminds me of some old roué with pouchy eyes and a cigar hanging from the corner of his mouth. He does not rise to greet me. Languidly thumps a tail, and leers from a dark and bloodshot eye. "We'll make a man of him yet", says Henry cheerfully. It appears that the dog has never left the compound. His owner had used him merely as a stud dog. There was something repulsive about him lying there. These bull terriers that I had longed for all my life. Lorraine cowed and suspicious, this dog repellent. "We'll make a man of him yet", repeated Henry sensing my dismay. I was doubtful.

(Note, May, 1945. I yet had to learn that Henry's optimism is generally sound. From playing a losing game at tennis to the days of Dunkirk).

As we left the harbour the breeze freshened. I didn't want tea. It had been terribly hot at Kalyan, and the smell of those pink and white flowers at the station sickeningly sweet. And tinned milk is horrible. Rainey seemed more depressed than usual. Neither she nor Luther took the slightest notice of each other. It was a relief to come on deck and see the rocky coast sliding past. The serang was shouting orders, the lascars in their sunbright blue running about and doing all the things lascars do do on a sailing yacht.

There are series of creeks down this coast, the entrances guarded by grim old forts, lairs of the pirates who harried the seas. Henry tells me they all but prevented the early voyagers of the East India Company from establishing their settlements at Surat and Bombay. The English Navy had attacked these forts. Clive had captured one. (Painfully conscious of the weakness of my history!).

It was past sunset before Lot's Wife came into Harnai. Against the still shining yellow west the turreted Fort reared up boldly with the shadowed grey-blue sea flinging itself up against the rock on which the Fort stands. Here Henry must land. Customs officials awaited him. In the fading light I could distinguish from here their bright turbans, their pale dhotis looped over very yellow boots. I could see baskets heaped with the marigold and pink rose garlands which would presently be slipped over his head. The dim warm sands we were approaching were crowded with Indians, and goats and babies, and bullock carts with solid wheels and hump-backed bullocks and babies, and slinking pi dogs, all moving in the afterglow like jewels against a background of shanties, and the dimness and grace of casuarina trees. It was fascinating.

And here came a boat out to us, and an official was describing to Henry in stilted English, details of the steamer wrecked in the monsoon. I heard his clipped voice through the jingle-jangle of the bells round the bullocks' necks as they lay chewing their cud in the warm sand. And by and by we too got into the boat, and then exchanged into chairs in which we were carried shoulder high through little plashing waves to the shore.

Another half hour and it was dark with the swift onrush of an Indian night. The jingling bullocks had gone, the crickets went "sing, sing, sing" and all along the strand moonlit waves were breaking up in bewildering green-white fire. Patches and fragments of this green fire were dancing all about us, for Harnai is lovely with its phosphorus. A strong tepid wind was blowing, and the moonlight was so bright the little marigold garlands round our necks gleamed orange.

We slept on deck. It was hard and I lay awake till three. The smell of the warm sea was strong. In spite of that charging wind it was stickily hot. Lot's Wife was rolling very slowly and deliberately so that the moon which was nearly full seemed suspended on a string which was automatically shortened and lengthened. Henry slept like some child. He was smiling. He had rolled up the sleeves of his pyjamas to the shoulder so that his arms gleamed strangely green-white. Lying on my back, pushing back the hair which blew about my face, staring up at the furled sail pointing like an immense finger to the misty stars, war was forgotten. I was completely happy.

Very early we were up to stretch our legs, and give the dogs a run. Luther instantly went berserk, scattering buffaloes in all directions, finally seizing one by the nostrils and dragging it to its knees. This took a lot of explanation to the mamledar[1] who was showing Henry round! "I told you we would make a man of him yet", said Henry after thrashing Luther till his arm ached . . . but I felt he was not quite happy! But Lorraine for the first time showed interest.

Amidst yells and shouts from the serang and the lascars we weighed anchor before seven to take advantage of the breeze before it dropped at eight o'clock. Then for three weeks onwards my purgatory began. Lot's Wife wallowed and groaned and rolled in the heavy ground swell, the sea heaving and sinking like violet diapered oil, the tar sticky in the seams of the deck. Misteri the cook was sick; Hyder Khan was sick, the pattawallas were sick, the dogs were sick . . . and I? I would have given the earth to be able to be sick! Daily Henry would sit at his pigeon-holed office table in his shirt sleeves. His collar and washing tie hung over the back of his chair, his jaw grim. Stubbornly he did his work, but the files when signed were not flung with the usual decisive slap on the floor. Stretched on my couch I would look past him at the windows filled rhythmically first with blue sky, and then with blue sea, blue sky, blue sea . . . Now

[1] Indian magistrate.

and again I would lift my head to look out of my own window. No. We *still* had not moved. There still was the old Fort with the fig tree afloat like a banner. We had swung round, but we had not advanced.

But at about one o'clock relief would come with the breeze. Then Lot's Wife sails briskly past white beaches and cocoa-nut palms cut out of shiny tin, and black basalt cliffs shaggy with golden-rose grass, and grim old forts with creepers gushing through loop holes, and intricate roots wrapped round bastions. Henry has brought books about the ravages executed by the pirates impartially on Dutch, French, English or Portuguese. He tells me of the doings of the Kings of Bijapur, of the Admiral Angria, and Shivaji the Mahratta chieftain.

Sometimes we run into a fishing fleet, and the jolly-boat is lowered to buy us pomfret.

To-day we saw floating in bright blue water, rising and falling like seaweed, a dirty yellow ribbon. A sea snake. Very, very deadly, but fortunately it seldom bites.

All this coast abounds with snakes. Especially fursas. An unpleasant death taking perhaps twenty days. You ooze blood not only from the wound but internally and from your ears and nose.

By the way, up and down this coast in the villages Henry tells me there are still a number of pensioners from Mahratta regiments.

"Oddly enough they *NEVER* die", he adds, "so a post has had to be created for an officer to visit every village every cold weather to see if Gopal really is Gopal or merely his great grandson!"

But not to seem superior Henry goes on to tell me retired members of the I.C.S. used to apply in person for their pensions at the India Office. He remembers his very first visit to London was accompanying his father who told him he had to show he was alive every quarter!

Devghad.

Henry buys me great golden hairpins of polished horn with cobras carved on them, and a big peacock feather fan on scarlet lacquered handles.

Daily we simmer and sickeningly roll till noon, then sail on to the next port, arriving a little before sunset.

Through those mornings of sticky heat, the tar bubbling on the deck, the glare from the heaving sea, servants and dogs lying in attitudes of misery, it was hard not to regret Mahableshwar with its roses and bulbuls, its aromatic wood fires in the chilly evenings! For the first time since marriage Henry and I could spend our mornings together, and here was I unwilling to speak or even think, wearily lifting a head now and again to see if the Fort still remained there as it had for hours.

But some evenings made up for this sort of thing. Jaighad, the Fort of Victory was one.

Five o'clock when we dropped anchor. A lovely land-locked harbour choked with native boats and behind them crazy shanties on stilts, and behind them again huts clambering up the cliff, forcing and squeezing themselves between cocoa-nut palms. Then right up in the sky the old Fort connected to the shore by its walls and bastions of black basalt.

We and the dogs climbed in greenhouse heat through the narrow spaces between the huts, though often we found ourselves actually in the huts. There stood about crowds of half-naked men and women in warm-coloured saris and caste marks on their foreheads, and babies with painted eyes, and buffaloes with wall eyes, and hens and goats and thousands and thousands of little, silver drying fish all mixed up. The sun was setting behind the precipice up which we toiled. It was suffocatingly hot. Though the harbour itself and Lot's Wife, looking like a toy, lay in shadow almost beneath the soles of our feet, yet the tops of the tall cocoa-nut palms over our heads were still in sunshine. The track was cut into rude steps, each step a foot or more high, and covered with dead leaves and rubbish. The blocks of stone in the walls had no mortar, merely fitting into each other by notches. "Think of the poor devils getting those up here!" exclaimed Henry.

We came under an archway with a wooden doorway still bristling with iron spikes to repel the assaults of elephants. And by and by we saw a few shallow excavations not much bigger than a grave. A dark-skinned man with tousled curls and a rag for clothing was emptying into one of these troughs some earth which he had carried up on his head. He and Henry were soon joking together. The man's teeth were very white.

"Think of that fellow's industry", said Henry afterwards. "First he cuts those excavations in the rock, and then he brings up on his head baskets full of soil from the river valley in which he can grow some rice. A Mahar. One of the depressed classes. I feel his caste has been badly treated, for a hundred years ago they were the mainstay of the army of the East India Company. They defeated a Mahratta army near Poona, and it was they who largely helped to cause the down-fall of the Poona Brahmin rule. And now we have disbanded all those Mahar regiments *and refuse to recruit them*".

I knew Henry had a great admiration for the outcastes. He had told me before how he had first come to value their courage. It was when the Bubonic plague first came to Karachi, and it was his first important duty to deal with it. One evening at the railway station he saw a train crowded as only Indian trains can be crowded, with untouchables leaving the city. He held the train up, and summoned their leader, who said they were dying in great numbers so were going to their country a thousand miles away. Now these men and their wives were of course responsible for all the sanitary work in the city. Henry palavering said "Get your people out of the train and go back to work. Tomorrow I myself will come to your homes and arrange a camp for you outside the city". After the old greybeards had consulted amongst themselves they agreed to this, and hundreds of men, women and children got out of the train with their bundles and babies and little tin boxes, in perfect order, and trailed away to their homes in the darkness. The following day Henry got the camp organised, and ever since he has taken every opportunity to support the claims of these humble folk to fairer treatment. Even now I know he is pestering Government for the resumption of military recruitment for the Mahar. These people are the representatives of the original inhabitants of India, the dark-skinned Dravidians who had been expelled by the Aryan invasions three thousand years ago and since been reduced to slavery. Contrary to popular belief, they are often unusually intelligent people, and just as pigs are only dirty because they are not given the chance of being clean, so it is with the Mahar.

We went on toiling, not a dry thread on one . . . I could hardly put one leg before the other . . . and then from that moist motionless atmosphere we came out on a great courtyard, and climbing onto a bastion were suddenly almost blown backwards by the wind which was almost a hurricane, tearing the breath out of our mouths!

Before our eyes nothing but the rough jade-green water of the Indian Ocean under a still flaming sky. Far below the sea thundered against the rocks, waves seeming to leap up to the crowns of the foreshortened palms.

There was a square old tower with a fig tree growing out of it like a banner of victory. We climbed to the observation post where a red reflector lamp throws its light miles out to sea. Our hands were crimsoned as though with blood. I thought of the raging war. This very lamp was on the look out for the German gunboat *Emden*! How far removed all this from the naked Mahar with his tousled curls bringing up the soil to grow his little patches of rice in the rock! But was this illiterate Mahar so far behind those who had burnt Louvain?

"Jaighad, the Fort of Victory", I thought letting my hand rest on the parapet.

"Don't do that!" exclaimed Henry snatching up my hand. "Just the place for a fursa this warm stone. And they are so lethargic they give no notice of their presence".

It is now the time of the Muharram, so all day, all night we hear without ceasing from the shore, the solemn note of the Dhol, lamenting the deaths of Hassan and Hussain. Across the sea come those muffled notes. Boom-boom-boom; boom-boom-boom.

As by day we wallow in the swell, or later sail past the coast with white strips of sand, the cocoa-nut palms, or its stern forts, we hear boom-boom-boom; boom-boom-boom . . . As at night we lie in the glare of the moon still comes from the shore that grave boom-boom-boom; boom-boom-boom. Never any faster. Never any slower.

Thus beats the patient, proud and steadfast heart of the Muslim; steadfast in endurance of the present, bowed to the will of Allah, proud in confidence of the future.

Boom-boom-boom. Boom-boom-boom.

Never have I seen anyone—except perhaps a general practitioner at home—work as Henry works. Hour after hour at his office table in the cabin, sticky in his shirt sleeves: then the moment he sets foot on shore, interviews and inspections. After a mere seven months, interested as I am, I still feel rather outside this Ma-bap life. Just now he is considering and investigating the conflict of interest between the rival coastal steamships; the Indian Bombay Steam Navigation Co., the British India and the P. and O., the recruiting of lascars, and pattawallas, in addition to the thousand and one problems brought to him at each port of call by the Indian magistrates—the mamledars—the petitions of the people and so on.

At Ratnagiri we are getting off the yacht to stay with the Muhammadan Judge and his wife. Then at Malwan we are camping with a Mr. Chuckerbutty. It is quite new to me that there are members of the I.C.S. who are Indians, so how much more would it astonish some of England's critics to know that the whole of the I.C.S. numbers less than a thousand to rule and look after the interests of three hundred million!

It must be tragically difficult for those Indians coming out to India after having been imbued with the English view of nepotism. For to the Indian mind it would seem cruel and unnatural for a young man not to help his relations and their dependents into coveted positions.

Judge's Bungalow, Ratnagiri.

The Tyabjis both very kind, but though on shore I still feel seasick, and Muhammadan food is rich. I have neuralgia, and a furious wind has been blowing for three days, rattling and banging at the jillmills so that sleep is quite impossible. In addition our beds consist merely of a board with a one inch quilt laid on it. Now I had been sleeping on Lot's Wife's decks, but I did have a mattress under me! One day a very pleasant young Hindu Assistant-Collector came to tea. I asked him about the Dhol whose solemn voice appealed to me so deeply. It appears he is much interested in music, and took much trouble in explaining all the different drums which Europeans describe indiscriminately as tom-toms, and moreover drew little sketches for me of each.

King Theebaw, ex-king of Burmah lives here in captivity with his daughters. Ever since we came to Belgaum Henry has been getting letters from these daughters beseeching him to find husbands for them. We went to call on him. I was a little inclined to be sentimental, picturing him eating his heart out in exile, till Henry briefly reminded me he had disposed of twenty-one of his brothers whom he feared by burying them alive, and causing elephants to trample on the pit. Theebaw was I imagine fairly happy with a tutor with whom he delights to study. The Palace was rather squalid, and overrun by little grubby dogs rather like Maltese terriers. The daughters kept clutching at me imploring me to use my influence to get them husbands. After Henry had had a long interview with the old king, I went in for a minute or two, having to curtsey to him, and back out of the royal presence.

The old reprobate!

His Burmese title was King of Kings, Lord of the World, and it was said that when war broke out he cabled to the King and Kaiser to stop it.

Malwan.

We are staying with Mr. Chuckerbutty, an Indian Collector whose mother was English. It is delightful to be on shore, though the earth still rises unaccountably to meet me! Mr. Chuckerbutty's camp is pitched in a very beautiful grove of cocoa-nut palms whose tall ringed stems shoot high overhead crowned with immense fronds. It is the first time I have been in camp. It is enchanting. We look like a tiny town under the trees, each tent having its own little drive leading up to it, picked out with white-washed stones so as to be seen in the dark. There is the Collector's own tent and office tent, and dining and drawing room tent. There is the Commissioner's tent and office tent, and our sleeping tent, and, of course, a number of smaller tents for all the servants and pattawallas. At a little distance are the bullock carts that have brought these along with all the stores. They are grouped in the shade with upturned poles, and the bullocks lying peacefully beside them are freckled over with sun and shadow. Every now and again they shake their heads with a chime of bells. Near by the men squat smoking bidis and playing cards.

Our sleeping tent is very large, a double fly, that is a sort of inner tent lined with a honey coloured material with little sepia fleur-de-lys printed over it. The outer tent forms a kind of passage all round, and in one corner stands a tub and washstand and commode for Henry, and in another the same for me. A single fly is not sufficient protection from the sun so we have to wear a sun topi whilst squatting in our tin tubs and pouring water over ourselves from a pint pot. That muddle of collapsible chairs and washstands and mosquito-net poles and beds with which Hyder Khan had bewildered me when I first came out to India, now makes sense.

One evening Mr. Chuckerbutty suggested bathing. He had gone to some trouble securing a native outrigger thinking it might amuse us to be towed through the water. He himself got into the boat, and there were two fishermen balancing on the tree-trunk attached to the side. We should both have preferred swimming on our own, but presently Henry said as he had taken this trouble we must make use of the boat. Accordingly I seized the trailing rope and was drawn swiftly along.

The sun had set.

Short choppy little waves slapped up against me, breaking in my face. It was not much fun. I swallowed too much water. The native boat with its little sail and the two men balancing on the outrigger were one moment hidden, the next visible. Somehow (I cannot imagine how) the rope, hard, wet and stiff, got round my neck. Just then Henry several yards behind felt he too must pretend to like being hauled through the water, so he grasped the trailing rope. The little boat appearing one moment on the crest, disappearing the next in the trough pulled me along, and Henry at the end with all his weight dragged me back. The rope round my neck was strangling me. I somehow managed to get two fingers between it and my neck, and frantically waved my other arm overhead in distress. This promptly sent me under. The boat was too far ahead to see what had happened, and Henry thought I was playing the fool. The struggling with one hand, the swimming with my legs, the coughing and spluttering, the rope sawing my neck off . . . the agonising thought. My poor Henry when he finds he has drowned me! . . . and then somehow he realised I was in trouble, let go the rope and came thrashing through the waves to me.

I had swallowed so much sea water I couldn't eat any dinner that night. Mr. Chuckerbutty was disappointed, for in the kindness of his heart, he had procured a quantity of oysters. They were so much larger than any I had ever seen before they repelled me, but Henry squeezing the little green skinned limes over them said they were excellent . . . and that night I thought he would die.

We always had the travelling medicine chest provided by Government for district officers, and castor oil and Dover's powders saved him . . . but the following day his insides were still in an uproar.

That evening I did a sketch from the shore. The tide out, the wet sands the most brilliant rose-gold, a line of cocoa-nut palms silhouetted against the flaming sky. On the shore a solitary woman holding a pot on her head, and gazing motionless out to sea.

Luther is rapidly becoming the bull-terrier of my dreams. Combination of buffoon, gladiator and sentimentalist. He accepts daily beatings without flinching, merely shaking himself with a loud rattle of hide, wagging his tail with a fatuous grin which says "That hurt you more than me". Life is very sweet to him whether it be chasing a buffalo or cow, opening his master's mail, bolting his dinner, or lying on deck on his stomach, his hind legs trailed out behind him like a court train. Watch him approach Henry buried behind the five weeks old English *Times*.

Stealthily Luther goes, paw by paw as though stalking. Reaching

Master he sits down before him very upright like a china dog. He lifts a paw, and places it on a tussore silk knee. The newspaper has not quivered. Now Luther is standing on his hind legs, and puts the other front paw up. There he pauses trembling visibly, the extreme tip of that whale-bone tail aquiver. Then a hind leg is drawn cautiously up, tries to find foothold, slips, finally succeeds. Still the newspaper never stirs. I am watching fascinated. Now Luther has managed to get his other hind leg up, and insinuates his head very gently under the newspaper. Quite suddenly Henry holds out the *Times* at arms length. Instantaneously Luther collapses like a pricked bladder on to Master's chest. There he lies in a swoon of sentimental adoration, his little roving dark eyes the only living thing about him.

Over that limp dead weight of sixty pounds odd Henry's eyes and mine meet.

Rainey, sad flotsam of war, bitter and contemptuous of us all three, continues to search for ticks between her toes.

Belgaum again. December, 1914.

Ever since I came out I've heard the name George Monteath always spoken with affection. George Monteath, Collector of Karwar, tiger and panther shot, naturalist, water colour painter and breeder of bull-terriers. Even if anyone could be found to dislike this man I doubt whether they would dare to admit it. His popularity has something almost fabulous about it.

George is as inseparable from his jungles as a tortoise from its shell, nevertheless you are always hearing scraps of information about him in the Club. The latest is that Charles, his beloved bull-terrier, has been carried off by a crocodile, and Minnie by a panther, and that he declares he will keep no more dogs in Kanara. Now he has written to Henry offering him one of their daughters. He is coming to stay and will bring her along.

This bachelor Collector is quiet, small, shy. In his shabby washed out grey-green jungle kit, rope soled shoes on his feet, he is a bit of the jungle himself. He has brindled hair, face as tanned as leather, and eyes shut up in short black lashes, as dark and twinkly as his own bull-terriers. He talks jungle "shop" between lips tightly closed in an almost inaudible voice. "A true Ulsterman", declares Henry whose own children persist in talking with their mouths shut!

"Sometimes you hear a tiger sort of singing to himself", George told me, "Not roaring. Just singing and talking" and he imitated a subdued kind of grunting, growling, roaring sound. "Last week I followed a tiger doing this. I just missed actually seeing him. He was always on the other side of a bush or tree, but not long ago I watched a fellow swimming the river, his shoulders high out of the water. He swam very strongly using his tail as a rudder. I watched him climb out of the water, shake himself and roll in the sand. Then he went off "singing to himself".

Well, next month Henry and I go off into the jungle and perhaps I shall hear this too.

The bull-terrier George has brought is a solid rather dwarfish-looking bitch, oozing with affection and happiness. She bustles into the room with her mouth tightly shut, though barking as though saying "Jolly well. How's yourself?"

She clambers into George's lap and platforms her head on his shoulder. It had never occurred to me till we kept them that bull-terriers were lap dogs! We call her Leprachaun . . . I don't know why—Rainey regards her sourly, but Lep and Luther become instant friends, sharing each other's charpoy.

We shall be staying with George at Karwar next month.

Christmas, 1914.

The McCullochs came from Poona to shoot quails and black partridge.

After dinner she played Chopin's Fantaisie Impromptu for me . . . and I sang. Then the four of us danced.

That night my dreams were punctuated by "Pop . . . pop . . . pop . . . ". Then a gentle repeated "*Sa . . . hib, Sa . . . hib . . .* ". At last I realised this was coming from just outside the half-doors giving on to the verandah, and that lights were flashing across the ceiling cloth.

Henry tore up his nets, and sprang up. Outside, Mr. McCulloch dressed, a pattawalla, servants with lanterns and general commotion. "Pop—pop—pop" still going on.

There was mutiny at the Jail and shooting. Henry and Mr. McCulloch, who by the way is Superintendent of Police, galloped off on the horses which had been brought round in the dark, and we two women sat on the bed under the nets trying to make sense of the bits of news we could get from the servants, anxious for our men.

The Jail was a small old building guarded by some sentries, and generally used for a few under-trial prisoners, but lately there had been an outbreak of armed robberies with violence, and a great number of tribesmen from the neighbouring hills were there awaiting trial. They were Berads, which means the Fearless Men.

It was not till eight o'clock on Christmas morning that our husbands returned both looking very tired. Instantly I noticed a smudge of blood on Henry's sleeve.

In the night a number of the Berads had broken out, murdering the police and seizing their weapons. They made off for the hills where they imagined some hundreds of their tribesmen would be waiting for them. The Indian Inspector had acted promptly, calling out all available men from the barracks, including a good many mounted sowars. By the time Henry and Mr. McCulloch had galloped onto the hillside it was like a battle field, and spasmodic firing was still going on. Wounded Berads lay scattered in the grass, and as the guard had used buckshot the wounds were shocking. Some seventeen lay dead, but numbers had escaped and were at large.

The men went to bed and slept all the morning.

Mrs. McCulloch and I drove to our Christmas service!

After that anxious talking through the night it seems strange to still call her Mrs. McCulloch. But Henry forbids christian names. He says when husbands get promotion it gives rise to suspicion if the wife has been on very friendly terms with the wife of the senior.

KANARA.

Belgaum is divided into three divisions, North, South and Central, over each of which is a Commissioner. Henry is now Commissioner in the Southern Division which is far the pleasantest of the three. Part of it consists of the uplands of the Deccan, growing cotton, jowari, sugar-cane and rice, and part of it is in Kanara. Kanara with its enormous jungles, also includes a sea-board of seventy miles with creeks and navigable rivers. It trades in teak, betel nut, rice, cocoa-nuts, silk-cotton and bamboo.

It is into Kanara we are now plunging.

Henry has six collectors under him. Each of these six collectors has three assistant-collectors or deputy-collectors under him. These eighteen assistant-collectors have three or four mamledars under them, and each of these Indian mamledars has fifty or sixty patels or kulkarnis under *him.* A patel being the hereditary head man of the village, without education but leader. The kulkarni is an educated man in the sense of being able to keep accounts. A section of all these people Henry will have to confer with whilst we are on tour.

The Land System contains important documents. The Record of Rights. Every field in the village has a definite number, and the right to that survey number should be accorded by the kulkarni (the meaning of the word in Mahratti being "the man who does everything"). His duty is to see that the register is kept up to date, and accurate, and Henry will have to see if his assistant-collectors or collector has verified this. Henry often remarks that the system is far more in advance of most countries, including England, where it is sometimes difficult to be sure of the title deeds of what you buy. Without this register the villager would not know whether a money lender or other member of the family would have the right to the nuts off certain trees, and so on.

All this sounds rather dull on paper, but explains why we have to take a whole "Office" with us into camp, office furniture, shorthand writers, pattawallas, mounted sowars (police) to carry despatches and so forth. This is the outward and visible sign of all that turns the wheels of the British Raj.

January 3rd.

To-day we go into camp for many weeks, making use of all that kit and stores with which Hyder Khan had so confused me on my arrival.

An exodus. The whole "Office" comprising Mr. Koimattur, the pleasant, educated Mahratta Assistant-Commissioner from Dharwar, Mr. Iyengar, the Madrassi shorthand writer and secretary, a sub-assistant surgeon, the havildar and pattawallas, two mounted police, the guard of five sepoys, not to mention one's own personal servants. Hyder Khan, Misteri the cook and mate, boy, ayah, a dhobi and bhisti, and sweeper, horses, syces, many hens and ducks and three bull-terriers. We shall ride or drive ourselves, but there are twenty-four bullock carts (two bullocks each) conveying the whole paraphernalia of "Office", double sets of tents, bedding, and the servants themselves. The bullock carts travel only at two miles an hour, so half go ahead by night to prepare camp, whilst the other half stay behind to pack up after the early morning start.

While Henry inspects, interviewing at each camp, his regular work goes on just the same . . . that is the never ending stream of reports from assistant-collectors and collectors; these ridden in daily by the sowars. Henry has to digest and sign them, and often accompany them by a long report written by himself before sending them up to headquarters . . . in fact here is the whole complicated yet efficient machinery of the I.C.S. which protects the ryot, which safeguards the revenue and keeps the country more or less free from pestilence and famine.

I am prickling with expectancy. I don't think of it as surveying some 4,000 square miles of forest but as entering a green fortress into which people disappear for months at a time . . . to reappear different.

We start by train already dressed in greeny-grey shikar cloth, breeches and coats with many pockets, and khaki sun helmets. The train dawdles along the outskirts of jungle past pools of lotus flowers, and great park-like trees of silk-cotton covered with red flowers. We arrive at Loanda at noon. There Sakharam awaits us in the dog cart. He is smart in his cold-weather livery, dark blue with a wide canary belt. Lot's bay sides are glittering in the sun. There are anxious moments as we drive through the crowded bazaar, the three bull-terriers spoiling for a fight with innumerable pi dogs. Our dak bungalow is at Astoli in the jungle some miles out beside a wide rock-stewn river. Here the Webbs, one of Henry's assistant-collectors, are camped in tents. Mr. W. has recently married. His wife Claire has a serene madonna-like countenance with a shy laugh, and very soft voice. She reminds me of a little brooding dove. Devoted to her husband, I yet have the feeling she finds the lonely life in the jungle hard to bear.

That night there is a full moon and heavy dew, so that sitting on the tiny verandah of our bungalow after dinner, the trees seem to watch with glittering eyes as the moonlight strikes on their wet leaves. There are fireflies snapping under the bamboos. Mr. Webb has a portable piano and a gramophone. We dance, the four of us. Odd to think a year ago I was learning the latest steps to this very tune in Cheltenham, "Little Grey Home in the West", and here I am dancing in the jungle, close netting over every window to prevent panthers from coming in, and the moonlight so bright that my emerald engagement ring gleams *green,* not merely dark, from my hand on H's. sleeve.

January 4th.

Lovely to wake feeling COLD. H. was sleeping in hot-weather pyjamas, sleeves cut off, and trousers shortened to the knee. To go to the tent which was his dressing-room, he snatched up a blanket, wrapped it round him, and thrusting his feet into an aged pair of pumps stepped gingerly out into the dew. There waited the guard. An order is barked by the subedar. Delightedly I watch Henry clutching at his blanket, bare legs showing beneath, stalk round the sepoys criticising button or rifle!

Mr. Webb has only some one thousand miles to administer as

against Henry's thirty-five thousand, so he will be staying on here for three weeks or so. I asked Henry exactly what does an assistant-collector do when in camp. This is what he told me.

"Well first of all his duty is to know the people. Every village has some petty tyrant, the tax collector, the policeman or the money-lender, and it is important that the villagers should feel there is some British official over them to whom they can bring their grievances. The big man may steal their land; the British surveyors have demarcated every yard, and as in the days of Moses any man who moves his neighbour's landmark should be punished. Webb must inspect the boundary marks, and stop the fierce quarrels that arise over any such theft. When he or any other assistant-collector sits in the chaura or village hall he may hear of damage done by floods which can be diverted by some co-operative labour, or damage done by wild boars or elephants, or roads which need improvement, or repairs to village tanks . . . in fact the countless interests of rural life. In the words of Virgil it his duty to be kind to the under dog, to repress the arrogant, and to teach the way of peace".

We made an early start. The cold made the horses restive. They resented the guard, they resented waiting, they resented starting. The jungle echoes and re-echoes with neighing in which the Arab horses of the sowars join. My black Leviathan pretends sudden affection for Ganpat, the mounted policeman's flea-bitten grey. He sidles up continuously, and shows his displeasure at my attempting to mount him by rearing to an alarming height. (He is seventeen hands!). At last Henry gets me up, but I can hardly hold my reins, they are so clumsy. Instead of the lovely little double bridle Father had had specially made for me with its supple inch-wide reins—this is a single bridle. The reins broad, coarse, cracked and mended with string. Yet the syces declare "It is the Memsahib's bridle. It is the bridle the Memsahib *always* uses. The bridle she brought with her from Wilayat".

Such useless, senseless lies. Leviathan that morning in rearing had snapped my bridle. Quite understandable. Why lie? H. is angry.

It is now his turn to mount. Larrikin lays his ears back and shows a white sickle to his eye. He begins to circle round, and the syce further upsets him by chucking at his head. Larrikin is over sixteen hands, Henry barely five foot seven. He has his toe in the stirrup, his knee almost in his eye, and Larrikin goes sidling around and around with Henry hopping after on one leg. I dare not laugh! Now the three bull-terriers hear monkeys and break away into the jungle a shrieking white line. Everyone has predicted we shall never bring them back from Kanara alive. There are so many panthers.

By now Henry is really angry, the servants completely losing their heads, "gabrao" as we call it. Rainey and Lep are sent back in disgrace to follow by bullock cart. Luther, Master's own particular dog is attached to Ganpat (the sowar) by a long rope, or rather Ganpat on his Arab is attached to Luther. Goodbye to the Webbs. We start. Horses still obstreperous. Luther dragging Ganpat after him, gasping, choking, his tongue starting so far out, it looks as though he must tread on it with his fore paws.

The road down to Supa is up and down, and striped across with shadow like the tiger who may be lying behind some bush or tree. It is soft and dusty enough to canter on. What fun! The sowar's Arabs, waving and flourishing their long tails over their backs, Leviathan ringing out excited neighs, and the quick beat of sixteen hoofs in the red dust. Moreover the feeling that this pleasure, this delight is really "work". It is important that I should keep Henry well, and able to carry on his exacting work, that I should be there as buffer between him and annoyance, exude oil when things go wrong. Years ago the old Duke of Wellington had written. "I know but one receipt for good health in this country, and that is to drink little or no wine, to use exercise, to keep the mind employed, and if possible to keep in good humour with the world. The last is most difficult to observe for as you must often have observed there is hardly a good-tempered man in India".

But it is quite unusual for Henry to lose his temper with Indians. The fact of the matter is that he and most of his fellows, kept against their will from active service to do what seems unessential work, are almost unbearably keyed up, thinking of Mons, Ypres, atrocities, the battle of the Aisne and so forth.

Seventy-seven years before the wife of another Henry Lawrence scribbled in pencil in her diary. "The wife who praises and blames, persuades and resists, warns or exhorts . . . upon occasion given, who carries her love with a strong heart . . . not a mere weak fondness . . . is the true helpmate".

But anyhow now all is peace. A ribbon of sky overhead, impenetrable growth on either side. Rope creepers. Flick and razor edge of sun and shade. Pull up a moment, and the silence is absolute. Tiger, panther, elephant, bison, jackal, deer, wild dog . . . yet never the snap of a twig, the quiver of a leaf to betray them. We feel we are being watched. Even the trees themselves seem to have eyes, for they are bound and strangled round their trunks with some fig parasite, so that only through chinks and small eyelets can the original tree be seen. They give the impression of doomed and anguished prisoners peering through. Then all along the high red banks are innumerable spiders' webs, and dark holes five inches in circumference. And even these look like eyes watching from the bank for a fat grey spider lurks in the middle like a moving pupil . . .

From the green silence we ride into a glade echoing and pealing with bird song. Bulbuls, golden orioles with their plaintive "peeho peeho", the sweet whistling of fruit pigeons, a hoopoe opening and shutting his lovely crest, "Uk! uk!. A golden woodpecker, minivets, barbets, ioras, bee-eaters, drongoes . . . they are all singing and calling till the whole glade rings like a church filled with boys' voices.

Just as suddenly as we ride into that bird-church we have ridden out of it. We have ridden in and out of one of those zones of song that interrupt the deathly silence of these jungles.

Henry fumbles in his memory for some classical allusion and by and by gets En Lochme from Aristophanes' *Birds*.

He points out that everything in the jungle has to fight for existence. Trees and flowers are armed with thorns. Even the sensitive plant which closes as you brush it is thorny. The gentle looking bamboo is spiked (is there a moral in this?). Henry seems observant all the time. I only sometimes, too often a mere sponge sopping up atmosphere. Henry thinks in form, I feel in colour. He arrives at a conclusion step by step reasoning. I jump blindly, yet somehow alight on the self-same spot. The combination makes for pleasant comradeship.

At Supa, that most lovely spot. The district bungalow is crouched on the side of the cliff, the verandah looking down, right down onto a tranquil pool where the waters of two rivers meet. There in that peaceful mirror is the tiny island shrine of Ramling, protected by a light shelter of bamboo poles supporting a strip of matting.

But I'm too tired and stiff and thirsty to look much. The servants already have everything prepared. Dhurries spread over the mud floors, beds made, and mosquito poles up: travelling bookcases open, water boiling for our tubs, and somewhere behind breakfast cooking.

The Maharajah as the servants call the old bearded sweeper, hurries forward with a brimming basin for Luther. The bull-terrier's face is streaked, his eyes half closed and red-rimmed with dust, his tongue covered with red paste, his sides going in and out like pistons. He is drinking so greedily the water slops over. "Follop . . . Follop . . . Follop . . . ". Then he pauses to break wind luxuriously.

As we go off to our tubs, he has hurled himself flat on his side, one rose-coloured ear inside out. Graciously he extends his limbs to be massaged one by one by the Maharajah. After all he has towed a horse and its rider for many miles.

What a dog!

Supa, January 5th.

Awoke to find white mist up to the rampart. Steaming and coiling, sometimes parting so that one caught glimpses of ghostly cocoa-nut palms suspended as it were in mid-air across the hidden river. Then as the sun struggled through, the mist rolled back, and the little Temple of Ramling is discovered sitting on the smoking water, there right below us.

We had our tea and toast brought out onto the verandah, and with coats over our night things watched the noisy jolly scene below, for the pool was now dazzling quicksilver, and men and boys were bathing with shouts and violent splashing. It must have been cold. Some were smiting the water so that it leaped and fell in showers of diamonds over their glittering bronze bodies, whilst half a dozen others swam out to the little temple, staying and hanging on to the platform. Bobbing blue-black heads in the water, and a great halooing and shouting which echoed and re-echoed in those wooded valleys. Then when men and lads had gone, down trooped the women and small children. Laughing, screaming, chattering. Quarrelling like seven-sisters birds they beat out their saris, and spread them out like long banners of red and blue to dry upon the sunny rocks. Some waded into the water, and bathed there, their hair unbound and dripping. As they came out their saris were pasted to their bodies so that they looked like Tanagra figurines, and all the while across the water blue smoke was curling up through the cocoa-nut palms with a delicious feathery smell, and green parrots flashed and screamed, pi dogs barked. It was a delightful scene. Sun, sparkling water, laughing voices. I felt for the first time I was seeing India. These were the same women one met on the road carrying pitchers on their heads, babies on their hips, the same serious men ploughing and working in the fields, but this was their real life, their background, their domestic scene. How often had I heard Henry complain ambitious young men in the I.C.S. are too keen to take, and retain, posts in the Secretariat, writing reports and recommendations before they have gained a sufficient knowledge of village life.

Well this morning we have been studying village life all right, stinks, cringing pi dogs, pink with mange and all. We splashed across the ford by the Irish Bridge. Mr. Koimattur, various pattawallas, and the three dogs accompanying us, the latter "heeling" so perfectly our heels threatened to strike their noses at every step. The poor little village is a huddle of country tiled roofs, their white walls spotted like Dalmatian dogs with the cakes of cow dung the women have plastered there to dry for fuel. And those same women I had heard screaming and gossiping down by the river, now stood smiling shyly at me, their saris drawn half across their faces.

The patel, the headman of the village, is here to greet Henry, also the kulkarni, the tax collector. Both are in long black coats buttoned to the throat, with white dhotis and bare legs. Henry inspects the office, the school, and the tiny dispensary attached. The school master is an enthusiastic Mahratta Brahmin. We see the copybooks of his pupils, and little chalk drawings, and a dusty cupboard where he keeps quinine pills. We learn that Supa, lovely though it is, is a hot-bed of fever. Indeed Henry had pointed out to me what swollen stomachs the almost naked children had, from their enlarged spleens. Now he is promising the schoolmaster drugs for the dispensary, and better equipment for the school. We stand and stand and stand, and the talk goes on and on and on, and as I can understand neither Kanarese nor Mahratta I begin to realise how very sticky I am, how very tired, how very thirsty. Henry when working is absolutely unconscious of such things. A relief when we are taken into a dark shed. Looming there from the shadows is a great domed Car of Juganath. Huge. Monstrous. Crushing in its effect upon one.

Abbé Dubois in his *Hindu Customs* had written of these great sacrificial cars more than a hundred years ago, but now Mr. Koimattur explains to me that the patel is telling Henry over there, that this car is still dragged out once a year. It weighs fifty tons, and it needs four hundred people to drag it. One can picture it decorated with brilliant banners of plantain leaves, and jungle flowers, dancing girls swaying and prostrating themselves backwards before those formidable crushing wheels. Cocoa-nuts dashed on the ground, lamps waved, the hysterical shrieking of pipes and blaring of conches, and rattling of tom-toms . . .

What does Mr. X, worn and red-eyed from overwork at the Secretariat in Bombay know of this?

This afternoon Henry and Mr. Koimattur have gone off in the dog cart visiting spice gardens, cocoa-nut patches and so on. No room for me. I'm content to explore the river above the Irish Bridge where the bright water is chiming and flowing between great rocks and tufts of grass taller than myself, and hundreds of pied wagtails very spruce and dapper are running amongst the sun-baked stones, making swift little sallies, snapping at insects: and weaver birds' nests hang like untidy straw bottles from the extreme tips of branches. Lovely that crystal clear river. Lovely the wagtails running and skipping about me. Lovely the soft skies of Kanara.

It dawns on me that if I want to paint or to write I must make a definite effort to do so, not just let it flow from me as heretofore. This is not to say that Henry is not richly appreciative of my singing, painting or writing. Indeed he is . . . but for the first time in my life I am living with someone to whom the Arts are something added to life, not growing out of it. Yes, something added. Rather like those pink tissue paper flowers you see pinned on to real bare branches, in tea shops or bazaars. Hitherto the Arts, the graces of life with perhaps animals have been the real background to my days. Animals fitting into the pattern as naturally as they do into the frieze of an Egyptain king, or a Bayeux tapestry, or the little dog couched beneath the pointed stony feet of some Ladye recumbent in her chapel in some country church.

Henry and Mr. Koimattur are late. The sun sets. The wooded hills whose reflections have been standing so brightly in the water below, are soft, and everything that is not olive green is silver, and very still. The speckled kingfishers like humming birds hover high above the pool with whirring wings. One falls like a stone splintering the water into silver, to rise from the widening rings with his prey. It is almost dark. A light shows in the temple, thrusting down its reflection like a sword, and the blare of a conch and an ominous knocking startles me. Little dug-outs bound together in couples, steal out from the shadowy bushes, and as they make their way to the temple the water dripping from the paddles drips silver, and the streaking ripples in that olive green water are silver too.

Perfect; perfect.

I had become accustomed to the deep organ note of the stirring insects I had first heard at Mahableshwar, but now as it ceased I was startled by an outburst of singing. The voices of those hundreds of pied-wagtails came streaming up to me on my verandah, a most lovely and unearthly choir. Darkness had fallen. I could only see a faint glimmer of water, but those joyous crystalline voices were still ringing through me, lifting up my heart, possessing me utterly . . .

Enchanted I leaned forward . . . and fell some four feet off the plinth onto rocky ground.

Henry returning in the dark finds Ayah bathing a strained and swollen knee by the light of a hurricane lantern.

Supa, January 6th.

Stormy start. My stirrup iron is missing. (Perhaps the Memsahib never had one. Preferred to ride without one!). Now my religious beliefs are hazy and unorthodox, but the one thing of which I am absolutely convinced is that we are all as important as another in the sight of the Almighty. Nevertheless these *stupid* sort of lies do try one.

But anyway my knee is far too swollen in spite of my dear old Tulsi's massage and fomenting to get into riding breeches, so it doesn't matter, and Henry hoists me up into the dog-cart.

It's cool. Clammy. The pool down there like a mirror breathed upon, the palms and huddled roofs grey silhouettes against silvery mist which even as one looks breaks into gold as the sun struggles through.

We splash over the Irish Bridge, Sakharam clinging to the step behind. We gallop madly up the hill, Lot's red rump tossing up and down like two ripe horse chestnuts. He has a mouth like iron. Henry vainly trying to hold him says a little breathlessly that Wellington when Colonel Wellesley must have crossed by that same ford when after capturing Seringapatam, and assuming the Government of Mysore he had marched a force up through Supa to aid the Bombay Government against the Mahrattas. "I wonder if my great-grandfather Alec . . . the one who got the Seringapatam medal, crossed with him here?" says Henry to me.

A most lovely drive to Khumbawada. Trickling streams and waterfalls. Birds everywhere, whistling, calling. "Be thee cheery. Be thee cheery", counsels the wood shrike. Bamboos gush up and spray over us like fountains. There are sago palms with hanging tassels like bootlaces: great kindal trees whose bark scurfs off and hangs in tatters, reminds one of wall paper in a deserted house. Strange flowers poke up through undergrowth, and along the high banks rise great turreted golden anthills, palaces in a fairy tale. Now a loud ringing call makes us turn our heads all ways. There he is. A Malabar squirrel big as a rabbit. Auburn . . . no crimson, he glints up there in a shaft of sunlight, his hanging tail a plume of pampas grass. Racing to the top of the tree, he twitches six feet straight up into the air, then launches himself into neighbouring branches.

"Listen!"

"Mahadeo! Mahadeo!"

We look at each other. The Mahratta war cry Henry tells me, bursting now from the throats of pilgrims journeying to or from some shrine. The shouting grows louder, and now we have come upon a number of bullock carts proceeding down hill. They are packed to overflowing with men with fresh caste marks painted on their foreheads, and women in bright saris, laughing, and children, and little babies naked except for the caps on their heads covering their cheeks. All the carts squeezed up and into the banks to let our dog cart, and the sowars pass, and the bullocks plunged and tried to turn, all but upsetting the carts, and the people laughed heartily and waved as though it were all the greatest fun—which it was!

Looking back over Sakharam's shoulder as he stood behind I could see the bored patient faces of the bullocks, stained purple and rose, and the purple tassels that swung from the tips of their painted horns. Sky blue beads and cowries were tight round their creasy necks. The pilgrims had been to the little temple of Ramling at Supa, Sakharam explained.

On we go between walls of painted jungle, the wavy narrow ribbon of sky overhead.

As the sun rose we came to the bamboo forests. There were parrots flashing past like green varnished aeroplanes. We saw a racket-tailed drongo, that astonishing bird with a forked tail of two thin wires two feet long. How do they remain undamaged flying through the thick jungle?

We passed Kanarese men and women with head loads of bamboos, the women very dark and ugly with no bodices, but ropes of black glistening beads falling over their breasts. Fine trees, deepest valleys, rushing streams and the skies a far softer blue than in Belgaum.

Suddenly we came upon our camp. A line of hooded two wheeled bullock carts along the side of the road which had travelled all night before us. Rice straw is scattered in the dust, and there the unyoked bullocks are chewing their cud. Hidden somewhere in the trees is the tiny dak bungalow. It can only boast four very small rooms, but some enterprising Indian member of the Public Works Department had seen that it should have an imposing entrance at all events. So there is a gateway . . . no gates . . . with two large pillars with balls on top.

Tents, beds, books, servants, and a crowd of cocks and hens and goats had left Supa the night before. They had lurched and bumped all through the night, but now we find tents pitched, beds made, baths ready, book cases open, cushions in the chairs, flowers in vases, and by and by dear Hyder Khan will bring us an excellent breakfast, and there will be salted almonds in a little silver dish for Henry, and chocolates in another little silver dish for me. Nothing forgotten.

The tiny bungalow is very dark, the unglazed windows somewhere up by the ceiling, and the walls painted a shiny navy blue. I examine various little flat insects, the colour of dead oak leaves as they move about these varnished walls. They have apparently no head, tail or legs. They move in any direction. They disgust me.

That evening I watch Henry in his shabby shikar clothes sitting at the door of his office tent. A great concourse of cultivators has come to see him. Some are on office chairs, others squatting on their hunkers. He is the arbitrator over the differences between themselves and the forest officials, the majority of whom are English, though some are Indian. *Kumri* is the burning of forest land for cultivation without plough. It is shockingly destructive and wasteful and so is forbidden. Mr. Koimattur stands there by Henry's battered travelling office table, a tall handsome figure in high buttoned dark grey frock coat, and rose coloured turban. (How odd it looks in the jungle!). Swiftly he translates all Henry has to say sentence by sentence into Kanarese. The figures nod gravely and gesticulate amongst themselves. Their fingers are long and supple with turned back tips. I love listening to Kanarese. It is like the sound of running water.

Early bed, for my knee is painful, but I hear Henry still in his office tent long after midnight, slapping down the files on the ground after signing them.

Khumbawada, January 7th.

Henry is shooting. He has disappeared into the still, sun-spotted jungle accompanied by some sixty raggle-taggle beaters together with Appa the sporting pattawalla who joyfully discards his starched white for khaki.

A long cane chair is carried out into the jungle for me some considerable way from the bungalow. Cushions, camera, war knitting, Hindustani Grammar and a bowl of bananas and limes. I shall lie there watching for birds and animals hour after hour whilst the sun slips five shilling pieces over me as he moves behind the leaves overhead.

How lovely these long and lonely days! Before I left England it had become the fashionable craze to take a week's starvation cure. Friends had told me of the clearness of vision, of thought, of understanding, the rarefied feeling which possessed them after the first two days discomfort. All clogging deposits of food gone. I too feel like that, freed from gossipy, unessential talk.

Some men come in from the jungle carrying a yard or two of bamboo, which they declare is full of honey. Their faces are very dark beneath the tattered turbans, and greasy ringlets fall on their shoulders. With their hatchets they split open the bamboo, and instantly clouds of tiny bees, like flies, are all round us. The servants who had crowded round to see, are panic-stricken, crying out, and madly flicking at the bees with their dusters, though they don't sting but are said to get into your eyes and ears. Even Hyder Khan usually so dignified, alarms me with the cloth with which he is defending me. Eventually the fly-bees are dispersed, and the honey tasted. It is very runny with a sharp lemony taste. Hyder Khan says it has a strong aperient effect. We shall see.

All the afternoon I lie there content to be enclosed by jungle. I see nothing. Absolutely nothing. Light. Shade. Silence. Then as the sky begins to brighten behind the leaves, I do hear something. I sit up expectantly. The noise is growing louder. It may be a barking deer, or even a tiger putting down his pads cautiously on the crisp dead leaves lying everywhere. It is coming nearer. My heart thumps. I have had my chair carried right away from the bungalow so that I shall see some wild beast. Can it be I am now afraid! It grows louder . . .

Out of the dead leaves comes a beetle.

Henry returns. No luck. He had heard a bull bison, and seen a cheetal. He is hot, tired and disappointed, but before going off to his tub sits at the small table which has been brought out from the office table and placed on a dhurry. The crowd of beaters gathers round. Others less punctilious might hand over the four annas or whatever sum had been arranged for, to their butler or head shikari, to pay each man. Not Henry. However weary he pays each man himself to avoid some sticking on the way.

I love the camp at evening. The bail wallahs in their grubby white squatting round their camp fire, its blue smoke curling up into the feathers of the bamboos, whilst a pleasant smell of cooking pervades everything; the sound of their voices as they play cards. Along the road in single file the bullock carts, ready for the night march. The cattle couched, some in sacking coats. By and by they will be unwillingly led to be yoked, their bells clashing and tonking irregularly. There will be commotion and shouts as the chests and bundles are dumped in the carts. Then goes a procession of twinkling hurricane lanterns as Ayah and the other servants disguised in thick cloth garments and country blankets, clamber in, and finally the whole procession goes creaking and lumbering through the night to the next camp.

I suggest to Henry it might be interesting to travel through the jungle at night. Perhaps that way we should see some of these animals who still remain obstinately hidden.

Henry is never startled at unconventional ideas.

"March by night instead of day? Why not? We will!"

January 8th.

Called at 3 a.m. Sleepy. Knee painful. Very dark and smells of cold. Why did I suggest this? The scantiest face-dip in icy water. Dressing somehow with numb fingers by hurricane lantern. They throw their light unexpectedly on ceiling or in a corner. I'm short of hairpins as perspiration makes them rust, and when my precious one or two fall on the floor I grope gingerly in the darkness with thoughts of snake or scorpion.

By the light of the hurricane Henry and I eat our chota hazri. Hyder Khan and others have gone last night, but Solomon, despised by the others because he is a Christian and eats pig, has turned out piping hot buttered egg. I wish however Henry had not surprised him spreading the butter with his thumb. All round us commotion, camp beds being taken down, mosquito nets folded, mattresses shoved into canvas bags. We hang onto the cushions as long as possible to hold between our legs to try and get a little warmth into us. Outside in the dark we can hear Lot snorting, and blowing his nose, and whinneying after Leviathan and Larrikin still snug and blanketed in their tent stable. But once started, though very cold, it's fun. The moon is not up, but the stout candles in the carriage lamps pick a feeble road for us through the darkness, and one sees glimpses of tree roots, the earth washed all away from them, on the banks on either side; and the spider holes; and moths are blundering round the lamps one moment silver or gold, the next black silhouettes. Once a glare of green eyes crossed the road. "Panther", say I. "More likely jungle cat", retorts Henry teasingly. A startling loud and frightening cry which might have been anything. Then the moon got up and one saw things in the light and shadow, and the dew was glittering like animals eyes on the leaves, and one remembered how only the week before Mr. Aitchison had been awakened by a heavy thump on his bed in the forest bungalow just in time to see a panther carrying off his beloved bull-terrier.

The rubber wheels go silently. Lot's shoes were taken off before we came into the district, and his hoofs are muffled in the dust. It is so cold we can't feel our noses or fingers. As the dawn begins to break there is a curious effect of disappearing shadows with daylight and moonlight mingling in silver grey under the trees. The Shama begins to sing. Very cold, very pure, very clear and echoing. Something between a blackbird and a nightingale. Most beautiful . . . and just before we arrive at Anshi a bear and four cubs shamble across the road.

Anshi, January 10th.

Awake to hear a shama in the grey light. Why have bird song or pealing bells always moved me so?

Henry busy at his office table. There is much more to see and hear to-day. I see three hornbills sitting on a dead branch looking exactly like those wooden toys balanced by beak and tail. Jungle cock scurry through the bushes. Monkeys big as children crash through the trees with their musical "Whoop". Then a barking deer . . . and in the hot still noon a loud "sawing wood" noise. Instantly monkeys are still. That's a panther "sawing wood". Butterflies idle past. I remember George Monteath telling he had seen the whole road covered after rain with red and black butterflies, drinking, wing to wing, and another time he had come upon a quivering purple pall . . . pall was the right word for they covered the carcase of the buffalo they fed upon. This hardly tallies with one's idea of the butterfly being the symbol of the soul!

Henry had gone off to shoot in the afternoon. At evening there came from the jungle the most awful and blood-curdling scream. Again it came. A little nearer . . . a pause and then yet again much farther off. It was the most terrible and desolate cry imaginable—not of this earth. What could it be? My heart went dump-a-dump. Once again that supernatural cry as of a lost soul, very far off now. Then silence.

My hair rose on my head. Never have I been so afraid. The servants came round pale beneath their dark skins.

"Khole Balu", they muttered.

Now when I was still a child I remember my brother Lloyd in the Forest Service writing home about a ghastly blood-curdling cry sometimes heard in the jungle, and never explained, but now it appears that Khole Balu is generally thought to be the cry of a mad jackal turned out of his pack. Some people think it is a jackal scared by the presence of a tiger. This seems unlikely, for it is so seldom heard.

I am lucky to have heard it.

Anshi, January 11th

Wish I hadn't suggested these night marches. Henry very taken with them. After breakfast and tub he gets what he calls a short snoozy bazy before attacking his work. Like Napoleon he can sleep at will.

I can't.

He and the dogs and horses went off in the cold darkness down the Anshi Pass to Kadra, where there is a good Forest Bungalow. Hyder Khan has decreed I am to follow later in a chair. Even Henry does what Hyder Khan says. Calm, superb, Hyder Khan stands superintending the fixing of bamboo poles to an arm chair. He has six fine looking scallywags with merry eyes and muscles rippling under their pinky brown skin to carry me. I settle in my chair. Taking off their black blankets and doubling them into pads they balance the poles on their shoulders and off we go at a cheerful trot down hill, two extra men jogging alongside. My men are careful not to keep step, so there is no swaying sea-sick motion, and perched up here I am able to see over the tops of trees, catching glimpses now and again of blue wooded ridges against the brightening East. When a man tires, we do not stop, another comes forward, slips in and smoothly transfers the poles to his own head. (Why do educated people think their kind of cleverness is the only kind?).

There are streams everywhere, and ferns, and birds and beasts call, and after the sun has risen velvet dark butterflies, big as birds drift by. The descent is tremendous, the hills rising up grandly behind me, and the two men in front of me foreshortened to dwarfs. Glimpses of the sea . . . And now we are below ghats it has got very sticky. I take off this and that, and wipe my face and neck. The men's naked bodies are glistening, their long locks dank. They smell overpoweringly, and I am stiff and cramped, tilted so steeply in my chair. Relief to reach the bungalow at noon. It stands within a kind of high stockade built to keep out panther and tiger. This gives it a Swiss Family Robinson look. Henry is there with the dogs waiting for me. It seems ages since he left me in the night! Poor Solomon is looking livid with mauve lips. Henry tells me his eyes have been popping out of his head ever since he learned the reason for that palisading. He is sweating to such an extent that his white coat is black between the shoulders. A tiger has been roaring round the bungalow all night it appears.

Later I learned the palisading was not intended to, and could not keep out tiger or panther. It was erected to protect some newly planted trees of the Forest Department from deer.

Forest Bungalow, Kadra, January 11*th*

Stickily hot here below ghats. Henry sleeps all afternoon with a palm leaf and not much else on. After tea I manage to hobble down to the river. Wide and shining under a vast sky, for the nobbly hills coming to the water's edge are here quite low.

Henry in candour tells me he is glad to be out of the jungle, that he had felt morbidly "shut in" these last few days. It had fascinated me, yet it is pleasant sitting here right out in the open with sky and air round one instead of leaves. A tiny breeze dries the sweat on our faces, and round the bend comes the glisten of approaching oars in the sunset light.

"It must have been about here George Monteath saw the tiger swimming across, and then after rolling at ease in the sand go off 'singing' to himself", I thought.

The sun set. Everything very quiet. Across the water still bright, the dark verge blue as grapes. Then quite suddenly and silently there flashed up the river seven large white birds, dead white, incredibly white against that blue verge.

Up the river they passed . . . and after five minutes suddenly, silently, flashed down the river again towards the sea.

"Henry! They must be the very whitest things in the world", I cried.

December, 1946. I have had a pot of purest white winged cyclamen given to me. They remind me of the egrets at Kadra! To my amazement Henry rather shyly remarks when I say so, "It's not the sort of thing I notice, or remember, but I *do* remember your white egrets at Kadra".

Kadra, January 13th

The horses are being marched down to Karwar to-day, but we don't go till to-night, sailing down the Kali Nadi in a native fishing boat. Poor Solomon. The tiger was roaring all night. How terrified he will be lying shivering in his bullock cart jolting through the jungle.

We were called about three, dressed, breakfasted and came down to the shore, a procession of bobbing hurricane lanterns through the trees. Dogs tightly chained to our waists. No sound of the tiger. Only the crunching of dead teak leaves like broken earthenware under our feet. The false dawn was breaking as we came out of the trees. A blessed coolness breathed on our brows; men's voices, the sound of splashing; we could just distinguish the fishing boat, her sails and her mast darker against the dark sky, and a lantern glowing in the bows. The dogs jumped on board nearly pulling us over, and instantly hurled themselves down on the mattresses prepared for Henry and me in the stern. (Why do bull-terriers do everything with such violence, even lying down?).

The air on one's brow was delicious, the night lovely.

Poor people in England! How dull their lives. Pictures of deserted London streets, a solitary cat, and lonely lamp posts rise before me . . . but perhaps England in wartime isn't like that.

The false dawn was over, and the true dawn coming up behind our backs, the hills taking shape, and the sky lightening so fast we could see the lazy sail was striped tomato and gold. It was filmy with rents so that in patches one could see the grey sky brightening to blue. The light wind dropped, so now with cries the four boatmen were pulling in the sail against the tapering mast. It looked like the netherside of a mushroom.

Two of the men began to row with the heart-shaped paddles which were tied on with string. They stood up pulling hard, their muscles bulging, then sat down for the following stroke, pulling lightly with muscles relaxed. One man had long ringlets falling to his naked shoulders. He inclined his head mournfully to the oars, singing a question in a minor key. The rower behind him replied, then all four men joined in with decision. One asking, one replying, all four confirming over and over again above the dip and the splash of the paddles and their squeak as they worked in the rowlocks of string.

I turned and lay on my stomach watching the sky swiftly flushing with light, the edge of the wooded hills in the East growing harder . . . and suddenly put up my hand, for the sun had risen and was blinding me.

Karwar, Judge's Bungalow

The loveliness of Karwar with its far flung bay, its wooded headland, its noble casuarina trees drawn up from the sand along the shore, is all that its little coterie of enthusiasts, Mr. Bell, the Maxwells, George, and others had described—but they had left out the climate! The Turkish-bath atmosphere, the languor and the loveliness. And *I* can't forget it for one moment! Brushing my hair, it wraps round and round my bare arm, and must be picked off strand by strand. Drops stand out on my forehead. I'm always thirsty, but to drink is waste of effort, besides it only increases one's prickly heat.

And the listlessness, the dullness of thought, the feeling of negation.

The dogs have prickly heat, and have scratched themselves raw. They are constantly charging into the sea . . . the worst thing possible . . . and come out looking like black sweeps with red eyes. For blue as is the sea far out, the little waves break inkily all along the white sands owing to some woody deposit which comes down the estuary at Sadeshaghad from time to time, making bathing out of the question.

We might have lost Larrikin the day of arrival. After marching from Kadra, at Sadeshaghad the horses were got onto a native fishing boat to bring them across the estuary to Karwar. As the boat began to toss a bit Larrikin played up, backed and finally fell with a heavy splash overboard. Commendably the syce had managed to keep hold of the reins, and Larrikin was forced to swim for half a mile, arriving rather done in.

George Monteath is Collector of Karwar, but this being the touring season, he has come in just for a few days only to meet Henry, so we are all staying at the Judge's Bungalow. It is hundreds of feet above the little town with its municipal buildings. We are carried up a rocky precipitous path in a chair hoisted on the heads of four sweating, singing men. Even so, as one mounts steadily through the trees, the curve of the bay mounting steadily with one, my thin white dress is stuck to my body, and I am prickling all over. Amazingly the men sing even as they plod. They have a sense of humour it seems. When they carried Mr. Sheppard's fifteen stone (Henry's predecessor) they chanted sonorously "Great fat pig! Great fat pig! Shall we throw him down the khud? Great fat pig!" Needless to say Mr. Sheppard did not understand Kanarese. George told me this chuckling.

Henry cannot stomach the thought of being carried. He attempts to climb up to the bungalow, but finally has to give in like everyone else, though he and George do climb once a day just before their evening tub to save their self respect.

The view is superb from both the Collector's and Judge's bungalows. The horizon is at the level of one's eyes. The headland muffled in jungle coming down to the water's edge . . . but to the left open sea with the island lighthouse.

Our beds are carried out onto a rampart to get the night breeze. There is something macabre about the rattling of the big palm fronds. They sound like skeleton fingers tapping. One of these great fronds falling on a man can kill him. But the sound I shall always associate with Karwar is the ceaseless banging of paddles against the sides of the fishing boats all through the long hot day, to attract the sardines.

Our host, Mr. Vernon, is kindness itself, but obviously a sick man.

His predecessor, Charles Boyd (Haileybury and Magdalen friend of Henry's) fell sick here too. His wife and small son also. George says it is quite unusually hot now for this time of the year, the humidity being very great. It may be so, but I could never stand this climate at any time. Stores are a difficulty too. No milk. Tinned butter which is rancid, and so on. The horses have gone sick (we were warned they would) and fat little Lep is now looking like a hobgoblin from malaria, and is living on chicken broth and quinine.

(I think of March winds roaring through the branches of the elms and the rattling of all the ivy leaves up their trunks!).

There's no energy to accompany Henry to the Municipal Pan Supari party and all the rest of it, but on Sunday we did go over to the little port of Belikeri (how Irish that sounds!) in George's battered Chevrolet, and one steamy day we went for a jungle prowl, George and Mr. Bell as guides. As we toiled sweating up the hill little odd shaped bits of blue sea and sky showed between dark leaves, and from all around came the endless "Ku-tur; ku-tur; ku-tur" of the green barbets, covering us like a cloak. The men put their feet down like cats. A bird-winged butterfly came bearing down on me, startling in its spread of wing. I kept asking Mr. Bell what bird was making this call or that, and finding me so interested he has offered to show his butterflies and birds. I had thought George had a wonderful collection, but he says they are nothing to Mr. Bell's.

Mr. Bell, the Chief Conservator, is another legendary figure like George. The tigers he has shot, the adventures he has had! Both men seem to belong to Kanara, and have no relationship with the outer world. T. R. Bell came out here in 1884. Grizzled-red, spare and lithe with a gait like a panther, he is decidedly distinguished-looking. The washed-out green shikar clothes, the trousers tight at the ankles to keep out jungle ticks, the espadrilles on his feet, are all worn with an air. On one of his rare visits to England he wore this same kit in Piccadilly to the indignation of a brother who insisted on walking twenty yards behind.

Two adoring sisters, Miss Eva and Miss Louisa keep house for him and make most exquisite and scientifically correct drawings of moths, butterflies and orchids.

After tea Henry and I are shown the butterflies. Cabinets of them. Perfect specimens, for T. R. Bell had hatched them out himself in the meat safes lined with net which we could see hanging round the verandah, so they were killed and set before they had a chance of damaging themselves. I felt a pang for this bright pinioned beauty which had never known the joy of expanding and closing those exquisite wings in a shaft of sunlight. Amongst these butterflies were some exactly imitating green leaves. George told me he had once seen hundreds and hundreds of them dancing and flickering all down the road to some unknown goal. Standing there in the road he had divided the stream, and they had passed him in twos and threes and dozens, flickering as brightly as newly opened beech leaves; they had danced over his head, all about him, disappearing a gauzy green scarf through the forest. How I wish I had seen that!

But for the birds. Birds, some of which I had only caught for the fraction of a second darting through the forest, but which had left an indelible impression of beauty to which my mind kept recurring.

What did I expect? I don't know. But not hundreds of careful brown paper rolls, tied round with black thread, each containing a feathered skin waiting to be stuffed one day to make a unique collection.

"Here's the common bee-eater".

I remembered that first cold weather morning at Belgaum Henry pointing out to me the bee-eaters on the telegraph wires, who had just arrived. Exquisite jewels, emeralds one moment, blazing bronze the next as they flashed off and on the wires. This the bee-eater in my hand? Here in another roll the hoopoe, its lovely crest closed. How often of late had I heard him calling "Uk-uk", opening and shutting his crest. And a fruit pigeon. Impossible to see these as they stripped the fig-trees in the compound at Belgaum, so thick the leaves, so green their bodies, but how haunting, their joyful-melancholy up-and-down whistle! I had made it the motive of my *Tale of the Matti.* The fruit pigeons had called over and over again "He is here . . . is here . . . is here . . . ", but finally as Huli the tiger had dragged away the body of the sacred white bull, sorrowfully, "He is gone . . .

is gone . . . is gone . . . ". And now here lay the fruit pigeon, hitherto invisible, for me to see how lovely the green of his body, how lovely the dove and lilac plumage of his breast, how bright the little orange feet! As in a dream I held the limp little rolls in my hand one after another. They had no connection whatever with the bright creatures that darted and flitted in my memory. I grew more and more silent, as absorbedly Mr. Bell opened his rolls. A minivet, an iora, a sunbird not much bigger than a thimble . . . a wagtail . . . Oh no. No. No! Not my wagtails with their crystalline voices streaming up to me like incense from the river banks at Supa!

A dreadful melancholy fell upon me. It was all I could do not to weep. That bright loveliness, those thrilling bird voices, just little feathered mummies smelling of Keatings and pepper. Man had done this?

To-night I asked Henry what he thought of the collection.

"Horrible!"

Note. T. R. Bell died on June 24th, 1948. The *Times* describes him as "one of the finest field naturalists India has ever seen, and few could equal his knowledge of life in the jungle, be it birds, insects or plants . . . A few years before the last war he came to London and worked in the Natural History Museum (a large part of his collection is now in the Museum) but the bustle and noise of a big city was not to his liking, and he returned to Karwar where he died as he had wished."

Yellapur. Forest Bungalow, January 19th

George Monteath brought us up the Arbail Pass in his Chevrolet, through grand forest scenery to this roomy bungalow where he has his camp. Delightful to be above ghats again; the cool nights, the agreeable warmth of the noonday sun filtering through the leaves. There are numbers of monkeys here, the big silvery langurs. They crash about in the branches with their musical "Wh . . . oop"—a lovely sound—and land wallop on the roof, and play follow-my-leader all over the tiles purposely to excite the dogs to frenzy.

Lep's face is punctured by deep tooth holes, and is swollen out of recognition: Rainey's shoulder is slashed and she limps; Luther has narrowly escaped losing an eye, and has an ugly tear down his cheek and throat. He had joined Rainey in her pursuit of a monkey, and it was *her* monkey and she whipped round and told him so. He was too much of a gentleman to retaliate, but faithful little Lep, still weak from her malaria, dashed in to his assistance, and then Rainey turned on her.

January 22nd

Went for a jungle prowl, *phirao* as we call it, before breakfast to see where George had shot his black panther. Coming in from the jungle you have to drop all your clothes into a bucket of boiling water, and then rub yourself over with oil because of jungle ticks, before you get into your bath. I wear only Indian gauze combies, a silk shirt and breeches, and into the bucket they go each day. But even so a large tick on my behind has left its head in, and made a painful sore. George's wrists are scarred with the remains of these tick sores, but the leeches in the rains are much worse. Every bush is alive then with the beastly things, waving and reaching out to you, and when you get back your boots will probably be full of blood. The sores they make are worse than tick sores. Lloyd, my brother, had told me that.

January 25th

Monkeys have a great sense of time. Regularly at nine o'clock each morning there is commotion in the branches of the trees, and down come the monkeys. They skedaddle across the compound, many of them with their babies clinging to them, and run along a low tumble-down wall, and then off into the jungle. At five o'clock the performance is repeated in reverse. The regularity of it reminds me of rooks at home.

But how astonishingly human they are. After fifty years Father still reproaches himself for having once thoughtlessly shot a monkey. Often he has told me of the mother's pitiful distress as she clasped and rocked the little dead body of her baby. Here every day I can watch these monkeys fondling and cuffing their children, and only yesterday I saw a mother, exasperated by her baby's fidgets while she flead him, turn him over and smack his bottom.

The Edies are in camp near by. He is in the Forest Service, and I knew them in Belgaum of course. He is big and Scotch, and she is the tiniest little woman I have ever seen, with a soft voice and sleepy blue eyes. She looks like a doll, and as though she should be lying in an oblong cardboard box, and have a hole in her back from which comes a string, and when you pull the bead at the end she will say "Mama", but instead she wears a pig-sticker, and washed-out grey-green like the rest of us, and talks "jungle". I suppose this is really of no more importance than gymkhana chatter, but it seems so to us. We are all very good friends, and often go for a jungle prowl before breakfast, the men carrying rifles. The shikari comes along too. He is a tall lean fellow with a dingy black turban. We all creep, crouch and double through undergrowth of karvi, putting our feet down like cats avoiding every stick which might crack. As we go looking out for *janwars* (wild animals) I notice at the same time the lovely ivory and buff and rose leaves of the young dalchini, and that cinnamon has three horizontal veins in its leaves, and that the black pepper vines clambering up the trees have peppercorns like clustering green currants, and that Nux Vomica, familiar from doctor's prescriptions, has tiny oranges.

On one of these prowls George and Jock stopped to show us the vertical clawings made by a bear, on the trunk of an arjun tree. Bears are more feared than tiger or panther. Jock told us of the deplorable incident which had happened not long ago to another forest officer, Mr. Aitchison. He was out shooting, and a bear was seen to go into a dark hole on the opposite side of the nulla. The beaters much excited, wanted to go in and fetch him out. Mr. Aitchison declared they were to do no such thing. However as he stood watching the cave through his field glasses, he saw to his horror that one of the beaters, disobeying him, was about to enter the cave. He shouted across the nulla, but almost immediately terrible screams rang out, and man and bear came tumbling out together. Putting its head down the bear proceeded to roll down the khud in a ball, the man clasped to its belly. Should Mr. Aitchison shoot? He decided to as the bear went rolling and bouncing down. He fired; the bear instantly uncurled, releasing the beater. He fired again, killing the bear; but when they got to the unfortunate man lying on the side of the khud, he was so hideously lacerated that he died before they got him to hospital.

Perhaps to dispel the little gloom which fell over us on hearing of this tragedy George related an incident which had occurred at Karwar just before our arrival. At a meeting it seemed there had been considerable heat over expenditure on the Public Library. An Indian pleader sharing the views of George the Collector, spoke strongly. However at a later meeting of the Municipality he opposed George with the utmost violence. When George asked him the reason for this sudden change of front, he replied reproachfully, "But Sir, the first time I spoke as a pleader. The second as President of the Municipality".

Out all day in the jungle. Drove back with Henry in the dog-cart. Bamboo forest in moonlight. Fireflies.

Green days and nights!

January 26th

This afternoon Henry and I drove in the dog-cart, Sakharam on the step, to inspect the broken bridge at Bar Nulla. It is holding up all the bullock carts which carry spices and bamboos and other merchandise down to the coast. The road was through glorious forest. Immense trees. I saw a bamboo forty feet high thrusting its plumes through the lower branches of another tree.

At the bridge the Mamladar and others were awaiting Henry. Larrikin and Leviathan were there too, as we intended to ride back, so the syces went off with Sakharam in the dog-cart. Henry was delayed a considerable time. When interested he is completely lacking in all sense of time, which astonishes me who seem to have an unconscious clock which ticks on so that if I wake up at night I always know the time to within a few minutes. Now sitting there on the bridge I begin to fidget, for I've got the three dogs on the chain, and the ribbon of sky overhead is beginning to turn a little pink, and what about panther? I dare not interrupt Henry, but at last they finish. "By George!" exclaims Henry suddenly aware, "we shall have to gallop for it". After some bucketing and bucking we are off, the dogs wild with excitement. The road is soft and leafy. The only thing is to make a noise, and to gallop . . . to gallop like hell. Henry shouts; I yell the Valkyrie's war cry "Ho Yo To Ho!" It grows dimmer and dimmer, the great trunks of the trees on either side of the road like the stringy grey legs of gargantuan elephants. The horses blowing and pulling our arms out, the dogs giving tongue, the sowars at a hand gallop behind . . . Oh what a lark! We shot like a screaming arrow through the ever darkening jungle. The excitement, the exhilaration of that flight knowing a panther might spring on one of the dogs! "Ho Yo To Ho . . . ".

It was dark when we reached the bungalow. Had it not been for the dogs it would have been inexcusable to bring the horses back so covered with soap suds, and smoking like chimneys . . . but oh what a lark!

In Belgaum I had seen the lustrous gold mohur tree, a gorgeous tiger-lily rose. Gold mohur, not called as so many think, after the coin the gold mohur, but after Mohur, the Peacock . . . the Peacock Tree.

In Bombay I had seen a frieze of leafless coral trees, flat against a vivid blue sea and sky, vivid green parrots tearing and plucking apart the vivid scarlet flowers.

Here in Kanara I had seen the noble silk cotton tree with its satiny crumpled blossoms of brilliant rose.

But to-day I saw in the green twilight of the jungle the Flame of the Forest blazing. From naked grey branches there sprang hundreds upon hundreds of little tongues of flame, each glittering in the shaft of sunlight striking through the tops of the trees.

Pentecost.

January 27th

There has been a certain outcry in the Indian Press, that the small herd of elephants kept by the Forest Department in Kanara is an extravagance. The Forest Department on the other hand maintains they are necessary to the forest work, pointing out that in Burma the private contractors keep large herds of elephants. But characteristically Henry is determined to go and see for himself, before expressing an opinion.

So today we motored to see the elephants actually working in the jungle. The sun was up, but it was still cool when we started. We drove down-down-down, and every moment it grew warmer and stickier. Now we were below ghats. We kept wiping our faces, and our handkerchiefs were smeary with red dust, and then suddenly and most oddly spanning the road was a leafy arch with "Welcome to the Commissioner" in white letters on scarlet flannel.

"Damnation", mutters Henry. This is the sort of thing he particularly dislikes. My heart sinks. He is going to be difficult.

Miles from any human habitation as we are, there are several Indian officials in black coats, bright turbans, and silken scarves over their shoulders. The brown calves of the Mamladar's legs twinkle backwards and forwards between the looped draperies of his dhoti. He carries a black umbrella. Little flags and pennons hang limply from trees and bushes. Henry will be angry.

The elephants are drawn up on the right side of the road swaying their trunks, flapping the flies off their faces with their ears, rolling very bright little eyes at us. Two had crashed away into the jungle at our approach, but now advanced shamefacedly. As we get out all the elephants lift their trunks to heaven, and salaam to their Commissioner, moved to do so by the cries of their mahouts on their backs.

Amidst a mass of undergrowth, under other timber, lay forty feet of solid teak weighing more than a ton and a half. Shankar, the male elephant with the freckled ears advanced ponderously. He routed about on the ground till he found a rope with his trunk. Tucking this into the side of his mouth, Shankar leaned back, put his whole weight into it, and pulled. The teak tree did not stir. Shankar of his own accord now twisted the rope twice round his trunk to get a better purchase, leaned backwards and with a determined look in his small roving eye, pulled. Still the fallen tree did not budge.

Now up moved another elephant, slowly and with great dignity. This elephant at her mahout's bidding moved to the farther end of the tree. There she lowered herself almost to her knees, and with her forehead shoved, at the precise moment that Shankar heaved. Once the tree shifted there was no more trouble. Sometimes treading forward, sometimes stepping sideways, Shankar extracted gradually his teak tree. He guided it by the path of least resistance. He coaxed it round a corner, he lifted it over an unavoidable stump, using first one side of his mouth, and then the other to avoid the strain on his teeth. The road had to be crossed to get the tree down to the river, and for the sake of its surface two trees had been laid down as rollers. Shankar brought his burden up to these, heaved it on the rollers, and a few moments later we saw that mountainous slate blue back flecked in sun and shadow moving through the jungle, careful not to brush the mahout on his back against the branches of the trees.

Picture us all following. The Indian officials nervous and anxious to please, aware Henry was annoyed with the flag and pennon tomfoolery, Henry and I, and lastly some pattawallas in starched white and a few hangers on. The whole procession of elephants, their mahouts guiding them with toes thrust through the ropes round their necks, dragged their respective trees down to the river, slid them in, to be floated down to the auction mart. There they will lie in the water for a year or two to season.

And now these earnest workers stepped cautiously into the river themselves, and all at once became rowdy schoolboys. They drank and drank and made extraordinary grunting, burbling noises inside them and I laughed to such an extent, that Henry with tears squeezing out of his own eyes was saying in a stern voice. "*Will* you be quiet. For heaven's sake control yourself".

Then the elephants, their little eyes twinkling with merriment, went into deep water, and suddenly ducked, so that the crouching mahouts were forced to spring to their feet, shouting, and even so were waist deep in water, and the elephants sank deeper, deeper, till nothing was to be seen but the tips of their trunks blowing bubbles. They played water polo with one of the tree trunks they had launched, and at last tired of buffoonery came out on shore to be washed. Each elephant has three mahouts, and must have a bath twice a day. He is scrubbed with a broken cocoa-nut shell, and he helps by squirting water over the loosened dirt. Shankar lay flat on his side in very shallow water, extending one huge leg after another to be scraped, behind him the wide exquisite reach of deep water, with reflections of the wooded ghats.

Clean, with that characteristic piggy smell gone for the time being, they lined up before us. We fed them on bits of sugar-cane which they took very delicately in their trunks and tucked away in their mouths. Then we gave them each a cocoa-nut, and carefully they put it on the ground, and with one foot crushed it just sufficiently. The mahouts cut out chunks of nut, and every elephant lifted his trunk to the sky, waiting for us to push bits of nut far in, back by his teeth. And an elephant's tongue is the softest, pulpiest thing I have ever touched.

Now they were to say "Salaam". They broke into an indescribable noise. Trumpets, trombones gone mad, squeals, motor horns and always an undercurrent of that burbling watery growling which had made me laugh so much, the sort of growling Grimm's dogs with the eyes like church towers might have made.

But Shankar would not say "Salaam". He would not, until a special lady friend of his was induced to tickle him delicately with the extreme tip of her trunk just behind his ear. Shankar salaamed.

Servants had come on the night before in bullock carts. There under the great matti tree a little leafy hut had been built to protect the Chevrolet from the sun, and another little leafy hut for Henry and I to breakfast in. It was twelve o'clock and breakfast was waiting now. Curry and fish and eggs and fruit, and little silver vases with jungle flowers on the table. Bottles of beer hung in an arrangement of wet straw through which the air passed.

Eating, Henry told me he had felt uncomfortable when Shankar refused to salaam. He had asserted that it did not matter, that the Memsahib was weary and desired breakfast. "Sahib be pleased to wait. Son of Satan, did he not kill his mahout last year?" Then Henry gave the decisive order that the elephants were to be taken away, but Shankar had at length salaamed, and we watched them all lurch away down the road to where their real work lay some distance off in the jungle.

It had grown terribly hot and sticky; flies troublesome, and the jungle seemed to shimmer to the whirr and rasp of cicadas.

"Glad we came", remarked Henry. "To say those elephants are an extravagance shows sheer ignorance of the facts".

I shall add what I did not learn till a later date.

A young couple we knew were camping not far from where the elephants were working. The wife had been asleep one afternoon when she heard a great yelling and commotion outside. She jumped up and running to the tent door was just in time to see an elephant charging her husband. He had his rifle, and tripped over some tent ropes behind him. The elephant was just preparing to trample him to death, when he, lying there on his back, fired, and instantly springing to his feet darted amongst the hobbled ponies close by. To his knowledge that elephants have a great dislike of horses he owed his life. The elephant had suddenly gone *mast,* mad, and had to be killed.

Complaints have been coming in that deer and pig are doing much damage to the Spice Gardens. Henry wants to investigate this and proposes to inspect one this afternoon without notice. For some reason or other I am disinclined to go, perhaps tired, or just out of humour. Henry unaware of this, or aware and ignoring it says "Come on", and now how glad I am I did go.

We ride there through the motionless patchwork of sun and shadow of the jungle. The Spice Garden is as romantic as its name. It is sunk deep down in savage steamy jungle, an oasis of sweetness and grace with its tall betel-nut palms, their stems silver and ringed. A great ditch with a great fence on the top of a bank had been built all round in the hope of keeping out deer, pig and even elephant.

Leaving the horses with the sowars we slip inside. It is like entering a great shadowed hall of a thousand and one pillars, thrilling with bird song, and the warbling of little water courses threading this way and that. Exquisitely erect, amazingly slender, those fairy pillars shoot upwards through the shadows to support their lovely fragile roof. Up every two or three of these quiet stems clambers the dark-leaved pepper vine with its clusters of pepper corns. Tilting our heads right back we can see fifty, sixty feet up, the clustering ruddy nuts amongst the drooping fronds which are, up there, still lit by the evening sunshine. As *pan supari* the crushed nut will be wrapped up with a little fresh lime and cardamon in a betel nut leaf, which will be neatly pinned into a green packet with a clove.

No one was there to meet us. We wandered through the shadows down dank little paths by the water-courses. Birds were calling and singing like boys in a church. We passed a bamboo ladder propped up against a tree, just a single bamboo it was, from which the branches had been hacked away merely leaving little stumps for bare feet to rest upon. Once there was a sad-eyed boy who slipped his feet through a noose of straw, and so climbed out of our shadows right up into the sunlit fronds above. Up there he gleamed a wondrous golden youth singing and swaying. He swayed his body so violently that the whip-like stems swayed also, and thus he changed, still singing, from tree to tree, careless as a bird.

We followed a little path thinking to retrace our steps, but instead it brought us to a little thatched house, just such a little house as one sees glimmering up through the water of one's basin. Here the little water-course joined a noisy stream which babbled and flowed right round the little house. Across the stream was thrown a bridge of green and slippery bamboo poles. And on the other side, as though Henry and I were expected, stood two varnished yellow chairs. A table was there too, and on it two marigold necklaces and two marigold bracelets, bright as fire even in that green gloom. And beside the flowers were six screws of newspaper such as one played shop with as a child, and two little limes. Gingerly we crossed that slippery bridge, and out came the owner of the Spice Garden to greet us.

He had a melancholy countenance, this Havig Brahmin, yet with a humorous look in his eyes, and with a crooked smile. His eyebrows slanted away to his turban, and his hands shook like leaves, as he stretched them out offering his little limes in welcome. He was talking in Kanarese and slipping the necklets of marigolds over our heads, his words sounded as musical as the water flowing all round us. The marigolds smelled clean and pungent. Still smiling he handed us the newspaper screws. Opening mine I found in the first some bits of petit-beurre biscuits, very crumby and soft. In the second screw were a few sultanas, and in the third yellow sugar-candy with bits of newspaper stuck to it.

Whilst the owner was pulling forward the chair for Henry with his shaking hands, I slipped past a pipal tree whose trunk supported the roof, and reminded me of Hunding's house in *Die Walküre.* Suddenly and unexpectedly I came upon a little flock of women peeping and peering from behind a door, their dim warm-coloured faces melting into their dim warm coloured saris. They broke away laughing and chattering like so many seven-sister birds. But there was one who could not get away. For she was penned in with the cattle. I saw that she was a child widow, for she wore no ornament, and was dressed in dirty white, and had her head shaved. But there was nothing down-trodden about the child. Her little face was humorous, almost cheeky. She stood there with her hump-backed cattle all about her, and chattered to me in Kanarese . . . and I am beginning to wonder if the whole afternoon was a dream? For little child widows, even though they be the widows of Havig Brahmins and not Brahmins, do not laugh, and the little glimmering house coiled about with singing streams was so very like the little houses that one sees in one's basin, and how did the husbandman know that we were coming, and why should little bits of petit-beurre biscuits be found so far from civilisation?

January 26th

This morning, Henry and George being busy, I went for a prowl on my own, taking Dugadu as Henry insists. I ask if anything untoward happens what use would the very timid Dugadu be? Found the forest machan for spotting forest fires. A crazy bamboo structure some seventy to eighty feet high. Somehow I haul myself up, though the rungs are so far apart my straining toe is almost on a level with my chin. Pass the tops of the bamboos, and come out into sunshine. How delicious it feels on my clenched cold fingers. One final effort, and I'm out on the platform, sprawling on my tummy and feeling like a frog that has climbed up a stalk out of the pond.

Over my head the soft bright skies of Kanara, and all round, mile after mile of unbroken tree-tops twinkling with dew in the level rays of a rising sun. I can peer cautiously over the edge at all the birds bustling about in the bushy branches below me. Somehow they remind me of demi-semi quavers and triplets! It's enchanting up here. An English servant would wonder what on earth I was doing up there in the sky, and the knowledge of him waiting down there would spoil enjoyment. But Dugadu will be content to squat on his hunkers, his arms clasped round his knees, just "sitting away" and "eating the air". What is the Brahmin saying? "It is better to sit than to walk, to lie down than to sit, to sleep than to wake, and death is the best of all".

The sun warms me. I am happy. Through the clear morning air come a dozen different bird songs and calls. I can see flirting and flitting about in the bamboos a flock of delicious little scarlet and black minivets, ioras too, and pipits. The pointed leaves are continually shivering and parting with the movements of tiny bodies. I recognize wee brown avadavats one remembers huddled in shut-eyed rows in London bird shops, here flitting about like winged seeds. The whole scene is twinkling alive with birds and dew drops and bird-song.

But the sun is getting hot. It strikes across my shoulders like the slap of the hand. The little birds are growing quiet. Only the loud "Cooch-lee, Cooch-lee" of the tree-pies seem like loops of sound, which carry one away down the ghats to the Indian Ocean breaking and dashing up against the roots of cocoa-nut palms.

Over there a column of blue smoke begins to rise steadily through the trees. Breakfast.

To "sit away", to "eat the air" has been very pleasant. To drink chicken broth, eat vegetable curry, and boiled eggs will also be very pleasant.

"Ho! Dugadu. Ao! Come".

Mundgod

A long and exhausting march. For the first ten or twelve miles we drove in the dog-cart. At that early hour the jungle has an aqueous look, as though one were travelling under water, the sunlight filtering through the leaves, all quivering from refraction. The melodious whistle of the "idle schoolboy" with its abrupt cessation startled us every now and then.

The empty road ran through avenues of spiders such as one sees in nightmares. They squatted above our heads in webs, whose stout threads stretched across the road from tree to tree. They looked like aerial lobsters up there, the sun shining through red speckly legs. The web would be two or more feet above our topis even in our high dog-cart, but Henry made a pretence of poking the whip through a web, and the mere suggestion of spider and web descending and entangling our heads and shoulders made me sick with apprehension. I knew he was fooling . . . but suppose in laying down his whip, its tip *did* just reach and catch in a web? Shivers ran through me, and I heard little of what he was saying, when Lot snorted, and shied violently across the road. A snake had somehow got caught in one of the webs up there. It writhed horribly. Its white ribbed belly glistened in the sun. The web stretched and bent and danced like elastic, but held firm, and as we looked back we could still see the snake coiling and uncoiling trying as it were to climb up its own body.

By the time we came to where the sowars were waiting, the jungle had quite changed in character: the trees were young teak, much smaller, and growing farther apart, so that we could see a jungle cat, a mouse-deer or many jungle cocks and their harems scurrying about amongst the dead leaves. I remembered that Lloyd and Minnie much preferred this type of jungle (more like East Khandesh than Kanara), finding it much more interesting, but I sorely missed the shade that made riding even at noon so pleasant, and we were parched, sweaty and very dusty at the end of our march. There we found that Luther and Rainey, who had gone on the previous night, had had a bloody fight. Lep, of course, had hurled herself in to protect Luther, and so after a long, long and most blessed lime squash, before bath and breakfast, I had to set to, unpack lint and wool and chinosol, and bathe and bind. Luther very sorry for himself. Rainey indifferent as always. Lep squirming with apology and affection.

Rest in afternoon, and in the evening the village. The Mahratta schoolmaster, slight in black coat, white dhoti, pink sock suspenders over his bare legs, was touchingly enthusiastic over the shabby little school where dust lay thick everywhere. He felt the children should learn geology of all things, and he had collected little bits of stone and arranged them in lids of boxes, neatly labelled. Eagerly he poured forth his ideas, gesticulating with small womanish wrists, and long double-jointed fingers. Henry was impressed by the old man's earnestness, and will tell the Collector to back him up.

The district has been terrorised by a tiger, and is petitioning Henry to shoot it. The old spectacled Mahalkeri (a sort of deputy Mamladar) informs Henry that more than one hundred villagers have volunteered to act as beaters without payment. This makes me smile. As though he would accept! I cherish for Henry an immense admiration for his uprightness, his scrupulous exactness in payments, in travelling allowances, in anything that appertains to his own advantage. So often reading old memoirs or diaries one is struck by the constant allusions to the Almighty, prayers for guidance and so forth, made by even the most fiery and dashing soldiers as well as civilians. This generation has dropped all that completely. Nevertheless the same high standard of honesty prevails out here in 1915 except in the rarest of cases.

Note, 1948

Can we say as much to-day? What about the wangling for that extra bit of butter or tobacco, the juggling with the dates of petrol coupons, the little present to the butcher, the service coupons used by civilians . . . the whole horrid smeary life practised by those who yet are so quick to deplore the growing dishonesty in post-office and railway.

"Scrounging" after the Great War. "Fiddling" after the World War. Our fathers would have had another name.

January 31st

All the hundred odd villagers have turned up. A scallywag army carrying murderous weapons of all kinds, hatchets, axes, sickles, long curly knives tied on to bamboos and lathis. Even the old Mahalkeri has turned out clutching a brass-bound lathi to avenge himself on the tiger who had taken one of his cattle. To-day it is to be a "beat". That is all these men yowling and yelling and smashing at the bushes with their sticks will beat their way through the jungle in the hope of driving out the tiger who may be lying up somewhere. (Extraordinarily plucky of them!).

In expectation of Henry's visit two young buffaloes had been tied up, but the tiger had touched neither, though its pugs were traced near. Tigers do not kill unless they are hungry. Sometimes they will visit a tied-up animal two or three nights before killing it.

We start off in the dog-cart, the medicine chest with lint, wool, and carbolic acid with us, in case any of the beaters get mauled. After a mile or two we get out, and a small procession, consisting of Henry carrying his rifle, myself, the havildar from the Guard with his rifle, the sowars, and a few coolies with axes, branch off in silence into the scrub-jungle. At this season of the year the teak give little shade, for the enormous brittle dead leaves keep noisily flopping off, and it is impossible to avoid their crackle and scrunch under our feet. Peacocks flee before us, a tiny mouse deer, not much bigger than a hare, and then Henry does get a fine cheetal. We go back to the dog cart, now putting down our feet carelessly, drive on, and the whole performance is repeated.

No luck! No tiger!

February 1st

The whole day has been spent in inspecting *talao*-tanks. A tank is a small natural lake strengthened by embankments for preserving water for the villagers and husbandmen. We started early. I drove. Lot went spanking along. Such a fresh blue, cold-weather morning. Little doves sunning themselves all along the telegraph wires. "*Yussuf kua men. Yussuf kua men*", they said over and over again. "Joseph in the well. Joseph in the well". Henry tells me no Muhammadan will shoot a dove because when Joseph was thrown by his brethren in the well, they, the little doves, did their best to tell Jacob. "*Yussuf kua men*". Till I came out here I had not realised, and I don't suppose others do, how the Muhammadan shares our Bible stories, how he takes Bible names, and that he is indeed a great respecter of Jesus as one of the Prophets.

The tank was a delightful sight, teeming with bird life of every description. Such a flashing and bustling and stirring interspersed by bird cries and calls. The sparkling water was covered with lotus flowers, not flat on the water, but lifting long necks to stare up at the sky. I had never seen so many birds in my life, all bustling about their business. Herons and egrets, and duck and snippets, paddy-birds sitting greenish-brown, but flying miraculously pure white. Kingfishers, and dazzling blue rollers, wagtails and bulbuls, long-tailed parrots, snake-birds with thin vertical necks sticking straight out of the water like a walking stick, and then six hornbills flying in a row. They alighted, almost invisible, on the dead branch of a tree, balancing their enormous beaks by their little tails, and as always making me think of those wooden toy birds you balance on the edge of a table.

Henry said all this coming and going of birds reminds him of Sind. There the *dhunds*, as they are called, are miles of marsh and water literally alive with water fowl of every kind. Henry's eyes, it seems to me, are always fixed on Sind. He will never be really satisfied till he gets back there, partly because he has a definite plan for carrying through the irrigation of Sind on a vast scale (the Sukkur Barrage) and partly because he knows the people there so well, likes them, and is liked by them.

This morning he was more interested in talking to the villagers than in watching the water fowl. He wanted to know if the Panchayat (which consists of the Brahmin and the richer people) allowed the "untouchables" access to this tank, and the wells. He said to me: "Just as Oxford University forbade the parks to 'persons carrying burdens'—and the notice is still to be seen—so the Hindus forbid the wells to the 'untouchables' on the firmer ground of pollution of the water. If this is so here, some new wells must be built for the untouchables for it is impossible to expect the Panchayat to break their caste rules. We have to be Fabians, content to progress slowly".

I don't know about Fabius after whom the Fabians took their name. He explains.

Mundgod, February 2nd

My first experience of a machan, that is sitting up for tiger or panther in a tree. As yesterday, we went creeping through the jungle in complete silence. It was more open, and here and there a really fine tree towered above its fellows. Against one of these were propped two ladders bound together to add to their length. The shikari signed to Henry I was to climb up. Some twenty-five feet over our heads was a small, a very small platform suspended by ropes to an overhead branch. Now Henry had stipulated I was to be high enough to be out of reach of the tiger, but this seemed a little overdone. "All right?" he whispered. Nodding and very excited I climbed up. The little platform about three foot square was at an uncomfortable slant as the ropes on one side had slipped down the sloping branch, but by hooking an arm round the trunk I should be safe enough. The overhead branch however was so low my pig-sticker caught in it, and my chin was pressed down onto my chest. Down there they could not see my discomfort. Already my ladder was being removed! I had made such a point of coming, rather against Henry's better judgment, that I had not the face to call out now. Henry had insisted that the havildar should be posted with his rifle somewhere pretty near me. He, the havildar, was creeping on, and the shikari motioned Henry to follow himself.

I was left alone on my steeply slanting platform.

Almost immediately my knees, doubled under me, got cramp. My neck was cricked. My nose tickled. But whatever happens one must not move one's hands. They attract the attention of a wild animal more than anything else. At such an early stage, it would not have mattered in the least, but I was so desperately anxious that Henry should get his tiger and that I should do the right thing! Something nipped my wrist. A big black soldier ant. Squinting round I could see several on the trunk beside me. I remembered how once Henry had been forced to throw himself into the Indus in flood to save himself from being eaten alive, and was very nearly drowned in consequence. I wondered how far off the havildar was! I could not turn my head to look. Absolute silence except for the throaty *"Pois, Pois, Pois"* of innumerable tree-pies as though they were calling for peas in French. When would the beaters start? The sun had passed from behind branches, and now from a space of burning blue it was beating full upon me. Sweat began to trickle down my face, and down my chest. I began to feel sick. Where's the havildar? Where's Henry? Supposing I faint? Would my arm still stay crooked round the branch? Sunny silence. Razor edge of sun and shade. *"Pois, Pois, Pois"*. And then . . . Yes. Very very faint, a little cry. Unmistakeable now. The beaters approaching. Forty minutes it had taken them, I could see by the watch on my wrist. But they were coming now. Sickness and cramp forgotten. Yells! Screams! Howls! and every now and again a peal of delirious laughter. All very faint and faraway still, but there was stirring in the jungle. Birds began to fly past me. A peacock came full tilt . . . and only swerved aside to avoid me just in time. At first the cries had seemed to form themselves into a formal pattern, a background as it were to the hot still jungle, the motionless trees, but now as they approached nearer the yells and demoniacal laughter were pandemonium, and unbearably exciting! I was staring into the sunlit bushes. Was that the stripes of a tiger? . . . or merely light and shade? Did I hear the snap of a stick? My heart thudded . . . a little click . . .

that must be the havildar . . . another click . . . Yes the sign of warning . . .

And after all no tiger. I could have cried with disappointment for Henry's sake as well as my own. He went out again in the afternoon, but I was too done and cramped. The villagers implored him to try the following day. He hesitated, but finally decided to keep to his original plan of marching on to Kalghati. Sense of duty again. Some lucky Forest Officer with perhaps many tigers already to his credit, will come and sit up for "Henry's tiger".

Khalgati, February 3rd

Nearly seven hours in the saddle, and such hours. Leviathan had a loose shoe, and frequently stumbled, so I hardly dared to go out of a walk. Wide open country, glaring lint-white, with little umbrella-like trees here and there, so that after the jungle I felt I had no eye-lids. To ease an aching back I rode a good part of the way astride, which is hardly comfortable on a side saddle! Saw a large field of feeding peacocks. Arrived at half past twelve, stiff, sweaty, dusty, to find for the first time, *bandobast* had broken down. Uncomfortable dusty little bungalow. Nothing unloaded. No drinks. No tubs. No breakfast.

Tegu, February 16th

Queer open tumbled country, stoney and low light-blue hills on the horizon. Outside the village this evening Henry and I found a quantity of stones painted chocolate and white. On one was the figure of a villager, and his little son, and some leaping animal. It appeared that all the village had been indebted to him in ages gone by, though we could not make out why. The other smaller stones were erected when his descendants died.

It was here I saw for the first time seats put outside the little school for the untouchable children to sit upon, so that they should not contaminate others by their presence.

There were one or two immense silk-cotton trees. Always they remind me of noble trees in some English park, and this to-night was intensified by a glowing red sky behind the branches, like a frosty sunset at home. Yet five minutes before how eastern the scene! The rays of the sun level, so though the sky above was very clear, dust rising from the herds of returning cows and buffaloes, shone like billowy clouds of golden incense in which the dissolving shapes of the animals themselves could be discerned in darker gold. We walked in an encompassing glory. "The hour of the Dust of the Cow", the Indian calls it.

Mugat-Khan-Hubli.

Flat typical Deccan country. Lint-white grass. Stones. Little round trees growing smaller, bluer and dimmer in the distance till they are merely horizontal streaks against the lighter blue hills. Rocks. Monkeys on top. Shabby little cotton plants. It all seems rather an anti-climax after the jungle. Shan't keep a day to day diary any more.

Henry's tiger has been shot!

Belgaum Cattle Show

Henry was Director of Agriculture for five years. He has had various cattle farms under him, and he is anxious to compare the famous Krishna Valley cattle with others.

The show is held in that dense grove of mangoes alongside the road. So dark is it under the trees, so quicksilver is the sunlight stabbing through the leaves, spotting the tree-trunks, the cattle, and their owners and patches of rice straw on the ground, that objects have no individual shape. Everything is split up into meaningless specks and dots of blinding colour. That triangle of blinding white may turn out to be a few inches of a bull's flank, that line of magenta perhaps a portion of a sock suspender, that brilliant point of transparent blue the sun picking out a glass bead in a bullock's necklace. All is a meaningless jumble of brilliant colour like confetti, but as we come in off the road, and enter the trees as into a building, the jig-saw puzzle sorts itself out, and we can see cattle dressed up in their elaborate jhools with holes for their humps to come through, couched on the ground chewing their cud, or being led about by proud owners. A fascinating sight! Here are some of the big Krishna Valley cattle Henry told me had been specially bred for this heavy soil, and here a few of the magnificent Gujerati cattle. Silvery white with immense spreading horns, noble necks and creasy dewlaps. (Oh! here was Itu in my tale of the Matti Tree!). While Henry was busying himself with Rao Bahadurs and Khan Bahadurs in their black coats with brilliant silken scarves worn across them, I stayed behind to dash off a rapid sketch of a huge white bull dressed in a pea green jhool with rose coloured lotus flowers appliquéd on it. He was led by a proud young man the colour of old gold, clad in shirt and dhoti and magenta turban. Henry had told me how this magnificent breed of cattle had been saved from extermination in the great famine of 1899 and 1900 by the efforts of Government. When we got home he looked up for me a number of the Journal of the Society of Arts wherein this great achievement is described. There is his speech on the subject, but it deals chiefly with irrigation, and what he wanted me to read was Sir Frederick Lely's description of how these cattle were saved.

Sir Frederick, after saying there had been no famine in Gujerat for nearly a century, and that the people were generally well-fed, living in comfort on fertile soil, goes on to say in August, '99 no rain had fallen, and it was realised that calamity was approaching.

> "It was pitiful to see the frantic efforts of the people to save their cattle. They searched about in corners and on the wayside for straws and sticks, anything that could be masticated. They tore the thatch from the roofs of their houses. They climbed the trees and plucked the leaves off one by one, so that to the brown fields and hungry vagrants, and wandering cattle was added yet another presage of mighty famine, lines and groves of skeleton trees stripped of their green foliage".

In the official weekly returns of the cause of death the native clerks kept entering "trefal". This was no new disease, merely the number of people who fell from trees in trying to secure fodder for the cattle. There were about two million cattle to be saved, and not a blade of grass nor a wisp of hay to feed them on "for it was not the custom of the country to store hay".

With the railways at command it was fairly easy to bring grain to the people themselves, but every full grown animal would eat up two truck loads before the rainy season came again. In Thana two or three hundred miles away grass was to be had, so it was arranged that daily a train should be loaded with it, and instead of returning empty should take cattle back to those pastures. Reduced railway fares were arranged, cattle were to be registered, fed and watered on departure and arrival, but the people suspected that Government wished to ship these cattle to Africa for beef for the soldiers in the Boer War, and to drag their waggons. Meetings were called, and finally twelve cattle were despatched with two farmers with them to report. These returned bringing with them samples of grass, and now the difficulty was that *all* wished to send their cattle. I wrote somewhere in my diary about Pinjrapols, and how the Indian will not take life for even his most diseased animals; and now on much the same principal as the Englishman says women and children first, these husbandmen brought all their most sickly and diseased cattle to be carried by train to the pastures, and the men working so hard to save the cattle "had the mortification of seeing scores of trucks depart loaded with refuse animals, many of whom died on the way". In the end however about 10,000 head were got off, but it was not a success, the "Gujerat cattle like their owners were soft and little used to roughing it. The coarse grass did not suit them. In the midst of rough plenty they died in hundreds".

By December it was realised that in spite of all the efforts of Government it was impossible to save more than a fraction of the two million, and that they must content themselves with saving the breed from extinction. A few well-bred young cows, some sires, and oxen were taken in camps limited to about 300, and given a daily allowance of oil-cake to supplement the poor grass. And now I am going to quote in full Sir Frederick Lely's words, as they are interesting and illuminating.

> "The management of the camps made us acquainted with qualities in the Indian cattle we had never suspected. The truth is the Indian cow and ox have a much better chance of developing

character than those of other countries. The cow has . . . for many centuries been esteemed as the holiest of animate beings. To kill a cow is an unspeakable sin . . . The Brahmini Bull has the freedom of his village. The cultivator's ox too is treated as a member of the family. He occupies as good a room in the house as his owner. On gala days he is painted with red, decorated with flowers, and fed with grain and spices. Now, if environment goes for any thing it is not surprising that after centuries of this human treatment the domestic cattle show some sign of "clubbable" qualities. When the first camp was started one of the rules drawn up by a European expert was that the animals should be sorted according to size. If big and little were enclosed together it was thought the little ones might get the worst of it. But it was soon discovered that the bond between Indian cattle was not their size, but their village. If they belonged to the same 'set' they knew one another and kept the most perfect order. They obeyed the herdsman's voice, and even the crack of his finger, and so far from hustling the little ones, they took care of them.

On one occasion . . . their good manners were sorely tried. It was the first day on which a basket of oil cake was brought into the enclosure. They were taken off their guard and with one consent rushed at the unfortunate man who carried it and knocked him over in their eagerness to get a piece. But a very short time was enough to bring them to a proper sense of propriety, and it was a pretty sight in after days to see them at the appearance of the basket range themselves in an orderly row, each one awaiting his or her turn. One incident I should hesitate to mention if it had not come to my knowledge on the best authority, an eye-witness whom I entirely trust, though I scarcely expect others to do so. In one camp in the Panch Mahals there were several sick animals who were set apart and fed with special food which some of the others saw and coveted, and, in order to get it themselves they lay down and shammed to be sick also".

SIR FREDERICK LELY, K.C.S.I., C.I.E.

Dharwar

It is always spoken of as a delightful station with an even better, because dryer climate, than Belgaum. But it just happens that we have struck a quite unusually hot patch for the time of year. Henry and I both feel it.

There have been many rumours here, especially in November, when the losses were so heavy at Ctesiphon, and when Kut was encircled. Henry had at that time traced the exaggerated rumours to the settlement of German missionaries . . . the Basel Mission from where we get our towels and dusters, and that most attractive grey-green cotton shikar cloth we always wear in district. On Henry's representation the missionaries had been interned. Now all is quiet in the district. Once again the regiments recruited here are proving their toughness, their martial prowess, and the local sympathies are wholly loyal.

Some time ago a notable Arab prisoner was sent here for internment. He was provided with a house under light surveillance. His name was Nuri Bey. Henry had made a special journey from Belgaum to see that he was not too strictly treated, and was very favourably impressed by the man. In his opinion the Collector had been unsatisfactory as regards the treatment of this Arab . . . just as he had been, in the opposite sense, with the German missionaries. So Henry had had him replaced. (An agreeable thing power).

Now Henry has been to see Nuri Bey. The new Collector, Mr. Moysey, is a very different person from his predecessor. He takes him out riding, gives him lessons in English when he has time, and has arranged for an English teacher for him at the convent here.

Note (written in 1946).

When Nuri Bey returned to his own country he was a strong supporter of the British, and has been ambassador in England, and Prime Minister of Iraq.

It was in 1917 that Henry met the famous Jaffa Pasha, Commander-in-Chief of Iraq, and he spoke of Nuri Bey.

"Nuri Bey? Nuri Bey?" exclaimed Jaffa Pasha delightedly, "He is my greatest friend. I keep his sister . . . he keep mine . . . " A pause. Then explosively "We are brothers . . . in . . . law . . . ".

At Dharwar I visit the school for training women teachers, as up-hill a job as training Indian women as nurses. Not for lack of intelligence, far from it. But for a woman to leave her home for such a thing damns her respectability for life. I watch them teaching the little children in up-to-date methods, and am given a little black handkerchief case most miraculously embroidered in the tiniest and most exquisite cross stitch it is possible to imagine. You cannot tell the wrong side from the right. The thought of the children's eyes makes me shudder!

It is here at Dharwar too I see an iron seat, the sort one sits in in parks and at the sea-side at home. It just fits into an oblong of high spiked railings. Going close to see the reason my astonished gaze falls upon an engraved stone bearing this inscription "These public gardens have been presented by Rao Bahadur . . . " .

Added many years later. Well this is no more ludicrous than the millionaire Parsi knight who having built his palace near Bombay fitted it with modern sanitation (then a novelty) and insisted on showing his guests the W.C's., pulling the plugs himself, before they went in to his dinner.

Hubli.

Big railway centre. Workshops, so a large population of Eurasians in their European clothes, exaggerated sun topis, and rather grubby white canvas shoes. Uninteresting cotton country, the plants look shabby. Hot. Flat for miles around.

I remember as a child at the sea-side straying one afternoon under the pier at low tide. The great black supports went reaching up over one's head. They were covered in barnacles and very silky bright green seaweed. There was a strange exciting smell, and the hollow sound of footsteps overhead. The sands and the sea were cut up into odd shapes by the straddling legs of the pier, and looked unfamiliar. It was a new world I had wandered into.

Well Kanara had been like that. A new world . . . but here I was back in the ordinary one.

Staying with the Collector and his wife. She is the most beautiful woman I have ever seen. A tall brilliant Jewess. She has become a Christian which does not make for easy relations between husband and wife, in spite of mutual affection . . . but there must be some other cause to account for the tragic expression in this woman's lovely face.

To-day I learn it. She is obsessed by the thought of cancer. Many of her relatives have died of it, including both her parents. Then her baby girl got it. She was sent to the Middlesex Hospital, and the unhappy mother stayed for many weeks till the child died. She is convinced that her other children will have it, and that she too will die of cancer.

Now before my marriage I had heard endless discussions on whether cancer was heriditary or not between Professor Almoth Wright and Professor Bulloch. Both, from the investigations that were being carried out at the London Hospital and St. Mary's were positive it was not hereditary. I was therefore in a position to reassure her. But it was of no use. She remained unconvinced. The fear for her children more than for herself, was with her night and day. She burned the candle at both ends, and broke it in the middle and burnt it there with unremitting toil to help the cause of the sick and suffering. She cannot sleep. She sits up half the night writing reports and so on. She has just collected the money for a Dispensary to be opened for women and children at Hubli. It is opened with due ceremony while we are here. Henry, the townsfolk, speeches, garlands and so on. And though this talented charming woman smiles and welcomes everybody, and makes a speech, yet the haunted look never leaves her eyes.

I have been so used to thinking in terms of Nature and wild animals it is a jolt to come up against human tragedy.

She died of cancer a few years later.

S.Y. Lot's Wife. Late February

On board again. We were becalmed. It was hot. There was a heavy swell on. The three bull-terriers had flumped down in a corner of the cabin. Henry was restless. Our eyes were glassy. I dared not move. A British India steamer passed, and seeing how we rolled, making no progress, offered to tow us. That roused one. Something to look at . . . but the hawser kept snapping and after two or three attempts she was forced to abandon us. Almost immediately a stiff breeze sprang up . . . it turned to wind . . . and before we knew it a gale! At first anything was better than that oily heave, lift and fall, but the seas were running very high. We began to get into difficulties. The Serang looking anxiously up at the sky which was covered with scudding cloud, decided we must make for Vengurla, a safe harbour. Already the day was beginning to close in. The waves looking like ink under the wild sky, slapped and thundered and burst up against the sides, and flung themselves over the deck. The wind shrieked in the rigging. It was growing darker and we were still some way from Vengurla. Kesu lay on the wet deck rolled head and all in a blanket, for all intents and purposes a dead man. Finally it became pitch dark. Secretly I was scared stiff. Henry and I stayed on deck clutching the side, trying to peer ahead into the darkness. My arm was through his. We were alternately jostled together and torn apart. "Listen", shouted Henry above the screaming of the wind, the crump and the thump of the waves.

I could hear a continuous roar as of breakers, and in the darkness we thought we could discern a dim whiteness, a pale blur. The Serang was yelling orders through the roar and the screaming wind, the lascars scrambling about, half seen in the dim light of hurricane lanterns . . . and then a tremendous crash and shuddering shock that hurled me on to Henry. Pandemonium in the darkness. Shrieks. Curses. Another shuddering shock that sent us both staggering . . . we must be on the rocks . . . the roar sounded louder . . . there were lights springing up all round us . . .

The whole of the Malwan fishing fleet had sought safety in Vengurla harbour as it was more sheltered. They were lying up here without any lights. We had crashed into them.

What a night! We were able at last to anchor, but not to land. The angle of our cabin deck was 45°. Everything crashing down and rolling across the floor. The noise, the groaning and creaking, the crash of breaking glass, the frantic efforts to keep oneself in bed, by arms and legs spread wide apart. Nothing to be seen through the streaming black glass of the windows as the waves burst up against them. The melancholy satisfaction that at long last Henry too had succumbed! If only the noise, the being flung about would stop for one second to give one a chance of taking hold of oneself . . .

When day broke we were able to get ashore. The little district bungalow is built on a projecting rock with the roaring seas on three sides of it. We see the dangerous rocks and the white foam bursting and sliding back from them unmoved, but when I go out onto the verandah which is enclosed with jaffery work, when I see the swinging seas up and down behind its criss-cross I am all but done for again.

Wonderful little Misteri. Pea-green under his dark skin, still trembling from the danger the Holy Virgin has saved him from, somehow he kills one of the chickens he brings along with him, and makes us chicken broth.

Never in all my life have I tasted anything so delicious.

Vengurla

Henry is not easy when ill. He has a heavy cold, and a cough that shakes his broad shoulders, and he is running a temperature. Nevertheless he insisted to-night on going to a Pan Supari party given in his honour, and there making a speech. In the shamiana it was packed, and suffocatingly hot, and though the sun was barely setting acetylene lamps hissed and flared over our heads. Mr. Koimattur's face was running with sweat as sentence by sentence he translated Henry's speech . . . and so was mine. Henry was constantly held up by violent coughing. Would he cut out by a sentence what he intended to say? No. There came the usual garlanding of pink roses and marigolds and jasmin, all drenched in rose water . . . very chilly and uncomfortable, trickling down your clothes and mingling with your own trickling perspiration. Bouquets betinseled, little limes, the red paste smeared on our outstretched wrists. Henry had a bright patch of colour on his cheek bones.

At last we came out from the packed shamiana with its red carpet and flags and pennons. The sun had now set, but the skies were still brilliant, and the sea a lovely jade green behind cocoa-nut palms that looked as though they were cut out of black paper. Henry went straight out onto the verandah which projects into the sea. He took off his tussore coat, his tie and collar, opened his shirt, rolled up his sleeves to the shoulder, called for a whiskey peg, and lay back in his long chair, eyes closed and the strong tepid wind charging straight off the sea, blowing and flapping at his open shirt where the sweat was standing in drops on his chest. Snapped furiously at me when I said this was folly.

There he stayed till it was quite dark.

The next day

Henry really ill. Can scarcely breathe. This evening he agreed to call in the sub-assistant surgeon whom we take around with us in camp. Henry had just eaten, as I thought, far too heavy a meal with the fever that he had. I left him alone with the timid little Indian. Subsequently there was much coming and going. Wood, blankets, kerosene tins filled with water, charcoal sigris. Hyder Khan told me a fire was to be lit, and all doors and windows closely shut. I could hardly believe him. The sub-assistant surgeon was in there for a long while. When at length he left I went in to Henry. As I opened the door I staggered. The heat was tremendous. The air so opaque from steam I could hardly see the camp bed with its mosquito poles, and that on it lay Henry with eyes closed, unable to speak. I could not feel his pulse.

Covering him almost entirely I flung open the doors and windows, and the strong air came streaming in from the sea. The little surgeon had closed every aperture, and had lit a charcoal sigri. He had wrung out boiling sheets in boiling water and wrapped them round Henry . . . and all this on top of a heavy meal.

No more sub-assistant surgeons. Henry has a constitution of iron. In a day or two he was well . . . and we were off to the Sinclairs at Castle Rock, home of tiger and panther.

His determination to work in spite of real illness reminds me of an incident in the life of John Lawrence. He was smitten down by abnormally high fever. The doctor considered that he could not live through the night. Early the next morning he came round to certify the death . . . and found John fully dressed, writing at his office table. He had work to do. Remembering a bottle of burgundy, he had drunk the whole bottle, and immediately fallen into a heavy sleep. Waking he had had his bath, dressed, and was busy at his table casting up settlement accounts when the doctor arrived.

Very like Henry.

Belgaum. Late March

We have returned home with a great clatter and dust of sowars. How large and dim, how clean and cool the bungalow. Our voices echo through the verandahs. The bull terriers charge in and out, the rugs flying away from their eager feet. How charmingly dainty the glass and silver and linen. How delicious the butter and milk straight from the buffalo instead of the tin. How luxurious that extra hour or two in bed instead of rising for forced marches. How comfortable not to live in a travelling chest of drawers; to wear a frock instead of breeches and riding boots, to play the piano—a grand—to go to the Club in the evenings, in short to taste the flesh pots. Till I put on a proper evening frock I had not realised how sunburnt I had become (what salt cellars!) and how dry and faded my hair! "Have you been ill?" asked fat kind Mrs. Fisher, the doctor's wife, with concern, and Dr. Fisher himself warned me to take it easy. "That great horse of yours is far too much for you. Why not give up riding for a bit?"

Not I.

It is only that I have seen and done so much in the past five months, taking part as it were in a continuous march through jungle, over maidans, down the coast, in cities, and townships and villages and hamlets, with every day a sowar galloping in to bring grave news from Europe, Mesopotamia, and East Africa to make a background of horror to otherwise supremely happy days.

I'm tired.

Since Christmas it had been the jungles, the soft empty roads striped across with shadows, the razor edge of sun and shade on every leaf. Strange blossoms. Fantastic insects. Harsh cries of bird and beast. We had inspected timber yards, and slides, and fellings, and spice gardens, and areas devastated by kumri, and ravaged by wild elephant. We had entertained and been entertained by Indian and European officials. We had visited Bijapur that glorious Muhammadan city with its hundreds of mosques and tombs. For that we had left by the mail one evening at about six o'clock, and at every stop there had been an official welcome at the station. Garlands of roses and jasmines, marigolds and champak drenched in cheap scent, staining our clothes and dripping down our necks. Soon the railway carriage became piled with wilting garlands, tinselled bouquets, and flat baskets of limes, plantains, and oranges which rolled beneath ones feet. The seats were covered, the floor and the little lavatory crammed, basin, seat, and floor. The heat, the lamps, the overpowering smell of fruit and flowers flattened by the kerosene I always have to smear myself with in these old railway carriages to keep off the bugs which infest their woodwork, was stupefying, and at every station the same thing was repeated. The door opened, and there below, a crowd of brown faces glistening with sweat beneath the hissing kitsen lamps. More fruit and flowers pushed in, more garlands, more speeches. By midnight we were both worn out. Henry had taken off his coat. I longed to undress. When the train drew into Bijapur Henry had determinedly turned out all lights. Wooden shutters, black gauze screens were pulled up over the windows. We sat there in the dark scarcely breathing till the hubbub outside ceased. At last the carriage was shunted into a siding, and we slept. The next morning when I pulled down my black gauze window it was to find the magnificent spectacle of the Gol Gumbaz, the greatest dome in all the world, flanked by its four towers, filling the window completely. It is easy to write of leaf and bird and beast, and even sometimes of man. But what of Bijapur offering me her forlorn appeal? I am dumb. My hand is still. The beauty and the decay, and the goats scrambling over tombs bring a lump to my throat. But I know no history. The most fatuous guide book can do better than I. Henry tells me the Mogul dynasty was brought to an end in Bijapur by Shivaji the Mahratta Chief, the Mountain Rat as they called him. I see the domes and the many slender minarets of the Ibrahim Roza silhouetted against a sad sunset, and I look on the tombs of the Kings of Bijapur and their pen cases painted with convolvulus flowers, and I am shown the great Turkish gun, the Malik-i-Maidan, whose muzzle is so big a man can sit inside, this great gun to whom the Sultans did reverence, and which used to be covered in cloth of gold, yes I see all that, but there is no perspective. It is all a piece with that small kid, its four hoofs bunched together as it poised on a broken tomb, or the clinking sound the carved stone chains made as they shifted in the wind, or that Henry and I are staying with Mr. Varley, the Judge, and that the Judge's Bungalow is a white-washed disused mosque, and that that first evening we go to the Gymkhana which also is a white-washed, disused mosque, and play badminton.

"Near me a Mussulman, civil and mild
  Watched as the shuttlecocks rose and fell
And he said, as he counted his beads and smiled,
  God smite their souls to the depths of hell".

Yes. I had read that in the shabby little green volume of Sir Alfred Lyall's poems on the voyage out. Well here it was, and little Mussulman boys in blue dungaree with broad red belts round their tummies darted about retrieving my feeble and wayward shuttlecocks . . . but Henry did tell me afterwards that Lord Curzon when Viceroy had strongly disapproved of the misuse of mosques, and they were being rapidly restored to their original purpose. Such details of no importance like a milk-white kid, and the sunlit leaves of a fig-tree looking like brocade in a dark archway, or the deep deep jade of the water lying before the Asar Mahal, stand out in my memory, and also that from Mr. Varley we went on to stay with the Parsi Collector and his wife, the Kabrijis. There were many female relations, and as is usual they all wore embroidered saris, and very high heeled French shoes, and gold-rimmed spectacles. But what I remember most of all is that when we had finished an enormous breakfast of porridge, fish, brain cutlets, vegetable-curry, eggs and marmalade, Mr. Kabriji pressed on me fruit which I did not want. He would take no refusal, and not wishing to offend I at last gave in. My custard-apple consisted entirely of innumerable fleshy pips. No one else had taken one, and I laboriously sucked and ejected hundreds of seeds feeling Henry's delighted gaze on me, amid the silence of the Parsi ladies behind their spectacles, and my kind host's polite questions answered with so much difficulty.

Yes. Till I can read . . . and digest . . . some Indian history, these trivial happenings are what Bijapur with her supreme beauty means to me, I confess . . . but back to Lot's Wife again.

We had visited the famous American Mission Hospital of Dr. Wanless . . . not the one at Miraj but the one on the coast. Rumour had it that he was taking leave and returning to the States. So from two hundred miles and more patients had come crowding in, on foot, by bullock cart, or in native boats, overwhelming the little hospital. The new up to date building with its marble operating theatre, its rounded corners, and glass tables and so on was unfinished, and could take but few. Doctor Wanless had shown us over the old building, dark with uneven mud floors and walls. Men and women had crowded in, in their panic he would leave before seeing them. They were lying on the floor between the beds. It was difficult not to tread on them. I brought away a confused impression of scarlet blankets, and bunches of flies on the hard pillows covered in ticking, of men destroyed with fever, a woman fighting for breath from heart disease, sick babies with painted eyes, children eating curry, children with opthalmia, sores, saturating heat, and always those bunches of black flies . . . and Doctor Wanless, that inspired man walking through it all, full of confidence and enthusiasm, the eyes of these poor people following him as though he were God.

And we had sailed on South and Misteri our Goanese cook is hanging over the yacht's rail, excitedly pointing out his property. He is a considerable land-owner, and in virtue of this he is explaining he has the right to sit in a chair when the Governor of Goa (no half-caste, but sent out from Portugal) is in Council. How strange that a man owning acres of valuable mango orchards, should choose to leave his wife and family to manage them, and come and cook for us for eleven months out of every year!

We had sailed on to Panjim. Panjim that picturesque little Portuguese town with its continental casino and bandstand, and the windows of the poorer houses fitted with oyster shells instead of glass. In Panjim harbour three or four German ships were interned. Rusty and dirty. The German sailors looked as though they could murder us. We hired a ramshackle victoria, and past cocoa-nut groves and mangrove swamps drive to old Goa, past very high walls within which the convents and monasteries seemed to hug their secrets of past centuries. We went over the cathedral at Goa and saw the tomb of St. Francis Xavier. Himself we did not see, for some disgusting American visitor had bitten off his big toe some years before, so now he is not shown. We saw the great silver candlesticks shown by a priest with immense pride, and for some reason or other I found something touching in that they were of unpainted wood with a thin, such a very thin layer of silver clumsily nailed to the front side only. We saw extraordinary dark old portraits, and furniture. We wondered what tales these convents and monasteries choked up in their palm trees, could tell. And then the following day we had motored up to Castle Rock, and here we were back in Belgaum at the beginning of the Hot Weather.

No! I'm not ill . . . but I'm very very tired.

April.

Back to station life again. No dancing. Quiet dinner parties. Giving out khaki shirts which arrive already cut out from headquarters: also knitting wool. Packing up the articles when finished. Y.W.C.A. meetings. Going to the convent to replenish towels and sheets and tray-cloths destroyed by the dhobi on tour. Taking the nuns and Mother-Superior little sugary cakes, not only for their own childish pleasure but also in memory of two much loved R.C. friends at home.

It's hot now. A brooding heat. Green leaves are showing amongst the fiery gold mohur blossom. One wakes to the endless repetition of the brain-fever bird. "Brain-fever. Brain-fever. BRAIN FEVER" he screams in an ever ascending scale till even I who never weary of the cawing of rooks, or the harsh cries of peacocks before rain, could wring his neck. Yes. It's hot. We ride early to the racecourse where all the little road-side trees are putting forth bright glaucous leaves which contrast oddly with the burnt up grass of the maidan. The crimson dust lies thickly on the roadside agaves. In the evenings we play golf. The links are ochre-coloured, and already the spear-grass hooks viciously into one's ankles. After, the Club. Lime squash, weak whisky pegs, and parched gram as we discuss the war news. Perhaps a little badminton at which I remain a hopeless duffer, and Henry excels as at tennis and squash.

War of course takes precedence of everything, but the shocking infant mortality, and the unintentional cruelty of the dhais (hereditary mid-wives) can't be ignored. The welfare of Indian women had been of special interest to Louise. She had laboured to alleviate their sufferings, and now Henry would like me to carry on her work.

This worries me.

I've been out here a year, but my ignorance is still great. It is all very well for the young wife of a junior Assistant Collector. She begins at the bottom, climbs slowly up taking a little more responsibility as she climbs . . . but here am I inexperienced, starting away at the top! I attempt to explain; but Henry in the course of his work has come across a remarkable woman, a Mrs. Brown, wife of a missionary out at Khanapur. She is a trained mid-wife, she speaks Mahratti and Kanarese fluently, and is only too willing to help, thus gaining the Commissioner's name and support in her work for women.

She came in this afternoon by the Mail. She turns out to be a racy and amusing person, rather nice looking, obviously enjoying the particularly good tea I've got for her, and all eagerness to win support for her poor women of the lowest castes amongst whom she works. She tells me hair-raising tales of the practices of the dhais. To begin with only the oldest and dirtiest clothes are used for confinements. The woman lies on a heap of old rags on the mud floor. All ventilation stopped with rags, and a fire burns. Relations and children crowd up what little room there may be. If the labour is unduly prolonged the dhai will in all good faith step on the woman's stomach and trample, or the patient may even be hung up by her long black hair! "But it's no use scolding the dhais or alienating them in any way", declares Mrs. Brown wisely. "It's an hereditary calling and they do their best. We've somehow got to educate *them* and then get the mothers to expect them to be educated". She went on to say what indeed I knew already that women will not go into hospital, and even if Indian girls were trained it would be as impossible for them after to go into the mofussil (district) to help their sisters, as it is impossible to train school teachers; for any but the most advanced Indian would consider his daughter by so doing was advertising herself as a prostitute.

It is arranged then that invitations should be sent out to a number of highly placed Indian ladies, and that Mrs. Brown shall come and talk to them on the simplest rules of hygiene. "But supposing they don't come?" I ask. "Never fear. They will *all* come, and bring their children, and servants too," laughs Mrs. Brown.

Contrary to expectation I am enjoying her visit. She is human. She is carrying on her work amongst the lowest of outcasts. "Poor dear souls. I would do anything in the world I could to help them, but . . . " here she leaned forward, a capable freckled hand on my knee, "I've told Mr. Brown I can't really LOVE them as he does . . . You see, my dear they do *stink* so".

(It was not long before that all-embracing charity of hers included them in love as well as service).

The ladies have been asked to come at three o'clock. Before two the dhamnies begin to roll up the drive, and disgorge women, children, babies and a few servants. They are all escorted by the pattawallas into the middle drawing-room, large, empty, and with a parquet floor. I peer through the hanging bead curtains unseen. There is a hubbub of high-pitched voices and babies crying. I can't speak a word of Mahratti or Kanarese. Few will understand Hindustani. I *must* wait for Mrs. Brown. But the noise is ever increasing so finally I part the beads and instantly I am surrounded as a crust of bread thrown into water is surrounded by minnows. But I should say gold-fish rather. For these Mahratta, Brahmin and Lingayat ladies are most gorgeously apparelled and loaded with jewels. Fresh caste marks on their foreheads, little pearls or diamonds in their noses, and wreaths of fresh jasmine resting on their low knots of oiled and blue-black hair, they surround me. They are evidently amazed that I wear no jewelry. Even the naked babies with their big eyes, bigger still from smeared bitumen, have golden anklets and bracelets. What a wishy-washy creature I must seem in my white and black spotted cambric dress with its black velvet sash. I smile. I finger their jewelry admiringly, I try not to see a baby is being held out to fulfil the wants of nature on my parquet floor, and then, thank heavens, Mrs. Brown bursts in with her infectious laugh, her huge sun-hat slipping sideways off her head. She takes instant charge. These brilliantly clad women are comfortably seating themselves, some on chairs and sofas, but mostly on the floor, and Mrs. Brown has them all listening spell-bound, as with animated gestures and laughter she talks to them. They nod appreciatively to each other in confirmation of what she says. Over and over again I hear the one word I can understand, *Bai,* Sister. It is clear they look upon her as a sister. It is all a great success, and I suppose I must consider the ever increasing puddles on the floor not too high a price to pay.

It is almost impossible to get our visitors to go, but at last we are left alone. Over tea Mrs. Brown confides to me that her husband belongs to a Faith Mission. That is neither of them have any money of their own. They have given up everything. Their bungalow, their mission hall, their dispensary have been built from free gifts. They are dependent for their next week's food, on what may or may not come in from headquarters. I am aghast!

"We just ask for the needs of the day", said Mrs. Brown happily.

"Once there was no money left in the house. Not one anna. It was on a Sunday, and at our 'breaking of bread', the native Christians put in their little bits of coins . . . but we had nothing . . . ! On the following day the bhisti and the sweeper would have to be paid. There would be no food for our babies. All my faith went. 'It will be all right', said Mr. Brown, but I was crazy with fear. He spent the night in prayer, and I cried and cried. The next morning came a cheque for a hundred pounds from a sympathiser in England. I've never troubled since that day", and Mrs. Brown laughed, looking into space all rapt and delighted as though she were seeing something hidden from the rest of the world.

It was after one of the subsequent meetings I learned she was the daughter of a rich settler in Australia. Member of a large family, tired of picnics and dances she thought she would like to train as a hospital nurse. Her people raised no objection. After doing three years she went on a holiday to England, and met her missionary. Her people threatened to disown her. She grieved . . . but she married him, and came out to India. They now have two boys, but she is not yet wholly forgiven by her family.

"And you don't regret it?" I asked.

"Why no. Sometimes I get tired and snap, but I wouldn't change my life for anything. I don't say I wouldn't like to see a theatre, hear some good music, and have a dress that wasn't made by the dirzi, and eat food I hadn't cooked myself. But a week would be enough. Here I have Mr. Brown and the babies, and when my time comes I shall pass straight into the arms of Jesus like that lovely old soul they fetched me out to last night".

I was embarrassed. Not Mrs. Brown. "Think what fun it will be meeting Abraham and Elijah with their long beards and all the other people we know in the Bible!"

Well . . .

Any Thursday

This is given over to mail. Henry is particularly anxious to keep in touch with the children. It is constantly in his thoughts. Many return to their families in England complete strangers. He is too busy to write himself, so before I can turn to my own correspondence, my mother-in-law, George, Michael and Bim must be written to individually. It was comparatively easy when in camp, but how to write with interest to children, of the routine of station life?

I write to the picture of George that rises before me. Fair-haired, extraordinarily unselfish little boy, whose leg was so fatally easy to pull, whose appetite was quite impossible to satisfy, who knocked over everything from milk-jugs to chamber pots. I see him silhouetted against heaving grey seas, patiently fishing off Buckers Rock, or perhaps holding out his hand to guide me over some rock he considers difficult to balance upon.

I write to Mike, the crimson-cheeked hazel-eyed little dare-devil, who something tells me, is secretly afraid of the Atlantic rollers he pretends to delight in, and who equally secretly sickens at the blood of a shot rabbit. Mike, who when I nervously announced his father and I were getting married, remarked with quiet satisfaction, "That's what we've been waiting for", and promptly on his own packed up a puffin's beak and sent it off to Derry to be made into a brooch for me!

I write to Bim, rising in the saddle, mile after mile following our jaunting car, when both her brothers had long before given up exhausted. Over the wet shining sands of Lagg Strand, splashing through pools of daffodil sea-water, right into the quivering brilliant sunset, on and on and on she trots . . . Bim the lint-haired little girl of nine whose solid determination to get just what she wants out of life seems to blot out everything else about her.

But have these pictures anything in common with the three children at their schools, with their prim little letters coming out to us? "Yesterday we played 'Johns'. We won by one wicket", etc., etc.

Well, I shall know some day.

Most mornings Henry has visitors, Indian or European. He sits at his office table, Luther at his feet, at the end of the long verandah, and I hear as an undercurrent to my own writing, the crunch of wheels on gravel, the murmur of the pattawallas' voices, and then the footsteps of the visitor as he makes his way over the polished tiles to the office.

But to-day Henry comes to me.

"Montgomerie, the Judge, is here, and he has got with him young X, an Assistant Collector, whom I shall bring along. Keep him for a few minutes, and tell me what you think of him".

"Well?" asks Henry five minutes later as the dhamny rattles away with the two men.

"Henry. He's *mad*!" I exclaim distressed.

"Poor devil! Yes. He was certified this morning, and I have just had to put my signature to it. They are taking him away now".

It seems that poor X had been strange in his manner for some time, and the night before had produced a revolver, and tried to shoot his stable companion. It had been a terrible night.

Haunted by the thought of that poor boy all day. He has no relatives out here.

I have been revising some essays I wrote in Kanara before sending them to the publisher. Seeing me very sticky and weary over my little portable Blick, Henry suggested my dictating to Mr. Iyengar, his shorthand writer, who happens to be free this afternoon. Mr. Iyengar is the tall, lanky, pleasant Madrassi burdened with innumerable female relations who are always ill, and always in need of money. He looks wretchedly ill himself, too often getting fever. In he comes in his little black cap, and voluminous dhoti falling over his bare legs, his face as always beaded with sweat. He seats himself with his pad. He seems even more nervous than usual, fiddling with his pencil in his long fingered hands with their bluish nails. I read out a sentence very slowly, and clearly. He asks me to repeat it. Nervously. Apologetically. I do so. He is clearly in great discomfiture. Now Mr. Iyengar is a first-class shorthand clerk, and from much singing I do speak distinctly, and I am sitting exactly opposite to him, whereas

Henry when dictating is often walking up and down, and has a pipe in his mouth. What can be the matter? Henry looks in.

"All well?"

"Sir! Sir! I cannot do it!" and Mr. Iyengar rises hysterically from his seat cracking his finger-joints in his distress.

"But what's wrong Read out what you've got down", says Henry bringing as always good common-sense into the situation.

In a shaken voice, almost weeping Mr. Iyengar reads out word for word what I have dictated, the first paragraph of "The Tale of the Matti Tree".

Henry looks at me.

"But that's absolutely right!" I exclaim.

"But Sir! Sir!" cries Mr. Iyengar now in tears. IT MAKES NO SENSE".

(N.B. Henry still reminds me of this. 1949).

But in that timid body beats a lion's heart. When we travel up to Mahableshwar we go by powerful car from Poona, but the "office", the clerks, the servants, follow by bullock cart, which takes two days. To Henry's astonishment Mr. Iyengar turns up for work that first afternoon.

"How on earth did you get here Iyengar?"

"By motor bike sir".

"Motor bike? I never knew you could ride a motor bike!"

"No sir. I had never been on one till yesterday when I went into the Poona bazaar and bought one. This morning I rode up here".

How he had ever survived those hair-pin bends where bullock carts come suddenly round, their drivers asleep, and go half plunging over the precipice of two thousand feet or more . . . a man who had never ridden a motor bicycle before! It is a complete mystery.

June.

Old friends of Henry have been staying with us . . . now to be my friends. First John Shillidy, Collector of Surat in Gujerat. He is the son of an Ulster missionary who has been out here for years. At once I recognise the affection and esteem with which John regards

Henry, but he is not an Irishman for nothing, and his audacious sallies are often directed at Government and its ways. Never have I met anyone with such a sense for the absurd. Where he is, is laughter. Henry and I are enjoying him immensely.

There comes a break in the rains. We mount John on Lot. A short burst on the racecourse, and then away over the downs towards Flat Top Hill. It's a laughing sort of morning, the wind fluting, thousands of little white orchids dotting the green, all growing individually like the flowers in early Italian paintings, and the hills over there blue as delphiniums.

"Ireland!" shouts John as we gallop. So it is. The brilliant slopes are strewn with grey boulders. Everything gleaming and glooming in bright sunshine and shadow, so that one moment the racing dogs are white as paper against the grass, the next almost invisible in shadow. Near Flat Top Hill as usual we put up, not a jack, but a fox, and start a grand gallop, the dogs giving tongue. We three separate to head off the fox. Leviathan is pulling my arms out . . . the fox gradually slows, the dogs put on a final spurt as he sinks on his haunches apparently exhausted. Almost delirious they press on, and as they approach, up pops the fox fresh as a daisy, and away he goes over the sunlit grass, laughing his heart out as his shadow races before him.

But the dogs are done in. They never learn this trick. As we draw rein, turning our sweating, blowing horses to the wind the three flop down, eyes and tongues starting out of their heads "Ha-ha-ha-ha-ha-ha-ha", we hear their panting above the whistle of the wind through the hole in the top of our topis.

How good it is up here on top of Flat Top Hill; all round us spread miles of rice and millet, gleam and gloom and glisten of floods. "Pateela! Pateela! Pateela!" call the partridges. To be so completely in accord with your companions and your surroundings: this is happiness!

John shows us his hands, amusedly. Strips of skin hang loose and there is blood between his fingers. Lot has anyway a mouth of iron, and he was naturally excited at getting out of the shafts again. Well I wonder what John's backside is like? Skin gets abnormally tender in Belgaum owing to the humidity. Each morning I rub the cake of soap under my knee, and then bind three inch sticking plaster. Yet I'm sometimes raw on my return. Leviathan gets a spot of scarlet raw flesh on his black satin neck where the reins chafe. Poor John. Well, he shall have a cushion on his chair.

Now another friend of Henry's. She is in her early thirties, intelligent, travelled, the kind of woman who prefers to dress smartly rather than becomingly, and yet can carry off the most extreme fashion without looking ridiculous. Just back from Paris as she is, she transforms my clothes with a skilful tweak here, and an upstanding bow there. Such poise she has, such sophistication, I am at first unable to recognise the genuine kindness and generosity under those mannered ways, but Mrs. Brown, of all people, recognises it at once.

Mrs. Brown has been in Dr. Wanless' Hospital at Miraj. She is back home now, and we all three motor out to see her. Antonia . . . as I have christened her because of her likeness to some Roman lady . . . fits at once into the little Mission household for some reason or other. We leave her talking to Mrs. Brown still in bed while Henry and I go off to see the Criminal Tribe Settlement close by.

These Criminal Tribes have been brought up to the profession of crime, from time immemorial. They have become such an intolerable nuisance that Government is now segregating them in camps. This will be a costly experiment, Henry says, but the idea is to see if they can be reclaimed. They live with their families in huts, have their own cattle, and are taught trades they can carry on inside the camps. The children have to attend school. Mr. Starte, an I.C.S. man is in charge of this particular camp. He is enthusiastic over its possibilities and the wonderful work Mrs. Brown is doing amongst the women and children. The people do look happy enough, but how tame the life must seem to the men! Henry is talking to one or two.

"You'll have your pocket picked as you stand here", warns Mr. Starte.

Sure enough, one of the men smilingly hands Henry's note case back to him, and my handkerchief to me. I fancy from Mr. Starte's smile they are allowed to show off their skill in this way occasionally.

The Bhat women are very picturesque looking, not dressed in saris, but in brilliant voluminous skirts, and black bodices sewn all over with bits of china and looking glass. They are very friendly to me. I suppose these people must not be allowed to roam the country-side and make a nuisance of themselves, but as we return to the Mission I find myself remembering how disconsolate and draggled the hawks and eagles look on their perches in the London Zoo.

From time to time we go up to Poona or Bombay for the Legislative Council meetings where Henry has to take a share in discussing political questions affecting the whole Presidency. Hence his title Honorable Mr. H. S. Lawrence. Legislative Council is something of a social affair for the women. They lean over the gallery in attractive clothes, their bracelets, and wrist watches clasped over white kid gloves. On the red-carpeted dais below sits Lord Willingdon, the Governor, immaculate in light grey frock coat and button-hole. With him Mr. Pattani a venerable old gentleman arrayed in dazzling white with silky white beard, and the two English members of Council, Mr. Carmichael and Mr. Sheppard, Henry's predecessor. Presently Lady Willingdon swims in with a large bouquet in her gloved hands. She is followed by an A.D.C. in white uniform, complete with sword. Lady Willingdon settles herself in an imposing chair beside H. E., looks about her, smiles and waves her fan at someone, hands her bouquet to the A.D.C. . . .

Those at home would be amazed to see the predominance of turbans and other Indian head-dresses. They do not realise that the white officials out here can be numbered in hundreds, whilst the population runs into hundreds of millions. They would be amazed too to hear the extreme eloquence of Indian speakers in the English tongue. True there is a good deal of repetition at times, and the sentiments are high flown, but you are spared the too frequent hesitations and "ur-ah", of the average Englishman.

Sometimes it is interesting up there in the gallery, more often boring, and sometimes horrifying, as when the orthodox Jain sitting next me, removed his head dress, searched, and found, and very carefully deposited what he had found between his chair and mine, to avoid the taking of life.

Lord Willingdon is always urbane and polite even when bored. I remember on one occasion his thanking a certain senior English officer who had spoken at great length and most confusedly. H. E. congratulated him on his speech, but enquired however whether he had been supporting or opposing the motion!

Antonia accompanies us this time to Poona on her way to Bombay. Coming to Poona means a night journey, therefore bug-bites for me, in spite of the fact Kesu rubs my mattress and mosquito nets with kerosene, and I go to sleep with a kerosene rag in my hand. The wood-work in the carriages of this old narrow gauge Southern Mahratta railway is infested with bugs from the coolies. Henry they do not touch. False dawn and the real dawn breaking, seen through a railway carriage window fascinates me wherever it may be. As we draw near Poona the drenched dark earth with forlorn pale pools staring up at the still dark sky reminds me somehow of Inishowen. Antonia seeing me sit up, declares briskly, "I'm going to make you a cup of tea. China or Indian? Both here".

Not a hair out of place, a gay scarf tied round her head, she produces the latest thing in tea baskets, and before many minutes we have fresh tea. She is the most efficient person I have ever met.

We are staying in one of the typical old Indian bungalows in Queen's Gardens. Big verandahs, deep eaves, mud walls and floors. Eminently comfortable and suitable for the climate. The Keatinges are immensely hospitable. There are always people in to breakfast and dinner. Gerald, big, bluff, bubbling over like fizzy lemonade with enthusiasm, fun, vitality and good stories. Polly with the frizz of hair and pretty eyes his equal. With one at each end of the table, talking loudly, enthusing, laughing, telling amusing stories, it is almost impossible to hear what any one is saying, and quite impossible not to be laughing too.

Henry takes me out one morning to the Agricultural College near Ganeshkind (Government House). The College is Henry's pet child. For when he was Director of Agriculture it was his duty to attend annual conferences with other officers of other Provinces at Pusa in Bengal. In his opinion the situation was badly chosen, not only being inaccessible, but also unhealthy. So when later Bombay was to start a College of its own, Henry in the face of the most violent opposition succeeded in having it built at Poona. He argued that people must be able to see what experiments were being made, and that the staff must have the encouragement of visitors, and the recognition of their work.

Note, 1949. His objection to Pusa was justified. Thirty years later Government scrapped the Pusa Institution and transferred it to Delhi.

We go over the College, and we move slowly round the farm, Henry and the Indian manager discussing the respective merits of silage towers and silage pits, and I seeing that the plains all round us of grass, and sugar-cane and millet are brilliant varying shades of emerald, whilst all the hills surrounding Poona are just the colour of a grape. And to-day Singhad, the Lion Fort, the hill-fortress which though twenty miles away, dominates Poona, is lifted high against an almost white sky, and is looking so close you could reach up and put your hand on it. Some day we are climbing up the little track which zig-zags up and up, steeper and steeper, and finally leaving shrub and tree and tangle behind, coming to fifty feet of smooth black basalt, flanked by great towers.

Up there the garrison was once held by one thousand of Aurangzeb's men. But Shivaji, that mountain rat, as Aurangzeb contemptuously described him, was determined to take the fortress. Tanaji, his favourite commander had crept with followers to this spot, and the great stratagem was to begin. The ghorpat is produced from its basket. (A ghorpat is a huge lizard found in these parts, and sometimes made a pet of). This ghorpat was called Geshwant: he was painted, and wore a collar of pearls. Tanaji had fastened a rope round Geshwant, and encouraged the lizard to run up the bare face of the rock, and disappear over the crenellated wall. Quickly Tanaji and his followers swarmed after with the aid of the rope. The three hundred Mahrattas overcame the garrison, but Tanaji himself was cut down by Afzul Khan, and Shivaji even in his triumph laments, "I have won the Lion's Fort, but I have lost my Lion".

But now I know more history than I did. I know how Shivaji in making peace with his Muhammadan enemy Afzul Khan, comes forward to embrace him in Eastern fashion, but instead wounds him mortally with the iron claws he conceals in his hand . . .

Another day I go to visit the Seva Sadan in Poona city. Seva Sadan means Service of the People. There Mrs. Ranade, widow of the famous High Court judge who was Henry's friend, is helping to emancipate women. She was overwhelmed by the death of her husband. It was Louise, my sister, who urged her to rouse herself, to eschew the custom of leading the ignominious lot of an Indian widow but rather to come forward, to help to better the lot of women and children, to educate women who had become mothers, perhaps at twelve or thirteen, and who did not know how to read or write, or be of any companionship to their husbands. Long had Louise pleaded and argued. At length she won the day, and now this noble woman runs the Seva Sadan which is ever enlarging its scope.

Our tonga rattles us through the smelly confusion of the bazaar. The narrow lane with its pools of rain water, blocked by bullock carts, and passers by, and a bull sauntering down the pavement pausing unmolested to pluck at this and that from the vegetable shops. Old dwelling-houses have rickety carved balconies, and sometimes a wonderfully carved door in blackwood. Little details detach themselves, as with cries from our tonga-walla, and a great ringing of bells we force our way through the crowds. I remember the Brahmin lady picking her way serenely through the mud, her red and blue sari looped between her thighs, and fresh flowers resting on her knot of oiled hair; the fakir writhing naked on a mattress of iron spikes; in a doorway a woman with a child's head forced between her knees while she searches for insects which she places on the child's outstretched palm, and then a little box of a shop glittering with thousands of glass bangles, standing in columns of ruby, of gold, of turquoise, of green and of blue, and next to it a garland-maker sitting on a shelf like an idol, stringing his garlands from the roses, the jasmine, the marigolds heaped about him.

The Seva Sadan has its home in a perfect rabbit warren of old rooms leading one out of another, all very dark, and so low I have to stoop to pass under the lintels. Mrs. Ranade is the most dignified and gracious woman. She shows me round with pride, and with genuine feeling and affection speaks of Louise as "my sister Mrs. Lawrence who persuaded me to do this work". She is now a leader of the advanced school of politicians and she tells me again how it was Louise who encouraged her in this.

Here in the Seva Sadan we see women of all ages learning to read and to write. There is one old white-haired woman who is laboriously striving to learn her alphabet.

"I'm afraid she will never learn it", said Mrs. Ranade, "but she is so happy coming here we let her come".

The women learn to sing and play instruments and to sew. They learn, unfortunately, not their own native work, but the most monstrous embroidery in Berlin wools on black velveteen. A terrible cushion cover is presented to me of flowers in that particular shade of pink of which the Indian is so fond, which suggests to us cheap confectionery. At parting they sing to me a long, a very very long hymn in my honour to the thumping of a portable harmonium. They sing loudly, their eyes tightly shut, their mouths so widely open you see their large tongues stained with betel juice . . .

We keep Indian hours, that is parting after the eleven o'clock breakfast till tea time. Henry at the Secretariat. I spend hours in my own rooms and the verandah, writing my novel, painting, learning Hindustani, knitting war socks. There is a lovely durantur tree with its mauve flowers just outside my verandah. A sun bird has its nest there, and there are showers of canary-like music all day. There is also the tub, and its high framework is covered with thousands of brightest blue tiny convolvulus flowers. Over these flowers hover and flicker all day tiny blue butterflies, just the same blue as the flowers. A charming sight.

Club and gymkhana in the evening after games. Henry and I are not what you would describe as gymkhana people, not being very socially minded, though Henry as a matter of fact can be the most exhilarating host, and make the stickiest party "go". But he has always set his face resolutely against the endless "treating" when after strenuous exercises, circles are formed under the trees, and drink after drink passes round. True the whisky pegs are usually almost colourless, and the drinks are often lime squash, but there is a certain amount of milk punch too, and in any case the remorseless bills coming in at the end of the month must stagger many a junior couple who feel they must do as others do. Anyway to drink and eat gram and chip potatoes at seven o'clock, when you are going to eat a dinner of many courses at eight-thirty seems to me stupid. As a family we were brought up not to eat between meals. I can hear Father exclaim with disgust "Elevenses, they call it. Low middle-class habit. Disgusting!".

I must confess those endless séances under the trees, wrapped in blanket coats, the sweat drying chillily on you, and the mosquitoes feasting on wrists and ankles seem boring to both of us.

Returning home tomorrow. I say to Henry "We've been married eighteen months. Would you like me to see a doctor?"

"I think we are very happy as we are. Don't you?".

I do.

Note 1948.

In these visits to Poona and Bombay for Legislative Council Henry met some of the Indians who later on were to play an important part in public affairs. With V. J. Patel, who became President of the Legislative Assembly of India (a dignitary corresponding to the

Speaker of the House of Commons) he began an acquaintanceship which developed into a close friendship of mutual laughing mistrust, if I may use such a contradiction of terms. One day in 1915 Patel moved a resolution to amend the law regulating the powers of Indians in self-government. The members of the Executive Council opposed the motion, and with the Government majority in the Legislative Council it was thrown out. At that time as I have just described the Governor presided in person at these meetings. That evening Henry asked for an interview with Lord Willingdon, and told him that the advice given to him by the Executive Council was a grave error. H. E. therefore appointed a special committee with Henry as chairman to examine the law and propose amendments, and with Patel, the original mover, as a member of the Committee. Sitting together Henry and Patel became good friends, both men always ready to see a joke. This friendship some could not understand, John Shillidy for instance who regarded "V. J." as he was popularly known, as the devil incarnate!

Ten years later when V. J. was engaged on a whirlwind campaign of seditious oratory, and Henry was a member of the Government, V. J. came secretly to Henry at midnight, saying cynically he was completely worn out with making these endless seditious speeches, and needed a rest. Would Henry therefore have him arrested and give him three months in prison? With characteristic humour he added, "This 'Crown of Martyrdom' would do me a lot of good politically".

Henry did not comply.

In 1919 he was over in England to be present at the debates in Parliament over the Amritsar affair, and the shooting down of the people by General Dyer. We were staying at that time in a residential hotel in Queens Gate whose inhabitants were chiefly old ladies, with a sprinkling of retired army people. Henry asked V. J. to come and dine with us. The inmates were startled for V. J. turned up arrayed in homespun white khaddar, sandals on his bare feet, and a soft Gandhi cap which he kept on indoors. Hitherto one had always seen him in European dress, and on greeting him I could swear his tongue was in his cheek. Now Henry's eldest son in the Coldstreams had just returned from Cologne, and was now at Oriel annoying his Uncle Reginald Thornhill by his pro-German views and deep pink politics. George had been loud in condemnation of General Dyer . . . that was understandable . . . but he also spoke a good deal of the tyranny of the British Government in India! So Henry had him in to dine to meet V. J. The latter on introduction familiarly thrust his arm through George's and addressed him as "my dear Lawrence".

It was amusing to see George's reaction. With obvious difficulty he concealed his Colonel Blimp's attitude. Needless to say we teased him afterwards. "But to put his arm through mine! To call me 'dear Lawrence' straightaway!" George stuttered with indignant surprise.

So much for the politics of the young.

How we laughed, Henry and I, when alone.

June.

Too much to do with people lately. Hankering after district life again. Wayside shrines always appeal to me. How often going along the Vengurla Road my eyes have turned to a white speck almost at the top of the hill away to the north. I persuade Henry to come and look at it this morning.

We've got a car now. Henry has bought Colonel Peebles' treasured Fiat. Before he went to Mespot Colonel Peebles would never take her out if it rained. We have no such feeling, and this morning out she goes in the drizzling Scotch mist, and moreover is packed with the excited Luther, Rainey and Lep who muddy the seat, and trample on us all the time. The horses are waiting for us a few miles out. We pass men wrapped in black country blankets, or with wicker testudos protecting head and shoulders. The dogs pour out of the car like a stream of milk. The little speck of temple up there gleams out from the changeful purple-grey hill.

Usually we gallop over the rice-fields; every dozen yards or so the horses snorting with excitement, their shoulder muscles rippling, bunch themselves together to clear the *bunds;* but to-day the going is too heavy. Great phids of earth fly from the horses's hoofs striking us in the face. Besides, the fields have already a mist of living green, and intoxicating as it is jumping that endless succession of rice bunds it would no longer be permissible.

In spite of the rain it was suffocatingly hot. The sky was blind and white, and Shivaji's Bubs, as the two hills are irreverently known, look almost cornflower blue against it, whilst from all around rises the unbroken chorus of frogs.

"Brekekekex koax koax".

Ploughing is going on here and there. We pass an old man yoked to his bullock, and it brings home the poverty of the people. Henry turning his face, with great gobs of mud on its pinkness, reminds me of the ryot we had seen at Jaighad carrying up the incredibly steep ascent his basket of earth on his head to fill the little pockets he had dug out of the rock in which to plant his grain, little pockets about the size of a dining-room table.

Soon we were scrambling up the hill side amongst rocks and dripping branches of lantana which soaked my habit, and filled the air with its curranty smell. Half way up the horses picked their way through the ruins of a temple. A peaceful spot. Birds singing in lovely disunion. The temple had heavily carved whirling pillars all in different faded colours. There were two white carved towers, Shiva and Parbati (those one saw from the road), and a tank with worn shallow steps. Everywhere drooped sprays of pink, waxy antigonum, and white orchids grew from the mossy trunks and branches of the trees. I cannot tell why, but I had the strongest feeling I was in Japan.

It was a sweet and lovely spot.

We decided to climb on to the top of the hill. The heat was overpowering, shut off as we were from all breeze. You felt the sweat trickling down your body. The horses grunted and sweated and stumbled striving to dig the tips of their hooves into the red laterite rock. We both clung to the single long lock left in their hogged manes for that very purpose. Ganpat the sowar toiled and sweated behind us on his little white Arab, no doubt thinking us mad.

With a final scramble the horses, their ears cocked, gained the top, and instantly a fresh reviving breeze was blowing in our faces, and there was the country spread for miles and miles below us, rice, jowari and sugar cane, while overhead cruised not a chil, but an eagle. In the relief of that breeze, the loveliness of the changeful view, we had not noticed from near by come a holy man naked to the waist, his long black locks blowing, his body shining and golden with cocoa-nut oil.

"Ram! Ram!" greeted Henry.

"Good morning to you and your lady", replied the holy man smiling.

Yes. He had lived in England. He vouchsafed no more. We did not ask.

"It is not often that anyone visits me in the Rains", he continued. He went on to say that as soon as the cold weather came he would wander from fair to fair, Nasik to Benares, Hardwar to Hinglaj carrying with him nothing but his blanket, his staff and his beggar's bowl. I thought of our twenty-four bullock carts and retinue of servants and horses and dogs, hens and ducks.

"Will you not come in and see my wife?" asked the holy man courteously. We slipped off the horses whose sides were still going in and out and followed him.

The house of the Sadhu had a corrugated iron roof. Outside was a sacred tulsi plant in a pot painted blue. A ship's bell hung over our heads, and I saw on it engraved the figure of the Virgin Mary daubed with red as idols are.

We entered. Small windows had sacking across them, and the little mud rooms had connecting archways so low I had to double up to avoid striking my topi. In the dark innermost room was the little wife, scarcely more than a child. We had heard a curious nasal humming as we entered, and now we surprised her bathing down the household gods and singing a hymn as she poured water over them. She drew her sari across her face. She hung her head. She seemed to obliterate herself in her agonising shyness into the mud wall. The gods glistening and wet squatted there in a row.

"Please excuse her ignorance", murmured our host.

With his own hands he offered us milk in brass lota. Did I hesitate after Henry's many warnings never to drink milk unboiled?

"You need not fear", smiled the Sadhu, "my wife is ignorant in many things, but I have taught her European hygiene".

Driving home, I sit in the front with Henry; the dogs still panting and very muddy are with Kalu at the back. We pass a pi dog Luther does not like the look of. Without hesitation he clears the door to tell him so, though we are travelling at five-and-twenty to thirty miles an hour. We hardly dare look round . . . Luther has picked himself up, and stands in the middle of the road shaking himself violently. H. brings the car to a standstill, and Luther comes trotting back looking a trifle self-conscious.

The pi is nowhere to be seen!

It is not yet decided whether Luther is to be shot. The unspoken opinion of the station is that he should be. Even I think so, in view of eventualities.

Henry has not made up his mind.

We had had Laurie Impey staying with us, and he and Henry were playing golf the other evening. I was riding, taking a sowar and the dogs with me. Through some trees I saw the figures of the two men and the sun-lit white of the pattawallas carrying their clubs. I went to watch them hole out. Later as I turned Leviathan's head to go, the dogs who had watched the proceedings with lowered heads and drooping tails, sprang into life. Luther losing his head in excitement flew straight for Leviathan's throat. Leviathan reared straight up in the air. Luther went berserk, leaping up again and again. Then Rainey and Lep joined in. Henry and Laurie were shouting at the dogs, and trying to beat them off with their clubs, Leviathan rearing up and down, up and down, up . . . so that it seemed as though he must fall backwards. The noise of the dogs, the shouts and cries of the men . . . suddenly with a great bound that all but unseated me

Leviathan broke away, the three dogs in full cry after him. We clattered on to the road all but colliding with a victoria of startled Parsi ladies coming round the bend. Leviathan plunged up on to a heap of stones, and my topi (which fortunately I was still wearing) crashed against the overhanging branches of a tree. Why I was not stunned I don't know. Leviathan up—down—up—down . . . on to the road again with a shock of clattering hoofs . . . up . . . down . . . How long this lasted I don't know . . . but at last the dogs were called off and Leviathan snorting and trembling in every limb allowed his bridle to be caught, and me to slip off. There was a vermilion tear of two or three inches long on the black silk of his shoulder. Had I been riding Ganpat's little Arab as I sometimes did for fun, Luther would have gained his object, that is seized the horse by the nostrils and dragged him to his knees.

The dogs were thrashed and chained and taken home. Leviathan was led away by Ganpat, suddenly quiet as a cab horse, his long tail swishing his hocks from side to side, and we went to the Club to sit down and have a drink.

At the time I had felt no fear (does one ever at the time?). The one thought "My poor Henry; first Louise killed by a horse. Now me. And before his eyes", . . . but it has left me unnerved. I feel what is there to stop Luther attacking any dhamny returning from the Club with ayah and children, or any victoria. Henry says "We'll only take him on unfrequented roads".

The following week we drive out several miles and have the horses waiting for us there. Henry mounts me, and had just got into the saddle himself when Luther leaps up and seizing his foot tries to drag—drag—drag him off! What on earth has possessed the dog? Luther, a baby could have played with! It is decided that none of the dogs are to be taken out with the horses again.

Nevertheless I am still unnerved. It is so inexplicable. I remember once at a dinner party at Devonshire House the man who had taken Mother into dinner had told her he bred bloodhounds. He spoke of their wonderful sagacity and affection, but added there was some deep buried instinct which was apt to declare itself unexpectedly; that you could not depend on them; they were liable, and for no apparent reason, to completely lose control of themselves.

Suppose Luther is like that? I become obsessed with the thought. I dread taking him out, even on the chain. The bull-baiting instinct of his forbears awaking in him!

I try to think of him oozing into one's lap, sentimentally platforming his head on one's shoulder. I think of him offering some minute pebble held daintily between his lips instead of his teeth, as he cannot hope to emulate Rainey as she circles round one proudly with an immense boulder between those punishing alligator jaws of hers. I try to see him asleep nose on paws, and his hind legs trailing out behind him like a court train. I remember him that afternoon outside Henry's office tent. The sentry uncomfortably shifting his feet, as again and again Luther comes up and piles little stones on his instep, and the wretched man's relief when Henry bursts out laughing, as he sat watching from the office tent. I think of him seeing a herd of returning cattle in the evening in a cloud of dust, and lying down in the middle of the road. My warning cry "*Luther*". Rising stiffly he advances on his toes. "*Luther!*". But he has shot ahead straight at the advancing cattle in spite of my shouts . . . and then a few feet from them stops dead, and looks back over his shoulder with lolling tongue, and little half shut black eyes saying oh! how plainly "Sold again".

I try to think of these things, but all I can see is a whirling leaping white fury at my rearing Leviathan.

July

Henry drops a bombshell. There is to be a big War Meeting in Bombay next month. We have to go to it. Lady Willingdon wishes me to speak.

My heart stops.

"I warned you you would have to speak in public", says Henry.

He had. I remember that sunny misty morning on Beachy Head,

the sound of sheep bells tinkling and twinkling all round us, and the sun's pathway across the sea twinkling like the sheepbells. I remember ugly red Meads transformed to a rosy city whose chimneys sent up gilded smoke like incense, and Henry, as we climbed the dewy slopes, and slipped in slimy white chalk, telling me I should have to speak in public . . . But how far away, how unreal speaking in public had seemed that glorious autumn morning on Beachy Head.

"You sing in public", Henry was saying, now seeing my face of dismay, "what is there to be afraid of?".

"How many people will be there?"

"Anything between five hundred and a thousand I suppose. Sarojini Naidu is speaking too".

He strove to sound careless, thinking no doubt these numbers would appal me.

As a matter of fact they comforted me for I remembered singing "Ernani" with a view to an engagement at St. James' Hall, and the question of singing at one of the Albert Hall concerts. Somehow neither of these had been so unnerving as practising voice production in the drawing room, and a visitor coming in with her needlework. "Don't mind me dear child".

"Write what you mean to say . . . every word of it", Henry was saying. "You needn't read it of course, but the fact of having it there to refer to if you do get stuck will give you confidence".

"But what am I to say?" . . . even as I ask I remember a little iron ring in the Sheraton cabinet at home, and Mother explaining the French Government giving these to the women who had poured out their jewelry, even their wedding rings, at the time of the Franco-Prussian War. I could tell them that! Think of the jewels of the Parsi ladies alone. Already the speech is writing itself.

The speech is written. Is learned. I say it in front of Henry. This indeed makes me nervous, but he approves. I say it in front of the looking glass, I say it in my bath, I say it silently whilst Tulsi is brushing my hair. I say it in the sermon on Sunday. I say it splashing through the rain on Leviathan, or going to the Club to play badminton.

We take the night mail. The bugs, the noise and the hissing Kitsen burners at the stations, the cries of "Hindu Pan . . . i", and "Mussulman Pani . . . " as the water sellers of the respective faiths pass beneath the carriage windows; the forlorn breaking of the dawn, and the wan pools of water in the dark hills. Lloyd and Minnie come to Poona station to see us pass through. The journey down the ghats to Bombay. Wonderful they look, half-hidden in cloud and mist, looming and glooming and frowning deep purple and brilliant green, laced with innumerable waterfalls . . . but I pay little heed. As we get below ghats it is suffocatingly hot, and stage fright is already making me feel sick. Bombay is unbelievably hot and sticky. We dine with the Wardlaw Milnes. I can eat nothing. She is a kindly Scotch body. She tells me she too is recovering from a chill. "Very usual in the Rains. Nothing but two good ounces of castor oil will do the trick". But I know what is making me sick. Stage fright.

The following afternoon by two the Town Hall is packed. Humidity and heat terrible. As in a dream I climb onto the platform past the ferns and crotons and flowers, where men and women speakers are gathered. Amongst them is Mrs. Naidu looking charming in an exquisite sari. She is an Oxford graduate and a poetess as well as an accomplished speaker. She has innumerable admirers who are gathered here to applaud her.

Their Excellencies come in with A.D.C's., Lady Willingdon brisk, corseted, flowers in hand, looking about her, smiling, nodding, waving a white gloved hand up at me.

Henry is sitting just below. I give him a sickly smile. Beside him is Sir Narayan Chandavarkar, a Judge of the High Court and a very learned man. Mrs. Naidu delivers a flowery address, and there is terrific applause. And now this thing getting up and coming forward is me. I mustn't fail Henry. I'm wearing the blue taffeta dress I was married in. A sea of faces . . . blurred as I'm short-sighted.

It's over. Fifteen minutes of it. Nothing forgotten. Tremendous applause. As much as for Mrs. Naidu.

Note by Henry. "When Mrs. Naidu spoke Sir Narayan Chandavarkar turned to me muttering 'Fustian', but when R. had spoken he was most moved, and said 'That's what I call true eloquence and poetry' "

The ordeal over I should be feeling all right. But I'm not.

Mrs. Wardlaw Milne must be right after all. Castor oil it shall be as soon as I get home. But I wake in great pain that night, and Henry wants to send then and there for the doctor. He wakes Hyder Khan who is sleeping on the floor outside our door. He gets a whiskey bottle, fills it with very hot water, and I clasp this to my already sweating body.

We get off to Poona by the following morning to stop with Lloyd and Minnie. Nice! A bit of "home!". Blood is thicker than water. I still think Lloyd is the handsomest man I have ever seen. They both declare I look wretchedly ill, and agree with Henry I must see a doctor before going on that night to Belgaum.

I soon realise I am going to have a baby.

Nothing written for weeks. A loathing for the colour blue, a passion for the smell of Elliman's embrocation. Every day feels like being on Lot's Wife. Already the shortage of doctors is being felt. Major Houston is gone. Doctor Fisher is on leave, a very sick man: after various changes of Civil Surgeons we are now left with a very young and inexperienced R.A.M.C. Captain. If he is so scared of a pregnant woman, what happens to that woman in labour?

The siege of Kut has begun.

We had two garden parties for Indian troops returned from Mespot. Indians love to "eat the air", as they call it, in a garden, and our garden after the rains is lovely. The well-head wreathed with bridal creeper and pink antigonum. Roses and balsams and dahlias and zinnias, plumbago and cosmos . . . These silent Indian soldiers who had been through so much, rested and ate the sweetmeats and smoked the bidis we gave them . . . but we made one bad mistake. The Indian has a childish love of fireworks, and stupidly we had not realised the bangs, the bursts of flame would now be distressing to men just back from fighting.

Colonel Peebles of the Norfolks is back on sick leave. He is very quiet, and his hands and face are the colour of tarnished brass. He has malaria and jaundice. We put him to bed at once, and there he stays for several weeks.

He is very low, and pathetically grateful for the little one can do for him. He confides to me one day, that years ago he had married a very young girl, little more than a child. He had been stationed at Gibraltar, and there the little child wife had picked up fever and died.

"If I get through this war I should like to get married. Someone near my own age who would be a companion. A woman of the world. Its very lonely".

"I'll look for someone", I promise, and think of Antonia.

One day I hear from his room feeble cries for help. Henry, pattawallas and I rushing in find Lahri, my Malabar squirrel, menacing him with grinding teeth from the lower rail of his bed. She had come in through the window.

I don't think I have written of Lahri in my diary. She is now a magnificent animal, about the size of a rabbit. She has coarse, almost crimson fur, with a creamy ring round her neck, a creamy chest, and a great hanging tail like a plume of golden pampas grass. When Bulbul was carried off by the chill a sympathising Forest officer had given me his baby Malabar squirrel which he had brought up from the nest by means of a fountain pen filler. She was then the size of a small rat, and had quickly attached herself to me. I'm afraid I wasted much time over her.

By the time we went into camp she was almost full grown. She travelled in a small box, and that first evening at Astoli with the Webbs, rather nervously I had let her loose. She went up a tree, made herself a great untidy nest, slept in it all night, and came running down next morning to get into her box and start off in the bullock cart.

Now she is adorable. See her swinging upside down, her feet hooked into a branch, as she crams rose petals into her mouth with both little hands. Her breath is sweet as attar of roses, for roses are her favourite food. She accompanies me everywhere, sitting on my shoulder, her long tail like a fox's brush hanging to my waist. She will play with a ball or your fingers as enchantingly as any kitten. I crumple her up and toss her over my head. She parachutes down though she is not a flying squirrel, and alights on my shoulder. Told to kiss me she puts two little chestnut hands on my cheek, and a small revolving tongue smelling of roses caresses me. She is quick as thought. One moment on my shoulder, the next up a tree sending her penetrating ringing call back at me. Everybody is fascinated by "Mrs. Lawrence's squirrel" for she plays readily with visitors.

And now I have spoilt everything by my stupidity.

There are no Malabar squirrels in the district and I thought to introduce them. A Forest officer got me a young male. I put him in a large cage on the verandah next to the one in which Lahri occasionally slept. They flirted with each other through the netting for a few days, and were shortly to be put together. Coming back from a ride I went to talk to the male, opened the door and began to fondle him. From somewhere appeared a crimson fury. Hurling herself on my hands Lahri bit me over and over again through my gloves. I could not pick her off. Henry heard my cries and came running with many pattawallas. At last she was got back into her own cage and I with my hands dripping with blood went off to the Civil Hospital to be disinfected and dressed. On my return, muffled up in lint and wool, there was little Lahri standing up, little hands clenching the netting, trying to attract my attention, desperately ashamed and apologetic.

A little cloud no bigger than a man's hand. What about the baby if *she* is so jealous?

The male squirrel is returned to his owner. But Lahri's temper becomes uncertain, though not to me. The pattawallas are now terrified of her, and I must confess I myself saw her chasing Appa, our shikari pattawalla all down the verandah, snapping at his flying heels like a dog. Henry has always been very fond and proud of her, but now he declares he must protect himself by a ring of bull terriers. Unfortunately the dogs themselves are frightened of her, for she springs on their backs. An absurd sight is to see old Luther flat on his belly, his head pressed down to the tiles, eyes beseechingly upturned for succour, while Lahri securely seated on his back rapidly grinds her teeth, and sends defiant ringing calls which echo again and again through the bungalow.

Henry has always taken her tricks remarkably well. Even that day of the dinner party when just as we were going in there came the sound of an overturned glass crashing into fragments, and Lahri flashed past us out into the darkness. She had played havoc. The damask cloth was patterned over with her dusty footprints now turning into muddy ones from the overturned vase. Butter was scored by her teeth, nuts and sweets nibbled, roses pulled out of the vases.

Lahri had been forgiven then with the proviso she should be shut up for dinner parties, but now the order goes forth Lahri is to be shut up all the time.

It will be lovely to have a baby of course . . . but oh my Lahri! Didn't Lady Sarah Lennox prefer the company of her pet squirrel to that of George the third? How concerned was Henry Fox at Holland House when the squirrel fell ill. He wrote in his diary:

> "Lady Sarah's mare is lame, and her squirrel ill. These two misfortunes do really vex her. The other (the king's marriage) sat very lightly on her mind".

And a little later he writes when the squirrel died:

> "Lady Sarah to comfort her has a young hedgehog who breakfasted with us to-day. She bought it yesterday, and continues to kiss it very much".

Dasera.

This is the Hindu holiday, celebrating the end of the Rains, when in bygone days the Mahrattas could once more sally forth to war.

The servants celebrate it by decking the emblems of their work with flowers.

This morning the syces brought the horses round, with garlands of roses and marigolds swinging to their knees, and anklets too. Leviathan looked superb.

The sweeper led the garlanded bull-terriers to the verandah, and if anything is sillier than Luther's fatuous white face surrounded by roses and marigolds I have yet to see it.

The dhamny bullocks followed with flowers on their stained horns, and the bhisti's bullock with its leather bag with the water squirting through the seams, had its garland too.

The malis have laid out their trowels and forks and watering cans made from kerosene tins all in a row, with bunches of flowers beside them and when I went to my bathroom, I found the metrani, not to be outdone had encircled the seat of the commode with roses, plumbago and marigolds.

Baksheesh all round.

BELGAUM, 1916.

Henry was always moving about his division. It was written of another, but would equally apply to him, "He set himself laboriously to learn how each kind of complex business should be performed from beginning to end, from the lowest to the highest step; having done that, he would reduce all his knowledge to lucid statement, so that what had been hard to him might be made easy to others. When he had thus instructed his officers of all degrees, he was extraordinarily patient and watchful in seeing they acted up to his instruction".

Now the touring season has come round again. I must stay behind. I protest, but he has so much ground to cover he will be moving camp every day. Too exhausting for me. I am left behind with the dogs and Lahri.

Lately a Colonel O'Brien has been staying with us; he is a Political in charge of the Southern Mahratta States. An old friend, good looking, a wonderful athlete. He has won the Army Running Championship for several years in succession, the last time when over forty! Henry will go for days without sparing time for any exercise at all, and yet turn up to play in some tennis tournament and probably beat his opponent who has been playing regularly every evening. Now he and Edward O'Brien are going to play squash together! It is impossible that Henry should beat him, but the games are quite close, and as I sit sweltering up in the gallery watching these two darting madmen, bandages round their foreheads to prevent the sweat pouring into their eyes, I'm proud and excited beyond endurance. Suddenly comes an arrowy thought "This will all be changed in the future. Not just you and Henry any more. A third person". To be jealous of your own child? I am horrified at myself.

Charlie Boyd has just come out from home to be Judge here. He is an old friend of Henry's from Haileybury and Magdalen days, the gentlest, most affectionate whimsical creature, slow in speech and movement, even thought, yet uncommonly able. His wife Gertrude is ill at home after the birth of their youngest child Christopher. As the disturbing cables arrive, Charlie makes no effort to control his feelings. He wears a perpetual woebegone look, and without embarrassment he wipes his eyes with the finest and most expensive linen handkerchief and moans.

I am not so taken aback as might have been supposed, for Charlie has looked almost as tragic when describing his own symptoms. He has permanent internal trouble, as one or two other men we know, and lives chiefly on *kanji* (rice water).

Charlie was a great buffoon and wag at college. And at Karwar I had heard how one hot day, after coming out of Court, he had calmly walked out on to the little pier, before the astonished gaze of his "pleaders", and plunged into the sea fully dressed. There was also that tale of the gymkhana when he had promised a prize worth a guinea for some event, and then presented a box of Beecham's pills to the winner. But better still, when engaged upon trying some important case, he went into camp shooting for a few days. The attention of the High Court Judges in Bombay was drawn to his absence, and they wired to him to know if the papers had been left in a sufficiently safe place. Charlie wired back "Papers safe. In pet panther's cage".

Even now, when a more cheerful cable comes in he begins to chuckle and play schoolboy jokes. Quite solemnly he will go and stand on his head in the corner and remain there motionless for a minute at a time; or pretending he is an elf, he will tuck up his long thin legs and spring with amazing agility on to the back of a sofa . . . quite the most unlikely person I should have thought to appeal to Henry! But they are good friends of many years standing, and Henry now suggests that instead of eating his heart out alone in the Judge's bungalow, he should come and live here and be company for me while Henry is in district. Odd in England, but not a bit out here.

We get on famously. He is knowledgeable about dogs and talks nonsense by the hour to Lep who almost swoons with sentimentality in his arms. He is intensely musical, and between us we hire a pianola from Bombay. We have Schubert and Schuman's songs and

Carnaval, Brahams waltzes . . . yes, and Waldteufel and Strauss too . . . But our great *pièce de resistance* is Beethoven's song, *Adelaide.* As soon as he gets back from Court, Charlie has tea in his room, changes, and then we settle down to an orgy of music instead of going to the Club. The malis come with their kerosene tins to water the ferns in the verandah, the declining sun streaming through the trunks of the trees in the park, turns the falling drops from the watering cans into rainbow diamonds, and passing on into the shadowy drawing-room picks out and fingers the old brass figures of gods on the shelf over the sofa, and over and over again *Adelaide* rings out, as he and I sing at the top of our voices to his pianola playing. Pedalling away astonishing expression out of the old rattletrap, sitting there with his eyes tightly shut, and an air of rapture on his face, "Ade . . . lai . . . ide".

Sometimes he plays Chopin. "This is Pachman's interpretation", he says, and then after he will play the same thing as some other well known pianist would play it, and then yet another.

Certainly this baby, Owen or Inishowen, whichever it is to be, should grow up truly musical. Every stitch in its tiny nightgowns is sewn to music.

But now a cable comes that Gertrude must have a serious operation. Charlie becomes permanently "weepy". Immaculately dressed and shaved he sits opposite to me at dinner, the tears rolling unheeded down his face, as he murmurs "Gertsie, my poor Gertsie". When the operation is over and real progress being made, I feel I must escape, for I am almost drowning in this green drawing-room with waters of music and emotion closing over my head. Kind Charlie fusses over my health. Now Henry is a bracing and astringent personality. I am not used to this too much sentiment. Not long ago I had confessed to a great feeling of homesickness, but to my indignant astonishment, Henry, instead of giving me the comfort I was expecting, rounded on me in no uncertain way! I was so astonished it was some time before I realised it was the best thing he could have done. Now I feel I must escape from too much solicitude. The longing for jungle life is almost physical. To hear a barking deer in the hot mid-day silence might brush away the small worries that are wrapping me round like cobwebs.

For after great difficulty, I have succeeded in finding a monthly nurse, an excellent woman who had once acted as Assistant Matron at the Jamsetjee Jeejeebhoy Hospital, commonly known as the "J. J". She has a French name, and this agreeably recalls my childhood, the security of the nursery with a smell of flannel clothes warming on the fender, firelight playing on the ceiling, and homely French remedies, *tisanes* and *eau sucrée, Eau de Mélisse, Pomade de Vigne* and such like. Nurse F. comes down to see me between two cases, and I find in spite of the French name, she is coffee-colour. Now that I do not mind for myself, but not only will she have no authority with the servants, but they will put every difficulty in her way. They will speak of her as just "kala log" (black person). Then when she meets the amiable M.O., her amazement and indignation at his neglect and omission of the most elementary measures, know no bounds. He has told me to engage her for mid-January. She declares the beginning of April too soon. Worse, I learn she is qualified to take a case without a doctor. Awkwardly I explain, Henry wishes me to have a doctor. I see the extreme distaste with which she views the prospect of working under a man she regards, I am afraid correctly, as incompetent.

In addition to all this, my dear Tulsi ayah must leave me to return to her former mistress back from long leave. She produces her much younger sister Rakma, whom she assures me is a far better lady's maid. So she may be, but she is aggressive and quarrelsome with the other servants, and straightway informs me she is a lady's maid and will have nothing whatever to do with the baby when it comes, and in no case would she ever go into camp. She pesters me continually to advance her wages. Now the servants all do this periodically, for, poor creatures, they are all more or less in the grip of money lenders; but Henry is very averse to advancing of wages because these debts are probably inherited from their parents. The Indian money-lender has established the custom that debts are to be paid generation after generation. To pay them off, the poor victims borrow more. One anna in the rupee to be paid monthly, which amounts to 75 per cent. per annum, a burden which cannot be paid in a lifetime. But Rakma storms and weeps and will not take no . . .

I write to Henry. I simply *must* get away from all this for a few days. He plays up, recognising urgency. He agrees to take four days leave. We are to go into Kanara, to the Forest Bungalow at Nagagali, deep, deep in jungle.

Now shall I take Lahri and turn her there adrift? Her importunate little figure standing upright in her cage, clutching the netting with her little thumbless hands, beseeching me to let her out, wrings my heart. But the wild creatures will mob her, even as the crows are apt to do here in the garden at times. She gets terrified . . . and anyhow, she will never consent to be left. That fatal pursuing quest of mine to find a little wild animal's soul! What am I to do?

Only a few days ago an Indian Superintendant of Police had brought me the most enchanting little mouse-deer for a pet. A little creature of exquisite grace, scarcely bigger than a hare, with tiny polished hoofs, flicking tail and dewy eyes and muzzle. I had hardened my heart and refused it, for now I realise how shabby a thing it is to teach these wild things to love one, only to betray them later.

Nagagali. January, 1916.

The horses had been sent on, but we ourselves went by train, for though Nagagali consists merely of a small forest bungalow buried in jungle, the line passes within little more than a mile. It will stop at the spot where timber is loaded, and put us down.

Henry has never yet bagged his tiger. Goats and bullocks have been frequently tied up for him, but so far the kill has failed to coincide with his advent, and he is too conscientious to extend his stay at any one place. But now we shall have three clear days at Nagagali. Two goats have been tied up. Surely something may happen this time. We discuss the chances as the train dawdles through sunbaked scrub and low jungle. Sliding past the windows are queer-looking trees, a lonely pool with hundreds of lotuses thrusting out their blooms on long necks. White egrets feeding. Branches shake, and with a loud whoo . . . p a monkey is springing throug the air. Now all the branches are agitated, and monkeys crashing along from tree to tree following the train and the smoke and the flying smuts.

Life clean as a peeled wand again!

The Guard, sowars and horses are waiting. Black Leviathan is almost scintillating in the sunshine as he shudders a fly off his withers, and whisks his long bang tail. The cicadas are reeling and rasping in every bush. The simmer, shimmer and sizzle all round! Then we enter the gloom of the forest . . . and almost at once the sound I had longed to hear again . . . a barking deer! Leviathan paces soberly as though recognising his responsibility to Henry's unborn child.

The bungalow is tiny and very dark. How familiar to hang one's coat on the crazy criss-cross of wood nailed crookedly on the wall, to wash one's face in the battered tin basin. A little tent has been pitched for Misteri, another for the guard, and a leafy hut for the horses. The dense jungle comes up quite close. We ask eagerly if there is any *khabar,* which means "news" but is understood only as "has there been a kill?" Unfortunately, no kill. I know Henry has set his heart on getting a tiger, and I do most desperately want it for him. Well, we have three days.

Three days, three lovely jungle days—but alas no kill. And tomorrow morning the mail will stop at the clearing in the jungle to pick us up again. We go to Belgaum, Henry will sleep at the bungalow and go on the following morning to Bombay where he is due for Legislative Council. And then—just as we are sitting down to tea the sound of excited voices! "Khabar!" The shikari talking volubly. A kill, and round it the pug marks of a large tiger.

But the short day is already closing in, khabar has come too late. I could cry! Henry's disappointment is evident; the shikari distressed. But why not try for him tomorrow morning, catch the afternoon mail, and go straight to Bombay instead of staying the night at Belgaum?

I plead, and at last, to the delight of the shikari, Hyder Khan, the various pattawallas and myself this is decided upon.

Henry sends a message over to Mr. Aitchison, a Forest officer, whose camp is not far off. Forest officers of course have endless opportunities for tiger and their list of trophies is long. How exasperating if this tiger falls to Mr. Aitchison and not to Henry! I am too excited to sleep much. What a glorious deep golden coat a tiger in this dense jungle will have! Not pale and sunbleached as the Mundgod tiger would have been in that thin scrub teak jungle.

Mr. Aitchison turns up for breakfast. I am in a fever to start, but the two men linger over the meal. I hear yet again how a former Commissioner Southern Division had been killed here at Nagagali, as the undergrowth is so thick he could not get his rifle up fast enough to fire. And I hear again of that time when the bear rolled down hill with increasing momentum, the beater clasped in his arms, and Mr. Aitchison had to make up his mind whether to fire or not . . . but at last we do set out. The two men and Appa with rifles, and the shikari and many beaters, wild-looking men with sinewy bare thighs and arms, and tattered turbans, once red, all carrying sticks, and axes. We file up the track already talking little, and in low voices, instinctively putting down our feet so that no stick will crack. At the spot where the two unmetalled roads cross the party leaves me. The kill is about three quarters of a mile away farther on. How I long to go with them, but Henry is adamant. I return to the tiny bungalow, very excited, thinking perhaps a little of the Commissioner who had been mauled by the wounded tiger, and of Henry's half laughing, half serious instructions as exactly what I was to do in the event of anything happening to him . . . and all the time my ears were cocked waiting for the crack of a rifle.

There it is. Another. *Another.* Three shots. I did not like that, and Hyder Khan looked grave. He said the first time the tiger must have been only wounded. I thought again of the mauled Commissioner.

About half an hour later a pattawalla who had been left at the cross roads to bring me news, arrived in a state of great excitement.

He poured forth such a torrent of words it was impossible to understand him, but I learned from Hyder Khan that Henry and Mr. Aitchison had drawn lots for places, and that the tiger a "*bahut bara walla*"—a very big one—had come out in front of Mr. Aitchison. An easy shot, but for some inexplicable reason the tiger was only wounded. Both sahibs had fired again, wounding him further, and now were following him up.

In my ignorance I walked to the cross roads (what a fool!). I sat there on a fallen tree. Not a sound, till a mouse routed in some dead leaves at my feet. Butterflies dawdled past.

I walked back to the bungalow; inside our kit ready packed, the strapped red canvas rolls of bedding. The servants ceasing their talking as I appear.

I walk back again to the cross roads. Silence. What could be happening? It was nearly half past three. Back again to the bungalow. This time I get Hyder Khan to unstrap the wooden medicine chest that a district officer always takes with him. I lay out the lint, the cotton wool, the carbolic acid, the little bottle of Chinosol. I pore over the directions in the medical book for dressing wounds caused by wild animals, the necessity of applying pure carbolic acid owing to the poison in teeth and claws. I remember the disastrous burns Minnie had given the Chief Conservator when he had been mauled by a panther. Now two more pattawallas arrive talking excitedly. Again it was impossible for me to follow what they said. Again Hyder Khan gravely explained there had been a great deal of blood and the two sahibs were following the bloodstains.

Now the sunshine was growing golden, the little bungalow very dark. I walked yet again to the cross roads. The jungle looked different in late afternoon. The sun striking a golden lance through the leaves in which the insects dance, whilst all else is dark and gloomy. I am wild with anxiety now! It will be too late to catch the Mail. That brings home the seriousness of the situation as nothing else could have done. Henry to allow anything to interfere with his work! I sit waiting in the bungalow, inadequately lit by hurricane lanterns standing on the floor. The cotton wool, the lint, the carbolic acid, scissors, clean boiled water in the basin . . . I hear the whistle of the Mail . . . our Mail . . . as it passes a mile away. No Henry. No beaters. No news. Nothing but the night noises of the jungle, the night itself as it presses up against the walls of the tiny building.

Then voices. Unbelievably. Lights approaching. Henry's voice, Henry's face, worn, strained . . . but here. Safe.

The tiger was not killed. He had been badly wounded, and had bitten through a sapling in his rage and agony. They had followed the blood-spattered leaves crouching through the karvi . . . and had lost him.

As most people know it is essential that a wounded wild beast be followed up and killed otherwise incapacitated by his wounds from obtaining his natural food he will become a man-eater. Obeying this unwritten law Mr. Aitchison and Henry had followed him up all day. Henry said the worst time they had was when they had to crawl on their hands and knees through a prickly bamboo thicket. One kept watch till the other got through. Till darkness made it impossible to continue they had pushed through karvi undergrowth expecting any moment to be attacked. Now first thing in the morning Mr. Aitchison would continue the "following up" getting some other Forest officer to join in. I knew without being told how intensely distasteful it was to Henry to be obliged to leave them to the dangerous job.

By now it was dark and very cold. Exhausted though he was, stiff with the sweat of the day dried on him, Henry said it was imperative that we should board the train which would be passing at midnight, for him to go on straight to Bombay (I to get out at Belgaum). After we had eaten something we were ready to start. The cold had made the horses obstreperous. Leviathan kept standing straight up on his hind legs, and finally Henry made me get off. Between the bungalow and where the piles of timber lay stacked by the line, was rather more than a mile of jungle. Here for all we knew the wounded tiger might be lying up. If near it would certainly attack us. With the hurricane lanterns bobbing in the blackness we set out for the railway line. Henry was close to me, his rifle ready to fire, the guard with their rifles surrounding us. I am not likely to forget that trek through the night. The blackness, the cold, the cracking of a stick, the snorting of nervous horses, the legitimately terrified servants and pattawallas, and all the while waiting for a growl, a roar, the launching of some dark body out from the bushes, in front, behind, at the side . . . What Henry was feeling I don't know. As for me I was so terrified I felt nothing but extreme nausea.

As the lights blinked out at last on the little platform Henry said in an unfamiliar voice:

"Look at the Guard. So prepared to fire at any moment . . . yet I doubt if their rifles are loaded!"

"What do you mean?"

So he asked them.

"Ne, Sahib. We have no ammunition".

The mail was two hours late. It was most bitterly cold. We sat huddled together on our rolls of bedding on the open platform, and now and then walked up and down under the stars. Henry told me why he had guessed the Guard's rifles held so importantly were not loaded at all. I have made him write it down in his own words.

> "In 1910, when I was Collector of Sukkur there was an outbreak of dacoities led by some daring robbers. I anticipated that an attack might be made on the District Treasury, which adjoined the Police armoury, and I told the head of the Police to strengthen the guard.
>
> A few days later I inspected the guards, a fine body of men. Before leaving them I ordered them to open their pouches. Scarcely any had any ammunition! I asked the Inspector why. His reply was that the men were ordered to the Treasury at once, *but no order had been given about ammunition*!"

This reminded me of the occasion when Sir Charles Napier inspected two regiments of regulars. The infantry regiment was composed of a very fine set of men. When their arms were examined Sir Charles writes "one soldier had a musket without a lock, another a lock without a musket. Here was a bayonet that could not be unfixed. One man had a weapon with a lock, the cock of which would not go down. Then came one which did not stand up. A fine handsome soldier six feet high, brawny and bronzed, his broad deep chest swelling with military pride, and his black brilliant eyes sparkling with a malicious twinkle, pretended to hold over his shoulder between his left finger and thumb a flint, his only arm! He was an epitome of political-military arrangement, a powerful soldier rendered useless by ignorance".

Henry and Hyder Khan went straight on to Bombay, and here I am back in the Bungalow crying out with Charlie "Ade . . . laide!"

You have begun your adventures early in life you little creature, Owen? Inishowen?

March, 1916.

Henry has got his tiger.

He and Mr. Bell were out together. Henry in his machan heard, to his surprise, a slight sound behind him instead of the direction from which the beaters were advancing with shouts and screams. From the corner of one eye he caught sight of the tiger flashing past between some trees about fifty yards away. He got a snap shot and the tiger dropped behind the trees. He heard no sound—except, I bet, the thumping of his heart! The beaters began coming up. They found the tiger stone dead, a bullet through the head. Mr. Bell, exmaining the shot was most complimentary. Little Owen-Inishowen shall have his tiger-skin to roll on after all.

A day or two later Henry got another panther—a most difficult shot. He was in a machan over the kill, and it was already growing very dark. Staring, he thought he saw a movement in some undergrowth beyond a fallen tree away to the left. Then the leaves became still—stirred again. On these occasions, it is almost impossible to know whether one sees or imagines. But now Henry, straining ears and eyes, thought he heard as well as saw, and he surmised the panther must be lying down hidden by the intervening fallen tree. What a situation! But after an eternity, as it seemed, the panther's head and neck, spotted like sun on leaves, showed beyond the end of the fallen tree. He shot him.

I said another panther. He and Louise had shot one in Sind as it sprang to attack. He had also got two fine ibex under unusual circumstances, a right and left as they escaped from a panther . . . the panther passing him close by, after the shots.

Just as a comedian treasures the rare opportunity he has of playing tragedy, so does Henry welcome the rare opportunity of showing he is a sportsman as well as a zealous official!

The Willingdons spent the day here.

We had a peacock for luncheon. Boiled. He was brought in with his whole panoply of tail-feathers stuck in. Excellent he was. Misteri is a first-class cook. He was trained as Mate in Government House, and his most treasured possession is a complete set of menus for breakfast, luncheon and dinner for every day in the year. A god-send to me.

"Henry. Will you shoot Lahri for me please?"

"No. I can't do it. I'll tell Appa to".

But Appa may only succeed in wounding her. So Lahri goes to the Bombay Zoo.

Good Friday.

Rainey and I are overdue. We are cumbersome and oppressed. Ayah tells me Rainey will have five puppies. She also tells me that the Nurse Miss Sahib knows nothing, and that I have several more days to wait, and that the servants and the pattawallas declare it will without doubt be a "chota sahib", for the Memsahib is so big and high in front. (How horrified Mother and Father would be at such talk!).

Nurse F. is becoming more and more critical of the M. O. She has now been in the house for more than three weeks, and these three weeks she has employed in telling me the most gruesome stories of incompetent doctors and how the situation was only saved by her. She undoubtedly is a most competent nurse and endlessly kind to her patients. It is extraordinary she can so disobey the elementary duty of a nurse as to fill her patient's mind with horrors. But how many nurses do! I can only imagine it is from sheer nervousness at having been warned not to do so, as one learning to bicycle inevitably goes over the stone he is seeking to avoid. In Nurse F's. case, I think, too, her sensitiveness to her colour forces her to glorify herself. Poor thing. I know the servants, out of my hearing, are insolent . . . Even Solomon, on the principle of a bullied boy bullying back when he at length gets the chance. The culminating thing is when she says meaningly to me, "I shall take very good care not to send for the doctor till the last minute, so the baby will be here before he is".

I confide this to Gertrude Boyd, and she promises she will send for the doctor on her own. For Gertrude is living in the Bungalow with us. She has just come out. A frail little slip of a thing with hair like silk, and green eyes. She has left Christopher, the baby, behind in England in the charge of the nurse who is looking after the little boy with hip disease. Charlie keeps murmuring "Gertsie", and looks at her as though he could eat her.

The weather is still trying. Stickily hot. Tiny eye-flies crowding into your eyes, and thunder growling all day. Rainey wanders restlessly about the verandah, flumps down on her side, only to get up, leaving a dark patch where her burning body rested. I wilt in a long chair with the peacock feather and scarlet lacquer fan we bought at Ratnagiri, and try to read the Pioneer. Its innumerable pages all get in the wrong order and the war news is bad. Kut has surrendered. Ferns and pots and hanging baskets of flowers are silhouetted like a futurist wallpaper against the red-hot garden where the casuarinas moan. Suddenly comes a scream from over my head. I look up and see the white ribbed belly of a daman rapidly slithering over the spaces between the bamboo poles which compose the lining of the tiles. The pattawallas are asleep, and anyhow, rat snakes are harmless, and rats are not, for they carry plague fleas, so I do nothing to save the poor rat, and lie there listening to the melancholy "Ka-weer, Ka-weer" of the koel . . . and God knows it is a melancholy sound. If only I had a book to read. A nice clean book. There are so many books here, but their covers are all spotted from the damp, they smell fusty, and their pages are eaten by cockroaches or stuck together with silvery fish insects. Even so, I have just finished Winwood Reade's *Martyrdom of Man*. A wonderful book . . . but not encouraging at the moment.

Everything is finished. Ready. The coolies have squatted in the nursery day after day plaiting up the cool fresh ivory and almond green rushes till the whole of the mud floor is covered up to the pale green walls. The last stitch is in the tiny clothes. The innumerable bowls and things Nurse F. and I drove down to the bazaar to buy, now just waiting.

Every night we take Rainey to her lying-in-room. A deep three sided box has been prepared for her, the fourth side sloping down and covered with cocoa-nut matting. She settles herself down in extreme melancholy, never attempting to follow us back to our own room. Really her indifference to us is humiliating.

Tonight I wake with a start, my nightgown sticking to me. Everything is quite quiet except for a little bell frog outside, and Henry's quiet breathing beside me . . . yet I know there is someone in the room. Our two beds are enclosed in a mosquito tent, and the room is not dark because behind our heads through open archways is my dressing room and on the floor stands a hurricane lantern because of snakes. Then our beds face through other open archways, and through my nets I can discern the court-yard and the jack-fruit tree and alamanda bushes quiet in moonlight . . . but I know someone is in the room. I wake Henry carefully. Shaking out his shoes for possible scorpions or snakes he goes round the room and dressing-room, and down the step into my bath room. "There's absolutely nothing there . . . " and then there came a very gentle, regular sound. It seemed to emanate from a bamboo erection in my dressing room behind whose chintz curtains hang my washing frocks. By this time I too am out of bed. We draw back the curtains and there lying uncomfortably on the bare floor is Rainey methodically licking five hideous little objects.

We give her water and try to make her a little more comfortable. Dear Rainey. So she had turned to us after all. Henry got me back into bed, and taking the lantern he went off through the connecting bedrooms to her lying-in chamber to see if she had dropped any of her puppies on the way.

He seemed to be gone a long while, and when he returned he was amused.

"So you thought Rainey came here because she wanted to be near us? *Why* Rainey came was because a stray cat had got in and is now having kittens in Rainey's bed. Now if Rainey and the cat have both managed it, don't you think you too could hurry up old girl?"

Rainey and her family are established under the tent of my hanging washing frocks. I dare not disturb her. She cringes as one approaches, but I thought I heard her tail whack on the floor. This morning her puppies are snow white with bright rose pink faces, tummies and paws. They remind me of the sugar mice one ate as children. Pink and white with tails of string.

It's been a hot day and sweating and fidgeting with prickly heat, I think of Inishowen, of the sea round the Big Rock, looking like ginger beer with purplish patches of seaweed heaving up and down like nets in the water.

After tea Henry forgoes tennis, and takes me for my duty walk. All day the mangoes in the compound have given rich dense shade, but now strong low sunshine is streaming under them picking out the bull-terriers and shining through their pink ears. The compound is only separated from the maidan by an agave hedge pushing up its great variegated tusks, and we come out on to wide spaces, dotted here and there with little flat-topped trees, wide spaces, the colour of a rather shabby lion-skin.

The Collector's new bungalow is nearly finished. It has a fairly long drive, and the Public Works Department are digging deep square holes on either side of it in order to plant young trees. But before the trees can be planted, the Lingayat subordinates have too often planted a corpse. For Lingayats bury their dead and in a sitting position.

For some return the P.W.D. can save much labour to the relatives by excavating a grave through the red laterite rock and sun-baked earth. Corpses when discovered by officials are of course removed, but there must be a good many left. What a gruesome avenue.

Luther and Lep have put up a jack and are away giving tongue. There is something glinting over there, and Henry and I can't make out what it is. He goes off to find out, leaving me on my seat stick. He is soon back.

"It's the corpse of a young girl. I suppose we disturbed them and they made off. They've propped her up under a tree, and she looked quite natural sitting there till I got quite close, and found her all whitened and bedizened and painted. Better not go".

Easter Day.

Rainey has half eaten one of her pups, and killed all the others. Horrible.

An undated entry.

John Owen Napier Lawrence was born at 11.30 on April 24th, 1916, Easter Monday, the day of the Irish Rebellion. There was rebellion too in the bungalow. Doctor and Nurse violently disagreeing over my body. Things went gravely wrong. The place was a shambles. Captain X lost his head. Panic-stricken he decided on certain measures. "You'll kill her", cried Nurse F. He argued. She grew more vehement. Primed for the past month with her ghoulish stories I gasped "Oh! you *mustn't*". So taken aback at the voice from one he thought unconscious he allowed Nurse F. to take charge! Rakma ayah is sent for. Terrified by what she sees Rakma refuses to enter the room declaring blood will cause her to lose caste. (Ayahs of course have no caste). In desperation Nurse F. sends for the sweeper woman, the untouchable! There are clankings of buckets, but I pass out.

Strange days and nights. Henry appears, kisses my forehead and disappears. The dim room, the creaking punkah, the cold and soaking perspiration and a crying, struggling bundle brought in from somewhere to try and get what nourishment it can, as this is supposed to relieve my condition. In its fruitless efforts it screams and tugs and fights and falls asleep to be awakened and forced to try again. Each feed takes over an hour and I am left more prostrate than ever. That this brutal struggling little monster has anything to do with me I cannot realise.

A week later a Calcutta specialist arrives. Sinking through my bed I hear him telling me I must never have another child.

"How can I help it?" I ask.

He becomes confused. "Your heart won't stand it apart from any thing else" he says in a loud voice.

I was too ill to see even Gertrude. There was no door between my bedroom and the drawing-room where the grand piano was, only many archways and hanging split cane curtains, and through them flowed gentle music, Brahms waltzes, *Carnaval, Kinderszenen,* and little bits of things Gertrude knew that I loved.

The Boyds had to go to their own Judge's Bungalow. Nurse F. was due for another case. It was impossible, owing to the war, to get a nurse. Finally, after cutting through endless red tape, Henry got permission for a German girl from the Concentration Camp to come in during the day to look after Owen whilst the unwilling Rakma saw to me.

Nurse F. went. She was honest enough to volunteer that my grave illness had been increased by giving me ergot so as to hurry things up before the doctor should come! (Note added later). I have never told this until now, when she has long been dead.

The monsoon had broken, and my inner windowless room, darkened by verandahs, back and front, was too dim to allow me even to look at picture papers had I been well enough. Everything smelt fusty, and bedding had to be dried daily, spread on a wicker contraption over a charcoal sigri. In a faraway room the baby screamed. Languidly I asked the doctor if he was all right. "Oh yes. Screaming is capital for babies. So good for their lungs". I was only too glad to believe him and promptly forgot the baby again. Henry, returning from Poona where he had been working with V. J. Patel, was distracted to find me still running a high temperature and lying supine. Saying nothing to me, he set out next day to Khanapur to the Mission Settlement, returning that evening with Mrs. Brown, the boy Granville, aged three or four, the baby Douglas in arms, an ayah, a boy, and the bull-terrier Ranee, who immediately had a scrap with Rainey. The ayah had never been in a car before, and had been sick over Mrs. Brown and the children. Mrs. Brown came straight to me, her big surgical bag in her hand, her huge topi slipping sideways, and goodness and charity shining out of her smiling face. She had left her husband, the Mission, the dispensary and the Criminal Tribes to look after themselves, and come straight along to succour me.

At once she discovered the source of the baby's screams. Poor little Owen. From laziness or ignorance the German girl had neglected to change him, and when his buttocks were raw and actually bleeding, she became, I suppose, too frightened to tell. Mrs. Brown's simple remedies cured him in a few days . . . but the knowledge of his suffering roused me from my indifference . . . I loved him!

All too soon that wonderful woman was forced to return. Without her skilled nursing I began to slip back, day by day. "We'll see what getting you up does" said Captain X cheerfully. I was only too glad to escape from my stagnant pool of a room. Somehow they got me half dressed, and lifted me into the victoria one evening. Oh! the live, fresh air, the dripping greenery, and, above all, the light—the wonderful light. Vultures wheeling in the windy blue . . . Everything green instead of dun and ochre as when I last saw it. We drove past the Club House nestling amongst feathery bamboos. All the bullock carts were there, the bullocks lying beside them, the children playing in their white frocks, their ayahs gossiping. We drove past the cemetery, with its swishing casuarinas, where so easily I might be lying. The south-west wind came charging towards us from the sea eighty miles away. O miraculous drive! Hills blue as the hills of Donegal. Downs dotted with myriads of little white orchids. Flocks of black and white goats and little shepherd boys piping in sun and cloud shadow.

Sakharam drove on to the Point, where the Parsi ladies sat in their victorias taking the air. Wise old Sakharam drove the victoria away from them, and let Lot stand facing the breeze. O the blue hills, the gleam and glisten of floods, the croaking of frogs, and the "Kra-krak" of a black partridge from the sugar cane.

Henry got out to talk to some Parsis. Suddenly I heard his voice raised in surprise. "Why, Doctor Leonard! What on earth are *you* doing down here?"

"Not Dr. Leonard any longer. I married a German, so they brought me down from Sukkur and interned me with my husband."

Henry brought her round to me; a big, fat, jolly-looking woman who was now pitching and sliding about like the green downs behind her.

"Your wife has no business here" I heard her say sharply. "Any doctor can see what is wrong with her. Get her home at once and into bed . . . ".

Poor Captain X. Wrong again. After unheard of difficulties, Dr. Gumprich is allowed out from the Concentration Camp to attend to me. An immediate operation is necessary. She is to do it.

I live chiefly on milk. No longer does the old dudhwallah guide his slate-coloured buffalo slouching through the trees to be milked in front of Hyder Khan. For Belgaum boasts a Military Dairy. In addition to many "buffs", there is a herd of the Sindhi cows, amongst the best breeds in the world, giving three gallons of milk a day. You can choose whether you have your milk raw, pasteurised or sterilised. It is all very hygienic. The milk comes in bottles, with a special patent sealed cap.

Yet I complain my milk has a "taste".

Henry gives orders that the bottles are to be opened only by the "Nurse—Miss Sahib" (Hyder Khan will resent this), so that there is no risk of interference when it reaches the bungalow.

When this afternoon's milk arrived, even in the green gloom of my lofty bedroom, Nurse and I saw a red deposit in the bottle. She opened the patent cap. It stank.

Calling a pattawalla, we send the milk into the office, which is merely through an archway.

"Will the Bara Sahib be pleased to smell?"

The Bara Sahib smelt; ordered the dog cart and drove straight to the Military Dairy. There he interviewed the Superintendent, a smart young officer. The records are turned up. Yes, here is the milk which had been despatched that afternoon to the Commissioner.

"A particularly high percentage of fat" said the Superintendent complacently.

Henry produces his putrid smelling bottle with the red deposit.

It was not till the next day it was discovered that the man who brought the milk could ingeniously remove the patent cap without being discovered. After taking what he wanted, he was in the habit of filling up the bottle from the tank by the roadside where the buffalows wallowed. Now day by day this tank was drying up. It was really not Genu's fault that to-day so much soil had got into the bottle.

How little Munshi would hug his bare feet and shriek between his peals of laughter, "Hikmat!" But no, on second thoughts, perhaps "Hikmat" is only good when practised by Mussulmans, not Hindus.

June.

After all this, there now comes a summons for Henry to go to Sind almost immediately, to take up the Commissionership. Three years ago, the Governor, then Sir George Clark, had offered him this post, but when Henry had given his advanced views on self-government for Indians at a Royal Commission, he had been reprimanded, and the coveted promotion went elsewhere. Now Lord Willingdon approved his liberal policy, and the prize was his at last.

It means a three-day journey with servants, silver, pictures, horses, dogs, etc. Train to Bombay, and then taking the small costal steamer and braving not only the monsoon, but the marauding gun-boat, the

Emden. It means settling in at Government House, incessant entertaining of officers and their wives stationed there, and influential people passing through on their way to Mespot, and Persia, the responsibility of five immense war hospitals in Karachi alone, Y.M.C.A. and all the rest of it, apart from the administration of a country as large as Ireland, and starting the great scheme of the Sukkur Barrage for which Henry was to be largely responsible.

It is clear that I must be left behind.

Owen is to be christened by the Scotch Padre from Poona. We did not care to have the Padre here, and indeed the Bishop of Bombay might have objected. But we were married in the Scotch Church, and they, of course, have no feeling against the marriage of deceased wife's sister.

Antonia has been staying here. She went off into the bazaar, returning with yards of crisp white voile, pin spotted with black and bordered with cheery red cherries and the brightest green leaves. The dirzi and she turn out the most Frenchified little frock for me, a trousseau hat is pulled to pieces and made incredibly smart. I tell Antonia I know of someone who is looking for a pleasant woman of the world as his wife. She seems amused and interested.

June 7th.

Owen was christened in the drawing room. The rain was thrashing down so the room was very dark, but the roses smelt sweet, and all the brass figures on the shelf behind the sofa glimmered. John Shillidy was here as godfather. He has given Owen an embarassingly handsome present of War Certificates to the value of £80, declaring it is his contribution to the war. Owen cried a little. He is christened John Owen Napier. John, after John Napier, inventor of logarithms, and John Lawrence, first Viceroy of India. Owen after Inishowen, e.g. Island of Owen. Napier after me.

Judge's Bungalow.

Henry has gone. I am here with Kesu, and Lep with thirteen fat roly-poly puppies, and dear old Tulsi, Henry having fired Rakma for her behaviour at Owen's birth. "The Memsahib's hair", exclaims Tulsi in dismay, "it used to be *gold*". Lovingly she spreads it out across the pillow and brushes it out with long soothing strokes, till very slowly it begins to shine again. It will be three and a half months before I can join Henry. I must reconcile myself to a more or less invalid life here with Charles, Gertrude and Mr. Montgomerie, the Assistant Judge who has joined us. Scotch, musical, with a Rabelaisian humour.

Little Gertrude fears horses, and is indifferent to animals. Nevertheless, we have become close friends. "I think you are both positively disgusting" I hear her exclaiming in her vehement way, as Charlie and I "flea" Lep daily, putting a hundred or more fleas at a sitting into the bucket of boiling water beside us. Fleas have to be seen to be believed here in the rains. For two or three inches above the mattinged floor there appears to be a mist. This is fleas jumping. Charlie is devoted to fat Lep, now so thin. He gets up every night to feed the six of her puppies he is bringing up by hand.

Oddly dissimilar as we all are, we make a kind of "happy family" and the Judge's Bungalow resounds with music all day long. Gertrude, though she looks so frail, sits at the grand all morning playing Bach's Fugues with the utmost decision and precision, her erect little head burning like a torch in the room so dark from the falling rain outside. After dinner, Mr. Montgomerie produces his gramophone. He has a fine collection of classical records. Sometimes I wonder what the effect of all this music will be on Owen.

Note added in August, 1920, *Eastbourne.*

To-day Christopher Boyd, who though only six is extremely musical, was standing by the piano, and with head on one side, kept gently striking a discord. "I like that" he murmured.

"Don't", ordered Owen from his meccano on the floor. "Well what shall I play?" asked Christopher, always sweet-tempered. "Oh, play some Brahms" says four year old Owen, not looking up.

The eyes of the two mothers meet. They do not permit themselves to smile.

Certain trifles, fragmentary incidents emerge from the quiet level of these days in the Judge's Bungalow. The pale rain-washed flowers on the dripping durantur trees all up the drive. The arrival of little convent-bred Nanny de Souza, with her frizz of black hair, her toffee-coloured eyes, and skin so dark against the dazzling white of her collar. Nanny scarcely bigger than a child herself, but saying with the utmost composure "Yes, Madam, he is a very big boy, but I shall easily manage him". Nanny, who after thirty-two years, is still a loyal and devoted friend of the family.

Then the relays of goats in the compound, twelve at a time, to supply sufficient milk and cream to Owen and the puppies, and how they always went dry after a fortnight! And the two African camp-followers in the hospital, sick unto death, nameless, and no one able to communicate with them; and my reluctance at leaving Owen, even in the experienced care of Nanny and Gertrude, when toothache forced me to Poona to see the dentist, and my having to stay a whole week there with Lloyd and Minnie; my absurd impatience to get back, to find in my absence that Owen had "found" his fingers. The intense surprise on his face when these wiggling things suddenly appeared before his eyes, was most comical. He lay there, moving them first quickly, then slowly; he did not realise they were his, for when his arms tired and fell back, he simply could not understand where the new playthings had gone! He was just as surprised when, lifting his little arms, they appeared again. Oh, and then an absurd incident when Gertrude and I went to call on the Commissioner who had succeeded Henry. Strange to walk up one's own drive, be greeted by one's own pattawallas, see one's own pots of crotons, coleus and caladiums along the plinth of the verandah which the dogs were for ever knocking over. We had just caught a sight of Mr. M. at his desk—Henry's desk—but instantly he had made his escape. Gertrude and I turned to go, but when we had got as far as where there was still a dark patch on the tiles where the blood had dripped from my hands when little Lahri bit me, a shout from Mr. M. in the portico brought us back. He had been kindness itself, and there he was smiling.

"Oh, do come in. I must apologise for running away like that, but I was wearing my office glasses, not my proper ones, and I could not let you see me like that . . . ".

Used as I am to Henry's superb indifference to what people say or think of him, I imagine Mr. M. to be joking. But no. He is known at the Club as Asquith and Lord Page 5, for in the catalogue of the Bombay outfitter, there is the picture of a dressy gent in immaculate sponge-bag riding breeches, and Mr. M's sponge-bag riding breeches are the talk of Belgaum.

Far be it from me to despise a love of clothes! Sir Charles Napier once had to dine with Queen Victoria at short notice. A drab waistcoat was all he had, but he remembered his valet was a dandy. "I dare say Nicholas has a fine waistcoat, I'll borrow it". He did. This does not appeal to me!

SIND

But strength was returning fast, and now life without Henry was but half a life. Living in his letters, I longed for the end of the monsoon when I could join him. Henry's ambition had always been to return to Sind as Commissioner. It was his "blue rose". He had spent all his early years there, knew the people and their language. Once when he made a speech in Sindi, an English reporter asked a Sindi pleader if he understood it. "Yes" was the reply, "except for a few words which were too classical for me".

Though Sind is nearly as big as England, he had been in every corner from the confines of the Punjab on the North to the Indian Ocean, 400 miles to the south. He had shot ibex on the mountains of Baluchistan on the West, and black partridges in the Sind desert on the East. He had known the Indus, that river 2,000 miles long, in all its moods, giving life to the people when the waters are controlled, but spreading death and destruction when they burst their banks. He had known it change its course eight miles in a single night, and had helped to build embankments to save a city from being swept away. Seven years before he had taken part in an irrigation conference, and there announced his opinion that its control meant life and death. Now the main task of his service in Sind would be to devise this method of control.

Sixty years earlier, in 1856, a far-sighted engineer had proposed to raise the waters of the Indus at Sukkur, running canals parallel to the river, down to the sea. This vast project was beyond the skill of the day, and beyond, too, the financial courage of the Administration. It was revived from time to time, but never could be brought to execution.

In recent years, the engineers and civil administrators had made great progress in harnessing the waters of the Punjab rivers which flow into the Indus, and their success, so beneficial to the Punjab, naturally reduced the supply of water for Sind. It was Lord Willingdon who finally decided the Sind scheme must be started. A great barrage was to be constructed at Sukkur. Henry was to take charge.

But it was not only achieving his ambition. Henry had a deep affection for the country and people. When we were secretly engaged he had talked continually of Sind, and the life I should some day lead there. When we were in Kanara, living in all that vivid beauty and interest around us, he had still talked of Sind. I remember him telling me how Sindhis take so much interest in wrestling and dancing, and that once a Baluchi chieftain, whose lands extended from the Indus far into the desert of the East, had summoned his retainers for a wrestling match. One strikingly handsome youth attracted the eye of Henry and Louise, who was with him. Henry said to his host "That lad has a Grecian face like the Great Alexander". "So he has" replied the Chief, for the name of Alexander is well known throughout the Province. Promptly he sent for the youth to be brought forward. He appeared, naked to the waist, magnificent limbs, tousled curls and the purest profile.

"Your name has been Mahomed Ali so far" declared the Chief. "Hence forth it shall be Sikander". (Sikander being the Indian variation of the name). And Sikander he became. Henry then asked the chief how far to the East his territory ran. His reply was "The river belongs to God and the Sirkar (Government). The desert belongs to God and *me*".

Many of these men are ruffians, but how likeable, with their picturesque way of putting things. There had been a riot among the Hindus of the Sukkur Bazaar. Hearing this, a chief came to Henry. "Give me the word. I will ride in with a hundred horsemen and there will be no more rioting in Sukkur".

When Hyder Khan left Belgaum with Henry, I asked him if he were glad to go. He replied with great dignity, "Here men are monkeys. There they are men".

Leaving Belgaum. September, 1916.

Owen, Nanny and I, Tulsi, Kesu, Lep and thirteen puppies and a pattawalla left Belgaum on our three day journey. Owen in a Japanese basket, and the puppies in a hamper through whose interstices squeezed pink noses and paws with nails like pins, and deafening shrieks of alarm and hunger.

How majestic the descent of the ghats! Leaving Khandala and the bluff called the Duke's Nose, familar to me from childhood from Father's description, the hills reared up all round us, dark and threatening, laced with white cascades leaping into shadowy abysses over ledges and shoulders of plushy green, brilliant beyond belief . . . and then the hills were all at once dissolving into a swimming dazzle of silver and lilac light, only to be blotted out entirely as mist and dark cloud rolled down again. But too soon, cool wet winds and waterfalls were left high up behind us. The wait at Kalyan below ghats was insufferably hot and oppressive. Owen wailed. The puppies shrieked.

We should have the whole afternoon and evening in the stifling heat of Bombay before sailing. Government was up at Poona, of course, and it seemed simpler to go straight on board rather than go to a hotel. But I had not reckoned on the heat between the drenching thunderstorms, nor that the boat would smell of bilge-water, nor that the electric fans would not be working till she started, nor that our portholes would be pressed close up against the slimy sea wall! However, it was too late to alter plans now. Settling Nanny and Owen, I took a ticca gharry and went off to see Lahri.

The Bombay Zoo had written some time ago, saying Lahri had not settled down very well. A visitor had offered to take her, having just lost a much loved Malabar squirrel, which had been a feature of the well-known wine merchants, where it had had the run of the place. Joyfully we accepted. So this afternoon I am seeing her.

As it happened, the manager was away in Poona, and his wife had gone home. A clerk at once offered to show me the squirrel. I followed him to the back premises.

"She isn't loose, then?"

"Oh *no*, Memsahib! She bites".

It was dark after the glare outside, and at first I did not see Lahri, looking half her usual size, crouched on the floor of a cage as large as the one she was very occasionally shut up in at Belgaum. This cage had a clean sanded floor, but there was no tree slanting from corner to corner, no branch, not even a perch, so Lahri's little hands and feet fashioned to grasp and grip as she swung from branch to branch were now on the flat, and her tail, that plumy, golden bush, had worn down to a mere bottle brush. There was no saucer of milk or water, no succulent leaves, no rose petals, no fruit. Nothing at all in that clean, roomy cage but Lahri crouched in a corner.

I thought of her at Belgaum, her hind legs hooked into some high branch as she swung upside down in the breeze, stuffing rose petals with her hands into those small revolving jaws. I thought of her sprawled asleep across my chest, her breath sweet from all the roses she had eaten. I thought of her wickedly alighting on the back of a bull-terrier, sending out her ringing cry of triumph while he flattened in abject helplessness. I thought of her at the top of the casuarina trees grinding her teeth defiantly at the crows as they tried to mob her, and then suddenly giving way to panic flashing down to find succour on my shoulder, her long tail hanging warm down my back. Lahri, swift, wild and beautiful! Lahri too much for everyone but me, and once too much for me when I fondled him who was to be her mate, and she sprang in crazy jealousy sinking her teeth into my hands and wrists over and over again.

"Lahri", I whispered choking.

The little creature, dark from lack of sun, and smooth instead of bushy, came to the wire netting. She reared herself up, holding to the wire with little "sunburnt" hands, the cream of her tummy showing. She stared at me with her unblinking completely circular golden eyes.

"Lahri! My little Bai!"

Paying no heed to the agitated warning of the clerk, I put my face to the netting. Did she remember? Did she recognise my smell, my voice? I don't know. But with those round golden eyes staring, instantly that tiny tongue began to "lick-lick-lick" through the netting with incredible speed.

I left her there standing on her hind legs, clutching the wires, looking after me, and suddenly letting out that tremendous ringing cry of hers . . . that cry that should be ringing through bamboo forests instead of the gloomy premises of a wine merchant in Bombay.

O Lahri!

The *Linga* has an evil reputation. She has a peculiar cork-screw motion even in calm weather, and now the seas were still in uproar from the monsoon. When we started Owen at first thought the motion was to amuse him, and laughed and chuckled uproariously . . . and then. Who was it said babies are never sea-sick? Little Nanny pea-green, with lilac lips and nails, but still methodical, in the course of the next two days changed him constantly in the intervals of being sick herself. Kesu, Tulsi and Lep are apparently dead. The puppies silent. I suppose the Captain is anxious about the German gunboat *Emden*. Nobody else is.

But "Journeys end in lovers' meetings". As we finally draw into the harbour at Keamari the following evening and can pick out Henry's familiar stocky figure in its tussore suit amongst the crowd on the sunlit quay I could cry with excitement. And here we are! And here he is! And Lep gaunt but ecstatic is jumping up at him bags aswing, and the thirteen puppies shrieking, and Owen in little Nanny's arms to be shown, and Tulsi hovering, and Mr. Iyengar smiling, and the people passing and jostling . . . Kalu smarter than I remember him is there with the Fiat. The towering blocks of the Port Trust Buildings, now being used as war hospitals Henry says, are luminous in the evening sunshine. Trams, goats, camels drawing trucks, and all the people with an entirely different aspect. What was it Hyder Khan had said in Belgaum, "Here men are monkeys. There they are MEN".

Henry puts his hand on my knee.

"Well? Is it well?"

We draw up under the portico of Government House. The sentry presents arms. Hyder Khan is there, his handsome bearded face smiling a welcome. He is more imposing than ever. The gold on his scarlet waist band considerably wider! It is sunset, and two pattawallas are lowering the flag from the flagstaff. Owen stares round-eyed at it as it comes fluttering down.

"Great Scott", suddenly exclaims Henry. "There's a Bara Khana to-night. Three dozen or more coming. I believe I forgot to say anything about it".

"Bara Khana?" A big dinner. I look down at my crumpled cotton. I've been travelling for three days and nights, and my boxes are still down at the docks.

Henry explains the situation to Hyder Khan. Hyder Khan is imperturbable. No doubt he is inwardly amused that the Bara Sahib should be so taken up with the arrival of the Memsahib that he had forgotten to mention either to himself or the cook that thirty-six guests would be dining at 9-30. But he merely shakes his head with that little characteristic sideway movement. "Tik hai, Sahib". And "Tik hai" it was.

There is a wonderful free masonry between Indian servants. Have you no flowers for your dinner party? No matter. The mali who arranges your vases to-night will see that your table is as gay as anyone else's. You are apt, on dining out, to recognise your own sugar sifter, candle shades or what not . . . so no doubt the dinner will turn out all right to-night. I am excused on the plea of fatigue, and long after I learn the only thing to mark it from any other dinner party was that the guests ate bread instead of rolls.

Note added in 1947.

I am here tempted to recall the arrival of Lord and Lady Irwin to India as Viceroy and Vicereine. Henry was at that time Acting Governor of Bombay, and we were privileged to entertain both the incoming and outgoing Viceroys with all their staffs at the same time! Now our Military Secretary, Major Vaux, was renowned throughout India for his excellent staff work. In no other Government House, not even in Viceregal Lodge, did affairs run with such clockwork regularity, or were A.D.C's. so assiduous in introducing, and in looking after the well-being of guests from the mightiest to the humblest. Lady Willingdon, with her hand of steel in a silken glove, had been responsible for this in the first instance, and Major Vaux kept up the high reputation. Now he had arranged for Lord and Lady Irwin's kit to be brought immediately from the docks that first evening, as there was a large dinner and reception at which the two Viceroys and their Vicereines would be present, and many reigning princes and all the élite of Bombay. But the incoming Military Secretary told Major Vaux his help was not needed. He himself had made the necessary arrangements for the baggage to be brought up immediately.

It did not come.

Dinner was put off half an hour. An hour. There we waited on in our bedrooms, all dressed up, waiting for the A.D.C. to come and fetch us. When he did, it was to say—"No luggage".

So Lady Irwin, looking like a shy little girl in the short frock to her knees, which she had worn coming off the steamer, had to be escorted around the room, having presented to her jewelled, brocaded princes, egrets clasped with diamonds rising from their foreheads, Parsi ladies, blazing with jewels, wives of merchant princes in Parisian trained dresses, and all the rest of us in full court evening dress!

Government House. Karachi, 1916.

We have entered on a new phase.

That whenever Henry leaves the Province a salute of twenty-one guns is fired; that there is a resident Assistant-Commissioner, who adds to his duties those of a Military Secretary; the flagstaff, the sentry and the Visitors' Book, where everyone passing through has to write his name, and such things are the outward and visible signs of this new phase . . . but to me, I think the real and startling change is the quality of light in Sind, the light which comes streaming in and pouring on one from every side.

After the submarine atmosphere of the jungle, and then the dimness of the Judge's Bungalow during the Belgaum monsoon, to be translated into this outpouring of incandescent light, together with the unmistakeably curious feeling that both desert and sea are close at hand, is positively startling. The landscape is like a silverpoint seen after a painting by Rubens.

Government House stands in its gardens and acres of rough ground, overgrown with oleanders and tamarisks, with many jackals slinking there . . . a paradise for the dogs! The house itself, built for the first Commissioner, our own Sir Charles Napier, I suppose is not beautiful in itself, but I find it very attractive. It is approached by four drives, and two very long wings reach out from the two-storied main building. As you mount the marble steps at that end where the Visitor's Book is kept, you see, reaching away in long, long perspective, the grey tiles, polished to such an extent they glimmer like water, so that chairs, tables, palms and ferns in tubs are reflected in their surface. The main entrance is under the high portico, and there is the sentry. Behind him, a group of cocoa-nut palms and other trees, and perfectly kept grass lawns with great clumps of brilliant cannas growing from the grass.

When Queen Mary (then Princess of Wales) came to stay, huge marble baths were installed, but they proved so cold in themselves, requiring such volumes of hot water, that the homely zinc tub squats in them now. According to Mr. Covernton, the Assistant-Commissioner, when the Princess of Wales stepped into her marble bath, the whole floor gave way, because although the P.W.D.[1] had guaranteed the floors would stand the great weight of the marble, they had omitted to calculate the addition of the royal body. I take this with a grain of salt. He is a nice creature, shy, amusing and diffident, all in a breath.

At the time of the royal visit, the then Commissioner had had the whole place redecorated. The drawing room, a fine rectangular room, had an apple-green carpet with bunches of wild roses on it. There were pale green brocade curtains with pelmets and puckers and

[1] Public Works Department.

flounces. I like neither. The carpet is taken up; the curtains taken down. Sea breezes shall blow unimpeded through the many arches. There is a parquet floor, and on this our Persian rugs shall lie under the really fine crystal chandeliers. The green carpet goes upstairs to the state bedroom. This opens into a sitting room for me, this in turn into the day nursery and the night nursery. At the other side of the state room are our marble bathrooms and a small office where Henry, getting out of bed in the night, frequently goes to work. An extremely wide verandah runs the whole length of the upper story, and from it we look out over the tops of trees and a great open maidan, and sand flats and creeks to Manora, the Fort that guards the entrance to the harbour. The other day an Arab dhow, flying the Turkish Star and Crescent came in. The battery fired across her bows. The dhow still came on. The battery fired again, this time sinking her. A launch was sent out to pick up the survivers struggling in the water. Poor bewildered creatures! It appeared that for months they had been sailing up and down the coast of Africa trading. They were unaware of any war. They did not know the Star and Crescent was a Turkish flag, and anyway, they had never heard of a place called Turkey.

Karachi is a city. Blocks of buildings, trams, docks, hospitals and commercial undertakings such as Ralli Brothers, Volkart, McKinnon Mackenzie, and so forth. Though there is a garrison of artillery at Manora, field artillery in Karachi itself, English and Indian regiments, transport lines and five great war hospitals under General Fowler, yet somehow the Army, no less than the Civil Service and its various branches who make up our little society in Belgaum, seem swamped by what are rather unkindly known as the Boxwallahs and their way of life. Few out of the odd one thousand two hundred Europeans, not counting Tommies, ride. The men seem older and less athletic and fit. One meets individuals who if they were not wearing tussore suits, one would picture catching the morning train to the city. Quite a few are stoutish, devoted to their game of golf in the sand on Sunday morning, with a heavy luncheon at the Sind Club afterwards. The bar at the Sind Club plays an important part in Karachi society. There business, war, scandal, is discussed over whiskies and milk punch, not war, tiger, sketching and games, as in Belgaum.

I don't fit snugly into this society as I did into little Belgaum.

All the same, I confess I like living in the Government House built for my kinsman. I like to see his lighthouse winking at me each night as I lie in bed on the verandah, like to hear of the Napier Mole enabling ships to come in from Bombay. I like to visit the Government Gardens which he had started to enable the troops to have fresh vegetables free of charge, and so get rid of the ravages of scurvy. I like to hear of his Artillery Barracks now used as a hospital, but which still remain as a model of what could and should be done for troops. There had been one of his usual rumpuses with the Directors of the East India Company over the expense. "Such barracks are expensive, no doubt", snorted the old man, "So are sick soldiers; so are dead soldiers. But the difference of these expenses is that the first is over and done with, the second goes on increasing like compound interest, and quickly strips the capital".

I like, too, to think of our horses stamping and eating where his beloved chargers tossed their heads. Red Rover, whom he had to lie down in his own tent to shelter him from the desert sun. Red Rover, brought to his bedside as he lay dying in England. Perhaps my Leviathan stands in Red Rover's very stall?

Leviathan has had tic fever whilst I was in Belgaum, and the English military vet. has prescribed linseed oil all over his feed. He loathes the oily mess. I scatter a few grains of gram to give him something to scrunch on, and I fancy gratitude in the bright eye he turns upon me as he lifts his nose from the bucket.

Hyder Khan has had made for me a Sindi necklace of sky blue beads, gold thread and gilt lockets fastened with purple and rose floss-silk pom-poms. Leviathan wears this Sindi fashion round his throat. Theatrical? Who cares! Henry himself approves. How beautiful, how noble he looks, pacing away slowly after the syce, his long tail brushing his hocks, his fine black skin scintillating and rippling in the sunshine, fancying himself, no doubt, a Derby winner!

The cold weather will soon be here and the flowers are lovely. Twice a week I send roses, cannas, balsom, cherry pie and so on down to the Dufferin Hospital. Twice a week the over-worked matron writes me a letter of thanks. I assure her this is quite unnecessary. To-day I get a letter brought to me as I sit searching through the menu sent up by Misteri for traces of bacon or beef. For amongst the guests to-night are Mir Ayub Khan, who, of course, must not be offered bacon, and Mr. Harchandrai, the Amil President of the Municipality, who, being Hindu, must not be offended by beef.

Reading my letter through, I don't know whether to laugh or cry at the folly of man.

The writer is the wife of a senior member of the I. C. S. She has heard of the flowers and the letter incident. She is a woman years and years older than myself. She reproves me in her exquisite writing for "lowering the prestige of the Commissioner in Sind" by permitting flowers to be received without written acknowledgment.

She worships position, precedence and so forth. It must have been a difficult letter to write, for in presuming to criticize *me,* the wife of the Commissioner in Sind, her husband being considerably lower in rank than mine, she (according to *her* views) was as culpable as the matron of the hospital in not acknowledging the flowers!

I force myself to remember that this respect for position in the I. C. S. is genuine. It is impossible not to laugh—not to feel superior—yet, at the same time, let us remember that the first orders passed by the British when they annexed the Punjab were:

1. Thou shalt not burn a widow.
2. Thou shalt not kill a daughter.
3. Thou shalt not bury a leper alive.

It was not the Commissioner in Sind the lady saluted, rather the spirit that guides the Indian Civil Service, the ideas that it serves.

Apropos of the lepers John Lawrence once received the following petition.

"Hail, cherisher of the afflicted.

Be it known to your enlightened mind that your devoted

servant has been a leper for many years. My limbs have fallen off piece by piece, my whole body has become a mass of corruption. I am weary of life; I wish to die. My life is a plague and disgust to the whole village, and my death is earnestly longed for. It is well known to all that for a leper to consent to die, to permit himself to be buried alive, is approved by the gods, who will never afflict another individual of his village with a similar malady. I therefore solicit your permission to be buried alive. The whole village wishes it, and I am happy and content to die. You are the ruler of the land and without your leave it would be criminal. Hoping that I may obtain my prayer, I pray that the sun of prosperity may ever shine on you. Ram Bukshm, Leper".

John found this poor creature just as he had described himself, limbless, lying beneath a tree and begging to be destroyed. Profoundly moved he exclaimed "I have no power to grant the permission, even were I willing".

"You will find the village will bury him alive without leave", said a native, who could not understand John's rejection of the petition.

And so it was.

But to return to my stickler for etiquette.

At Government House at the end of the verandah, there is a Visitor's Book, but elsewhere the usual custom prevails. That is, nailed to the gateway of each bungalow is a little box with "Not at Home" painted on it. The new comer has to drive round and deposit his or her cards therein, a very lengthy and tiresome proceeding. My critic watches to see whether Mrs. So-and-So, or the young unmarried men have come themselves, or whether they have sent a servant to drop their cards, as is the usual custom. If the latter, a caustic note in that fine, beautiful writing is at once written.

Again ridiculous. But this lady has many good points. At heart she is truly kind. She works extremely hard, attending meetings, touring, visiting schools and missions and hospitals, even riding camels if necessary. This cannot be easy, for she is an old, old woman whose head shakes, with eyes so blind that her rouge has a hard line and she smudges her bristling eyebrows as she darkens them. But truly she has a kind heart, carrying out her duties with zeal and efficiency. She is in an entirely different category to Mrs. X and Mrs. Y., both of the Railway. Mrs. Y., considering she should have been sent in to dinner before Mrs. X., was heard by Joe Covernton to hiss in tones of concentrated hatred "Your husband began as a station master . . . and . . . (in a menacing voice) *not on the main line*".

Mercifully I, who have no head for tables of precedence, have nothing to do with arranging the dinner table. Mr. Covernton does that, and a plan of the table is printed in red and black in the printing press which stands in our grounds. The plan is laid by my plate so that I can see at a glance who is who. Henry and I sit opposite each other at the sides . . . like the Lord's table! Joe Covernton is of the greatest help in coaching me as to who is who. With his pleasant, rather apologetic smile, his fair school-boy sort of look, he reminds me all the time of young George in Clayhanger. He flushes when embarrassed. To-day Henry learned that he had been nearly drowned last week when his "tom-tit" turned turtle, and he and his companions were rescued just in time from beneath the sail. Joe himself had never alluded to it.

At one dinner party, Mr. Harchandrai was sitting next to me. Hyder Khan offered him a tray covered with every kind of liqueur. Very carefully he considered each of these, then asked for something not there! By rights he should not take any!

Mr. Harchandrai is rather laughed at for wearing the Sindi gold cloth cylindrical "top-hat" with a "plate" on top, for strictly speaking, it is only the Mirs of Sind who are entitled to this head gear.

I visit the Dufferin Hospital pretty frequently, going round with Dr. Curjel, or one of the sisters. When I ask what is the matter with a patient, the answer is almost invariably "Oh specific", so in desperation I said one day "But what *is* specific?" It turned out to be what is now known as V.D.

But a number of women did have that dreadful disease bred of darkness and lack of fresh air, when their bones become so soft they twist into extraordinary shapes. I remember one poor creature who had become almost a ball. A pleasanter memory is of a young

Afghan, separated from her stony mountains by mile upon mile of desert. She lay like some superb animal, her chin cupped in the palm of her hand, surveying us with long, laughing eyes which were almost hidden by their lustrous lashes, a rich colour mantling her dark cheek. The nurses said she was always laughing. No word of Hindustani could she speak and not a nurse knew Pushtu. So it was that the young husband came to translate daily; and such was the love these two bore each other a screen had to be placed round the bed. The other patients drew their saris across their faces, murmuring "It is not good to show love thus. *Bahut sharam ate hai*—much shame is coming".

Attached to the Dufferin Hospital is the Louise Lawrence Institute. This has been built by her innumerable friends and admirers to carry on the work in which she was chiefly interested, to train Indian women to go out into the mofussil as midwives. The building is here, the money, the equipment, including a life-sized model of a pregnant woman which can be opened and handled . . . but the women to be trained are not.

Committee meetings on hot mornings. Under the monotonous purr of the electric fan we sit, clean paper, beautifully sharpened pencils and rubbers in front of each one of us. The Collector is in the Chair, suggesting somehow Savile Row, cedar-wood boxes and the aroma of expensive cigars. Next to him the Judicial Commissioner, with rumpled brindle hair and eyeglasses perpetually falling off his nose as he jumps about in his enthusiasm for the cause, his burning pity for suffering womanhood, his intense admiration for Louise. Then the City Engineer, with accent so richly Yorkshire I feel he must be play-acting! The washed-out looking matron, the excitable little Parsi . . .

But for all our talk, the Indian women fail to come.

Last Sunday Henry and I rode out in a downpour of sunlight through the loose desert sand, past clumps of posturing prickly pear to Louise's other memorial, her desert tomb. It is a replica of one of those old Sindi tombs you may come across in the sand and the stones, still lovely in their crumbling decay. It stands there, conspicuous in that intensity of light, on its sandstone knoll, looking on the one hand to the distant hills of Kohistan, and on the other, away to the sea. Under the richly carved dome the shadowed casket has a large Christian cross in relief. The desert wind sings round the eight pillars and their carved capitals, twitching up loose sand all round the low boundary wall.

It is recorded that a Baluchi shikari said:

"Sahib, when I learned of the death of the Memsahib, then was I afflicted with great grief. In all the country of Sind there was not such another Memsahib".

"Throughout the Province she was the People's Physician, a name synonymous with healing. She alone has been called Sister by Mussulman ladies, Mother by the women of the people everywhere. She won the affection of wild men and hostile women, of Mussulman men and of Brahmin women, whom the Hills called Mother and the Plains Sister".

So the record goes.

Already the Mussulmans are making of the tomb a holy place. Little chiraghs, that is, wicks floating in oil, are placed on the plinth at night, their tiny flames guttering and blowing in the wind.

I suppose in years to come, when the stones split and gape and crumble as in those other tombs one sometimes passes, the origin of the lamps will be lost though still they may be lit. For I remember that from the endless stream of motors and carriages rolling out from Poona to Ganeshkind for some reception, the guests may see on the right hand side of the road, little lamps glimmering from two humble graves. These are the graves of two unknown Englishmen, dead these fifty or a hundred years. Nobody knows their names nor why they are buried there, but Indians still bring votive offerings and the little lamps still flicker and gutter there every night.

Much has to be crowded into the weeks before we go on tour. Schools, missions, hospitals, Y.W.C.A., Y.M.C.A., and above all, the "Sind Women". In a building nearby, women of all castes and creed are toiling voluntarily through the hot hours at war work. Machining, cutting out, packing up great cases, making out lists and orders from subscriptions collected by them, they supply the hospitals not only here, but overseas, with "comforts"; but "comforts", to Henry's indignation, have to include such essentials as bed pans, bed rests, towels, sheets and pillows, which it should surely be the Government's duty to provide. Many of the "Sind Women" are long overdue for leave, anxious with men-folk at the front. It would be strange if little jealousies and bickerings do not occasionally arise with so many working at close quarters in heat and discomfort, with parcels, packages and packing cases everywhere impeding them. But what they accomplish is magnificent.

There is not much time for Owen or seeing the country, but Henry and I do ride most evenings out in the desert, or we go down to Clifton, scrambling and slithering down over the sand dunes planted with the creeper brought over from Australia to prevent them being blown away. There is always a wind blowing—sometimes half a gale. The sands below us stretch out for miles with the long line of breaking waves, catching the light of the setting sun as they break. But whatever is that? The whole shore seems to be on the move. "Crabs", says Henry, laconically. And it is! Hundreds upon hundreds of crabs hurrying along high on their legs. Horrible in their numbers. They are pugnacious, and stand up to attack Leviathan, their eyes on sticks. He rears up snorting, till he grows to disdain them, but Rainey, beautiful white devil that she is, dextrously seizes one after another and tears them limb from limb. Luther and Lep are clumsy and often get nipped. We pass a dead pi-dog. Crabs have clambered on to it and are feasting—you can hardly see its body . . . disgusting! Worse than the Kanara spiders. We put the horses into a gallop and here the wet, shining sands are firm and ribbed and we go galloping into the sunset . . . the sound of the galloping hooves "ga . . *rump,* ga . . *rump,* ga . . *rump*", and splashed by the waves and buffeted by the wind and blinded by the level rays of the sun, I forget the crabs.

Wind, always wind. Things banging. Papers scurrying off your table. Stones in the vases. Everything covered with a thin film of white sand in spite of the constant flicking of the hamal's duster.

Living here, I have thought more of Sir Charles Napier in the past week or two than in the whole of my life. Though it is nearly eighty years since he left Sind, legends and tales of him are still rife (as, indeed, they are still of Alexander the Great!). I suppose if your transport is camels and your bullock carts have the same solid wheels they had at the time of Alexander, 325 B.C., 1842 and 1916 A.D. are much the same. It is not so much the man as a soldier, but as an administrator I think, the effect of whose vigorous and, no doubt at times, eccentric policy is still felt. He himself had said "The enforcement of obedience is like physic—not agreeable, but at times very necessary".

In his own journal he wrote "We have no right to sieze Sind, yet we shall do so, and a very advantageous, useful, humane piece of rascality it will be".

"Autres temps autres mœurs". Those men had swords in one hand and Bibles in the other . . . well now, if we have thrown away the sword, haven't we thrown away the Bible too? How often this honest entry in his diary, of seizing Sind, is quoted spitefully, yet I have never once seen reference to the fact that when he left Cephalonia for ever, the Greek peasants "voluntarily" cultivated a small bit of land which he had left uncared for, and year by year they never failed to transmit to him the value of the produce without disclosing their names.

Here in Sind this scarred, wounded old man, this old rattletrap, as he described himself, put down many abuses, especially those which appeared to be female suicides, but were found to be murder of theit wives by their husbands.

> "People of Sind" he proclaimed. "You who murder your wives outrage your religion as much as you outrage ours. Some foolish men among you believe that the English are easily deceived, and you have in a vast number of cases hanged your wives and then pretended that these poor women have committed suicide . . . You shall tremble if a woman is said to have com-

> mitted suicide in your district, for it shall be an evil day for all in that place. The English Government will not be insulted by such felons. The murderers shall be sent to labour far away over the waters, and heard no more".

Then again when the Brahmins protested that suttee (the burning of widows) was "religious custom", Sir Charles had retorted cheerfully that they must therefore, of course, follow their religious custom, but he added, "My country also has a custom. When men burn women alive, we hang them and confiscate all their property. My carpenters will therefore erect gibbets on which to hang all those concerned when the widow is consumed. By all means, let us all act according to our national customs".

A Chief interceded for a man who had merely killed his wife. Sir Charles observed: "But she had done no wrong".

"No, but he was angry. Why should he not kill her?"

"Well, I am angry" said Napier, "why should I not kill him?" And did kill him!

His picture hangs in the dining room with all the Commissioners who have followed him, but he has a whole wall to himself. He is in a poshteen, his whiskers and moustachios wild, his brilliant eyes looking out through great horn-rimmed spectacles.

> "He is wonderfully well preserved for a man of sixty-seven" wrote Dalhousie. "When it is recollected what a life of hardship he has led. What climates he has braved, how riddled and chopped to pieces with balls and bayonets and sabres he is".

(He got his first commission when fourteen years old).

Well, we are shortly going on tour, and from Hyderabad will visit his battlefield of Miani, where "Generals had to fight like privates".

The Circuit House, Hyderabad, November, 1916.

We are housed here. Red, and substantially built. Hornets in all the rooms. A job to keep Owen and the dogs from getting stung. I see my first Mason wasp. They stuff up every small aperture, like a keyhole, with rubbish.

We visit the hospital, and the gaol, and watch the convicts making carpets, rugs, sheeting, towels, and slippers. We visit various schools. I loved the Kundunmal, the Amil Girls school. Modern and airy its walls were washed a delicate blue the colour of summer skies at home. Amils are Sindi Hindus. The young girls wear a charming drapery of fine white muslin over head and shoulders. Their legs are encased in very tight silken trousers clasping their ankles with an embroidered band. Timidly they rise as we enter, and with their long liquid eyes, and their very slender legs, they remind me of a herd of lovely gazelles ready to dash away at our approach.

Hyderabad is a quite extraordinary place. Every house has a fantastic erection on its flat roof to snaffle the perpetual wind and guide it down into baked rooms. It appears to be a confused huddled sort of city dominated by the magnificent golden citadel with its immense bastions, gateways, crenellated walls and turrets, and round towers. And yet it is not the Fort by which I shall remember Hyderabad.

It is by the pink oleanders . . . and the lovely Talpur tombs standing alone in the windy desert outside the city.

These great tombs are built of burnt brick and are quadrangular buildings with central domes, and with turrets at each corner. Their facades gleam radiant with turquoise and royal blue tiles, nearly every one differing from the other in design. Over the immense pointed archways verses and quotations from the Koran are inscribed in Sindi-Persian, and the flowing curves of those light blue, and dark blue letters remind me of my old Belgaum munshi explaining "That is for beauty's sake". The caskets are under the domes and are of white marble with marble fretwork. The surrounding courtyards are paved with plain kingfisher-blue tiles from Hala. The gold sand, the gold burnt brick, the blue sky, the blue tiles, and white pigeons cooing. What a resting place!

It was from Hyderabad that Henry had received a message that the Indus was in high flood and had broken an embankment which regulated it twenty miles away to the north. It was threatening to break the embankment at Gidu Bandar four miles away from

Hyderabad. At mid-day in a Sind July he rode sweating through four miles of watery wastes never knowing when he might not blunder into the water courses hidden beneath the surface. At the embankment men were striving to save their homes with sandbags. The river flood was within a few inches of the top of the bund, and a sudden gust of wind might have slopped the water over making the first gap, and the whole torrent of the river would have swept the village away and devasted the country beyond.

"It was watching those Sindis and the way they worked in a crisis that makes me confident the Sukkur Barrage will be a success", Henry declared to me. "People say the Sindi is lazy, but all these years I've stored up the lesson I learned that morning, and I mean to act on it".

MIANI.

Hyderabad, November 13th, 1916.

This morning Kalu motored us out to Miani. I remember years ago Stephen Coleridge rolling out to me in his grandiloquent voice that much quoted passage of Sir William Napier on Miani:

> "Thick as standing corn, and gorgeous as a field of flowers . . . they filled the broad deep bed of the Filaillee, then clustered on both banks, and covered the plain beyond. Guarding their heads with their shields they shook their sharp swords, beaming in the sun, their shouts rolled like a peal of thunder, as with frantic gesture they rushed forward . . . with demoniac strength and ferocity. But with shouts as loud and shrieks as wild and fierce as theirs, and hearts as big and strong the Irish soldiers met them with that queen of weapons the musket and sent their foremost masses rolling back in blood . . . The ferocity on both sides was unbounded, the carnage horrible. The General seeing a 22nd soldier going to kill an exhausted Belooch chief called to him to spare him. The man drove his bayonet deep and then turning justified the act with a homely expression terrible in its truthfulness accompanying such a deed. "This day General, the shambles have it all to themselves".

I remember having read that at Miani there were two surgeons only to attend to all the wounded; the others mere assistants without experience and very young.

Well at least things must be better than that in France for Egbert. But I feel sick misgiving all the same. He has written of the "unimaginable and awful sound of the guns". Brave as he is, I feel he would hate that noise. I determine to send him a pinch of dust from the battlefield of his kinsman.

To write of these brilliant days of ours in camp brings a feeling of shame, when vast numbers are even now fighting and dying in heroism, in misery, in despair. I feel this particularly on this old deserted battle-field to-day.

In a deeply shaded garden, red oleanders blooming all round, there is a monument to those fallen with the names inscribed on one side. Near by a blindfolded camel plods his ceaseless circles, the wheel creaking and groaning, but the water steadily rising in the little earthen pots to spill and flow down the little water courses of the garden. Sir Charles loved his horses to foolishness, but he loved all animals too, and now looking at the camel I remembered he was the only commander in India, besides his hero Wellington, who saw as carefully to the welfare of his animals as his men. Of the camels he wrote: "Those poor patient creatures are cruelly overladen, and when they sink under the weight are beaten and have their nostrils torn to pieces by pulling and working to make them rise". So he decreed that every camel should have a brass plaque with the number of pounds it was to carry according to its strength. 300 lbs. for the strongest. 200 lbs. for the weaker.

It was very peaceful here. Those fallen should sleep well, forgetting the terrible heat of the day when they rested with wet towels about their heads, and all movement had to be made by night. Even so, many fell victim to heat stroke, and Napier himself the soberest and most abstemious man in the forces suddenly reeled one day and was only saved by throwing himself on a table and the doctors near at hand bleeding him. It might indeed have been better had he fallen at Miani. For though he had achieved this brilliant victory, and every soldier native or British adored him, and he felt with them he could go anywhere and do anything, yet the thanks of Parliament were not voted till February 12th, that is, within a few days of a year after the battle! But the Duke had written in his own hand of "the two glorious battles of Meanee and Hyderabad".

"This is enough", said Charles, "now I ought to die, and have the Duke's speech graven on my tomb".

Nevertheless Sir Charles had felt the delay of Parliament as a personal slight on his beloved soldiers who "had received no recognition of their heroic courage and endurance". For this was the man who declared: "A man of high breeding is hand in glove with his men, while the son of a millionaire will hardly speak to a soldier." And, "All my life the idea of making soldiers do what I did not do myself has been odious to me". The man who would not ride on a march, and often carried a weary man's musket; who wrote: "I treated every soldier as my friend and comrade, whatever his rank my feeling is of love . . . it is hard to express but it is as if I had known them all my life and only forgotten their name. When I go into Portsmouth I feel inclined to take the first soldier or sailor by the arm and walk with him certain of knowing how to talk to him of matters with which he is familiar"—the man whose statue in Trafalgar Square was raised almost entirely by subscriptions of the common soldier that he loved.

Thinking of these things Henry and I came out of the garden into the white glare of the battlefield, every milk bush, every pebble casting its short midday shadow. Kalu's face above his tunic glistened as he bent to swing the handle, and we could hardly sit on the seats of the car, so hot they were.

Yes. Sir Charles, I thought, would be glad of that shade, of that klink and tinkle of water for his men. Kind, truculent, touchy old man, always fighting for his soldiers' rights or his own . . . and for yours too!, I thought as we passed the well with the stalking blindfolded camel. I thought of all those camels dead more than half a century ago which he had befriended. For it had been his custom to unexpectedly call out a camel from the file in order that its load should be weighed. And woe betide the man responsible if the weight were found excessive!

"Lord Bentinck by abolishing flogging has left no punishment when an army is before the enemy. I did *entre nous* make free with the law, breaking one and using the other. I shall be hanged one day!" So he wrote in his journal.

Yes, as we moved away, and the rising and falling of the Persian wheel fainted on that bright hot air, and I looked back over my shoulder at the shady garden where the men slept by red oleanders and running water I thought "Sir Charles would be pleased".

My brother was never to receive that pinch of dust from the battlefield. The very day we were wandering over the Miani battlefield, November 13th, 1916, he was killed in the great push at Beaumont Hamel.

November, 1916. *S.S. Jhelum.*

The Commissioner's Camp consisting of Henry, myself and Owen and Nanny, and Mr. Covernton, the Assistant Commissioner, Mr. Iyengar, Henry's shorthand writer, the sub-assistant surgeon, all the pattawallas, and the whole paraphernalia of office, together with the Fiat, Kalu, chauffeur, three horses and dog cart, five bull terriers with their string cots, goats, chickens and ducks, and Misteri the cook, and all the other servants came on board the *Jhelum* to-day at Kotri about five miles from Hyderabad on the opposite side of the river. The *Jhelum* is the flat-bottomed paddle steamer on which the Commissioner is conveyed up and down the Indus on official inspection during the cold weather. The *Jhelum* itself has only three cabins, and a small forward deck with fixed awning. Here are easy chairs, tables, a standard lamp, and seats running round the sides. In the centre is a capstan, and when we stick on a sand bank, which I gather may happen several times a day, the crew man the capstan, running round and round chanting, trying to get her off by means of the anchor which they have previously fixed on another sand bank.

They, the crew, the pattawallas and servants, the car, horses, dogs and poultry, all live on a flat the same size as the *Jhelum* which is fastened to her by hawsers. It seems we tie up each evening. Horses are exercised, goats browse, and the servants pitch little tents for themselves.

The river here at Kotri is more than a mile wide. This morning as we chugged peacefully upstream Henry is watching for magars, rifle ready. I, talking to our pleasant little Eurasian captain, explain I have always disliked the idea of taking life, but perhaps I should not mind shooting a crocodile. "I used to think that", said the little captain thoughtfully, "until I saw one cry".

Am much amused, and, crossing to where Henry waits with his rifle, tell him how Captain De Souza, having heard of "crocodile tears", imagines they are a fact, and pretends to have seen them.

(N.B. I was too clever. In later days I, too, saw a crocodile weep).

We tie up for the night. The last sound in my ears, the Indus swishing and sucking up against the side of the boat.

Following day.

Awakened by the usual disgusting sound of our servants and patta-wallas hawking and spitting in the dawn, reinforced now by the crew. We have got up steam. Breakfast under the awning. The river a dreaming loveliness, very pale and very enormous under a very pale and enormous sky. A flock of pelicans flying in a V overhead.

That morning, in my long chair, I watch the man in the bows rhythmically throwing the lead and chanting out the depth. *"Sarre panch Fut! Sarre arth Fut!"*—five and a half feet, eight and a half feet, and then unexpectedly, *"Arrhai Fut!"*—one and a half! "Look out", shouts Henry from his table. Too late! I'm shot out of my chair. We are on a sand bank. Now all is commotion. Rugs and dhurries are rolled back. Chairs pushed to one side. Paddle-wheels thrashing. The small boat lowered and rowed to another sand bank where the anchor is dropped. Then the capstan is manned, the crew tramping round and round to Owen's great delight, as he watches from little Nanny's arms. The crew are singing loudly as they go. "Highly improper verses" confides Mr. Covernton, smiling, and they get sweatier and smellier every minute as they stamp round and round on their bare feet. Eventually we are pulled off.

Henry returns to his files, and I to my long chair, in a trance. The vast sky and the vast river are divided by one blinding line of mustard, sliding by. Great golden Sindi boats, laden with grain, with their huge rudders turning this way and that, dream past with idle sails, and there are little fishing craft with a spidery circle of net, and the graceful figure of some Mohana woman bent against the long steering pole. Here is a white crane on the side of a small boat, patiently fishing for his master, so tight a ring round his neck he cannot swallow his prey for himself. Glassy sky. Glassy water. Hours fused in glare seem to stand motionless like reflections in a mirror.

How is it possible for Henry to continue working so methodically?

The next day.

First experience of malaria. Desperately aching back and bones. Icy trickles down my thighs. Whisky bottles filled with hot water around me, and every rug, coat, blanket, Henry's eiderdown as well as my own, even the cushions off the chairs piled on me—still I shiver and my teeth rattle like castanets. Aspirin, quinine. Temperature 103°. That night I feel I am climbing most laboriously up a hill. When I get to the top, something will happen. It does. Sweat breaks out. Blessed relief. Presently sheets wringing wet, pillow a poultice. Laborious changing.

Next day, utter prostration. We keep running aground with a tremendous jolt; the men chanting, the tramp of their feet, the tumult of the paddle wheels thrashing uselessly. I lie in my black, airless cabin. It has no daylight, being merely the passage the breadth of the boat, with a limp curtain hanging at each end. Owen and Nanny have the one good cabin in the hull, with windows all round and a bath room attached. So I crawl out on deck. Disinclination to eat, speak, read, sleep or even live. Glare on the water. My head aches; my arms lying so limply are yellow as a goose's legs. Third day temperature up again. Lie shivering and shuddering in my black cabin. Find the *Jhelum* quite *detestable.* Henry, first sharp, at what he calls my unreasonableness, then using his weapons of silence and aloofness! (He has never in all these years had malaria).

Make it up. Nice!

Sukkur.

Our tents are pitched by the side of the Indus, in a grove of palms . . . not tall, soaring, graceful cocoa-nut palms as in my first camp with Mr. Chuckerbutty in South India. These are date palms. Much shorter and stouter, with scurfing trunks. Henry is standing on the bank staring at the river intently. I ask him if he is watching for wagus (crocodiles). He explains that in the first scheme the Sukkur Barrage was to be built above the Sukkur Gorge. This had been turned down. The Barrage is now to be built on this exact spot where all our tents are pitched, under the date palms.

I am beginning to realise the great importance of the Sukkur Barrage and why it takes precedence of all else in Henry's thoughts.

Sind is a strange country. Rain falls seldom and then probably in thunderstorms of great violence. The people live on crops grown wholly on water derived from the river Indus by canals which run perhaps thirty or forty miles. The inhabitants worship the river as an inscrutable deity who in varying moods may give them bread or destroy them. When in the early summer the snows melt in the distant Himalayas the river rises and water enters the canals and cultivation begins; but the supply rises and falls uncontrollably and ceases after four months. For the rest of the year the people have no work in the fields and thus live aimless lives on the edge of subsistence.

The Sukkur Barrage is designed to cure this unemployment and to enable the fields to be cropped throughout the year with a supply of water scientifically controlled. If a dam were constructed across the bed of the river the water could be held up to a point where it would flow down all the canals from Sukkur to the sea. Moreover with a longer season the crops could be improved—wheat in place of coarse millets and long staple cotton substituted for short staple. All this would mean a vast revolution in the economy of several millions, and amongst even the officers who are concerned in carrying out the scheme there are grave doubts of its success. Some declare that the Sindi peasant is the counterpart of the Irishman, shiftless and thriftless, and will never settle down to steady work; whereupon Henry, himself an Ulsterman, declares Irishmen given the chance all over the world have risen to the heights of opportunity whether in crime or honesty. What of Roberts, Kitchener, Parnell? He had found, he says, in odd corners of Sind patches of perennial water on which the Sindis had created flourishing gardens. Vehemently he foretells Sind will attain great prosperity in thirty years, and adds that any way it is a question of life or death in the present. For in the North, the Punjab Government have control of the waters before they reach Sind, and have already established several colonies of irrigation. Unless the Sind system is working before they develop any further schemes, little regard will be paid to protests from Sind at having their water taken. If the Sind system is established, and the Punjab improvement destroys the livelihood of Sind, Sind must win the decision. Hence the urgency for speed, the need to overcome the reluctance of conservative landlords to make a change in their normal way of life, the need to pacify the conflicts of opinion amongst the official team.

Added in 1948.

It took Henry three years of incessant work to prepare the scheme, and eighteen months to secure the support of the Government of Bombay and the Government of India. The seal of approval was finally set on this work of Henry's when the Government of India declared officially: "We consider that this scheme, when constructed, will revolutionise cultivation in Sind and convert it into one of the most prosperous tracts in India. The credit for this most satisfactory achievement is due primarily to the Honourable Mr. H. S. Lawrence, C.S.I., Commissioner-in-Sind, who has controlled the local authorities in the various departments concerned so as to prevent controversies which have in the past so greatly interfered with the systematic preparation of a well-considered scheme, and has with a most inadequate staff evolved a project that is more complete in detail than has ever been attained before".

It goes without saying that Henry had had nothing on earth to do with the construction of the mile-long dam. Sir Charlton Harrison and Sir Arnold Musto designed and built it—a triumph which Sir Montagu Webb described as "a work that no superlatives can over-praise, and that future generations will surely regard as the Eighth Wonder of the World". Over ninety years before one Major William Baker had originated the plan. The intervening years had been one long pigeon-holeing of reports between London, Simla and Bombay. With great courage, Lord Willingdon, as Governor of Bombay, even while the war raged, caused a new scheme to be prepared. It had been Henry's job to overcome the opposition of the landholder to the changes in their mode of life and in the agricultural system, and to show that the revenue expected would support the cost of the scheme.

Once again finance threatened the project, but thanks to the determination of Lord Lloyd, who had succeeded Lord Willingdon as Governor of Bombay, Lord Willingdon (now Viceroy) opened the Barrage in December, 1932 . . . "A work of the utmost importance, that will bring under cultivation a region to be measured in millions of acres", declared the *Times* in its leader.

* * *

The river here is nearly a mile wide, and swift-flowing, even in the cold weather. I shall never forget the beauty of that first evening in camp. As the sun set, the sand banks turned to a cold blue which darkened to chocolate, but the river flowed like an immense tide of ringed rosy-golden oil under a flaming sky. Far across lay the low black bank and the black silhouettes of date palms and a Persian well. Presently, long cool milky fingers of light were slipping themselves through those rosy waters, and gradually these fingers closed together till the whole river paled and lay like a moonstone beneath the still flaming sky.

After breakfast it warms up in the tents. They are lined with yellow, and the sun, striking like a sword through the date palms, fills the tents with golden glow. Now Nanny baths Owen. His little body plump as a partridge, shines like silver from the brown water drawn from the Indus, for it is opaque with silt, though silky-soft. (It makes delicious tea).

Henry's day begins . . . An unceasing stream of visitors, hour after hour. Not the humble husbandmen I used to watch squatting in a circle round his chair in Kanara jungles, but influential zemindars (landholders) arriving on horseback or in victorias, bumping gently over the sand to the tents, or on camels: or wealthy banias in their hard little red hats, who have jogged out from the city on their skewbald ponies, or a mullah on his camel, or white-faced missionary women in big sun-topis in a tonga . . . But whoever they may be, they all want something, and by two o'clock Henry is at times completely exhausted. It is Mr. Covernton's duty to first interview these visitors, and then escort them across to Henry's tent. This morning he comes over to the "drawing-room" tent to tell me that one of Henry's visitors wishes to pay his addresses to me—may he come? (Do I detect humour in that shy smile of Joe's?). He then ushers in Khan Saheb Sirdar Imman Bakhsh, of Napierabad, an imposing, bearded figure of marked physical beauty. His presence seems to fill the entire tent. His square-cut beard and his patent leather boots are black, but everything else is dazzling white, from a colossal turban of seventy to eighty yards in length to unusually voluminous trousers, and the fine white shirt falling over these to the knee. After the usual salutations, which I have now learned to give in Sindi, the following conversation takes place, Joe acting as interpreter.

Joe: "The Sirdar wishes to thank you in person for your help in civilising his kinsmen".

R. "I?"

J. (smoothly). "Yes. Your kinsman, Sir Charles Napier, ordered the Sirdar's ancestor to be blown from the mouth of a gun".

R. Inarticulate murmurs.

J. "Sir Charles accused him of having stolen two hundred camels, but far from having stolen the camels, he was the means of finding and punishing the man who had really done so. Therefore Sir Charles, instead of blowing him from the mouth of a gun, paid him 300 rupees and granted him lands and a pension. The village was called Napierabad, and now the Sirdar has come to thank you for having civilized his people".

It is a little difficult to think of appropriate remarks, but no doubt Joe makes them!

Much occupied all day with thoughts of Sir Charles. Natural enough after the Sirdar's visit, and when anyhow Sukkur is so marked by his by-gone presence—the old island fortress of Bukkhur, to take one thing alone. I wish I knew more of the old man. Mother used to deplore our lack of knowledge of our forbears. I did not even know it was he who had first planted the seed of the barrage. He had written: "Hitherto the Indus has created and destroyed the harvest at its caprices. In June and July the country is one great expanse of water, and the grain shoots up like magic. Suddenly down goes the rise, and all is parched by the terrible sun. The grass bears this for some time, the earth holds moisture, and if a second rise of water comes, grows rich and heavy crops, but if the river does not rise in time enough, or not at all the crop perishes altogether. Now with our system of sluices . . . "

After four years of his administration Sind had begun to export grain, and in 1836 he was writing "She will become the granary of India".

My friend Stephen Coleridge had been an enthusiastic admirer of the Napier brothers. I well remember him declaiming to me in that magnificent voice of his the storming of Truckee from Charles' journal. "Such are British soldiers. Where mortal may stand in fight they will. Every man of these had a medal; two of them had three on their breasts. Never was the Durani medal so honoured. Their deaths have cast a glorious halo round that order. They died gloriously but uselessly on that sad cliff in the Cutchee hills . . ." To this Sir William had added (and I can hear Stephen rolling out his moving words): "There is a custom with the hill men that, when a great champion dies in battle, his comrades, after stripping his body, tie a red or green thread round his right or left wrist, according to the greatness of his exploit, the red being the most honourable. Here those brave warriors stripped the British dead, and cast the bodies over, but with this testimony of their own chivalric sense of honour and the greatness of the fallen soldiers' courage: each body had a red thread on both wrists". Fine.

Now my third brother is called after Sir Charles, and many anecdotes about the old warrior stick in my memory. There is, of course, the great hero-worship he felt for the Duke of Wellington, and the astonishing praise bestowed by the Duke time and again on the three brothers. Have we not got the bronze cast of the Duke's hands in the dining-room at home? Do I not wear as a ring, the big pearl waistcoat button which the second Duke, picking up his table knife at dinner, sawed off and presented to Mother in token of the family friendship? And do I not know that when Ensign Arthur Wellesley had been spoken of in Irish society as a "shallow, saucy stripling" Sir Charles' father, Colonel Napier had declared with singular prescience "Those who think lightly of that lad are unwise in their own generation. He has in him the makings of a great general". Now Sir Charles almost worshipped his father, "Strong and beautiful in body, powerful in mind, he seemed to his sons superior to any man they ever knew", wrote a relative; and forty-two years after his father's death Charles was writing, "No man of his time equalled him. Sir John Moore and the Duke of Wellington came nearest". Is it too fanciful therefore to surmise that the feeling for his own father planted the subsequent seeds of veneration for the Duke? I wonder! All these trifles, and many others lie submerged in my memory, but oh! how I wish now that I had paid more attention as a child to the tales of Sir Charles as an administrator, whose capacity for government won the admiration of Sir Robert Peel; of whom Byron wrote: "A better and braver man is not easily found. He is our man to lead a regular force, or to organise a national one for the Greeks. Ask the Army! Ask anyone!" He had turned Cephalonia into a model island, erecting a lighthouse, building a great mole, sweeping away slums, and making fine broad roads. He had made covered markets, passed beneficent laws, built a girls' school, and in five years a mountain road a hundred and thirty miles long covering passes over five thousand feet in height.

Of his work in Sind I have already seen something myself. I determine now to learn more of this "benevolent despot". I shall read his journals, for whether a man wish it or not most surely does he betray his real self in his diary.

Had tea with the Mission ladies in Sukkur. Miss Piggott is astonishing. On her leisurely camel she penetrates to remote desert hamlets. Missionary though she be, I suspect the practical and medical side of her work appeals to her most.

There were Indian sweetmeats, and as one approached the table, flies rose with a roar, reminding me of blue-bottles arising from blackberry bushes after rain!

Tea over, I made that speech which Mr. Crouch had spurred me to write and deliver in Hindustani. As a matter of fact, the women understood only Sindi, still the intention was good! Many of the women had earnest and intelligent faces. The faded blues and orange and tan of their saris and tight trousers were a joy. They seemed delighted with my sisterly approach . . . but without deliberately reasoning it out, I have decided, in spite of Mr. Crouch and Mrs. Brown, that my job is not to take an active part in this sort of thing, but to keep Henry happy, amused and untrammelled, so that he can do *his* work, his most exacting work—before all, his work on the Sukkur Barrage—without dissipating his energies. (This, by the way, is not necessarily so self-indulgent as it appears on first sight).

Nevertheless, I shall not pretend these days in camp are not sheer excitement and delight.

We go into Sukkur bazaar. Down by the quayside where the flat-bottomed Indus boats, with their strange sails and rigging, tie up to load with grain for Karachi, and immense yellow mounds of grain are standing there like pyramids, with black squawking crows scuffling and fighting all about them. It was along here that Bachal Shah, the fakir of the Mohana fisher folk, wandered on his return from Benares and other holy places. Miss Piggott had told me all about him. Muhammadan though he was, yet could he quote to the Hindus from their own holy books. One day he would enter the bazaar in a nobleman's gold brocaded coat, and the next, wearing only a rag of a loin cloth. Moslems cast their rupees at his feet, and when he sank to rest on a sack of grain in some bania's "go down", the trader would afterwards send the sack of grain as gift to this man of alien faith. Little children loved him, for often he would play cowries with them, and such was his skill with a gun, he shot the very fish in the river. Some sixty years before, Miss Piggott had said, a Punjabi dancing girl found her way to the Pir, seeking peace. Thrice did he tell her to sacrifice her jewels of shame and cast them into the river Indus. Twice she had turned sorrowfully away, but the third time, she had flung them far out into the river. She became the chela or disciple of the Pir; but first, to purge herself of her sins, she had made the pilgrimage to Mecca, and so became a Hajiani. She returned to Sukkur purified, and when Bachal Shah died, she lived on alone to tend his shrine, revered alike by Hindu and Mussulman. Now she, too, is dead, and buried at his side. We must ride out to their tomb one morning.

These early morning rides! Emerging numb from one's tent, the sun rising a red ball from the mist, the sand reaching coldly blue, the fidgeting horses snatching at their bridles, ready to leap out of their skins. And then the dew-drenched pink tamarisks suddenly breaking up into twinkling rainbow drops in the long level rays of the sun; doves sitting on the telegraph wires like small clay pigeons. Green parrots flashing from tree to tree, the groaning of the Persian wheels rising and falling across the wide water . . . (Henry complains I'm like Sir Charles: "The only pace known was a hand gallop").

I have ceased to look back over my shoulder at Kanara!

This morning, we wandered along the banks of the river instead of riding. The water is so cold Lep and Rainey won't go near it, but it is impossible to keep old Luther out. The current is very swift, the brown water goes sliding by the cliff-like banks, its surface broken by treacherous little whirlpools where you may see a stick caught, struggle and get sucked under, to be seen no more. Luther keeps close in, splashing and blundering through backwaters from one sand-spit to another. This icy water and the hot sun of mid-day is bad for his liver. There may be crocodiles too, and this morning he is in sudden difficulties. He spins round and round . . . his head disappears . . . and before we ourselves have taken it in, Lep has taken a leap down . . . splash! into the water she had refused to go near. Little Lep is swimming out to him, swimming round him as his head reappears, poking her nose at him, encouraging him, and somehow getting him to flounder to the shore, where he stands shaking visibly, a sheepish look on his old face.

Brave, faithful little Lep.

Khairpur State. November 13th, 1916.

Henry has to pay an official visit to Khairpur . . . the Land of Happiness—a misnomer. The state is about the size of Wales, but most of the land is arid desert, and little inhabited, the population being rather over 200,000. The Mir is himself an independent ruler, i.e., he has his own courts of justice, his army, a section of the Imperial Service troops, and his own system of taxation. The Collector of Sukkur, Mr. Moysey, can only advise him if he hears of serious scandal (there is plenty). The Wazir is an Indian official selected from the British Service, and the Political Agent would make enquiries through the Wazir when necessary.

Henry tells me when he was P.A. he had stayed at Khairpur with a small party. The food was execrable, rotten fish, etc. Henry had sent a message to the Wazir that under the circumstances they would prefer to eat Indian fare. Within an hour back came the message the cook had been sent to jail. Now the food would be good. Henry pictured the outcry that would arise in the native press. A cook sent to jail because the Collector did not fancy his cooking! He protested to the Wazir, but the Wazir declared the man was sent to jail for theft. He had stolen all the food the Mir had caused to be sent up from Karachi and Bombay for his guests. Again Henry protested. This time the Mir exercised his prerogative of mercy, and the man was deported.

Our visit has been exciting. Gorgeousness and squalor. Pageantry and over-eating and making conversation at interminable state banquets. Intrigue. Red carpets. Rams fighting, fireworks, treachery and whispers of murder. Everything one is led to expect in a petty native state in fact.

Khairpur was within easy motoring distance, but the Mir wished for an official reception so we had to go by train. The old gentleman has his own ideas. One idea is that he must eat a mango every day of the year, so the world is ransacked to enable him to do so. As a mark of great favour he passes on his half eaten, half-sucked mango to someone else to finish. Supposing he does this to Henry?

Travelling here is far more comfortable than in the Southern Division. The Commissioner in Sind not only has his own steamer, but also his own coach which is shifted from train to train as desired. We have a bedroom, a bathroom, a kitchen in addition to the large saloon furnished with chairs and couches. There is also a whole compartment for the servants. One is thankful to think of them travelling in comfort. To be squeezed into third class carriages, unable to lie down at night, fruit skins littering the place, and blood-red expectoration from *pan* eaters, bundles, tin boxes, children and babies, unversed in the most elementary ideas of hygiene, sweepers, coolies, everybody mixed up in a tight breathless impacted mass of noisy humanity! Nobody loves travelling as the Indian, but it is impossible to think of Hyder Khan, so majestic, so spotless, in surroundings such as these.

The train got in at dawn, and we were shunted to a siding. Cold dressing, and peering through the window at tall pampas grasses silhouetted mauve against a pink East, as we ate our chota hazri. Cold and shivery too stepping down out of our carriage behind Henry, so resplendent in his dark blue uniform, gold lace and sword. Mr. Covernton was in uniform too. His high velvet collar up to the chin, and a row of bright buttons down his front. But Mr. Moysey, whom

I spy on the platform amongst a seething crowd of officials and servants, is in immaculate frock coat and trousers with a beautiful crease. So too is Mr. Taunton, the Assistant Collector, and the Wazir, a tall distinguished-looking man wearing a small brilliant turban. Mrs. Moysey is down there too. She and I are like two hen birds, neat but uninteresting in our coats and skirts amongst all this bright plumage. So too are Nanny and Owen.

The band strikes up. Red carpets. Flags and pennons everywhere. We are all garlanded, and icy drops of attar of roses trickle down our necks. Henry is slowly and carefully inspecting a magnificent body of men in bright bottle-green uniform with baggy vermillion trousers and dazzling white gaiters. They look oddly French. In the background against the babul trees is a restless confusion of horsemen, and here before us is a huge barouche on swaying springs, the sort of thing in which the dowagers of last century took "carriage exercise". But this barouche is not drawn by fat carriage horses, but to my immense delight, six camels, now snarling and bubbling, looking down their noses disdainfully, from long lashed eyes, their hocks touching, their hind feet spreadeagled. Into this barouche Henry, the Wazir and myself clamber. Doors are slammed. Other barouches are behind for Mr. Covernton, the Moyseys, Mr. Taunton and Nanny and Owen, but drawn by horses. And now we are off swaying and lurching at a great rate under flags tied on to trees, and between rows of sightseers in every conceivable colour of turban and blanket. Picked horsemen thunder along ahead of us, and others behind, in clouds of dust burnished now by the level rays of the rising sun. On each side of our carriage the two elder sons of the Mir are riding with drawn swords. On my side gallops Mir Ali on a beautiful liver-coloured Arab who, blackened with sweat, bounds and caracoles and snorts besides me flourishing his long tail and flinging great flakes of spume from his bridle on to my lap. I know about Mir Ali. He is in disgrace with the Mir. He has been to Cambridge. His ambition had been cricket, but now it is to go to the war. The Mir won't hear of it. Mir Ali is kept here caged in this little state. He is allowed no money.

Although he rides superbly he is already a little fat. There are tales of women, and drugs and drink. The other brother is fatter and slothful and contented. He has not been to England. The Wazir, his back to our six galloping camels, is bending courteously to Henry pointing out this and that. He has a harassed, a haunted air. No wonder. His two predecessors were poisoned. The heir is a sickly boy of ten or twelve whose mother dare not let him out of her sight for fear of poison. Khairpur, the Land of Happiness.

We surge along through the crowds, our two galloping escorts on either side. We pass under an archway, and from it thousands of pink rose petals flutter down on to our topis, into our laps, all over the barouche.

The Faiz Mahal is a large rose-coloured palace built to accommodate His Highness's guests. It has dog-toothed columns and many little chabutras and thousands upon thousands of yellow chrysanthemums, all in pots before it. The rooms in the Palace are lofty and very, very cold. Good Persian rugs lie on the crudest Brussels carpets. There are many musical boxes, mostly broken, and chiming clocks which don't go. There is very red mahogany furniture from Tottenham Court Road, and the chairs and sofas are almost impossible to sit on, so hooped out they are with broken springs. But in one of these lofty rooms there are a silver sofa with carved back and three silver chairs, all upholstered in vivid emerald-green velvet. Instantly I remember that Christmas present I had so despised as a child. A box of sham silver furniture for my doll's house. "People don't have silver furniture", I had pouted. But here it was.

Mrs. Moysey, Nanny, Owen and I were hidden away high up in a gallery looking down into this room. Very cold and our tums rumbling with hunger. Far below, all foreshortened, Henry awaited the formal visit of His Highness. A thunder of guns announced he had left his own Palace. He arrived a rather frail old man with clubbed white beard, gorgeously apparelled in rose and pea-green brocade, a sheaf of white egret feathers springing from the front of his jewelled head-dress. After mutual greetings he and Henry sat on the silver sofa, holding each other's hands.

The following conversation took place.

H.H.: "Are you well?"

H.: "This is your kindness. I am well. Are you well?"

H.H.: "Thank you I am well. Is your health good?"

H.: "Thank you my health is good. Is everything good with you?"

H.H.: "Taking one thing with another all is well".

The visit lasted but a few minutes. Then the Mir left. More guns to announce his departure from the Faiz Mahal. Swiftly he was driven back to his own Palace. When a quarter of an hour had elapsed, more guns, and Mr. Covernton and Mr. Moysey fetch H., and he drives away to repay the ceremonial visit.

Again they sit on a sofa, hand in hand.

H.H.: "Are you well?"

H.: "This is your kindness. I am well. Are you well?"

H.H.: "Thank you, I am well. Is your health good?", etc., etc.

An immense breakfast then follows for us all before we set out for our strenuous sight-seeing of the town, the dispensary, hospital and technical school. This last is a most fascinating place; airy and clean. Boys are educated to read and write and draw. They learn turnery, tailoring, shoemaking and carpet making, this last from the carpet factories of Amritsar. The Persian pattern is written on a piece of paper, rather after the fashion of musical notation. The "Leader" remains standing, singing out from the paper in his hand, a "note-stitch". Whereupon boys pick up the colour, knot it into the warp, at the same time singing out themselves what they have done. Leader and chorus follow without a break, so the Persian design appears song made visible.

In addition to the carpets, dusters, ropes, shoes one is accustomed to see made in government jails, there are pottery and tiles such as I had gazed at on the facades of the Talpur tombs in the desert outside Hyderabad. Persian designs in turquoise and royal blue on white grounds, and to me still more beautiful, tiles and great vases in quite incredible kingfisher-blue which seemed to throb in its brilliance.

There were scarlet-patterned lacquer bedposts and chairs, toys and balls, these last opening one after another till the tiniest enclosed a seed. There was iron work, and calicoes printed with ramping elephants and birds, and pyjama girdles of rose or magenta and emerald silk, double, but so fine they would pass through a ring, their ends finished off with an entwining design of gold and silver thread starred with tiny pearls, which design was captured and finally bound into a long golden point. There were embroideries of all kinds, and gold lace on brilliant velvets; and the tall Wazir, looking taller than ever in his well cut grey frock coat buttoned to the chin, took us to see the best and fastest embroiderer of all. This was a little boy of perhaps ten years old, who, as his fingers stabbed in and out, making an all-over chain-stitch design, lifted up his face. There were two red sockets in place of eyes.

This embroidery is taught from the earliest age. A pitiful sight to see a row of little children on the floor, ceaselessly bending back the fingers of their right hand with their left to make them supple. This may go on all day for weeks.

The next stage, they are given a needle stuck in a wooden handle, and with this they practise stabbing in and out of a bit of cloth, faster—faster—faster!

At last, a thread is put in the needle, and from beneath their flying fingers flow wonderful designs of leaf and flower.

The Afternoon

Under a huge shamiana, the flag with the Star and Crescent waving on top, red carpets, Persian rugs, pots of flowers, we are all assembled to watch the sports. Very hot and sticky. His Highness is in a high silver chair. Henry sits on his right hand; then I come, and Mir Ali, now out of his riding breeches, dressed in a vivid emerald velvet coat encrusted with gold lace and huge baggy white trousers, and patent leather shoes, is seated on my left. What can I say to him? It is easy enough to enthuse about this and that to his fat, smug brother; but handsome, discontented Mir Ali is eating his heart out. Is he despising his velvet coat, these savage games and wrestlings we see? The whole barbaric splendour of everything? Is he thinking of Cambridge and his friends he made there, now fighting in Europe while he idles here, bored, drinking, eating too many sweetmeats, having too many women, not allowed out of the tiny State, intrigue and the threat of poison all about him? Away on my left, past the harassed Wazir and the Moyseys, are his fat younger brother and the sickly little boy who is the rightful heir. The child's velvet jacket is almost covered with gold lace, his high head-dress glittering with gold . . . But I must be paying attention to what is going on.

Before us, the dusty maidan, and away on the other side the crowd looking like a long line of "hundreds and thousands" sweets in their varied clothes. I bring out my sketch book, and get an impression of the dance of the Makranis. They form a circle before us. They are dressed in loose wide-sleeved shirts of mignonette-green worn over very baggy mauve trousers and canary turbans. How strange to see such exquisite taste in colour after the hideous mixtures in the Faiz Mahal. Round and round they go snapping their fingers, lifting bent knees, uttering sharp cries, faster, faster, while the two men in white strike their drums with furious intensity.

Now rams fighting. The rams are being held. They rush forward. A shattering sickening noise as their skulls crash against each other. The two animals waver uncertainly, they withdraw, another rush and again the sickening sound . . . This goes on till one staggers, falls and does not rise. No time to feel upset. Tent-pegging. The wonderful riding, the dust, the flashing horses, and now immediately in front of us the "Dance of the Pathans". The twenty or thirty of us in the shamiana are stirring with anticipation. Men all in white are running forward with braziers full of red hot coals with which they trace out a circle. And now come the Pathans. Tall beautiful young men with blue-black locks falling to the shoulder. Dressed in white they are, their shirts worn outside their trousers, but kept neatly into the figure by a black waistcoat. With shouts and cries they proceed to dance and leap bare-footed over the red-hot embers, and as they whirl faster and faster, their hair flying out horizontally, the two perspiring figures in white come rushing up with their braziers piled with fiery coals which they fling exultantly onto the track, causing the dancers to leap and yowl in pain and ecstasy . . . And then the Sindi wrestling; the Camel Corps, the men running beside their galloping camels, and actually and amazingly leaping on and off as they gallop full tilt in clouds of dust . . . So it goes on till the shadow of the shamiana is reaching right across the maidan, the sun sinks, the temperature falls, moment by moment. We shiver. All at once it's cold. "It's a passionate climate", as Sir Charles' daughter once wrote.

Sukkur. Camp.

How much pleasanter our tents under the stars than the Faiz Mahal.

Took the dogs for a prowl by the river this morning. The morning sun lighted the plumes of the pampas as they bent in the wind. Returning a little ahead of Henry, I was startled by a huge negroid figure in brightest pink, crazy with drink and bhang exploding, as it were, out at me from some tamarisk bushes, with loud cries. I was stiff with fear, but already he had collapsed at my feet, a blubbering, quivering mountainous jelly. Running up, Henry found him to be one Ghazi, a former syce. He crawled on his stomach, sobbing, uttering incoherent cries and clasping Henry's ankles. A more revolting object I never saw. It appears when Henry left Sind, Ghazi had become a follower of the notorious Pir of Kingri, the "Vice-regent of Allah". The Pir was the head of a heretical Muhammadan sect who was regarded by many thousands of Sindis with fanatical devotion. These men, known as the Hurs, would and did sacrifice their lives and property, and commit the most horrible crimes at the "Holy Man's" bidding. He had a fort ten miles from Khairpur, which Henry had once visited; there was a chamber deep down in the ground with a water cistern to cool the air. Here the Holy Man took refuge in extreme heat. He was alleged to have tortured many men and women. The Mir of Khairpur was terrified of him, and was much alarmed at Henry visiting him!

Note added in 1946. In this last war the Hurs rebelled and a brigade of troops had to subdue them. They numbered hundreds of thousands, mostly in the Makhi Dhand (marsh of flies) district. After the rebellion, the Pir was tried and hanged.

The Pir was a thorn in the side of Government. Amongst his many villainies, he was reported to keep some wretched man in a very small cage which he carried about with him. (Years before Sir Charles Napier had come on a similar case). Now Ghazi, writhing at Henry's feet, tears coursing down his face, great loose blubber lips, rolling eyes, told Henry he proposed leaving the Pir's service and coming back to him!

I tell Henry if he does, I go.

Ghazi had come from a slave family imported from Abyssinia by the Mirs of Sind. Like the ladies of Hogarth's day, the Mirs chose their attendants for their hideous features, and Henry had followed the fashion. But, in addition to this quality, he had been devoted not only to his master, but to his horse. However, Henry could not in any case re-employ him, for apart from his habits of bhang and drink, he might infect the whole of the Moslem staff with his fanaticisms!

Note added later. When the Pir paid a ceremonial visit to Henry, he was escorted by hundreds and hundreds of his wild followers, and I watched many of our respectable pattawallas slink away and join in his procession. So in this strange country there are religious pitfalls even in engaging a syce.

Undated.

To-day, Henry told me he was going to visit an "old friend" of his, who only by the mercy of heaven had managed to keep himself out of jail.

"I found" said Henry, on his return, "a most charming and benevolent old gentleman who told me his sole occupation now was 'to sit in the shade of a tree, to watch the young wheat growing and to think on the mercy of God' ".

Now I knew that this same man only a few years before had committed every imaginable crime! Before we were married, Henry had told me "Some of the zemindars are awful ruffians, but somehow you can't help liking them".

"I never see an ugly Belooch or ugly Scindi man", wrote Sir Charles, all those years ago, and perhaps the wonderful physique, and good looks, and the merry ways of these rascals, impel one to like them.

December, 1916

I waited for Henry for two hours at the station this morning, sitting outside in the car. Why I know not, but the experience was extraordinarily vivid, and looking back, this particular wait declared itself as an experience when one was drinking in the "feel" of the country with every breath. So it had been that morning at Supa, watching the men and youths swimming around the little temple of Ramling, and later, the women and children bathing and spreading out their saris to dry over the sun-warmed rocks.

Maybe there is something in this climate of Upper Sind at this time of the year, with its iron-cold midnight and blistering hot midday, that flicks one's impressibilities like a whip. Then, a station in India is always a bustle of variegated crowds, some of whom have been camping with bundles and babies and brass cooking pots on the platform all night, waiting trustfully for some train or other, which may come in some time or other, to take them to some place or other, near where they want to go. Anyway there was so much to look at I had not a dull moment, and drew innumerable little sketches in Owen's scrap book as soon as my fingers were warm enough.

The sun shone through the mist making a dazzle of gold. Figures, either squatting or propped up against the wall, were invisible (bar an eye or the tip of a nose) in their blankets of orange, umber or shrillest green. Additional little fringed shawls, often of crude pink, were tied over their heads. The Sindi believes if his head is warm, he is. He is right. But just by the car stood a Hindu youth in dirty white shirt and three-quarter length white trousers. He had no shawl or blanket. He had thrust the fingers of both hands into the tiny pockets of his black waistcoat. His body faced me, but his features were in profile as those of a figure on an Egyptian frieze. He was shivering visibly. Fever perhaps, for every moment the sun was gaining strength. Pi dogs had uncurled and were scratching and basking in its warmth. There was much coming and going of the little family parties to the two water-taps labelled respectively *Hindu Pani* and *Mussulman Pani.* By and by, when the Mail should come thundering in, Mussulman and Hindu vendors would trundle water along the platform past the carriages where packed passengers hung out of doors and windows, crying aloud their cry to which I had become so accustomed on our travels: *"Hindu Pan . . . i", "Mussulman Pan . . . i".* But for those now waiting there were the two distinct taps to which they hurried, carrying at arms length brass lotas or cheap tin kettles, from which the water spilled. How strange these two similar waters, side by side! I am reminded of the waters of the Rhone and Arve, flowing in one bed without mixing.

The station yard waxed brilliant in sunshine. Parrots flashed and shrieked. Little stripey squirrels whisked up tree trunks to remain there apparently glued. Half a dozen coolies squatted in the shade, smoking bidis and playing cards. Though the shadow of the wall had turned their dirty white garments to deepest blue, yet this blue itself was luminous, so brilliant the light around. Kalu had wandered away to watch the gambling. Different from them, in his erect figure, his starched white uniform and dazzling buttons, and yet how alike in his love of smoking and gambling! Sindi women passed, pitchers on their heads, their long earth-coloured chemises falling over the tight faded blue trousers. They were screaming to each other, not quarrelling as one might suppose, merely conversing cheerfully in their high-pitched strident voices. Now a camel lurched by, his neck see-sawing. The woollen trappings and balls swinging by his swollen-looking knees and hocks, were scarlet and black, the peaked saddle worn crimson. His rider had baggy indigo trousers, a mustard coloured coat, a dull red turban and a scarf worn cross-wise. There is nothing drab about Indian poverty! The poorest woman wears ornaments of brass and her arms glitter with bangles. And now a drove of tiny donkeys pattered by in the dust, almost hidden under their immense burdens of grass. Often one's stomach muscles grow taut at the sight of the sores on their withers and quarters; but to-day, sores are hidden beneath their loads.

The train is very late. It is hours past breakfast, and I begin to feel a little sick in the sun for I have not brought black glasses, and then my attention is attracted by the sight of an old fellow with a bushy white beard and immense and complicated white turban. He carries some stringed instrument and a bow. He settles himself down in the dust and drawing the bow across the three strings he distracts me from the thoughts of sickness by the most sweet and poignant music.

He is an old, old man and his eyes have a faraway look. Somehow one could not picture a young man playing this particular instrument. Its frail, plaintive voice suggests laughter long silenced, sobs long hushed. Sweetness and passion now thinned away to ghostliness. This is the heritage of old age.

Kalu draws near and explains this is a taus, so called because of the perky little peacock at its end. The music with its etiolated passion entrances me. I long to play it. The old man hands it up to me. It is quite cheap and rudely made. The little peacock has had his crest broken off and it has been stuck on again, but a little crookedly. I long to possess it. I ask the old man to sell it to me. He shakes his head. I press it. And finally it is mine. The mail rushes in. There is the usual commotion and hubbub, and here comes Henry, looking, as always, clean and unperturbed even after a night journey. Hyder Khan is close behind, and Mr. Iyengar and various pattawallas. Driving home I display my treasure, caressing its polished body, its little peacock. Henry, too, is fascinated by it, for we share appreciation of our roving life and what it brings. I lay it carefully on the top of the travelling piano and gaze at it as we eat our late breakfast. The tents are very hot now, full of amber light from their yellow lining. Henry goes to have a tub. I go around asking the servants, the clerks and pattawallas if they can find someone to teach me how to play my taus. I am told it is extremely difficult and there is no one. Apparently the tuning is an art in itself. I turn one of the pegs and a string breaks. I lay down the taus. It has a reproachful look. I am striken by remorse. I have taken the old man's treasure. I picture him trudging along the dusty Sindi roads under the babul trees carrying his shoes, in silence . . . a blind man without his dog. And here, the little peacock with his broken crest is doomed to perpetual dumbness.

What have I done?

Henry amused me this evening as we sat in our tent, warming our toes at the little camp stove. He said Lord Kitchener had once visited Khairpur when he was Collector of Sukkur and Political Agent for Khairpur. But I will try to tell it in Henry's own words.

"Kitchener was en route from Delhi to Quetta and I had to make arrangements for his entertainment. The Military Secretary, Birdwood, told me they had heard that there were fine specimens of old Persian swords in Khairpur, and the Commander-in-Chief would like to see them. A number were brought out for his inspection, which Kitchener declared were modern and worthless. One, however, he pronounced as "passable", and he would like to buy it.

"Alas!" said the Wazir, "it belongs to a most venerated High Priest".

"Priest?" exclaimed Kitchener, "What does he want with a sword? I will get him a splendid Koran from Cairo".

The Wazir said "I will do my best to persuade him".

Kitchener: "Very well. I shall be passing through Rohri on the fourth morning after to-day. Send it to meet my train".

But when the train passed through Rohri, the sword was not there. Birdwood wrote to ask me why. I made enquiry from the Wazir, and the reply was the holy priest had sent it off by a trusty messenger. This man had a bad riding accident and entrusted the sword to another.

The latter reached the station, worn out with fatigue, and went to sleep and did not wake until the train had passed. The priest recognised then that it was not the will of Allah that the sword should be delivered to the Commander-in-Chief. So there the matter ended. Lord Kitchener's collection was not enriched.

Larkhana. December, 1916.

Very wide shady roads here and most glorious babul trees. The place was laid out by Colonel Mayhew in well designed gardens. The Eden of Sind.

We are in the P. W. D. bungalow which, being built for the hot weather of Upper Sind, has small deep-set windows and very thick walls to allow no sun to penetrate. So now, in the cold weather, it looks, smells, and feels like a vault. A low white mist loiters about it from the canal close by. But Hyder Khan, buttoned to the chin in a brown checked coat over his starched white, soon causes a roaring wood fire to be lit in the big open hearth, and this evening Lady Kemball and I (oddly enough, we have both brought long-sleeved wine-coloured velvet dresses . . . very cosy . . .) stretch out grateful fingers to its crackling and dancing, while the unused punkah with its dingy fringes, hangs motionless overhead. In spite of that stagnant cold, there are clouds of mosquitoes in every room. They twang like a banjo, filling up every pause in the conversation. We wrap rugs round our legs, have hurricane lamps under the dinner-table, and burn incense.

I awake in the dark. It smells of dark and cold. There is a faint, far off music, which I at first mistake for the mosquito banjo band. But it is growing louder. Harsh, yet musical, too. Like some uncouth and yet somehow beautiful orchestra pierced with the shrill notes of piccolos.

"Henry, what *can* that noise be?"

He never minds being wakened up, as he can instantly drop back into sleep. Now he explains in a sleepy voice it is country carts, with solid wooden wheels, bringing grain into the town; that the wheels are purposely left ungreased so that if the oxen stop plodding, their sleeping drivers will awake and goad them on. Unromantic . . . and yet somehow there is something strangely beautiful in that procession of mingled sound coming out of the night into the dawn, louder and louder . . .

In the morning, Henry and Joe Covernton are busy with officials. Lady Kemball and I sketch. Difficult, impossible with her chatter, which is ceaseless. Crossly I tear up my bridge, with its reversed half moons in the water, which so easily might be a bridge in England except for the slanting palm in the background, and wander off by myself. A handsome bearded Sindi is advancing on a minute donkey. He is sitting on its hind-quarters, not its back, but even so he has to hold up his feet so that they should not trail on the ground. Fascinated, I watch him approach, feeling any moment he will begin to "punt" himself along as men used to on velocipedes! With vanity he poses for me. Beginning at the lower end, he is wearing scarlet shoes with curly toes, full faded blue cotton trousers, a pea-green and scarlet check shawl swathed all round him, toga-wise, and draped over his orange turban. (Not at all like England!). The donkey has merely a rope round its neck for bridle.

Of all tiresome things, it is clear that Lep should be "in purdah". Not only have we Luther to contend with, but hoards of pi dogs, and the pis in Sind are not like the miserable diseased curs of Southern India, but vigorous, very large and often savage. Indians tie a bag over a cow's udders to prevent the calf from sucking. It gives me an idea. Nanny and I make Lep a pair of drawers from some crimson and white striped cotton crepe. Now Lep is the jolliest, most uninhibited dog I ever met. The cheery confident way she bustles into a room, barking, though still keeping her mouth tightly closed as though saying "jolly well. How's yourself?" endears all hearts. But now, though I am most careful not to laugh nor even to smile as I put on her drawers, she becomes abject. She stands humped and motionless, her tail clapped down over the red and white stripes, her eyes, though not her head, following me imploringly.

But what can I do?

Indian Gelert

West of Larkhana some of the isolated peaks in the Kohistan Hills rise to nearly 7,000 feet. Kuta Ka Kabr the Dog's Grave is one of these. On its summit is a cairn.

Many, many years ago, nine hundred years or more, there lived near Dhariaro a Mussulman from the Brahui country. He was weighed down by a burden of debt, a debt of one hundred rupees. He had little hope of ever being able to repay this debt, and his only solace in life was a huge Baluchi sheep dog, whose bushy coat was thick and white as wool. His value was great.

There came a day when a certain Hindu of Dhariaro, who was the poor Mussulman's chief creditor, sent to him saying that he would wait no longer for payment, and that all those goods which the Mussulman had pledged would be sold immediately unless the money was forthcoming.

"O Dog!" cried the old man. "I am a poor man and without resources. What can I do?"

And the great white dog looked at his master with faithful eyes as though he wished to help him, and he thrust his nose into his master's hand as it hung there by his side.

Then the Mussulman put on his shoes, and taking a staff set out for Dhariaro, the dog following him. The dog seemed to realise that his master was troubled, for he paused not to investigate bushes as was his wont, neither did he circle stiffly round the village dogs on his toes, his hair lifted all down his spine, and his teeth bared. No, he kept close to the Mussulman looking neither to the right nor to the left, so that all the village dogs slinking out from behind mud wall or thickets of cactus and prickly pear murmured amongst themselves. "What is this? Is the great White Dog sick?"

Meeting the Hindu, the Mussulman with troubled mien and gesticulating hands begged for more time in which to pay his debt.

This the Hindu refused.

"What can I do?" exclaimed the old man. "Allah knows I have nothing more of value in the whole world. With difficulty can I fill the bellies of my dog and myself".

Then the greedy eyes of the Hindu fell on this dog of noble stature, with coat thick and white as wool.

"I will take your dog as additional security", he said quickly, "and the matter may rest for the present".

"Nay Seth", cried the Mussulman. "Excuse me this! Thou art my mother and my father. The dog is my servant and my friend".

And the dog licked his hand.

The Hindu repeated his terms.

Then the Mussulman was sorrowful, for though the dog is an unclean animal, did not Muhammad himself consider that a dog pure white was not unclean? And did not some even say that white dogs issued from the navel of Muhammad? And this dog had been a servant and a friend to him for many days. So he was grieved at the Hindu's new conditions, yet was he compelled to agree with them.

Turning to the dog he said:

"O my Friend and Servant! Henceforth this is thy master. Be faithful unto him as thou hast been unto me. Guard his home and all that is his, and return not to me until such time as he himself sends thee back to me".

And then the Mussulman turned away, and returned to his house alone. The way seemed long.

And all the village dogs, yellow dogs, and black dogs, thin dogs, and dogs with sores on them, rushed out to snarl and to snap at the old man. And his heart yearned after his noble protector with the coat like white wool. "The Hindu will feed him with grain, and grain is no fit food for a dog, royal like my dog", thought he with sadness.

And the village dogs barked excitedly amongst themselves: "Doubtless he is dead, the great proud White Dog who bared his teeth at us".

Now some days later thieves broke into the shop of the Hindu, and carried away many valuables. The Hindu was disconsolate, but the dog remembering his master's command followed the trail, his nose close to the ground. He found the spot where jewellery and other valuables had been hidden. Returning he took the dhoti of the Hindu gently between his teeth and led his new master to the place so that he might recover all that he had lost.

Great was the thanksgiving of the Hindu. On a piece of paper he wrote a message to the Mussulman telling him of what the dog had done, declaring that in gratitude he returned him to his old master. This he tied round the dog's neck with a piece of cord, and so thick was the dog's white fur scarcely could it be seen. Then the Hindu sent the dog back to his old master free!

The dog ran like the wind. He charged through the village so that the astonished village dogs were parted on either side of him as water is parted from the bows of a boat. But the Mussulman seeing him coming thus from a great distance was seized with anger:

"By fleeing thus from thy master thou hast heaped shame and dishonour on my name", he cried, and taking hold of a hatchet he killed his dog.

Dying the great beast rolled over, so that the paper on which the Hindu had written could be seen half buried in fur.

Then the Mussulman reading cried out with a great voice: "I have killed my faithful servant and friend!" and he wept.

In token of repentance he buried the dog on the mountain near by, building over him the cairn known to all around as the Dog's Grave.

And now it is not known whether the peak of Kuta Ka Kabr is the cairn miraculously grown, or if the cairn itself has given name to the whole mountain.

And I thought of another Dog's Grave in far off Wales, where the purple mountains guard valleys green as velvet, and the rain falls fast and often. Gelert of noble heart had been left by his master to guard his sleeping child. When the master returned from hunting the child's bed was empty and the sheets all bright and clotted with blood.

And seeing Gelert with blood about his jaws, the father in his grief and anger slew the hound, only to find the child sleeping unharmed, and a dead wolf killed by the faithful Gelert lying near by.

How different the graves. The one on the stony mountains of Sind, the other in the green valleys of Wales, but both testifying for all times to the faithfulness of the dog.

In Camp, Kambar. Christmas Day, 1916.

Cold. Cold in the tents on waking. Pattawallas and servants hawking and spitting in the darkness outside. A shivery business washing at the little camp-washstand in the corner beside the bull-terriers on their string cots. Tightly buttoned in their coats made from numdah cloth, they remain completely buried under their country blankets which move up and down with the hidden saluting tails. Finally we emerge from our tents with numb fingers into misty pink air. Tamarisks and date palms and ground are grey with dew. The shawled servants are creeping between the many tents in tucked up attitudes, enveloped in orange blankets. Nanny and Owen, like the bull-terriers, are still invisible under bed clothes. Impossible to imagine we shall be sweating in an hour or two.

Lady Kemball appears at her tent in a saucy little hat, rubbing her hands.

"You must wear a topi", announces Henry.

"Oh, I *never* wear topis. I look a positive fright in one".

"Rosamond will lend you one of hers", he insists. But the sight of my khaki pig-sticker is too much. She confesses to owning one after all, and produces an almost brimless thing covered in white-chip straw with a bunch of pink roses on it. Ruthlessly we tie a large khaki cotton handkerchief over it, but the white frilly blouse showing beneath her coat we can do nothing about. She is positive she won't need the topi, and she has no black glasses. "You see, if I do feel the sun I can put up my umbrella". (What will the duck feel about a white sun-umbrella and a white blouse?). But we say no more. Lady K. is so plucky and so cheery. We all feel for her. Her husband is on his way to England to answer questions about his failure to press on from the Dujailah Redoubt till the Turks had had news of his presence. Underneath her cheery chatter must be an anxious heart. No one would guess it—a typical Englishwoman.

The sun is shining through the mist. We stretch our limbs in the feeble warmth like numbed flies, and set off. Some of us ride, some of us motor over the sand track strewn with rice straw for our convenience. Bullocks meandering along with their solid wheeled carts pause to pluck at the straw, but the abrupt cessation of the creaking wheels wakes their sleepy drivers, who urge them on with shouts, twisting their tails. Little stripey grey squirrels flash across the road and seem to nail themselves against the trunk of a date palm; parrots shriek; we pass a high blank mud wall and a woman in a long terra cotta chemise and faded blue trousers looks after us, a pitcher held on her head.

The Jheel at Changro is sheets of pale blue water under a pale blue sky, dotted with little islands of pink tamarisk and reed, faint blue hills in the distance. We clamber into flat-bottomed boats where water is seeping in. Handsome, larky Sindis, with tousled curls, standing waist deep in water, push us off with tamarisk branches. They are naked except for a loin cloth and a little felt embroidered cap, cut square, covering their cheeks. Their shoulders are magnificent, their skin a warm, pinky brown. They are smiling and excited at the prospect of sport and the certainty of duck to eat; but every now and again they pretend to be miserably cold, their teeth chatter, they shudder exaggeratedly, they burst out laughing. It's all part of the game.

The boats go off in different directions. Henry and I are deposited on a squidgy little portion of ground, about five foot long. The punt is pushed in close under the shelter of a tamarisk bush. We squat there with Henry's Purdey and Greener, and the bags and boxes of fours and sixes, whilst the others take up their scattered posts and the beaters go off far in the distance. Henry and I are almost invisible in our greeny shikar kit. I'm pleased with the stripey green and brown stuff

I got at Abu Bukker to cover our topis, perfect camouflage. I sketch our man sitting there in the punt, watching and listening so attentively. His skin is brown madder. There is a broad silver ring around his big toe. I'm sitting in a puddle myself, but the sun is getting hot and all around are the delicious fluty noises of water-birds as they go unsuspectingly about their business between the little islands of tamarisk. Henry whispers their names to me. Red crested pochards, with brilliant beaks; pintails; a blue coot; and many others—all trafficking about the little canals and pools between the rushes. A mallard stands up in the water, beating his wings. Diamonds flash. I love it all.

And then our Sindi comes to life. He has heard the faraway voices and cries of the beaters. Now a quite incredible hour or two for me. There is a sort of silken scream of wings, and rushing towards us and passing over our heads, are hundreds . . . thousands of duck. Never had I believed so many birds existed. Gauzy skeins, very high up, others crossing them on a lower plane, others still lower. Hundreds . . . thousands of birds. Bang! Bang! Bang! Henry is blazing away. So are others. I, crouching beside him, am loading as fast as I can. His gun is smoking. The birds are falling "splash" "blonk", into the water and the coolie plunges after them. As the old zemindar once said to Henry: "Sahib, they are falling like rain drops from heaven".

"Give me a four", cries Henry as a solitary mallard, a flashing emerald, comes directly at us like an express train. A swerve, and "blonk", he too has fallen with a heavy splash. The Sindi has got him, beating wings, a knife across that lovely neck, and the living jewel, now just a lump of bloody meat, is pitched into the bottom of the boat to join that tangled heap of bright feather where now and again a twitching wing, a gasping bill can be seen. "*Halal karo*" shouts Henry angrily as I cry "Oh, it's not *dead*". The knife is produced again, but your Sindi is a Muhammadan. He must cut the throat of the bird while it is still alive, but whether it is dead after is a matter of indifference to him.

Henry is a good shot. He is merciful, and will not take chances. He is shooting splendidly. It is not like that day when his old friend Khair Bux consoled him: "The Sahib shot magnificently but Allah was merciful to the birds". Clearly, he is enjoying himself. I am glad. He so seldom takes a day off. Our surroundings are lovely. The thousands of birds streaming overhead are incredible. This is the best duck shooting in the world, but squatting there in my puddle, breaking open his gun, pitching out smelling cartridges, thrusting in the four or sixes as required, always I am conscious of that tangled heap in the punt, which in spite of his repeated shouts "*Maro*! *Maro*!" quivers here and there.

By twelve o'clock he has shot a hundred and seventeen. The corpses are laid out in endless rows. Their beautiful markings admired . . . But I, for one, am reminded of Mr. Bell's collection of Kanara birds, lovely little jewels, skinned and carefully rolled up in little paper cases . . . Yet this is *different*. For all the Camp will feast (some of the beaters will eat as many as six duck apiece!). Sowars will be sent off to catch the train at Larkhana, despatching any amount to the hospitals in Karachi.

We have an enormous spread ourselves, provided by the local zemindars, who feed with us. Mountains of rice, roast kid and pilau. We eat with our fingers.

Lady Kemball confesses the glare off the water has given her a headache. With a stifled sigh, I hand over my black glasses, and then *I* get the headache! Back in camp for tea. The sun is setting, a glowing ball between the scurfy trunks of the date palms. There waits Owen, jigging up and down in Nanny's arms. He is like a little white woolly bear in his knitted coat and bonnet, framing his rosy cheeks and silvery hair. Outside his tent we finish decorating his Christmas tree—a growing tamarisk, pink with blossom, and now with crackers and toys and candles thrusting out among its sprays. I sing Weckerlin's "Noel" to him. The temperature is dropping minute by minute, there are white wisps of mist. We light the little candles. Owen reaches out his arms . . . the ghostly tents all round . . . the servant's fires . . . the date palms against the smoky west. What a strange Christmas! Lovely, but oh, my head aches.

Boxing Day.

I awake in the night with a jerk. Frightened. Someone in the tent. I lie motionless. The matches are over on Henry's side. Our little low camp beds are barely a foot off the ground. We have no nets. His bed touches mine. I grab at him and whisper: "There is someone in the tent". Instantly awake he snatches up that automatic torch which emits a feeble light if you grasp and relax, grasp and relax. He flashes it around. There is no-one there. He gets out of bed in the icy-cold and from the outer corridor brings back the hurricane lantern and sets it on the dhurry in the middle of the tent. It casts its wavering light on the golden ceiling with its little *fleurs de lys.* Nothing. "You look very flushed old girl". He puts a hand on my forehead. "Have you a touch of fever?"

Perhaps I have and yet . . .

Henry falls asleep. Something heaves violently beneath me. My mattress is lifted, and me with it . . .

"Henry. There's someone under my bed!"

My mattress subsides again, and from beneath crawls on its stomach one of the huge yellow Sindi pi dogs.

Lep should be in purdah. This in camp is not possible. The guard are instructed to watch out, but the pi must have slipped through.

December 26th.

To-day the shooting was not so good as at Changro. Yes. I must have got a touch of the sun yesterday. Head bad.

December 27th.

The others go off. I stay in bed. Fever.

December 28th.

In spite of aspirin, and hot water bottles, and mountains of rugs and clothes my temperature creeps slowly up and I can't sweat. Nothing to mark the hours, but the icy tent growing gradually warm, then blazing hot, with the top luminous, and later the west side. Finally the slant of the tent-ropes silhouetted black with fuzzy gold edges. Through the open flap I see the smoke of the fires as the servants prepare the evening meal. We return to Karachi next week as their Excellencies Lord and Lady Willingdon are coming to us for an official week. Endless inspections of schools, hospitals, Y.M.C.A., etc., and receptions and state dinners. My head is buzzing with quinine. I'm deaf with it, and burning hot and shivering with cold. I MUST shake this fever off.

Straight from his shoot Henry comes in. He sits down on my low little camp bed in his shikar clothes, a smudge of blood on his sleeve, the mud drying on his jodhpurs. I screw myself up to say "Do you know I think perhaps I'm ill . . . not just malaria".

He gets out the medical book all officers take on tour with the official medicine chest. We pore over its pages. It can't be malaria, for my temperature though not very high creeps steadily up each day. Ah! here is something which seems to tally with my various symptoms. Henry reads aloud. "Unconsciousness then supervenes, swiftly followed by death".

Startled we stare at each other . . . then burst out laughing. All the same we had better get back to civilisation.

Commotion. Sowars gallop off to Larkhana with orders and telegrams. The Camp prepares to break up. I am rolled in rugs, and Henry picks me up and carries me to the car. By bright moonlight and in bitter cold Kalu bumps us away over the straw-covered road, fifteen miles to the station. There our special coach, with its bedroom, dining room, bath room and kitchen awaits us to be hitched on the train.

The station master wires to Kotri to keep the mail train for us next morning. It is held back as long as they dare, but as our train eventually steams into Kotri, the mail train steams out. This means waiting in a siding in blazing sun all that day. Never shall I forget the breaking back, the splitting head, the heat and the perpetual sound of *Chirri Miri* outside. Lying down as I was on the hard and narrow bed I could not see the half-starved little boy jigging up and down on the line below, slapping his ribs and naked stomach. I could not see his upturned face exaggeratedly distressed, but breaking now and again into smiles as he whined:

Chirri Miri dé Saheb.
Meskin admi hain Saheb.
Bhuk se mou jate hain Saheb.

Alms! alms! give, Sahib.
Miserable men are we, Sahib.
From hunger we die, Sahib.

But it is so familiar at all the stations we ever stop at, as familiar as the pi dogs slinking from carriage to carriage in hope of picking up food, that lying there I saw the little boy as plainly as I heard him.

Chirri Miri dé Saheb . . .

Dear old Dr. Nazareth is there to meet us at the station. Vaguely I remember being put to bed by a nurse. Not in our room, for the Willingdons will of course have the state rooms, but downstairs along the long long verandah. Burning, I fall asleep to awake in pitch darkness, bathed in cold sweat, and not knowing where I am. All my bedclothes are on the floor. I call and call in bewildered misery, my teeth chattering, my bed shaking. After what seems an eternity Henry comes in in his pyjamas. The night nurse he had left sitting up with me feeling very tired (poor soul, she had already done a day's work in Dr. Nazareth's Home), had gone to lie down in an adjoining room, and had fallen asleep. She is very deaf. Henry had to shake and shake her to wake her up.

The next day he learns I am apparently suffering from both malignant malaria and typhoid. The Willingdons are even now on their way up the coast on their yacht.

Poor Henry.

To save Henry as much as possible their Excellencies stayed on board their yacht. Otherwise all the official programme was carried out. Dinners, receptions, garden parties, inspections of hospitals, schools, etc., etc. I was desperately ill. My recollections are of a tight iron band round my head and my feet perpetually bathed in icy sweat. Two nurses, kindness itself, and jealous of each other. The deaf one was the senior, but it was such an effort to make her hear, I much preferred Nurse H. with the preposterously swollen legs which caused her to groan perpetually. What I craved for was my dear Tulsi who was not admitted to my room. Thirty days and still no fall in temperature. A world-famous bacteriologist was passing through Karachi from Paris. Crashing through medical etiquette Henry insisted he should see me. The two doctors attending maintained there was no object as the tests proved conclusively I had typhoid, not paratyphoid. Nothing could be gained by further opinion. Henry waved this aside.

"You see. He'll say 'paratyphoid', not 'typhoid'," I whispered to Henry.

He did. But the other men were right too. It was that having battled through typhoid I now had started paratyphoid. Henry and I discussed in a dreary sort of way what to do with Owen if I didn't pull through. Vi Fenwick, or Gertrude Boyd? Mildred Quin, his godmother, was too preoccupied with the discovery that Denis her boy was stone deaf from an accident.

The Willingdons departed, Henry was obliged to go on tour. He sent an S.O.S. to Mrs. Brown. She, splendid creature, cheerfully faced the three and a half days' journey, and arrived complete with Ayah, Boy, two babies and a bull-terrier. But the nurses resented her, the servants resented her Boy and Ayah as just "mission log", so deeply grateful though I was, it was perhaps a relief when she eventually returned to Khanapur. Nevertheless she quickened the dreary march of days, describing her life so vividly that I was able to see her milking the buffalo, separating the milk, handing out some to assembled women for their babies, producing oil for running ears, eucalyptus to keep off mosquitoes, interviewing women before they set off to gather wood in the jungle or work in the tile factory, gathering a few flowers, going off to her tub, and just sitting down to breakfast when three typical Mahars appear in tattered red turbans and earth-stained loin-cloths. The old fellow with a stubble of white on his chin and mat of white hair on his chest advances, "My grand-daughter has been in child-labour for seven days. Will the Mother come, for her hands bring luck?"

I could almost see her jamming on her topi, and getting her bag, and bumping off in the sidecar of her husband's motor bike. "When I got there all the village women were crowding round the door of that smoky little room", she told me. "The dhai, a terrible old crone, was poking up the fire under an earthenware pot for the ceremonial bath after the birth. That poor little mother was lying almost unconscious on a heap of filthy rags. But after an hour or two more of rabble and work the baby did get born, and a son too . . . ".

And I could see her sallying forth, a basket on her arm, mingling with the stream of country folk flowing to the bazaar. Women supporting baskets on their heads with one arm which winked with many glass bangles, chewing betel nut, screaming greetings and jokes to one another. Men driving little donkeys with hens tied insecurely on their backs, slow moving bullock cars in whose dark interior one caught glimpses of faces . . . Yes, I saw it all.

"You see my dear, I gave up a good deal when I came to India", explained Mrs. Brown with that refreshing candour of hers. "So I wanted to make the *best* use of my sacrifice. Of course we could have sent to Belgaum for our European stores, but we felt if we did we should be living much above the people we had come to help. And what could be more helpful to get the real language and idiom of the people than to eat their food, to go to the bazaar, talking to the village women, asking after their families, how far they had walked in, and so on. I would go round where the country folk squatted, their wares spread out on cloths in the road". (I could see them, their eyes screwed up from the sun, their shadows in sharply defined blots; and the sun striking dazzling points of light from tin pots, and nails, and glittering glass bangles and brass rings set out in rows before them). But Mrs. Brown continues: " 'Oh my Mother', cries one woman looking up with a beaming face, 'There is fortune and good luck in your hands. See, he is well. He is *yours*', and she holds up a scrap of a naked baby with great eyes bigger still from the bitumen they are smeared with; and perhaps the next cries, 'I have hidden the finest potatoes, sister, till you should come. No one else must have them'; or, 'Here is a seer of little onions sorted out the same size for your pickles'. I do *love* these people in spite of disappointments and dirt and disease, and dirt, and again dirt. And they love us! Once I overheard Phakira, an old servant, describing us and our ways. 'Yes, they are queer, queer people. They just pray to a Great Spirit. And although they can't see him he sees and hears the Sahib. They have no money. They never beg, and yet their stomachs are filled, and ours are filled too. He is a good master. Yes, they are queer. He sits *here*', pointing to a chair as he laid the table, 'and she sits *here*. He will never sit down till she walks in like a Ranee. Then he holds her chair till she sits, and then he gives thanks to the Spirit, then serves her first'. '*Serves her first*. How can that be?' exclaimed his friend standing in the doorway, shocked at the husband waiting on the wife! 'I have always to show HER the food first', repeated Phakira. 'He is a great man my Sahib. He is a God' ".

Mrs. Brown dramatised it all with her humour, and her infectious laugh and general gusto of life, so that even Father, who puts nonconformists, radicals, drunkards and people who are rude to social inferiors and cruel to animals all in the same category, would have been entertained by her tales, absurd as well as tragic.

Well, she has gone back now, dear woman, enchanted with a few clothes for herself, plants for her beloved garden, toys for the children in the settlement.

Henry was out in district. He has taken old Luther, his very own particular pal. Sowars bring me in letters daily when they bring in stuff for the Office. When he was at Gidar Bunder he was riding through a village followed by a pack of yelping pi dogs. There was a high embankment by the road, and the leader of the pack, a big yellow fellow, almost twice as big as Luther (Sind pi dogs are enormous, like the goats), went in front, and getting on the top of the bank made offensive snarls. Luther charged up the bank, lifted the pi with his shoulder, tossed him into the river Indus, and forged on ahead without even turning his head at the splash. He is a *lad*!

A day or two later, Henry writes Luther is not well. He is troubled about him. He thinks of sending him in on the condition I do not attempt to nurse him. And then, *Luther is dead.*

(Hyder Khan let out a year or more later that Henry had to shoot old Luther himself, he was in such terrible pain, on account of a snake bite he thought, and that the tears ran down the Sahib's face as he did it).

Meanwhile I was convalescent, and Lep had given birth to another thirteen puppies. For some reason or other my legs and thighs had become enormously swollen. Monstrous. "Typhoid legs", announced Nurse H., "That's how I got mine. Getting up too soon after typhoid".

She, poor soul, could hardly waddle, suffering terribly from elephantiasis which she chose to call "typhoid legs". "You must lie up and let me do everything for you". Unfortunately Sister M. also wanted to do everything for me.

These women, kindly capable nurses both, were tragic figures fighting for existence. Sister M. was a Eurasian, not bad looking, but with the hyper-sensitiveness of her kind, and with serious and increasing deafness. Nurse H. was pure European, and so looked down on her senior. Already her legs were as thick as a child's body, and her medical training must have warned her that amputation might have to be resorted to. To be at Government House gave these two dissimilar women kudos. Also there were servants to wait on them, airy pleasant surroundings, practically nothing to do. Me they regarded with romantic sentimental affection. Husband, child, position. To them a sort of fairy princess. Why should they leave when they could minister to me? Here, Nurse M. need not strain her ears. Nurse H. as night nurse could lie on her bed all day, and rest her legs all night. How could I tell her that it was her carefully shaded light, her starched apron, the turning of her pages, and too often her snores that were giving me such poor nights? To send these women away was like pushing two drowning people off my raft. I was in no shape to do this in my present weakness.

Yet I felt Henry was paying out needless sums of money each week.

"If you put your legs down you will get "typhoid legs like me", warned Nurse H. every day. I did not really believe her, and yet, supposing?

I had a wheeled chair in which I could trundle myself by my arms about my bedroom, sitting room, and on to the verandah where Owen played, whirling the dirzi's machine. The P.W.D. had managed at last to get the exact shade of sky blue for my sitting room walls, which had so taken my fancy in the Kundunmal School at Hyderabad, where all the little Amil girls in their tight silk trousers and with long liquid eyes had looked like gazelles. Hyder Khan had put up the pictures I brought from Belgaum. Over the door is the almost lifesize one I did of Luther. He stands out startling white against a plain dark background; Lucy Locket came in, looked up, saw it, growled, all the hair on her back rising; Lubin the same. He began to bark furiously. Strange! I had always understood animals could not "see" pictures.

Twice a day my legs were fastened up into cylinders and steamed. It was very hot anyway, and the sweat used to trickle down my face and off the ends of my long plaits, and all the while I felt the one thing that would cure me was to bathe in the sea. I was obsessed by memories of Buckers Rock at Culdaff. I could see in fancy the waters like ginger-beer surging round Buckers Rock, lifting and sinking purple tresses of sea weed . . .

We send horses with hot filled legs to stand in the sea. When I was quite a little girl I remember Father pointing that out to me; and in Bombay don't the race-horses and the polo ponies stand in the waves? Don't we send Leviathan and the other two down to Clifton?

I tell Henry I KNOW bathing would cure me. He is no respector of doctors. In fact he goes too far, and does not give them the benefit of experience which even the stupidest must have over oneself. If the sea would do me good, and I can't go to the sea, then the sea must come to me, he declares. Lot is sent down in the dog cart morning and evening to Clifton returning with great glass containers full of sea water. Dear Tulsi, her seamed brown face beaming with happiness is admitted at last. Squatting on her hunkers she bathes my thighs with iced sea water rhythmically for an hour at a time, twice a day. Slowly the swelling subsides. Like the horses I am cured.

When will doctors realise it is often the patient who knows what cures him? I remember Mother as a young girl telling me that she had, when living in Paris, a friend with consumption. This poor girl used to implore the doctors to let her have an open window, feeling it would help her breathing. Naturally at that time it was considered madness. Mother remembered a long suffocating journey to Italy with the windows kept rigidly closed because of poor Virginie. In the light of present knowledge she had often thought of the young French girl, and her piteous appeals for air.

Apropos of doctor's mistakes, I am reminded of one of Henry's tales. For some obscure reason, characteristic enough of his original and unpredictable turn of mind, he had decided to attend a Sikh religious conference at Hyderabad. There in a huge shamiana he squatted on the ground amongst perhaps a thousand of the faithful, their beards all enmeshed in silken nets. Amongst them however there was another Englishman, or rather a Scot, a red-headed raw-boned giant who Henry discovered was a district officer from the Punjab, either already a Sikh, or on the verge of initiation. It appeared he had once been taken very seriously ill when out in camp. The doctor had ridden out and told the bearer that the Sahib could not possibly live through the next twenty-four hours, and to get a coffin made. The following morning Mr. MacAuliffe was still alive though barely conscious. Outside his tent we heard what we all hear in India if we have to be called at dawn for a train, a shoot, or something equally important. "Sa . . . hib. Sa . . . hib!" in a low voice repeated over and over again regular as the ticking of a clock.

It penetrated through the sick man's semi-consciousness.

"*Kya hai?*" he asked weakly.

"*Sahib ka daffan, Sahib ka barkus aya*" (Sahib's cemetery-box come).

At the sight of his own coffin outside the flap of the tent MacAuliffe sprang from his bed reaching out for his khansamah in fury . . . and did not die.

But to return. My two nurses went on hating each other to the end. Poor Sister M. with her dark skin and increasing deafness. What will happen to you? And Nurse H., always in pain and becoming more and more crippled by those monstrous legs. Who will look after you? What will you live on?

The next step. I was weak as a kitten, but I KNEW I should get better if I went for a ride on Leviathan. Everyone in Karachi, and many in Sind and elsewhere know Leviathan. He is almost thoroughbred, 17 hands, jet black with a bang tail like a race horse. He rears, he bolts, but not with me—at least not to matter. Old Dr. Nazareth who is far more understanding than most doctors, says yes, I may ride him just for a few minutes.

Henry is away, but Mir Khan the sowar will be there. Almost trembling with excitement I come out on the steps in my starched white habit, hanging now so loosely on me. There is my darling, my beautiful Leviathan, his satin coat, his bright full eye, and the little Sindi necklace of sky-blue beads and gilt lockets, and rose and purple silk pompoms. I kiss his nose, and blow in his nostrils and do all the silly things one does do to a much loved horse. Mir Khan puts me up and we pace slowly down the drive past the morning glories, and the pink oleanders, and our printing press, out through the gates, past the Frere Hall, over the level crossing and on to the soft sand by the side of the road, Leviathan's tail swishing from hock to hock. I had said I would be satisfied with a few minutes, and not to go out of a walk that first day. But Leviathan, feeling the soft loose sand under his hoofs, remembered our gallops. He shook his head, whinneyed, half reared, and with one gigantic bound almost unseating me, was away. For a few seconds glorious. That strong elastic stride, that give and take of the bridle, and then the sudden hard tightening down into a hand gallop. Then I realised how weak I was. Already terribly, terribly out of breath. The charging wind from the sea tore the words from my mouth as I tried to soothe the wildly excited horse. Parsi ladies driving back from Clifton in their victorias half rose to stare after us as we thundered by. The sand stinging my face half blinded me. Mir Khan on his white Arab was left far behind, but Leviathan was determined to leave him farther yet! Now I was so exhausted I might roll out of the saddle any moment. I was clutching on to the pommel, my double bridle all in a mess, the breath pumping out of me . . . He might pull up at the end . . . he *might* . . .

"S-S-Stead . . . y my . . . Boy. St . . . eady . . . ".

Leviathan did pull up trembling and blown, the veins big on his neck, soapsuds everywhere. Mir Khan came up. "*Memsahib bahut jaldi gaia*", he exclaimed in anxious, half-reproachful tones.

I could just manage a guilty sort of smile to imply the gallop was intended. It was better to have it thought that I had disobeyed orders, than that Leviathan had bolted. It was not vice. Just sheer joy at having me on his back again. But who would believe that? For Leviathan did bolt with men. With me it was just at times he would "take charge" but with no vice.

Nobody ever knew. And Leviathan did lift me right out of that sick-room atmosphere of boredom and jealous nurses on to my own plane of busy, delightful life.

Note added in 1945.

My beautiful Leviathan. Twenty-seven years ago. Yet how often I dream of you. Always the same dream. For months you have stood in your stall for some reason forgotten. But to-day I will ride. Conscience-stricken I wait for you to be brought round. But what is this? An enormous gaunt horse moving towards me with wagging tail and the stiff tied gait of old age, deep hollows above the sunken lustreless eyes. Psychologists explain.

April 24th, 1917.

Owen is a year old and gives a fancy dress party. Eighteen babies and little children come with their mothers and ayahs and nurses—tiny peach-skin fairies, butterflies, columbines, dewy flowers, and so forth. Owen is a water baby. The dirzi has sewn the smallest browny-pink shells and sea weed on the scrap of pale green chiffon he wears. He has always meant "Inishowen" to me, with its rocks, its swinging green crystal seas. At Belgaum I had prepared his nursery to look like a sea-cave. There were swooping sea gulls, and silvery fish, and now to-day the dining room looks under the sea. The pale green walls with the light filtering through the palms on the verandah always have an aqueous light anyhow, and in the middle of the long table is a great aquarium alive and darting with gold and silver fish, trails of green creeper about it. Instead of a plate each child has a large flat mother-of-pearl shell from the Gulf set before it, and suspended over their enchanted heads sways and swims an immense jointed paper fish some fourteen feet long which Hyder Khan caused to be made at the Japanese shop. It has electric lights inside it, and realistically it dips and sways in the breeze from the overhead fans. The servants and pattawallas have entered into it all as only Indians can. The malis have turned Owen's high chair into a sort of throne with green creepers, very delicate and light looking. Sir Charles Napier from the wall looks down at all these little golden and brown heads, these excited upturned faces as they gaze enchanted at the paper fish floating above them. He adored children, and they him.

How different the impatient "Incessantly have I been worried to go to balls, parties and dances. Charlatanry. Quackery—effusions of fish and folly" from the sad "I doted on that little child. I would have given my own life for him. And now he is gone".

An odd and depressing thought to reflect on the ephemerality of these flower-like, butterfly-like little creatures! These transparent eyes with their blue-whites, the silkiness of these curls, the little round milk-white teeth, the dimpled loveliness of these tiny hands will some day belong to some old gentleman with corns and bunions and a pendulous belly, or some scraggy old woman with stringy neck and a moustache. Old age is so rarely beautiful out of books.

April 28th.

H. showed me to-day this letter which came when I was ill:

> February 22nd, 1917.
> My dear Lawrence,
> You will remember that I spoke the other day about the extracts from the old Punjab Records which have just been published in ten volumes. I am having a copy sent to you from Lahore which His Honour hopes you will accept with the compliments of the Punjab Government to a distinguished scion of the Lawrence family.
> Yours sincerely,
> J. F. THOMPSON.

(The Lieutenant-Governor, Sir Michael O'Dwyer, is called His Honour, not His Excellency).

Government House, Karachi, April, 1917.

Thanks to Mrs. Brown's moral courage the G's. baby is not going to die. It has even begun to put on a little weight.

The G's. used to be at Belgaum. I knew them of course, but we had not very much in common beyond a great love of dahlias. They were full of health fads, yet in spite of this, or because of this, were perpetually ailing, and the small boy was sickly and puny. Amongst other things Mrs. G. was convinced everyone ate too much. Just before Owen and I left Belgaum another baby had arrived, and soon afterwards they were transferred up here. The new baby, a pretty little girl, failed to put on weight as she should, and before long, to everybody's distress began to lose. It was pathetic to see her becoming transparent. She looked like a green-veined snowdrop. Her mother refused to call in a doctor. She was a firm believer in plenty of distilled water. The baby had a bottle of this always in its pram to suck at will. She became a "water addict". The teat was never out of her mouth, her tiny frail hand resting on the bottle. Nanny, in horrified tones told me she was now no heavier than at birth.

Mrs. Brown had been very friendly with the G's. when they were stationed at Belgaum, so soon after arriving in Karachi she went off to see them. I warned her how distressed everyone was, watching the baby dwindling day by day. She came back raging, and half crying. She said she must pray for guidance as to what she should do. That evening she left me to the nurses and went early to her room. The following morning she went off to Mrs. G. and said bluntly. "You are a wicked woman not sending for a doctor. That child is going to die and you her mother will have murdered her with your ridiculous theories". Naturally Mrs. G. was furious. Undaunted Mrs. Brown went on for she had prayed "for guidance" and this was what she had been told to do. She declared the child was being starved to death. Given proper nourishment even now it might not be too late. There might be a slender chance of saving its life. If she, Mrs. Brown, were given an absolutely free hand she would do her best to fight for its life.

Well, Mrs. G. gave in at last. The constant drinking of distilled water was stopped, and the child began to take a proper feed instead. It is now putting on weight.

Mrs. Brown came back from that interview shaking all over.

"I said dreadful things. Dreadful. I don't know how she ever will forgive me. But I was fighting for that little lamb's life. It was the only way".

Karachi, June, 1917.

At Belgaum the monsoon has broken. The rain thrashing down, the earth smelling like a hot-house freshly watered. "One deep calleth to another because of the noise of the water pipes: all thy waves and storms are gone over me". The psalmist might have written that of Belgaum in the monsoon. But here, though gloomy bellying clouds continue to pass rapidly as though on a slide over our heads, not a drop falls on the parched, pallid land beneath. (Sometimes rain does not fall in Karachi for three years, sometimes for five). It is dark. Always a strong wind, sometimes in gusty squalls. Shutters rattling and banging, vases blowing over, the newspapers scurrying down the verandah pursued by perspiring pattawallas. Yet it is not hot. That persistent wind is cool. In fact I am often chilly, though the clothes stick to one's back, and there are beads of perspiration on every face owing to the intense humidity. Health is good enough, though some of the men are afflicted with persistent boils. It is an unbecoming time for all. The wind blows the women's hair all ways, our faces are the colour of candles, and because to powder is not possible they gleam like candles too. That dewy peachlike bloom on the faces of the children at Owen's party has faded away. The little creatures are the colour of tallow, and my once lovely Owen has bruises under his eyes. For there is something in this monsoon air that drains all colour away. Even the mules in the mule depot who came from South America have lost their rich black and brown coats and are bleached to dun. These mules deserve a book to themselves. Those who have to do with them get much attached to them in spite of their devilry. The poor brutes were practically blind when they came out of the ships' holds. It was touching to see them rolling on the sands, at Keamari, squealing with mad delight at freedom again.

Frankly I find Karachi in the monsoon detestable. I feel like a lump of sugar slowly disintegrating in a tumbler of water. Maybe I should have gone for a change after typhoid as Dr. Nazareth suggested. But how possible with so many threads in one's hands?

There is talk that Nanny and Owen and I might go to Ziarat in Baluchistan, but there is a good deal of unrest with the tribesmen there and it may not be safe.

Undated.

We have hatched out a baby crocodile. He was an inch or two longer than the egg in which Nature had packed him. He is able to take care of himself immediately. We were told he would snap angrily when just emerged from the egg. He did. This baby, swimming vigorously round the footbath in which we put him, at once attacked a stick Henry thrust into the water.

The Bridegroom and the Pir.

In the desert you may come across tall poles surmounted by the glittering Crescent and Star, and kept upright by radiating cords from which flutter innumerable bright rags, votive offerings from the faithful. These poles usually mark the tomb of a Pir or Holy Man, and a descendant or follower has taken up his quarters as custodian of the tomb. I was riding past one of these this morning under a lowering monsoon sky, the flies buzzing round my head, when I heard a terrific din and saw a brilliant crowd approaching. Mir Khan, pressing up on his Arab, explained it was a bridegroom visiting the Pir. We pulled up to watch them go by.

The bridegroom was seated on a little chestnut tat with gay feathers between its ears, and choker necklace of cowries and beads. The bridegroom himself was wrapped in an orange blanket and carried a green umbrella. Before him danced backwards a negro striking a tabla with both hands, and all round surged and danced and tom-tomed and piped a great crowd of men and women in the most brilliant colouring. Rose and turquoise, pea-green, magenta and vermilion; which last seemed the embodiment of the squealing pipes and shouts and cries and tomtoming. Somehow this flickering, jigging kaleidoscope of colour seemed even more brilliant under those dark monsoon skies than had it been on a sunny day.

There was something biblical about it all. The words shawms and sackbuts and cymbals came to mind, and memories of little pictures from that Book of one's childhood. Line upon line.

Anyway it was a cheerful scene, and whatever miseries of poverty and sickness, failure of crops, and rapacious moneylenders lie ahead for that bridegroom, this was a happy hour for a great concourse of people . . . and me.

The Flagstaffs

There are now two flagstaffs in front of Government House, Karachi. The very tall one flying the Union Jack and the very small one flying a Sindi flag of bright appliqué calico patterns such as you see on the Pir's tombs. The pattawallas felt that the "Chota Sahib" ("the little Sahib") must have a flag to show he is in residence, the same as the "Bara Sahib". It is their own idea and they have erected this. Owen helps to run down the two flags at sundown.

Certainly Indians have a genius for amusing children.

Government House, August, 1917.

Karachi prides itself on yachting during the monsoon, whereas Bombay contents itself with merely racing in the safer cold weather. The "tomtits" frequently upset. Mr. Crouch interests himself with fervour. He takes me out . . . I hold the stop-watch for the start . . . but I prefer riding in the desert to clinging for my life to a "tomtit", ducking from the boom, drenched in water, and feeling rather sick, and even a little scared at the thought of being trapped beneath the sail.

To-day Henry and I crossed the almost dry bed of the Lyari and motored out over the desert to Magar Pir. The low monsoon clouds dark as mulberries were sliding in rapidly from the coast, sagging so deeply it seemed as though torrents must burst from their bellies. This way and that spread the pale sand, and even the clumps of prickly pear, and many-fingered milk-bush were tones lighter than the sky.

Out here queer volcanic-looking hills stick abruptly out of the desert, and between them you see triangles of further pale sand, and milk bush. There are hot springs here, and pilgrims come for miles to be cured of skin, and other diseases . . . But we have come to look at the magars. Henry has warned me I shall be sickened. I am.

There is a grove of date palms and other trees, perfect illustration for a child of the word "oasis". In them is a swamp full of little islets intersected by channels of slimy jade-green water. These little channels are blocked and crossed by what appear to be tree trunks or sand banks, but on coming closer are seen to be gorged crocodiles. There is something quite disgusting about their number, their sluggish evil appearance with half-closed eyes, quite apart from the loathsome smell, and the bunches of black flies settling on them. Instantly I remember how Father always declares that snakes have a peculiarly loathsome smell for him. I feel the same about these magars. Later beggars with horrible skin diseases clustered round us thrusting almost in one's face limbs covered with sores, or rotting with leprosy, but they were not so disgusting as those lethargic sacred crocodiles, that stagnant green water, and the buzzing clusters of black flies.

Coming home, the charging wind in our faces, we passed two beautiful old golden Sindi tombs, rich with carving, bare rocky hills rising abruptly behind them. Louise's tomb was prompted by such as these.

A few miles from the city out in the desert is the Gaol. We were riding past this evening when we saw the big "Black Maria" bumping over the sandy track, and a holloaing figure running behind—a prisoner having "missed the bus!" It amused me, though it did not surprise, for it is quite a usual thing to see convicts in irons being taken from one prison to another sitting under trees, smoking bidis and playing cards in the most friendly way with their guards.

But the sight of this man reminded me of rather a touching story Mr. Crouch told me of this very gaol the other day. It seems there was an old peasant serving a life imprisonment for murder. Not long ago he was released, having been in prison for twenty years. He made his way home only to find that his house had long been pulled down, and no trace of any of his people remained. Wandering back to the gaol he implored them to take him in again. There was no place for him in the world, and he missed the gaol flowers he had tended for so long. They were sorry for the old man but explained they could not take him back. However, some kindly disposed official suggested to him it might be possible perhaps to get re-arrested on some charge or other. The old fellow went back to the city, broke a window, and triumphantly returned to his only "Home", where I am glad to say he is to stay employed as mali for the rest of his life.

Riding in the desert I'm constantly wanting my painting things. Last night the sandstone rock breaking through the sand in horizontal shelves, had glowed like nasturtiums, and racing alongside the mail train we had galloped into the sunset through sand scintillating like rosy fire! Henry had promised me, though, that Kalu should run me out into the desert this evening to sketch. And now, of course, no light. Flat. Dark. A breathless ominous evening. Every breath you take like drawing a bucket out of a well . . . But it is better to seize the car while I can, so seldom can Henry spare it. Umar sits alongside of Kalu to carry my easel and painting things. Umar is the old pattawalla who always keeps in the background. He has a white beard dyed a fiery red with henna. Lep and Lubin clamber in with me at the back. We go out past the gaol along the track patterned by the cushiony pads of camels. We pass flocks of goats, goats quite different from Dekkan goats. Large high-standing creatures like calves, with very small heads with Roman noses, and ears of absurd length dangling on either side. A mournful evening. Mournful pallid sands lying supine beneath mournful black cloud. Sage green clumps of prickly pear striking conventional attitudes of woe with uplifted palms . . .

Leaving the car Umar and the dogs and I plough sweating through loose sand up to Louise's tomb lifted pale and solemn against the dark sky. For once the wind has dropped. Not a dry thread on me. An ugly evening, an uninspiring evening. I'm defeated before I begin. It is so hot my hand sticks to the paper, the air is so saturated with moisture nothing will dry. Everything is running in a mess: the legs of my camp stool sink deeper in the sand. There is a deathly silence broken only by the buzz of flies round my head, and the snicking jaws of the dogs as they snap at the flies buzzing round them. Exasperated I pack up and tell Umar to take my stuff down to Kalu waiting there half a mile below. Then turning to the East I am startled, confronted by the truly awful apparition of a cloud which has reared itself up and seems about to topple over on top of me. Here at last is inspiration. Snatching up a fresh Whatman board and my palette I send Umar on with the dogs saying I shall follow in a minute or two.

At that moment from beneath a lid of cloud, the sun low in the West suddenly stares out illuminating all the desert in an unearthly glare, picking out the little figures of Umar and the bull-terriers approaching the waiting car. And in the East it lights up a little blur of gold at the base of the toppling black cloud. Even as I watch this little blur of gold seems to be growing. Fascinated I stare. It is rising like incense against that cloud which now is black as ink. The gold is rising and rolling as it rises. It seems to be boiling up to the very zenith. Unexpectedly I am all at once TERRIFIED. Snatching up my things I begin floundering and running down hill through the loose sand, fast as I can. The heat, the stillness is frightful. Something is going to happen. I see Kalu standing there beside the bonnet of the car. Then the two bull-terriers make a sudden bolt and leap over the unopened door, and at that moment the car begins to move apparently of its own volition. I see Umar turning back to me . . . an appalling noise. I'm on the ground. I can't breathe . . . I can't get up . . . Everything is quite black . . . I'm choking, I'm being beaten . . . I gasp . . . I try to get on my knees . . . I am forced down. What is it? WHAT IS IT? Is it the end of the world?

Seconds? Minutes? I don't know. Gradually breathing becomes easier, the weight lifts off my body. It is becoming twilight. I struggle again to get up. *"Memsahib tik hai?"* Umar's face is close to mine, but the wind tears the words from his mouth. His dark face is white like a miller's, his red beard white too. Thunder bellows, lightning zig-zags, but now a cold rain is pelting like bullets, and every moment it is getting lighter. Kalu, white from head to foot, is staggering against the wind fighting his way from the car. The two between them help me to the car where the two dogs lie cowering on the floor.

When we get back to Government House the stones rattle out of my clothes all up the marble steps, and along the tiled verandah. Gravel and stones and twigs are embedded in the skin of my scalp so that I cannot help crying out as Tulsi tries to brush my hair. Bloodshot eyes, lashes white, mouth full of grit, skin flayed . . .

Henry had been terribly anxious. Ships had been sunk in the harbour, ticca gharis blown over, houses collapsed . . .

The force of that sudden blow of wind had caused the car to move on, and Kalu had only just had time to jump in and get the brake on more securely. As for Umar, it was thought he had saved my life by dragging me to the ground, and laying his body on mine. I weigh under eight stone now, and the wind in a bad dust storm has the strength of a hundred devils.

Dear brave old fellow.

BALUCHISTAN

August 17th, 1917. Going to Ziarat.

The train crawls across the desert. Outside the black gauze screen and the tightly shut window, sky and desert are fused in blinding light. The coach bumps and lurches, the wind raves, and dust sifts in under the door, drifting in ridges across the floor, lying thick on the table, the chairs, the couches. The skin of my face is tight and my finger tips gritty. We have been travelling since yesterday morning. Nanny and Owen are quiet in the bedroom. Bull-terriers lying outstretched on the bath room floor. Henry and I loll in the saloon. He is in a Roorkee chair, in pyjamas for coolness, reading the crumpled pages of the *Pioneer*. I am blinking out at the incandescent sand and sky through the wire screen.

As a matter of fact it is not too bad. Rain fell last week, and yesterday when we got to Hyderabad it was to find that the Indus had overflowed, and the walls of the great Fort rose from sheets and sheets of water. The desert was miraculously green, and cattle were greedily grazing on little islands lifted above the miles and miles of water. Here in the carriage we have plenty of ice in a zinc bath, and the little overhead fans are playing on a damp sheet stretched across the carriage. Even at Lakhi last night there had been floods, but here on either side of the train there is nothing but dazzling white sand, and the harsh sunlight has drained all colour from the broken rampart of mountains away to our left. It was quite bearable till at Gopang I had stupidly opened a chink of window to throw something to a starving pi dog, and the sizzling heat seemed to flay the very skin off my face, and burning dust and papers scurried across the floor. Henry was not pleased!

But now sheets of water were appearing again, quite close, just as at Lakhi. Lovely in their unexpectedness. And crowding palms, and white buildings.

"Why, what place is this?" I cried out.

"Mirage". Henry didn't look up.

"No! It's water. Quite close as at Hyderabad, and Lakhi".

"Mirage", repeats Henry aggravatingly.

At that moment the train trundles past the skeleton of a camel. White picked bones: the skull a little apart.

Henry looks up. "Poor devil", says he, "So near the water, but just too weak to get there".

But I recognise something mocking in that tone of pity. I look again for the fair sheet of water, the domes, the flat-topped white buildings, and crowding palms.

Just scintillating sand and sky in front, and the hooped ribs of the camel being slowly left in the desert behind us.

Mirage.

In the train. Nearing Sibi. August, 1917.

An expanse of incandescent sand, and far off, yet filling the windows, a towering rampart of hills, drained of all colour. And now towards that rampart over the shimmering dazzle, two or three terrified wild asses galloping away from the train, their shadows brightly blue racing after them.

Nearing Quetta. Cooler!

The miracle of this Harnai railway! The tremendous defiles crossed. We both run from one side of the carriage to the other to miss nothing. Henry marvelling at the engineering feats of Buster Browne, and I at the stoniest Doré-like gorges, cliffs rearing up bare as your hand, the dry torrent bed dizzily deep below.

Added in 1947.

Maud Diver in her "Unsung" has a vivid account of "Buster" Browne, that high-spirited boon companion of British officers and Pathan alike. We read of his passionate love of music, his gift of mimicry. How he would always take more than his share in danger and hardship. How too he would join the wild tribesmen round their camp fires singing their ballads, the only white man amongst them.

How he would sit between the tribesmen each talking a different dialect of Pushtu, and acting as interpreter for them. Who in this generation knows anything of "Buster"? For him, and his predecessor on the Great Trunk Road, Sir Alexander Taylor, I have searched in vain in my encyclopaedia, though names of insignificant Browns and Taylors are recorded there. Yet John Nicholson declared when dying "If I live through this I shall let the whole world know who took Delhi. Taylor did. Remember to tell them Alec Taylor took Delhi".

Ian Hay once wrote: "We all think we know something of India . . . its military life, its official and vice-regal activities . . . but of the men who have built it up, and held it together, we know nothing . . . the men who preserve forests, who build dams, and canals, who cause two blades of rice to grow where one grew before. We take them for granted, and to a great extent they take themselves for granted. That is why we never hear of them. They work behind the scenes, facing emergencies, devising expedients. They see to it that in spite of official vagaries above, and seditious propaganda below, the dams hold, the canals irrigate, the grass grows, and the British Raj endures".

Quetta.

We are five thousand feet above Karachi. In winter the cold is great, so the Residency has fitted carpets, curtains, upholstered furniture, and no overhead electric fans. Even now the nights are cool, although it is the hot weather, but used as Henry and I are to sleeping on the wide and empty verandah under a fan, or, as in the last few weeks, with the strong monsoon wind blowing off the sea, I felt last night at the Residency like a butterfly shut up in a box. Sleep was impossible.

Came along by narrow gauge to Kacch, arriving at the little dak bungalow at sunset. Desolate slate-coloured hills with no trace of vegetation, and between them a narrow road strewn with boulders, and reflecting the bright sky as it coiled in and out to a mountain, silhouetted distant and imposing and blocking the end of the valley.

The usual dak bungalow supper, murghi that had been running about an hour or two before, and "broon custard". Delicious to feel chilly.

Kacch. August 19th, 1917.

Slept under blankets. Delicious. Fresh and excited we left early in a procession of tongas, some with one pony, some with two, but all jingling with bells, driven by cheery handsome youths with tangled black curls falling to their shoulders, and very dirty sheepskin coats. The narrow track covered with loose stones wound up between the barest stoniest cliffs, but gradually tufts of a bushy plant rather like lavender began to appear. It had a strong pungent smell, and is known as *khush bu* (sweet smell). Presently we crossed a wide dry torrent bed. Cleverly the tonga ponies picked their way between the larger rocks, one wheel rising up over a rock, the other grinding down over shale and gravel. Then the first juniper tree appeared. A little Noah's Ark tree with a smell as pungent as the khush bu's. These junipers grew larger and more important as we climbed, the ponies trotting, walking and galloping in turns. The sun was hot. The air deliciously light and thin. We began discarding clothes. A sense of well-being, not experienced for days, pervaded Henry, me, Owen, Nanny, dogs and all! We changed ponies, had tiffin, climbed on changed ponies again and when we finally arrived at the mountain village of Ziarat some 9,000 feet up, the junipers were tall and stately and clothing the steep hills, and the whole floor of the valley was carpeted with waist-high lavender-coloured khush bu, whose fragrance in the sun mingling with that of the junipers was truly intoxicating.

Unseen beyond the immediate crests of the hills, others were rising higher, and there we were told the junipers dwindled again till the tree-line was reached; and on the bare hill tops there was nothing but rocks and stones and spiny humps of prickly plants like hedgehogs, under the sky.

Our tiny bungalow has been lent by the kindness of the Acting Governor-General, Sir Henry Dobbs. It is perched on a small plateau on the hill-side amongst stones and great tufts of khush bu. There is just enough space for a tent or two for the servants. Our kit is dumped down in the dust of the valley road, to be carried up later by coolies past the Acting Governor-General's own bungalow with its walnut trees, and willows, its pleasant little lawns and running streams.

The altitude has given Henry a headache, and he goes to bed. But it invigorates me. I feel grand!

Never shall I forget that first evening.

At day-break little shepherd boys had led their multitudinous flocks out of that mountain valley, up higher still into the clouds, their sandals carrying them securely over rock and loose scree which slid and rattled down behind them. All day they had stayed in the clouds, and now at sundown they were bringing the flocks down again into the valley swimming below them in amber light. We could hear the faint calls of the lads from one side of the valley to the other, crossing over our heads, weaving arabesques of sound in that quivering golden air. Moment by moment these calls grew louder and clearer. We could catch a word or two of Pushtu, and echoes from the gorges tossed them back again and again, so that at last the whole valley was ringing with the sound of voices and the baa-ing of the flocks. Then I understood why it had been said of a little English child brought up in these hills: "It is not only that his eyes gaze always at the horizon, but his voice sounds as though it calls from hill to hill".

As the shadows fell, and it grew chilly the rattle and slide of shale became louder and nearer; the sheep and the lambs, the goats and the kids came trickling down the precipitous slopes on opposite sides of the valley, seeking protection from wolf and hyena, to mingle at last in one immense flock which merged in the twilight. The baa-ing ceased. It grew cold. Then on that silence, in that darkness fell the most poignant cry in the world, the cry of a lamb lost on the hills. Again and again, and yet again. Always unutterably forlorn. No one who has heard it will wonder why Jesus spoke of the lost sheep for parable.

August 20th, 1917.

Henry left this morning.

I'm to share this bungalow with the Wooldridges. Colonel Wooldridge is an old friend of Henry's and is now in Mespot. Mrs. Wooldridge is up here with her daughter Betty. Betty is only fifteen but looks much older. Very tall, and strikingly handsome. Keen on horses, dogs and shooting, and has large well-shaped feet which look larger still in the flat roped-soled shoes everyone wears on these hills.

Here at this tiny Ziarat, Owen, Nanny and I are to spend the next ten weeks.

Ziarat itself is a curious little collection of official buildings. Scattered about the hillside are a few small bungalows for the "politicals". One or two have pleasant little gardens with willows and walnut trees, a scrap of vivid lawn and many roses, hollyhocks and cherry pie. Everywhere the sound of running water. But standing all around, unwelcoming, watching suspiciously, are the stark aloof hills of Baluchistan, of rocks and stones and juniper trees.

Even to the hillmen the Post Office is probably the most important place in Ziarat. Every morning the tonga-walla starts out on his thirty-two mile drive down to Kacch, from where the line goes flashing this way to Persia and that to Karachi. And every evening the dak rattles back into the valley with a last weary canter, bringing letters, and perhaps a visitor from Quetta. Visitors find the little low white Post Office charming, in spite of its corrugated roof, for beside it is a strip of brilliant turf, and the building itself is almost hidden by gigantic sunflowers and slanting strings, up which sky-blue rose and purple convolvulus climb.

Close by grows a ragged juniper in a horse-shoe of white-washed stones. Here on a dusty bit of matting the faithful pray five times a day, standing, kneeling, prostrating, their eyes turned to Mecca. Just beyond in the open space wicked little Baluchi cows loiter. Their teats are so small, no fingers but a Pathan's could grasp them. There is usually a camel or two snarling, showing discoloured teeth, and tall bearded men in long felt coats worn as capes, because the sleeves are sewn up, swagger across to the bania's shop. Groups sit there on their hunkers. There is much guttural talking, and often a snatch of song.

This is where Owen, Nanny and I are to spend the next two months. What a change from the formal life of Karachi, the dinners and receptions, the inspection of schools and hospitals and missions, the endless committees and interruptions, and never sure of having a moment to oneself. Here no prickly heat. Pungent air. Informal meals in a room so tiny one can scarcely squeeze round the table oneself. A great appetite, and the whole day to sketch, to play with Owen, to climb, and the evening to watch the wonderful spectacle of those cliff-like hills on the opposite side of the valley gleaming, not rose, not gold, but shining gilt, terrible in their beauty against the violet East.

(It occurs to me if anyone should ever read this diary how surprised they will be. My India seems so different to other people's India).

August 25th, 1917.

Amusing to see how the altitude affects even the rumbustious bull-terriers. Lubin, Lucy Locket, and stout little Lep and her pups pace solemnly up the tracks, two legs on the same side moving together like a camel's. The hill-men themselves breathe so hard you hear them before they round a corner. These men, almost without exception extraordinarly handsome, have slit the nostrils of their donkeys to aid their breathing. So far it does not seem to have occurred to them to do this to their women to enable them to carry heavier loads. When it does, no doubt they will.

These poor women! Their lot is as hard as the stones and the rock that strew every yard of their path. No sandals for their feet, only sandals for the men. I meet them toiling up these terrific ascents their bare toes clutching on to rock and stone. They are bent almost double from the mussack of water on their back, clutched at by both hands beneath their chin, and round their neck slung before them their youngest child in a shawl. Carrying water, wood and grass, bearing children, beating out the felt coats of their men, what wonder their hair is frowsy, their faces a srough and lined as the bark of a juniper tree?

The women speak only Pushtu, but their men have a slow guttural Urdu, very easy to understand, for the same reason I suppose that it is easier to understand an Englishman speaking French, however fluently, than a Frenchman. In their willingness to enter into conversation with the stranger the hill-men remind me of the Irish peasant.

Sketching this morning I heard the hard breathing that precedes anyone toiling up these tracks. Round the bend came a young bearded Pathan, naked to the waist, blue-black ringlets falling to his shoulders, and one arm linked carelessly round the neck of his donkey. Our conversation went like this:

"*Salaam Memsahib. Salaam*! From what country do you come? Your husband is doubtless a *Bara Sahib*. How many sons have you? One; and two by another wife? *Shabash*! Well done! Why did you leave your country of Sind where your husband holds high office? Because of fever? Ah! Sind is an evil country".

He edged closer . . . too close . . . looking over my shoulder.

"Why do you apply paint to clean paper after this fashion?"

I explain I am painting the hills.

Genuine astonishment I feel is breaking over those handsome features behind me.

"*Kuch faida kya hai*? For what profit?"

At first this seems unanswerable. Then I remember that time when going through the Roz Marra with Munshi in Belgaum I had failed to recognise the letter alif with so many twists and twirls and flourishes and Munshi had explained "The writer has put those in for beauty's sake".

So now I tell my Pathan I'm painting these hills for "beauty's sake".

His face clears immediately.

"*Beshak.* Doubtless! Sind is an evil land but here the mountains are beautiful. And the water and the air completely good. From the juniper trees, and from the flowers a sweet smell comes out. *Khuda ka Mulk,* God's country".

The wild lavender loosens its scent on my skirt, my shoes, my hands, and even on the dogs' limbs.

There's a difference in each day. Nothing stale. Wish Henry were up here.

August 28th, 1917.

I could laugh when I remember there had been some talk of my bringing Leviathan. We thread our way along three footpaths with shadowy abysses below and sheer perpendicular rock above. The valley road strewn with loose stones, going down to Kacch thirty miles away, is the only place I could have ridden him.

The air is so thin here one is liable to sunstroke. Betty has a touch of the sun. She should be playing hockey and studying for her Oxford and Cambridge, but owing to the war her mother brought her out here . She is alternately rude, affectionate, inconsiderate, and even given to tears. At first I am astounded. Then it was like being in mid-stream and seeing both banks . . . for I recognise I had acted in precisely the same way with my own mother, and that her solicitude when I was unwell roused in me such savage self-consciousness it could only find relief in temper. Hating myself, my rudeness, and temper I yet persisted in them. Probably it is the same with all adolescents. I sympathise with Betty as much as with her mother. She is certainly a most beautiful girl with fine eyes and teeth, and a glowing complexion. Both she and her mother are very friendly to me and charming to Owen, and the dogs. I realise now, without knowing it I have missed the close companionship of women. Clothes-talks, and needlework, etc.

Ziarat started as a convalescent camp for troops from Quetta, but the altitude was found unsuitable. Then various mothers came up to have their babies, but the babies found difficulty in breathing, and one died, so that too was stopped. Now it is the delightful summer residence of the A.G.G. and "politicals". The "politicals", if cliquey, are friendly. With these tiny bungalows in such demand, well might they have resented me butting in from another province. Nothing of the sort. Sir Henry Dobbs is not in residence, but the Maconechies and Chevenix-Trench and others are all that is kind, and see we get supplies of wood for burning and cooking, milk, fruit and vegetables through the Tahsildar. We even have a little house woven for us out of juniper.

The children here have donkeys and ponies with panniers or ring-saddles, but I feel Owen at fourteen months is too young for this. His devoted pattawalla Hassan Shah carries him everywhere.

August 29th, 1917.

Owen's first picnic. We went to Karby Kacch. A deep narrow tangi down which flowed a little stream babbling pleasantly. Mrs. Wooldridge was packing up the tea baskets, and I hastily sketched the Pathan chokidar who watched her interestedly. He sat there, a magnificent eagle-like man in creamy draperies, and a carelessly tied mustard-coloured turban with a long end, two glossy corkscrew curls falling on to his breast. A brass bound jezail was held loosely in the dark small hands lying across his knees.

Mrs. Wooldridge, without thinking, looked up and offered him a bottle of soda water.

"Memsahib, why should I drink Man's water from a bottle when God's water is running at my feet?" was his dignified reply.

Why indeed?

This place should be called *khush-bu,* not Ziarat, for everything smells. It is not just the wild lavender which the tribesmen bruise idly in their fingers as they pass, the wild lavender whose aromatic odour clings to my skirt and the limbs of the bull-terriers; nor just the green of the juniper which smells like hot blackberries in the sun, and its splintered bark like cedar wood, but *everything* smells—the sweet briar plucked at by the goats, the little wild white roses, the honeysuckle, the mignonette and cherry-pie from the little gardens, the thyme and mint, and a dozen other humble little plants the Pathan crushes with his sandal. And all these clean smells mingle on the wandering mountain airs, and are refreshed by thunderstorms each afternoon. Never before had I realised the delight one receives from this sense of smell. It rises like a golden cloud behind the backs of your eyes. Intoxicating. Inextricably mixed up with the flashing magpies, the bold hills and acute gorges, the evening voices of the shepherds and their flocks . . .

The faith of the people is Islam of course. Austere: reflecting the landscape about them, and those hills which do not please so much as inspire awe. In the South the teeming multiplicity of animal, bird, and vegetation had been reflected in those tortuous temple carvings where monkeys, gods, palms, tigers, elephants and wild boars are combined in one pattern. Those carvings whether they be in stone, or silver, or blackwood and sandal-wood seem an expression of Hindu thought, not merely of the superstitious faith of the ryot in his polytheistic worship, in trees, cities, hills, streams, tools of husbandry, and so forth, but also of the highly complex religious thought of the educated Brahmin.

But here all is hard, simple, bare. The ragged juniper, the ferocity of the precipice, the beak of the raven, these are suited to the circle of stones on the mountain side, where the Pathan, taking off his sandals, steps in to pray.

The trees alone cry out this difference. Compare those trees we used to ride by in the jungle, wrapped around, enslaved, strangled by some fig parasite, with these grand old patriarchs on the cliff defying frost and snow, lightning and earthquake for centuries. Tearing torrents have washed the earth from their roots, so that thus exposed they look like the fingers of a man clenched in agony. At times through the topmost greenery is thrust a single upright limb like a bared sword. And what is the dreadful secret of those stark junipers, white as bone? You see them on some high spot against a diamond blue sky the mountain wind shrilling through their nakedness, or gleaming out from the black shadows of a tangi like a tree of white coral, and the words spring to one's mind:

> *"I am the master of my fate*
> *I am the captain of my soul".*

September, 1917.

At the humble little Zenana hospital I heard an extraordinary story this evening.

Two or three years back they had as in-patients the wife of a tribesman and her baby, both with shocking wounds. The woman had come down into the valley to get something for her baby's cough. She took the mixture back in an empty soda-water bottle. The baby she carried in the usual fashion of these hill-women, that is slung in a cloth from her neck, bumping against her breasts at every step, while on her back was the mussack, taut with water, which is invariably carried by any returning from the valley. It was already turning cold in the evenings and I can picture her trudging up the little track past our bungalow grunting and sniffing loudly, the breath bursting from her open mouth so that it hung like smoke on the frosty air. At the top of the track you are confronted by an abyss across which you look to precipitous slopes, and higher hills rising into the sky. The woman was therefore compelled to turn sharp left onto a narrow track cut by the P.W.D. from the side of the bluff which rose many hundreds of feet above her. It was merely the pipe-line bringing water used in the bungalows, from a spring farther up the tangi, but the Pathans and the rest of us (except those with indifferent heads) use it as a path. The bristling face of the rock touched her left shoulder now and again, while her right foot trod at the very edge of the khad, dropping away to the torrent far, far below. The hill woman followed this track which is all in shadow at sunset, though the summit far above gleams an unnatural gilt. She followed it past the little locked well-house where the grass round is soggy and bright with forget-me-nots, and then she branched off into another tangi. I know it. It is gloomy, and very steep. Stones and long knotty roots of juniper reach across the path. It was growing dark. Out of the shadows ahead stepped another shadow. A wolf.

Why this wolf should instantly spring to attack the child is not known. It ripped the mother's chola down and tore at the clothing holding the baby. Screaming in fear and desperation the woman flung the baby from her over the khad, where it caught on to one of those little prickly bushes.Then the wolf attacked the woman herself . . . At that moment some youths came racing along the pipe-line shouting and singing to keep away evil spirits as they often do. The wolf hearing them sheered off. Attracted by the shrieks the Pathans found the unfortunate creature, her hands and face dripping with blood. The baby was extricated from the bush down the khad, and mother and child were got down to the Zenana mission. Both eventually recovered. This was the story I was told this evening at the Mission. I was also told that if a wolf loses her own cub, she will sometimes seek out a child, and suckle it and gambol with it as her own. I was assured by those whom I must believe, that a few years ago one of these wolf-children was to be seen in Quetta. It went on all fours, it had corns on its hands and knees. The wolf mother had given of her own milk, and had finally lost her life in trying to keep it for her own.

There are many Christ-like faces in these hills. Yesterday I met a dark golden figure walking towards me out of a smoky golden sunset. And as he drew near I saw that his features were the features of the Good Shepherd, and over his shoulder was a lost lamb, its long hind legs hanging. And though the sun was set the after-glow traced a golden halo round his head.

That is not to say that there are not evil faces too, wild, passionate and even murderous. But scarcely a man you meet, whether he is an old patriarch with creamy beard and hawk-like eyes, or whether he is some golden lad naked to the waist whose tousled curls rest on his shoulders, or yet again some older man in the prime of life, his black puggaree looped about his ears and neck, and across his bearded mouth, so that you see little but the aquiline nose and the bold glance, whichever of these he is he will share that wild animal grace, that almost insolent beauty which seems the birth-right of these hill men.

But as Sir Charles Napier said years ago, "The women are scarcely human".

The three of us have long been planning to climb Sut, 11,000 feet.

To-day we set out meaning to ride on hill ponies. Mine is a bright chestnut with a wall eye, so tiny and with such a narrow chest that both his front legs seem to come out of the same hole. I feel ashamed crossing my legs over the hard native saddle clamped tightly on to such narrow little sides! But my pony is full of heart, and when we gain the comparatively flat "pipe-line" all three little rats break into a canter. Now this is all very well for Betty and Mrs. Wooldridge who not only always ride but also hunt astride; but the pipe-line is about three feet in width (less in places) and it occurs to me, riding merely by balance as I am, that if I duck too abruptly from a projecting rock or thorny bush, or if my pony crosses his legs, we shall inevitably go over the khad together.

We pass the little locked well-house. The forget-me-nots are all dead, but the hoopoes are still there, and traces of the picnic fires of the baba log, the baby people, who had picnicked there with their ayahs and nurses. We turn up the tangi where the hill-woman had struggled with the wolf, on and on, higher and higher, steeper and steeper, twisting our fingers in the ponies rough manes to prevent the saddles slipping over their tails! Gradually the junipers become more and more dwarfed till at length we are above the tree line altogether. There is nothing here but great boulders and prickly thorny plants, and the hills rising up all around. The ponies are amazing, never making a mistake. Sometimes their four little hoofs have to bunch on one small rocking stone. The only sound is the scattering of the stones from their hoofs, the swish of their tails, the sound of their breathing. They are beginning to get distressed. We dismount, and, leaving them, climb these last few hundred yards. The mountain air is so thin and shrill it seems more like an evaporation than something to breathe with. We ourselves are now terribly out of breath. It is an effort to put one leg before another. We can only take a few steps for the pounding of our hearts. Will the top never come?

It is only a few feet away but seems impossible to reach . . . but we are there! Khilafat before us soaring in the clouds in magical isolation. But we scarcely look, for our one idea is to sit down to ease the ache in our legs, and to regain our breath; but the "hedgehogs" of spiny growth are humped so cruelly close together there is nowhere to sit! Here and there are scattered the ivory and black quills of porcupines. Mrs. Wooldridge is seized with mountain sickness. As soon as she is sufficiently recovered we are thankful to get down to the ponies without looking any more at Khilafat down which clouds are creeping. After all we are only four hundred and fifteen feet lower ourselves.

It was nearly dark when we reached the "pipe-line", and very cold. The air stiff with frost, every bush numb. A kind of madness seized us and the ponies too. We galloped along that little winding three foot track with the black abyss on one side of us, and the bluff with its projecting rocks and thorny bushes on the other, singing, shouting with *joie de vivre.* I felt as though I had ridden astride all my life, though as a matter of fact the slightest peck of the pony would probably have sent me flying! . . . and there at our little bungalow Owen eating bread and milk in front of a crackling juniper blaze, his cheeks like poppies, and Nanny waiting to hear about our day, and the bull-terriers shoving around and whacking our legs with sterns like sjamboks.

October, 1917.

Till the beginning of September, afternoons had clouded over at about four o'clock, and heavy rain had fallen for half an hour or so. The temperature dropped perceptibly, thunder growled in clouds hiding Khilafat, and for a time the valley lay wet and dark, between hills featureless but blue as bright delphiniums. But then the sun would break through again, dyeing the stones in the torrent bed and flooding the whole valley in light.

But that is all changed. Now the days are cold and glittering, the nights numb. The politicals have all gone. The little bungalows shut up till next April, for Ziarat will be under snow in a month or two. Already the little streams running down the hills are silent by morning. The flocks have moved down to their winter quarters. The Wooldridges and I linger on, but supplies of wood and milk are getting very difficult. The Tahsildar will go down the hill next week, and the Pathans themselves soon after. Everything is taking on an exaggerated clearness. The hills are glittering blue glass by day, and at sunset they almost terrify by their brilliance against that pure emerald sky. The lavender carpeting the valley is long dead and mummied. Birds seem to have vanished, except the ravens looking bigger, blacker than ever as they beat heavily off some dead juniper branch. "Kor-rok kor-rok".

Owen has come on wonderfully these two months in the hills. He runs now, and is brimful of intelligence. Apple-blossom skin deepening to poppy in front of our wood fires, enormous dark eyes and a cloud of silvery hair. He still has a bottle the last thing, and it is amusing to watch him placing one finger with an air of great importance on the valve at the opposite end to promote an easier flow. He found this out for himself.

I wonder what Lady Willingdon would think of him now! Before, she had described him as a "Vision of Loveliness". Someone else had said, "You always give your animals names beginning with L. You should have called Owen "Lovely"; and dear old Doctor Nazareth maintained "he is the picture of what a beautiful healthy English child should be".

Both Henry's mother and mine were good looking, and my grandmother and her sister were considered the belles of Paris. The Empress Josephine sent especially for them having heard so much of their beauty. Their mother, the one who was born in the prison at Rouen at the time of the French Revolution, was certainly exquisitely beautiful from her portrait. She owed her life to her sex. *Sans culottes* were walking up and down outside the cell awaiting her birth.

The Governor of the prison was a free-mason, so too her father. The Governor had given orders the child was to be spared if a girl. It was the best he could do for my great-great-grand-parents Martin.

October 14th, 1917.

Tremendous packings up. Even the beds we slept on. Persian camels, much smaller and darker than our Sindi camels, to take our kit down to Kacch. We and the servants and dogs all go by tonga. I now have Blanco, Colonel Lumsden's treasure with me. He is tremendously powerful, and the idol of his master, but I don't think he has a gentlemanly character somehow, and is not loveable. We rattled down the awful roads from 9 a.m. till 5-30 p.m. Train waiting at Kacch. We did not arrive at Quetta till 3-30 a.m. Henry was waiting, and we all went to the General's bungalow for the rest of the night, stiff with cold and fatigue.

October 16th.

Arrived in Karachi 7 p.m. having left Quetta on the previous day. We had come from ice and great frosts to a heat wave. Instantly prickly heat began. The colour seemed sponged away from Owen's face, and Ayah looking at me moans, "*Memsahib ka munh kaisa kharab hogaya*" (Memsahib's face how bad it has become).

On the 29th of the month the Viceroy and Lady Chelmsford come for four days. Already terrific preparations in progress. Ziarat seems a dream.

GOVERNMENT HOUSE AGAIN.

Someone once said of Simla, "It is impossible to hear yourself speak because of the grinding of axes and gnashing of teeth". For the first time I have been getting a glimpse of that side of life. The seating accommodation in Government House dining-room is limited to about forty people. The scheming and effrontery of certain people to get themselves invited to dinner, in addition to the "Receptions" after, or the "Garden Party" and so on, is unbelievable.

A certain Colonel demanded an interview with John Shillidy (who is now married and Henry's Assistant-Commissioner in place of Joe Covernton). The Colonel complained that neither he nor his wife had received an invitation to dinner. John, driven and overworked, promised to have the matter looked into. It then transpired that the Colonel and his wife had only arrived in Karachi the week before, and had not even troubled to write their names in the visitors' book. (No-one is received at Government House till this has been done). Politely John pointed this out. The Colonel was blustering and rude. Thereupon John revealed to him that even had he written his name down he was not sufficiently "senior" to be invited to dinner when space was so limited. The Colonel flew into a rage, using offensive language. Now John has the kindest heart, but he does not suffer fools gladly, and somehow I don't think those two will get an invitation even to the "Garden Party!".

Government House, November 2nd, 1917.

The visit is over.

The party consisted of:

His Excellency, and Lady Chelmsford.
Honourable Joan Thesiger.
Honourable Mr. A. H. Grant I.C.S., Foreign Secretary.
Lt.-Col Maffey C.I.E., Private Secretary.

Lt.Col Austen-Smith I.M.S., Surgeon.

Lt.-Col Verney, Military Secretary.

Captain Holland Hibbert, Captain J. A. Denny and Captain E. B. Baring, A.D.C's., and Reginald Coupland.

In addition to this little lot we had to put up an English valet, a lady's maid, and over ninety Indian servants. For these last innumerable little tents were pitched in the grounds, and amongst the tamarisk bushes, and behind this tree and that bush lurked an armed English tommy, or an Indian sepoy, or police, either British or native.

John Shillidy, and George Birch (the Eurasian Assistant-Commissioner—a truly wonderful person whom I have not yet mentioned for some reason or other) stage-managed the whole thing in a masterly fashion. Everything moved on oiled wheels to the minute. This sort of thing: the printing press in the grounds had printed in little books the timing of events from the beginning of each day to the end, the seating in the motors and so forth. As I say, all moved on oiled wheels. The only complaint came from the Indian servants, each of the ninety of whom demanded a bedstead instead of sleeping as is usual on a mattress on the ground, and from the English valet and the lady's maid who ordered and were refused champagne. Henry has set his face against champagne ever since the war, and so it appears has His Excellency.

The latter and my brother Lloyd were friends at Winchester, so he knows of my connection with Sir Charles. He appears to have considerable knowledge of him and to be uncommonly interested at finding himself here. It is almost as though he expected to hear the quick impatient step of the fiery old man coming down the verandah. He stands long before his portrait in the dining room. There Sir Charles looks rather like a Skye-terrier peering through his tangles of hair. "What an *extraordinary* looking man!" murmurs His Excellency. Then he turns and studies me intently at his side. "A truly remarkable family likeness", he murmurs half to himself. Now Sir Charles himself had written, "Whilst shaving I admire my courage in trusting a razor in the hands of such an ill-looking rascal as the glass reflects".

Henry's face is as impassive as a Chinaman's, but I forsee I shall not be allowed to forget this.

Henry has had the brilliant idea of turning his office into an "oyster bar" from 7-30, when we shall all be prostrate after the day's official inspections . . . a brief and blessed interval before the official dinner parties which begin at ten o'clock, and the reception held after. Colonel Austen-Smith says that H.E. must not be told. It would be too risky for him to eat oysters in his present state of health. The "bar" is an instantaneous success. The relief of that short relaxation from official correctness, tight uniform, tight boots, and impeding swords! Quantities are devoured each night with corresponding hilarity. H.E. somehow gets wind of it and insists on joining the party to Colonel Austen-Smith's dismay. He thoroughly enjoys his dozen, and wants more. Henry beckons to Hyder Khan. To his amazement Hyder Khan, the imperturbable, shows signs of distress. "Sahib, there are none", he whispers. "*None*?" repeats Henry incredulously, for dozens and dozens come in each night, and the pattawallas have orders to go on opening till stopped.

But one of the A.D.C's. (in mercy I will withhold his name) had raided the "bar" before it was officially open, and had gorged and gorged . . .

That night he nearly died.

At every meal I have to sit next H.E. It is a little difficult to be intelligent, attractive and tactful for sixteen consecutive meals, especially when you have been seeing the same person all day, but in addition to this Henry had entrusted me with a singularly delicate task. That was to let the Viceroy know that the Commissioner-in-Sind had to pay from his own salary very heavy expenses in excess of the small sumptuary allowance he was entitled to. In addition to this he had to provide motor transport for endless important visitors who came to stay. We shall of course be very heavily out of pocket from this visit alone. Well, I must have carried out my task all right for the words sank in, and the allowance was raised . . . though not in time for Henry to benefit.

The visit has been a great strain. The actual standing and waiting is no fun in itself in this climate. Then, till one experiences it, it is impossible to guess how the most familiar names evaporate when one has to present person after person, knowing the deadly offence caused if Mrs. Brown is called Mrs. Green and vice versa. After dinner Their Excellencies sit on different sofas, and guests are taken up for a set conversation of two minutes. It may be that the seated one is in the middle of a sentence, but seeing her hostess (me) advancing with the next victim, she does not know whether to rise and immediately make her curtsey, or to finish her sentence! It is just as bad for the Vicereine herself, who would have been so much happier to escape into the country with her sketching things! Lady Chelmsford was shy, and was known to refuse to open a conversation for fear of committing a gaucherie; and an A.D.C. had prepared a list of names and their official titles which she more or less concealed in the palm of her white gloved hand. Now one guest was equally determined to make no opening. The two sat in an oppressive silence. Then the lady consulted her list, and finding the silent man was General X, Director-General of Army Remounts, plunged:

"And how are the horses?"

But how difficult to refrain from these fatuous remarks! I remember once accompanying a certain popular Governor round a Maternity Home. We passed through the wards where at the foot of each bed was a tiny cot occupied with its brown baby. Then H.E. turned to the lady doctor—a dour Scotch body—and enquired brightly, "And now you must show me your men patients".

But to return to our visit. It came to an end late last night. When Henry and John Shillidy returned from the station, in spite of our exhaustion, our aching swollen feet, we all three executed a war dance under the chandeliers. Stamping, capering over the parquet, snapping our fingers, emitting cries of relief and joy . . . to look up and see

Hyder Khan advancing with drinks, not a flicker on his handsome bearded face.

For Hyder Khan the relief too was great. On these occasions the armies of strange servants descend on a place like a swarm of locusts. The responsibility for our own silver was great.

"They have taken much, Sahib, but the silver itself is safe", announced Hyder Khan.

December 17th.

The "Linga" had taken us down to Bombay for Legislative Council. Sea perfectly calm. Stayed at Government House. How superbly Lady Willingdon has drilled her A.D.C's. Never will you find girls retiring to pin up a pretendedly torn dress because they have no partner! Yet all is informal. There is the State Bungalow, and the various guest-bungalows scattered about on the cliffs looking out to sea. The guests have every comfort, cars to take them about, the private beach down through the woods to bathe from, the Viking's boat with the horse's head to dive from. Everything in fact to please. Whilst we were staying there a young cadet bound for the college at Quetta arrived in Bombay. H.E. knew of him, and an A.D.C. went to meet the boat and take the lad round the bazaar, to see the Towers of Silence and so on. He was brought up to luncheon, and came to a dinner-party that night. The following morning more sight-seeing, and in the afternoon escorted to the Mail which was taking him to Quetta. Now Quetta in December has an ideal climate. That first week the young man was writing home in all good faith, saying he thought the heat and hardship of soldiering in India had been grossly exaggerated!

But what I remember chiefly about our visit is the fence running along the top of the cliff covered with clear sky-blue Morning Glory convolvulus.

Blue sky, blue sea to the level of one's eyes, and those lovely blue convolvulus with their angel-faces.

Umerkot. December, 1917.

Christmas Camp this year consists of old friends, with the exception of "Wings". Some time ago when Henry was meeting a boat from Mespot he noticed a rather disconsolate-looking young man, and made a point of speaking to him. Discovering that he was a Canadian airman who knew no one in India and had no plans for Christmas, Henry asked him to come along . . . and here he is. Since landing he has been stationed up in the Punjab, and he is clearly unnerved and indignant at the dilapidated planes he is expected to fly. He talks openly of his "jumpiness", which is probably the best thing for him. He is enjoying every minute of his leave, and gets on well with the other guests.

Added in 1947.

On page 19 of his book *Bomber Offensive,* Sir Arthur Harris writes of this time, "We lacked everything in the way of necessary accommodation, spares and materials for getting our aircraft serviceable . . . In the end I got so tired of having to fly myself, and to send out my crew, in utterly unairworthy aircraft that I resigned . . . For instance it was not unknown for an aircraft to take off on operation on wheels with naked rims, because there were no tyres, and with axles lashed on with doubtful country rope because there was no rubber shock-absorber rope. We flew on single ignition engines which the Air Force at home had long discarded as unworthy. Lord Beaulieu . . . came round the R.A.F. stations, and saw for himself the appalling state of affairs that existed. Sir John Salmond came to enquire into our shortage of spares and equipment, a state of affairs not lightly to be forgotten or forgiven".

We in Umerkot of course knew nothing of this and put Wings' "jumpiness" down to "war strain".

Outwardly we are a cheerful set of people gathered here for the next few days to forget anxiety and over-work, to spend long hours in the open air shooting quantities of game, to eat enormous meals at night, and to sleep soundly under blankets and eiderdowns. We are a mixed bag.

Colonel Peebles of the Norfolks again on leave, more his old self than when down with jaundice and malaria last year in Belgaum. (What must he think of his Fiat now scratched and shabby, choc-a-bloc with guns and kit and game of all kinds, as we go careering and bumping over desert sand, and splashing through water?).

Colonel Willmore, I.M.S., silent and troubled over his wife's obvious ill health from her devoted work in the Karachi hospitals. Their dear little girl Una Mary who "mothers" Owen though he is twice her size.

The rest of us are what old Sir Charles would testily have described as "Civil-villains".

"Crouchy Pouchy" the judicial Commissioner. I've described him before. Round-shouldered and big with pince-nez perpetually bouncing off his nose. Brimming over with enthusiastic schemes for the betterment of mankind. The uplift of Indian women. The starting of clinics at home, especially Bath, for the treatment of rheumatism which he vows is far more prevalent than anyone knows. Ready at any moment suitable or unsuitable to hold forth on these subjects.

A young I.C.S. couple.

A police officer. Almost completely silent. He intrigues me for he is in the C.I.D., and I feel any time he might have passed me disguised as a fakir or something.

Last but not least Charles. Charles is one of my very best friends . . . A hard rider. Loving solitude, wild flowers, and Mogul architecture . . . but we bicker. He argues for the sake of arguing. It is no exaggeration to say that if I felt chilly and came in exclaiming "It's warmer to-day", he would retort "*I* thought it much colder". "Well, let's have a fire lit", I would put in very very quickly, and so get what I want.

"Wings" gets on with all these dissimilar people. What a funny bunch to find in Akbar's birth place. Moguls wiped out as though they had never been. Who will be here in another three hundred and seventy-five years?

This old Rajput Fortress stands on the threshold of the Sind desert. On the one side its crenellated walls and bastions strike down into the loose white desert sand, on the other into marshy ground and scrub tamarisk and sheets of water stretching right away to Delhi. Bare tree tops are studded with storks, cranes and herons, like fruit.

It was at Umerkot under the shelter of an Ak bush that the fugitive mother of Akbar gave birth to her illustrious son. Humayun broke and distributed a pod of musk to his chieftains saying that this was the only present he could give at the moment, but that some day the fame of this son "would spread all over the world as this perfume fills this chamber".

Now, three hundred and seventy-five years later, this old fortress is enclosed in a deep and shady garden with sloping lawns where the hoopoes raise their barred crests, and plunge their curved bills into greenest turf. "Ak AK", cry the hoopoes as though remembering Akbar. There are many flower beds, and malis squatting under the great babul trees mending the little babbling water courses which run this way and that. There on the brink of the desert we hear all day long the clappering of storks, the whistling wings of water fowl, and the lost harsh cry of the wild peacocks from the sheets of water to the north. Could anything be more strange? We turn our back from this wetness and greenery and bird life and climb up worn steps to the southern parapet to look on desert. Old cannon fire out the parrots who have nested in their mouths and make us jump. We walk along the ramparts peering over. There right down below come a drove of little burdened donkeys on their way to the village. They are foreshortened to us up here, but one can see they are sinking over their fetlocks in loosest sand.

"On April 4th, 1843, our troops had entered the Fortress of Omercote after astonishing exertions and resolution, the mercury standing at 110° and the heat hourly augmenting". So wrote Sir Charles, and he goes on to give this touching incident.

> "On one of the long marches which were almost continual the 25th Sepoys, nearly maddened by thirst and heat saw on of their water-carriers approaching; they rushed towards him tearing away his load, with loud cries of 'Water! Water'. At that moment some half-dozen exhausted soldiers of the 22nd came up and

> asked for some. At once the generous Indians forgot their own sufferings, and gave the fainting Europeans to drink. Then they all moved on, the sepoys carrying the 22nd men's muskets, patting them on the shoulders and encouraging them to hold out. They did so for a short time, but soon fell, and it was found that those noble fellows were all wounded, some deeply. Thinking there was to be another fight, they had concealed their hurts, and forced nature to sustain the loss of blood, the pain of wounds, the burning sun, the long marches, and the sandy desert, that their last moments might be given to their country on another field of battle".

December 23rd.

A line of camels came padding across the desert, each head fastened to the other's tail, necks see-sawing like snakes, and black and scarlet woollen balls and tassels banging against their knees and hocks. This evening we heard the Nar, the camelman's pipe.

We were roasting Kulu chestnuts, holding out our hands to a glorious blaze of babul branches when we heard a very little sound outside, a coaxing sound, a soft buzzing hum, and with it those mellow and sweet notes that earthenware gives when struck.

Outside in the moonlight eight or ten camelmen had made a fire and were squatting round it. The moon itself rode very high and small and white, and it was not moonlight but the light from our open door and their own firelight which picked out the huge complicated turbans, the wild-eyed features, and the breath hanging like smoke on that cold air.

From the Nar, the double pipes, the earthenware pot, and the stringed instrument whose point was resting lightly on the ground,—from these four came that primitive hum which was more felt than heard. We all listened there in the doorway. Then stirring seemingly from the ground, a delicate little air was forming itself, just as one sees the wind of the desert drawing delicate whorls and spirals more and more rapidly together till at last a "dust devil" is twitched up and goes speeding across the desert.

Just as rapidly rose this air, and one felt at any moment it threatened to break into storm . . . yet always this quietness, this softness, this measured haste . . . and through that the clear bell-like voice of the earthenware pot detached itself as the nervous hands of the man who smote it detached themselves from the darkness shining richly orange in the firelight.

Buzz and churr and hum. On and on and on. Eyeballs flashing out of the darkness, a little half-crown of light on either cheek of the man with the double pipe. Rising and falling with incredible speed those two little spots of light! Firelit toes working and twitching, the flying hands of him who smote the pot crooked like the claws of a tiger . . . this is the music of the desert.

And all at once it was over.

Nobody stirred.

The burbling and snarling of unseen camels rose in the silence, and the steps of the passing sentry . . .

When Colonel Peebles had had his sick leave with us in Belgaum he had confided to me that if he came through the war he would like to settle down. Would I find him a wife? He was not the hearty confirmed bachelor everyone imagined. Many years before he had married a child-wife, and after two or three months she had died. Now he would like to marry again. Someone not too young. Someone who would make a good companion and hostess.

At once H. and I had thought of "Antonia". A woman of the world. Travelled. Appreciating good talk and good wine. A kind heart. A sense of humour and plenty of tact. The sort of woman who loses neither her temper nor her keys. When the Colonel had returned to Mespot I mentioned him one day to "Antonia". She laughed saying "Well I am approaching the forties. It might perhaps be pleasant to settle down with a congenial companion. Who knows!".

I have her photograph here, and to-day showed it. He shied away like a frightened horse.

"Yes. Yes. Very handsome. Extremely smart . . . but I don't think it would do. No! it would *never* do".

He became embarrassed. "I'm quite sure she could never care for me. No. It would never do".

This brave soldier back from fighting was in a mortal funk, reminding me of that time when Lahri had dived in through the window, perched herself on the bedrail, and crouched there chattering at him ready for the attack!

"No. It would never do. I couldn't live up to her".

His terror was comic . . . but was it?

Was the little girl-bride beckoning to him across all those years? Did the pressed moss rose-bud still smell more sweetly than a sophisticated carnation?

I think so.

But what shall I say to "Antonia?" . . .

Nanny has gone to Goa for her yearly holiday. I have brought into camp a sergeant's wife to look after Owen. Her small boy some years older than Owen is here too. I like neither Jimmy nor his mother. She is a slattern and a shrew, though unpleasantly obsequious to Owen . . . at least in front of me. Jimmy, poor little boy, has pipe-stem legs, and a face drained of all colour. He swears, and he lies, and is stupefied by a constant cold for which he uses his sleeve. His father is fighting in Mespot. Looking at Owen so radiant and intelligent and half as heavy again, I realise how *unfair* life is to its Jimmies. This little boy is typical of all those barrack-square children that so moved Henry Lawrence to compassion, giving him no peace till he had started his schools in the hills to give them a better chance.

Jimmy, Una Mary and Owen have a little Christmas tree in the garden where the hoopoes run. The children love rolling down the very steep lawns. Over and over again, down they go, and Jimmy for the time being is like any other little boy.

Note. October 20th, 1948.

These schools were for the children of English soldiers, a hundred years ago. The three Lawrence brothers took the keenest interest in them, Henry apportioning a third of his income towards their upkeep. But to-day the Bishop of Lahore writes to *my* Henry:

"We are going through many difficulties in India and Pakistan.

The two Lawrence Schools in my Diocese—Sanawar and Ghora Gali—have already undergone great changes. Sanawar is down to about 100 boys (no girls) of whom 80 are Hindus and Sikhs. Ghora Gali closed the Girls' school, and the boys are now mostly Muslims! *Tempora mutantur.* Education goes on in English, and there is still daily chapel, as they want to preserve the Lawrence tradition".

Christmas Day, 1917

Henry and I wandered into the little bazaar very early in search of a Christmas present for me. Nothing at all but grain, and empty kerosene tins . . . and then all at once hanging amongst the kerosene tins we see a gorgeous square of Bokhara silk, damask rose with clumped masses of bottle-green embroidery which brightens here and there to almost laurel-green, and dims to almost blue where the dye has varied.

Charles maddening. Arguing just for the sake of arguing. I threw my gloves at him half in fun, half in anger. They knock his pipe out of his mouth. Very slowly, very stiffly he stoops and picks it up, his eyes half-closed as they often are. He said nothing. I am ashamed.

In our ride this morning . . . little desert rats popping in and out of their holes all about us . . . Henry and Charles were talking of Gul the camelman.

Gul is a short thick-set Baluchi with full blue cotton trousers tight in at the ankle, and an enormous turban which dwarfs his face. Gul's beard is red from henna rather than nature, for he has carried on his work for thirty years. Yet even now he is able to ride across the desert for twelve hours on end without visible fatigue.

His riding camels are the large light-coloured ones carrying their heads high and nobly. Gul prides himself on their smooth gait, and with justice. He was once lent to Henry for a month or so, and Henry tells me how it was possible to read a book whilst padding noiselessly along, and how one night he had slept peacefully from nine o'clock till six the next morning wedged in behind Gul in the high peaked saddle.

But Gul is really assigned to Henry Montgomery, Assistant-Collector of Sukkur. As the latter goes about his business Gul regales him with observations on the peculiarities of former employers. These are lively, and Henry Montgomery has told me that to listen to them made him forget the heat, the stinging particles of sand, and the miles of scrub and stunted thorn stretching away to a quivering horizon . . . forget even the smell of the camel. Gul too has a store of old Sindi tales and legends. Montgomery has taken some of them down. Saswi and Panhu he declares is "one of the greatest tales in the world". But here is "the Palace of Butter", for I believe it is supposed to have occurred in this district.

Many, very many years ago a King in the Kingdom of Sind took to himself a new wife from another country. The little Princess was but a child, so though she was possessed of great beauty, and with all the coaxing pretty ways of a child, yet her thoughts were often vain and foolish. But the King was so enslaved by her charm that he was ready to grant any foolish request that she might make.

It was one morning in the early days of their marriage, that as they sat at their meal, the merry eyes of the little bride fell upon a great dish of butter set amongst the meats, the rice, the fruits and the sweet-meats. Laughing and clapping her hands she cried out to the King her husband:

"O King! That I may have a Palace of Butter to be my own delight!"

The King's face grew thoughtful at the senseless request. He did not answer. The Shahzadi pouted like the child she was. There was silence between them. Then without a word the King rose and went out.

The King went straight to his Hall to take counsel amongst the councillors of the Durbar. He called too for famous architects to be present. These he asked if it were possible to build a Palace of Butter, so bound was he by the beauty of the little Shahzadi.

All the wise men present agreed that it would be as easy to build a Palace of Butter as a palace of wood or of mud or of stone. "But", said one, "surely the sun will melt the palace".

All faces grew grave, and the King on whose face a smile had come, frowned in displeasure and disappointment.

There was silence.

At length rose the Wazir, eldest and wisest of all present.

"With the help of the birds of heaven, O Badshah, this matter may be achieved. Let the birds of heaven be summoned by royal proclamation".

Then the brow of the King cleared again. His smile came forth, and all the councillors and the architects began to talk amongst themselves. The King commanded, and a proclamation was published by beat of drum calling upon all the birds of heaven. For in those far off days, when as yet truth was spoken upon earth, the birds spoke also, and were the friends of men, and obeyed the order of the King.

So now all the birds came out of heaven by their tribes and their castes, innumerable for multitude. From the mountains came the eagles and the ravens and the hoopoes with their dainty crests. From the countryside came the soft-voiced doves and pigeons. From the sandy desert came the sand-grouse, and the humble little pipits the colour of dust. From the jungle came peacocks glittering like jewels, and black partridges and flashing green parrots. From the Royal River came hundreds of flamingoes rose and white, trailing their long legs behind them, and heavy pelicans turning and wheeling together as by word of command. And from the marshes of the delta where the Royal River loses itself through many mouths into the Arabian Sea herons and great grey cranes, and hundreds and thousands of duck and coot and geese. All the birds came out of heaven so that they made a great awning right across the sky, and the sand of the desert was now in deepest shadow.

In the shadow was set the throne of the King, and of the Princess his bride; and a space was marked off where the Palace of Butter should be built. From the boundaries of Sind were summoned the clans of the graziers under their headmen, thousands upon thousands bearing each man on his head a pitcher of butter. From all the cities were commanded the architects and masons, the carvers and gravers, the illuminers and embossers, and the painters upon tiles, and also those who fashioned cornice work, and the moulders of gold and silver vaulting.

All were standing expectant in that deep shadow caused by the birds in the sky, ready to begin to build the Palace of Butter, when a single shaft of sunlight fell on the beard of the Wazir so that it glistened like silver.

Quickly the Wazir looked up, and then down. Trouble gathered on his brow, "O King. There wants one yet. One bird is absent. Chandur Pakhi, the Wizard of Birds, is not here. If we have not the wisest of all birds our toiling is in vain".

Then the King was very wroth for the delay, and the Shahzadi beside him frowned and complained and wept, whilst all around stood the multitudes idle, and chill, shaded as they were from the light of the sun by the multitudes of birds.

Heralds were sent forth to the North and the South and the East and the West. The herald who went to the East travelled in haste for two days, and on the third day he saw with a great lightening of heart Chandur Pakhi, the wisest of all birds seated in deep thought upon a stone.

"Salaam aleik um", said the herald.

"Salaam aleik um" replied the wisest of all birds.

Then the herald asked him why he stood thus aloof when by royal proclamation all the birds were come to the King. "Come quickly", said he.

"Nay", said Chandur Pakhi. "I come not now. After three days I come".

Bearing that answer swiftly and fearfully the herald returned. The King who all this time was still waiting in the shadow of the birds, was even more wroth, and the Shahzadi wept and wept. Yet what could be done to appease the King's wrath and to dry the tears of the Shahzadi? It was *lachar,* that is, "needs must"; and for two more days the King and the Princess sat.

On the third day early in the morning men saw, flying without haste across the desert, Chandur Pakhi. When at last he arrived he made salaam before the King's feet.

"Wherefore, O Chandur Pakhi, hast thou not obeyed my royal proclamation?" demanded the King sternly, "and wherefore camest thou not with my messenger?"

"Let not the King be wroth," said the wisest of birds. "I made delay, but I made it of constraint. For I was engaged in considering my award in an important matter of arbitration".

At this the Shahzadi forgot to weep, and the King wondering asked "What arbitration, O Chandur Pakhi, O Wizard of Birds?"

"A vexed question of dispute, whereon the parties had spent many years in litigation, and on pleaders many lakhs. And last of all they made me arbitrator. The question being 'Whether there be more of men or of women in the world?' "

"And thy decision, O Chandur?"

"I have given that the women be many more".

"But how is this?" cried the King, forgetting all his anger in wonder, "Are there not in my kingdom twice as many men as women?" and the little Shahzadi laughed aloud with the tears still wet on her cheeks.

"O Badshah" replied Chandur Pakhi the Wizard of Birds. "In a suit of this kind it is necessary for the judge to have some rule, and some standard of judgment, and I, in my arbitration, reckoned in the number of women, not only such as bear children and suckle them, but all persons whomsoever that be governed by women's words, and by women's vain desires".

A long while sat the King in thought; then rising he gave order: "Disband ye this great concourse of artisans and craftsmen; return the herdsmen to their herds; dissolve the curtain of the birds in the heaven. Be those vessels of butter a gift to the poor in charity. And upon Chandur Pakhi, Wisest of Birds, do I confer hereby the title of Khan Bahadur!"

Tales such as these are the cherished possession of the people. And to the simple Hindu villager the gods themselves are linked—Krishna and his milkmaids, Rama and Sita . . .

In England what a chasm between epic and romance and the ordinary man!

These few days should have been a real holiday for Henry. But as a matter of fact he is never separated from his "Office", meaning shorthand writer, clerks and pattawallas. When "Wings" and Colonel Peebles and the rest turn in early after the long hours spent in the open air, Henry removes himself to his "Office", and wraps a rug round his legs for warmth and to keep off mosquitoes. The table will be groaning beneath papers and files. I, snug in bed with hot-water bottle, hear him slapping down file after file onto the floor, and the following morning the pattawallas will carry out the flat wire baskets overflowing with papers on which he has written comments.

But he has been out once or twice, shooting pretty well, getting twenty to thirty birds at a time, which satisfies him. Owing to heavy rain this year the birds are not collected in a few definite spots as usual. In all something over six hundred head of duck, snipe, partridge and quail have been shot. Not enough for our party to send down hundreds of duck for the benefit of the soldiers in Karachi as we did last year, but enough for me to get heartily sick of wild duck! We have the popular "All Blaze" which is a sort of stew of all the game together; but Misteri's speciality is to bake a crusty loaf, scoop out the inside, put in a wild duck, who in its turn has a partridge inside it who has a snipe inside it, who has a quail stuffed with green chillies inside *it*. The lid of the loaf is put on and all are cooked together and the result is indescribably succulent. None of the goodness being lost, much in the same way as a gipsy cooks a hedgehog in clay with all his prickles on.

Till he came to India Henry had done little shooting. At Kaira, his first station, he fired off one hundred cartridges without stirring a feather! His hundred and first however brought down two birds, neither of which he had aimed at! However it encouraged him. A far cry to the hundred and seventeen he shot in under two hours last Christmas at Kambar.

One morning he made an expedition to see a salt lake, and found a natural phenomenon which he declares beats his understanding. I was not with him. He had driven into a country of low sandhills rising about a hundred feet from the desert, here all stubbly with undergrowth. He passed two valleys with lakes in them about a mile or two in length, and one lake was blue water, whilst the other was pink water. He was told the water of one was sweet, the other brackish. He climbed a third sandhill, and saw another lake, and this was white, glistening in the distance as though covered with dazzling snow. He found it to be encrusted with salt, and as though frozen almost solid. The salt was from ten to fifteen inches thick, covering the lake from shore to shore. Men were working at it, cutting it through with pickaxes and washing it in the water which lay beneath and then shovelling it to the side of the lake to dry for market. There is a great dearth of salt in the land, and at once Henry is making arrangements to supply salt from this faraway lake, on a very large scale.

This is the sort of useful thing the district officer on tour discovers and makes use of.

Regretfully our heterogeneous party prepares to break up, leaving the old Fortress and the improbable juxtaposition of camels and sand, marshes and storks. Maybe Akbar, that most tolerant of emperors, has distributed amongst us some of his tolerance like that pod of musk "whose perfume" his father said "fills this chamber".

SIND, 1918

Mirpurkhas, January 5th, 1918.

Our Christmas party broke up on the 4th, Henry driving Owen and me, Jimmy and his mother the sixty odd miles here. Cold. Glittering sun, tamarisk trees, pampas grass silvery, miles of marsh. Storks and peacocks sitting on the tops of trees. We got over the ground very well, but had one mishap. Following the banks of the Jam Rao canal we went over oozy swamp, in which the Fiat sank to her axles! Owen in great distress. He toddled up and patted the bonnet to reassure her! Henry always has sowars cantering alongside the car on these journeys, and now they galloped off and collected some twenty men who managed to get her out, with much pushing, pulling and yelling. Owen wept, thinking this must hurt the Fiat. Later eating our luncheon at Pithoro I watched him stoop and try to swing the handle. Not bad for twenty months.

The thick-walled bungalow purposely built to keep out every chink of sun. Dark. Very cold, and twanging with mosquitoes. Both Henry and Owen have fever. Jimmy and his mother also unwell. Henry went to bed on arrival. That night I undressed in the bath-room so as not to disturb him. He had fallen into a restless sleep. It was shudderingly cold in the bath-room. There was the steady "string band" of the mosquitoes. By the faint light of the hurricane lantern standing on the floor, the zinc tub half filled with ice-cold water looked repellent. Through the wall I could hear Jimmy crying, and his mother being sick.

My eyes were gritty from the drive. I always use an eyebath with zinc lotion. On the board nailed to the dark wall I could just see the eye-bath and blue corrugated bottle, which Ayah had unpacked before going off to her own quarters. By sheer force of habit I picked it up to read "To apply night and morning". Unfortunately Henry had had some strong lotion made up for a skin trouble on his scalp, also "night and morning", and it was this I poured into my eyebath. The instant agony was terrifying! I did not know whether my sight was destroyed. There I was quite alone. Had Henry been in the habit of getting fever I should have called him, but he was not; and he had seemed so suddenly and mysteriously stricken down that I was loth to rouse him. I could still hear Jimmy's mother being sick and Owen wailing . . . Ayah was somewhere outside in her unknown quarters in the dark. There was nothing to be done. Shivering with cold, terror and pain I crept under my nets, and lay down beside the tossing Henry.

By morning the eye was closed, but less painful, though now the other eye had become affected, in sympathy I suppose. Henry was surprisingly better. Nurse and Jimmy also . . . but Owen much worse.

Outside the hot windy glare. Inside the bungalow, vault-like and cold. Owen moaning, and now and again screaming with a high-pitched scream sounding almost like a laugh.

Where had I heard that before?

In the children's ward at the Dufferin Hospital in Karachi. Meningitis, Dr. Curjel had said. The child had never stopped night and day for fifty-six hours. Then it died.

Now I envied those mothers (hitherto pitied) living humdrum lives with a doctor round the corner. Of course we did have the Assistant Surgeon who always travelled around with us, but what use would he be? I remembered the man at Vengurla who had half killed Henry.

All that day Owen's high singing moan. That terrible cry, half laugh. His little hands flying to his head, then dropping to pick feebly at his sheets, only to fly up again horribly strong. My Owen. How easily Death could persuade so small a heart not to beat.

That evening I went to Henry, still weak and shattered from his fever. "I think Owen has meningitis. We must have a doctor . . .".

"We will catch the mail to Hyderabad first thing in the morning" said Henry.

Quietly, confidently, without fuss, arrangements were made. Hyder Khan of course would be responsible for the moving of the whole establishment, servants, bedding, horses, dogs, tents and dog cart. Mr. Iyengar for the moving of the Office, pattawallas, clerks, sowars and their horses. Henry telegraphed to Dr. Holland, that wonderful little missionary doctor. He was waiting on the platform at Hyderabad as the train drew in. He did not like Owen's intolerance to light, that scream and the picking at his sheets. Four big double teeth were trying to come through at once. The penny-whistle scream pierced one's heart night and day. If only little Nanny were here! Though dear Tulsi was devotion itself. Then I went down with dengue fever. Temperature 105°. The incredible aching in one's bones. If *only* little Nanny could get back from Goa. At last! Blessed little Nanny. Stumpy little figure with its toffee-coloured eyes and friz of black hair, the spotless print dress and white shoes. "Poor Madam. Don't worry. I'll say some 'Hail Marys' for our darling".

January 14th

We are able to come down to Karachi.

January 20th

Owen saw the welcome to the 28th Baluchis on their return from East Africa.

February, 1918.

How we move about! What distances we cover!

Henry and I have been staying at Bahalwapur for the Lieutenant-Governor's shoot. I left Owen at Sukkur with Mrs. Barlee, the Judge's wife, as we have to return to Khairpur after Bahalwapur. We went to the shoots (which by the way are not so good as ours in Sind) dashing along deep sandy tracks, threading our way between tamarisks in wagonettes drawn by four or more mules, two wheels usually off the ground. Very good fun.

The first evening His Honour told me what a trial the native band of pipes was to him. At times they played at dinner marching round the table in true Scotch fashion. I said I like it. "Very well. You shall have it", retorted he grimly. We did have them, and as they marched round and round the table as we dined in the tent I was as deafened, and as exasperated as he said I should be! We had the rollicking charming air of Zakhmi Dil, the Punjabi song of the

Wounded Heart whose sentiments unfortunately are quite unprintable.

Sir Michael O'Dwyer is a very fine fellow. Able to a degree. Henry says he has the shrewd look of a typical Irish peasant with those high cheek bones of his.

We were in tents, but we went one day to the Palace and saw the state jewels. We were shut into a room, and the coat worn by the Nawab at the time of coronation was shown to us. The brocade is entirely hidden in pearls, the raised pattern in large pearls, the background in seed pearls. As it was lifted carefully pearls were pattering off and rolling all over the floor! Hence the closed doors. We were invited to lift the coat. Its weight was such it was all I could do. It is only worn for a few minutes.

Khairpur State, 1918.

The tents were burning hot by day, and freezing cold at night at Bahalwapur. But never had I felt anything like the cold of these dim immense rooms of the Faiz Mahal. We all have streaming colds. Owen is heavy and cross. Lubin is desperately ill. All the dogs went sick at Umerkot, and are still under the weather. Now Lubin seems to be consumed by raging fever before our eyes. His body feels like a hot coal to the touch. His tongue and nose are like cracked leather. The Muhammadan vet belonging to the State says malaria and snake bite. He knows no more than we do.

Miss Piggott, the missionary from Sukkur, has been trying to inculcate methods of cleanliness into the dhais (hereditary midwives). It is impossible to persuade them to remove their innumerable bangles. To-day I have to examine them. This is just asking elementary questions. The necessity of washing their hands, and so on. Much shyness and giggling, but very friendly. I "pass" them all, to Miss Piggott's relief!

We are due at the great desert Fort of Kot Digi for a shoot. I can take my snuffling peevish Owen with me, but I shall have to leave Lubin behind. I have been laying endless handkerchiefs dipped in iced water on his poor head. Ayah promises to do this for me, but I hate leaving him.

This reminds me somehow of George Monteath once complaining "You always tell me all the things I want to know about the dogs in your letters, but why do you never mention Owen? I should like to hear about *him* too".

Such a thing had never occurred to me, that a middle-aged bachelor would care to hear of a baby a few months old. And now Owen has just a head cold . . . but poor Lubin is *in extremis*. I hate leaving him for one night.

To add to everything the Mir has sent over a phara (deer) of his own shooting, and it is lying out there as I write, and nobody to see to cutting it up. Eyes glazing. Flies buzzing.

The Mir has phara fed regularly in a clearing of the jungle. Then one morning he seats himself in a bough-made shelter. Through the narrow opening between the leafy roof and the sunk seat (for all the world like an opera box) the Mir looks up the rides cut in the jungle which radiate in all directions from the clearing before him. Down these rides the phara steal to feed as usual. Whereupon His Highness picks off one after another.

Last year Henry had been forced to take part in this sickening entertainment. H.H. insisting he should use his own rifle, an ornate affair with butt of emerald green velvet embroidered in gold and silver thread. Henry vowed he would never do it again; and this time he told the Wazir we should all much prefer to see the wild pig fed.

So early this morning he and Antonia and I sat and waited in our "opera box", our legs underground, our topis brushed by leafy boughs, before the slim trunks of trees leaning over the grassy rides, which radiate like spokes from the hub of a wheel.

Suddenly a most melodious long-drawn note sounded through the jungle. There appeared a man in voluminous blue trousers, fawn shirt, and yellow turban, swishing in a basket of rushes, the grain.

"*Ahri Ahri, Mudi Yah!*" he was calling sweetly, scattering the jowari all about him in the clearing. Down swooped the long tailed greedy parrots, and then right at the end of the middle ride a shadow suddenly appeared. The shadow advanced and became a big tusked boar, grey-brown with spikey wiry hair, and runaway hind legs. He was followed by two grey sows and a family of six piglets, tawny brown, striped with black. And now down all the rides, singly and in groups trotted the wild pig, hurrying yet timid, while the ousted parrots screamed up into the trees to swoop down again glittering in the patch of sun where the grain was scattered. One great boar delighted us by the way he chased off all who came near his circle. Another heard our whispers, and his warning grunts drove his neighbours out of sight, all except one old sow who arrested her piglets' flight as though saying where food and fear are, food comes first. Once again and yet again the man returned with his basket, raising his musical voice "*Ahri, Ahri, Mudi. Yah . . . ahri . . . Ah . h . h . h .*" summoning pets who loved him, yet vanished when he moved.

An enchanting spectacle.

Henry hears that plague had broken out in Larkhana. We motored there early this morning. The town is completely deserted. The doors of the houses marked with a cross. The only living thing I saw was a cat crossing the road.

February, 1918.

Lloyd and Minnie have been touring in Khandesh this cold weather. Last week Minnie got jungle fever. They were in tents. She stayed in bed for a few days, then her temperature being down got up at tea time. Lloyd said, "Better have supper in bed the first day". She did. Her temperature rushed up, she became delirious, and within an hour was dying in his arms.

They were two days' march from civilisation. One of Lloyd's forest guard fashioned a coffin of some kind, and Lloyd brought her into Surat where she lies buried.

S.S. Jhelum, February 26th, 1918

"*Waghu ko pakro, Shabash Juwan . . .* !"

Came out of my cabin in time to see the klassis joyfully hauling on board the crocodile H. had shot. Henry had Owen by the hand and both were peering down at its long jaws, for it was dharayal, the fish-eating kind. It sprawled on the deck, its pudgy hands spread out. I always think there is a hideous suggestion of evil in those pudgy human-looking hands with their curved nails, but now this poor brute looked so helpless, its bulging body corded tightly round, that even though it was dead somehow I felt a little sorry. But was it dead? Those eyes, not the little eyes of the common crocodile . . . but large and dark blue like a bullock's, seemed to be looking at me.

"Henry, I do believe its still alive", I exclaimed.

"Nonsense!"

And then I saw tears brimming.

"But it's *crying*!"

"By George! So it is!"

Incredulously he had bent to look, instantaneously leaping back dragging Owen. For those long jaws had opened like a pair of scissors, and were clashing to.

So Captain de Souza and Herodotus were right after all.

Dreamy days. The Indus carrying the sky. The cry of the serang swinging the lead. Henry bent over his table under the awning. Me in a long chair knitting war socks, my eyes on the bank as they slide slowly past. The water talking against the side of the boat.

There passes a Mohana, one of the fisher folk, an enormous pot balanced on his head, a long pole resting on his shoulder still dripping with water. For the palla-fish is in season, a most delicious fish like a salmon but with a more delicate flavour. It is caught in the strangest way on a huge earthenware pot called a dillo. The Mohana balances himself on this, his tummy fitting over the circular opening, his legs hanging over the sides. Upstream he propels himself frog-like, while his hands clasp the upright pole with its net at the bottom. When a palla is in the net, miraculously (and no one who has not tried to balance himself for even two seconds on a palla pot can guess how miraculous a feat it is!) he hauls up the dripping pole, lifts his tummy from the opening, drops the palla into the pot, and either paddles on frog-like again or floats down stream. It is an enchanting spectacle to see these golden pots, and their naked glistening riders topped by a small scarlet turban, drifting so peacefully down the broad pale surface of the river.

Sohani

To-day we passed Sohani's pillar, a sunned obelisk watching on the stony rocks of Lunko near the village of Hillayo. Hundreds of years have probably passed since the villagers raised this pillar to Sohani, but the legend goes that even now one may sometimes catch the faint cry over the flood "O Sohani, come", for Mahar was Sohani's lover, and nightly he called "O Sohani come".

The Mohana girl was beautiful, as even now these fisher folk are famed for their looks. Her father had married again, and daily his wife beat her, and made her life a burden to her.

Nightly as Sohani lay on her string cot she listened for that faint cry tossed across the waters of the river. "O Sohani come". Then the girl would steal down over the stones her bare feet knew so well, to where the dillo rested at the water's edge. Clasping the pot hard to her breast she used to push fearlessly out into the stream to cross to her lover.

But the step-mother seeing the wet sari each morning spread out to dry on the stones, watched, hugging herself with hateful joy. Nothing did she say, but secretly she changed the dillo for one still unfired which would founder in the water.

That night there came no call, and many nights passed, and still Mahar did not call. Sohani lay wakeful, sick with apprehension, yet helpless. And then one night exhausted, she fell into deep sleep and still sleeping heard the cry "O Sohani come!".

In one breath it seemed Sohani was awake, and over the stones, to the brink of the river. Seizing the unfired dillo she launched herself out on to the moonlit waters.

"O Sohani, faithless Sohani do you come?" Over the water came the cry.

But what was this? This uneasy sensation beneath her body? The dillo itself was shuddering and disintegrating beneath her. The little waves thick with silt were breaking in her face. With a supreme effort she raised her head above the waters and cried before she sank, "O Mahar, I come".

Henry Montgomery had told me this story. In his volume of verse he wrote some verses on it, and the last lines are

"Wherefore the stone stands here on Mahar's hill
And still to-day they call it Sohani's Stone.
Because Hate kills and dies, but Love remains,
Run River rolling on your silver silt".

Palla is exceedingly rich, and Henry was emphatic I should not eat it more than once a day as it would give me boils. Antonia pooh-poohed the idea. John Shillidy teased her unmercifully saying she would disfigure herself. As a matter of fact when she got to Calcutta to stay with her cousin the Bishop, life was a misery for weeks from boil after boil. She had eaten it for breakfast, dinner, and potted like char for tea.

The lovely lazy days drifted by. They call this two thousand mile river Darya Shah, the Royal River. He is indeed a despot, able by his whims to make or mar the lives of his subjects. One year he may roll his vast floods thick with silt down their appointed course, feeding canals, and watering hundreds of miles of cultivation, but another he may wilfully turn aside leaving rice and wheat to perish, trampling down embankments, covering villages under hundreds and thousands of tons of water, driving men and women, children and cattle before him. They say the people of the East prefer the rule of a despot to the equable rule of the West. In Sind the Hindus worship Darya Shah, giver of prosperity, of life itself as well as death, Lord of tributaries and canals, the great river rising in the snows of the Himalayas, and finally losing himself in the Arabian sea!

Day by day his presence impresses itself upon me. Drained of all colour by day, black as coal at night, lapping up against the sides of the *Jhelum* as I fall asleep.

See his waters opaque with silt sliding silently past. Here are treacherous swirls and eddies. There in that smooth reach, a hole big enough to take a man's body, suddenly yawns. Watch that tree tossing down in mid-stream. It is seized as though by invisible hands. It spins round . . . One end suddenly rears high above the waters like the hull of a sinking ship. It disappears. No. There far down the river it has risen to the surface again . . . and is this madness? It is returning. For some inscrutable reason the Royal River chooses to turn back on itself, sliding over the surface of its down-moving waters. Slowly, surely the tree, like some victim of a barbarian, is brought back to the scene of its torture, to be seized again, spun round like a straw, and sunk.

Hear the Royal River eroding his banks. A wide crack suddenly appears, a great portion topples forward with a splash, subsiding in an oily yellow swirl. In the space of an hour you may see the whole of a sand bank devoured.

The Royal River flows past villages and shrines, past feeding peacocks, past the quays of Sukkur where hundreds of crows are fighting amongst the mounds of grain which the flat bottomed boats will bear to Karachi, and so to the Persian Gulf; past the lovely island of Sath Bela from whose Sikh Monastery the bells ring out so sweetly. Past Sir Charles Napier's Fort of Bukker; past high steep banks feathery with pink tamarisk, or with sweet smelling babul; past the creaking Persian wheels, under mighty bridges, and past sandy spits where the crocodiles sun themselves. How many happy days we spent on the Royal River. How many sunrises we saw with the mountains of Baluchistan faintly blue on the horizon, how many sunsets watching the golden-rose waters sucking and racing past, the date palms on the bank rising like jet into the brilliant air, while high overhead, stringing out against the early stars, chains of flamingoes pass. Such peaceful days . . . our only sadness, Lubin, ill. He is wasted with fever. When we reached Kotri I got the sweeper to lift him out on the bank. He stood there looking round him in a strange way, more like a greyhound than a bull-terrier, his back arched and nobbly, his legs wasted. Blanco in his great strength and beauty suddenly hurled himself on our Lubin knocking him down.

Never have I been so angry with an animal. There has always been something alien about Blanco.

In spite of his blue blood he is not a gentleman.

Government House, Karachi, February, 1918

Back again, having covered two thousand five hundred miles in the past few weeks.

This morning felt like a Turkish bath. Steamy blue sky, and sweat starting out at every movement. Felt too languid to ride. We had Owen and the dogs in the grounds soon after seven, but even by then Henry's tussore coat was dark between the shoulders, Owen's face beaded all over, and the fat little hand he had pushed in his daddy's must have stuck there. But the bull-terriers whirled round just the same as ever, blundering into us and each other, charging into tamarisk and oleander, in and out of steaming sun and shadow, silver-bright and lavender blue, eyes in happy slits of heat and exhaustion, paddling luxuriously in the little water courses that bisect the grounds, lapping as they go, then pausing to drink in good earnest till they are fit to burst, "follop! follop! follop" and breaking wind audibly; reminding one of the zemindar who, doing the same, had remarked to Henry contentedly "My belches are sweet as rose water" . . . and then charging off once more to rout out a jackal or wild cat, Lucy Locket, Lucifer, Laverock, Lakhi and Blanco . . . but our dear Lubin not amongst them! He is still ill, though Haji the vet hopes even now to save him.

Henry and Owen were standing hand in hand looking up at the brilliant morning glories sprawling all over the jaffery work at the bottom of the tennis court, when I noticed Blanco standing. He looked somehow odd. Apart. I called him. He took no notice. Then I saw spurting from his leg a fountain of bright blood.

Blanco weights eighty pounds. Somehow Henry got him in his arms, holding too at the same time the gushing artery. He staggered off to G.H. I could not leave Owen at twenty months alone in the drive. He was too heavy for me to carry. So I had to hustle the little chap along as best I could, knowing Henry would never know where to find the cotton wool and bandages, etc. We got to the visitors' marble steps, and I pushed him into Mrs. Shillidy. Tearing up the long polished tiles of the verandah I met a terrified pattawalla running towards me, "Where's the Bara Sahib?"

"In the dining room", he called out without stopping.

And in the dining room I find Henry slumped over the table. His silk suit is blotty with blood. I have never trusted Blanco. Is he bitten?"

"Help Hyder Khan. I'm all right", he sighs.

Behind the screen in the "go-down" through which the meals are brought from the kitchen, stands Hyder Khan grasping Blanco's leg, Blanco himself is flat on his side on the table.

"The Bara Sahib says I must not let go", explains Hyder Khan pressing the severed artery. Blood stains stand out brilliantly on his stiff white clothes. He the Muhammadan to whom dogs are unclean!

At that moment in rushed Colonel Willmore in his pyjamas. Called up on the telephone, he had bicycled from his house at the gates of Government House.

"Where is he?"

Henry feebly lifts his head. "Behind there".

"The dog ! ! ! The pattawalla has just telephoned to say *YOU* were dead!".

Heat, blood, and carrying that dead weight on an empty stomach had been too much for Henry.

As for Blanco, he was driven off to Haji who stitched the artery and sent him back again saying he must be kept absolutely still.

Whoever kept a bull-terrier still when he didn't want to be?

He slept on my bed. His leg oozed on to the sheet which covered me, but the stitches held.

The Engine.

Henry has definite ideas on the spending of money in war-time. No replacing of faded shabby chintzes. No buying of toys for Owen's birthday. (They are certainly an exorbitant price). So I tell Hyder Khan to have made in the bazaar a small unpainted wooden engine. "Not bigger than that", and I hold my hands some six or seven inches apart. It should not cost more than one rupee or two at most.

Days pass, and the engine has not appeared. I complain, for Henry and I will be away in Lahore for Owen's birthday. Hyder Khan makes excuses. Still it does not come. I fear it will not be ready in time. At last he says reproachfully "The Railway Workshops are very busy, Memsahib". "The Railway Workshops?" I repeat with a little feeling of uneasiness, "What has that got to do with it? I ordered a little engine no bigger than that from the bazaar. Just unpainted wood". Hyder Khan agreed, but I could not help noticing he rubbed one bare foot over the instep of the other, which he does on the rare occasions when disconcerted.

And a day or two later a pattawalla came to me as I was writing out a simple talk on astronomy which I am giving to the Tommies (chiefly cribbed from Sir Thomas Ball's "Story of the Heavens").

"Memsahib, Baba-sahib ka ingin aya".

I tell him to bring it up, without turning my head.

But the pattawalla does not go. I repeat the order.

"Ne jata, Memsahib". Not able to come, Memsahib.

Now filled with apprehension I hurry downstairs. There under the portico by the sentry, who is sending sidelong looks of admiration, stands an enormous green painted engine, with a shining hump of brass on its back, and behind it an upholstered truck in which to seat Nanny and Owen.

I am aghast. What on earth am I to do? At that moment Owen appears on the top of the marble steps. He stands stock-still, his face above his smock becoming slowly crimson to the ears. Then with a squeal he flings himself on the monster.

Now Henry has two kinds of anger. The cold silent kind . . . and the not-silent kind. It is that kind I get now. Words like blows fall about my ears. He will not have it. What was I thinking of? It is to be returned instantly to the works . . .

And there is Owen in a kind of transport, his chubby arms round the funnel, his hands patting the bright brass . . .

No wonder Henry is angry.

The engine is clearly meant as a "gift" hoping for favours to come. Bluntly, a bribe.

Henry never accepts "gifts".

Therefore he must pay for it. It will cost a great deal of money and his policy is not to spend unnecessary money in war time. He is always preaching this.

Moreover rolling stock is gravely short, and time has been taken from the Railway Workshops to make an extravagant toy for Government House. An impossible situation.

N.B. The engine did not go back. It was too heavy to drag, except for a few yards by Hassan Shah, but Nanny used to sit in it all morning in the garden doing her sewing, whilst Owen washed it down, filled the tender with buckets of pebbles, and polished the brass. Never was there a better investment . . .

I am painting frescos on Owen's nursery walls.

An "efelant" as he calls it, tigers, the "ingin" and "Moushie", all much of the same size. "Moushie" is a little mouse who comes to his call every evening as he sits eating bread and butter and drinking milk, his legs buttoned into a pillow case against mosquitoes. "Moushie! Moushie!" calls Owen in the sweetest little voice, and from under the wainscot out ventures Moushie, catches hold of the bread, and tugs and tugs till he gets it.

But now I'm in a quandary, for another, and yet another Moushie comes too.

What is to be done?

Government House, Karachi. April, 1918.

I have noticed a peculiar taste in the bread. The French word *moisi* exactly describes it . . . an earthly, mouldy down-the-well sort of taste. I tell Misteri to be sure and scrub the bread-pan well out. "*Acchha Memsahib*", but the taste persists. Henry declares he does not notice it. Finally I tell Misteri he must bake the bread for us, as in camp, (he hates baking bread). But Misteri's bread tastes exactly the same as the baker's. Biscuits, scones and puddings, all have this pervading taste. It repels me. It gets on my nerves. I eat little. I haver on to Henry about this taste, rather tiresomely no doubt, and finally he bursts out "Well if you must know, it's WEEVILS. Karachi is eating bread which the army has returned from Mespot as unfit for human consumption, it's so full of weevils".

Well . . . Well . . . Did not Sir Charles Napier himself write in the Peninsular War, "Though not a bad soldier, hang me if I can relish maggots"?

It appears that the Medical Officers had got Henry down to Kiamari where the wheat lay in immense mounds on the quay side. As he looked, these mounds were wriggling. The M.O.s urged him to condemn it. Henry, his own stomach crawling, but knowing the serious shortage of food in Sind, stoutly declared the people must be fed, so the wheat must be eaten.

Government House, Lahore, April 16th

There is much grumbling that Government is still here instead of the Hills. It is certainly hot! But Sir Michael O'Dwyer has the same inflexible sense of duty that I admire in Henry.

In spite of the frizzling heat His Honour and Henry played several sets of tennis this evening. Henry is forty-nine and H.H. fifty-four. When I was dressing languidly for dinner, and Henry emerged from his bath parboiled, and with his iced peg in one hand and only a bath towel round him, and sank back in a long chair, I was worried at his exhaustion; but he charged me not to "let on". So at dinner I chatted brightly to H.H. how much Henry had enjoyed the games.

April 17th

Lady O'Dwyer confided to me how dismayed she had been at "Micky's complete prostration the evening before". I felt a hateful hypocrite. Too late for me now to admit how worried I too had been! Fatal, the first step in deception. You must go on.

A pleasant and charming woman. She told me of the difficulty of refusing "gifts". The latest ruling is that officials may not accept even flowers or fruit. This at times gives great offence, but is wise. Recently a new A.D.C. had accepted for her a basket of flowers in all innocence. Just in time another A.D.C. more versed in the ways of the East shifted the flowers to find a diamond bracelet beneath.

I in my turn told her of that charming old Sindi lady who came to call on me, the front of her victoria tied up in printed sheets, and all the pattawallas having to turn away as she shuffled down the verandah shrouded from top to toe in her white cotton burka. She had brought for Owen some little mud animals such as can be bought in Marwar bazaar for a few annas. The old gentlewoman squatted there on the floor, and caused the tiger and the elephant to walk, to Owen's great delight, explaining to me meanwhile, of course she knew of Government's decree, but that no one could object to mud animals of so small a cost. I sent a scribbled note to Henry in his office. Back came a scrap of paper. "Better not".

The old lady protested. She was hurt. Wounded. It was embarrassing.

But the following day the petition came which Henry had taken for granted would.

Her son wished Government to grant him a particularly valuable bit of ground on the river.

April 24th

Owen two years old. The Shillidys are arranging a birthday party for him. I hate not to be there. Well, I'm glad he's got his engine.

Government House, Karachi. May, 1918

Constantly getting fever. Yet blood tests show nothing. They suppose because of all the quinine. The sweating is trying. Have to change sheets every night as well as nightgown, and I've gone so thin I bind my wedding ring round and round with silk to keep it on. Fact of the matter is I've never got over that evening near Larkhana.

John and I had ridden farther than we intended. Had to gallop to get back before dark. The horses bolted, and we made no attempt to hold them. (It wouldn't anyhow have been any use). It was grand giving them their heads along the straw-covered track under the great babul trees. My breath was completely pumped out of me, and my cotton habit saturated in sweat when at last they slowed down to a canter. As the sun set an opaque white fog from the canal enveloped us, and our wet cotton clothes became chilly poultices. That evening dining on the *Jhelum,* exhausted but full of well-being, my glass of very weak whiskey and soda half way to my mouth, I was suddenly paralysed by unbelievable pain, my arm fixed in mid-air like a statue's. It was Mrs. Willmore, the doctor's wife who saw my predicament. I was unable to speak. She got me a medicine glass of neat brandy, and held it to my lips, but for some time I was unable to drink. Eventually she enabled me to lie down, and later undressed me. But for several days I was only able to breathe an inch instead of an ell, as it were. I was terrified of moving, and as a matter of fact have never really felt myself since.

There has not been much chance of rest. One thing on top of another. First the Blanco affair. Then we went to Lahore. Then we had Sir Charles Monroe, the Commander-in-Chief, and his staff staying. He was fascinated by Owen's calves. I found him stooping and gazing entranced, murmuring to himself "What a 'forward' he'll make some day". Then a guest got enteric. He was not seriously ill but was not an easy patient, storming and raging against the doctor's starvation diet of only a very little milk, even when convalescent. Then darling fat Lep died of pneumonia, and Rainey has red mange from the last jackal she killed in the compound, and all the time nursing my Lubin. It seems impossible a creature can live with a head that so burns to the touch. The Khairpur vet thought snake bite, Old Haji here thought a babul thorn had broken off and was suppurating. Now a hard lump has developed on his stifle joint, and Haji is positive it is hook worm. Whatever it is it entails endless fomentations. A pattawalla brings the charcoal sigri and kettle, and

Ayah and Nanny and I apply freshly wrung out cloths at intervals of two minutes for half an hour at a stretch. At the same time one of us bathes his head in iced water. It comforts him. Everybody loves Lubin with his clownish ways.

Haji lances the lump, and now the end of the worm should appear through the wound, and we shall wind it round a match, a little every day till at last the whole worm is withdrawn intact. This is the explanation of those wriggly seams one so often sees down the calves of the people. But no worm appears from Lubin; and daily he becomes more wasted, his eyes brilliant, the whites blue as the whites of plover's eggs.

It would be better to put him to sleep, but Haji is dead against it, and the old boy has such a heart, that at Henry's step he always lifts his head, and hitches a black lip to grin at him. But I feel I cannot go on much longer. It is not only the nursing, but these increasing night-sweats prostrate me. I have had night dresses made of thick Chinese crêpe to try and sop up the perspiration, and each night Ayah lays two fresh sheets and a large bath towel by my bed. At last it is decided Lubin must be put to sleep. Haji is to come to-night at eight o'clock. It is one of our bi-weekly dinners. I tell Henry he must make my excuses. Henry comes along dressed. He finds me crouched over poor Lubin stroking his burning head, and those ribs starting like hoops through his sides. Tears are trickling down my nose. Unwillingly Haji brings out a white cone to administer chloroform. Lubin had been practically unconscious lying flat on his side, one pink ear inside out . . . but at that moment he opens a sunken eye, hitches up his lip and grins while the extreme tip of his tail quivers.

"Sahib. How is it possible for me to kill a dog who laughs at me?" exclaims Haji sinking back on his heels.

Lubin is reprieved.

Henry has to go to Bombay. John fetches an English Army vet. He says it is hopeless. John will be present.

It is over. Prussic acid. Instantaneous. His head just fell back. My Boy.

Well I may as well make the others happy. Blanco is to be let off the lead to-day for the first time for six weeks. I put on my old shikar suit. It has been raining, and there are great puddles standing between the scrub. The dogs shall have a jackal hunt.

I tell the pattawallas and the sweeper I don't want them. The whole pack, Lucy, Lavrock, Lucifer, Link, Lakhi and Blanco are charging in and out of the bushes giving tongue. It is still drizzling with rain. Suddenly I see Blanco standing motionless, looking supremely self-conscious. I am reminded of that steamy morning just six weeks ago. He is there in the middle of a puddle. He does not budge . . . and now I see the water all round is becoming crimson. He has done it again!

Splashing into the puddle, lifting up his front leg high as I can, I half lift, half propel him on his hind legs to Government House, shouting at the top of my voice for help. Blood is spouting out. I try to keep my thumb on it—his other leg this time . . . Blanco seems to weigh a ton . . . he is oddly passive. Pattawallas come running. Kalu and the car fetched. We stagger in, and covered in blood and mud and rain drive furiously to Haji's.

As we turn in at the gate . . . oh what is this? A hand-cart pushed by the sweeper, and on it stretched out flat on his side my dear, my dearest Lubin.

Government House, Karachi. June, 1918

The consultation is over.

Here is the verdict.

Both my lungs are affected. I must not kiss Owen. I must lie absolutely still in bed. If I turn over quickly I might bring on a haemorrhage. I hate blood. I hate the look of it. I hate the smell of it. And already twice I have all but died of haemorrhage. Once after a major operation performed as a last chance by Sir Frederick Treves . . . and then again when Owen was born.

I protest I have no cough. But at once I am reminded of Major X . . . who had no cough but died last week in hospital after only three weeks illness, of galloping consumption. Of course I know this, but it seems an odd thing to remind me of it. I can only suppose it is to induce me to submit to treatment. One doctor insists I must be innoculated with tuberculin. I get very excited. I say I absolutely REFUSE to be done. I tell him I went to see Bernard Shaw's *The Doctor's Dilemma* in company with Sir Almroth Wright, that I was a friend as well as a patient of his, and I knew that he was absolutely opposed to inoculating with tuberculin, as was also our mutual friend Professor William Bulloch of the London Hospital. "Besides", I finish, "I KNOW I have not got it. My temperature and losing weight like this is just malaria".

One doctor says nothing, but the other explains that consumptives never believe they have it. It is a recognised symptom. He is very kind . . . but it almost seems he is forcing me into it.

Tomorrow I am giving that lecture on astronomy to the Tommies. I've drawn and painted a huge diagram of the sun in eclipse with the promontories bursting out in violent flame. Then two days later there is this combined Y.W.C.A. and Y.M.C.A. garden party at G.H. I have set my heart on this being a success, and I had to fight hard against the Collector's wife, and others who think the sexes should be kept apart! I sit up in bed and argue to the two doctors that for this at least I *must* be present. They press me gently back on to my pillows, telling me I may bring on a haemorrhage by getting so excited. Well then, I must go and meet Henry at the station from Bombay to-night and tell him my bad news myself. This too is forbidden. I persist in knowing it is not tuberculosis, and all the while hovering behind is the picture of "Blood". Would it ooze out of my mouth, or come spurting out as from Blanco's leg? Would it be warm and taste salty? Would it look all blotty and bright on my sheets and night-gown . . . and oh! how ill I feel. I only weigh seven stone eight, and these night sweats are terrible. Every night I change not only my nightdress, but my sheets at least twice.

It was dear John who had persuaded me in Henry's absence to this consultation, and now it is John who goes to meet him at the station. I forget and sit bolt upright when Henry comes to my bedside, explaining anxiously he mustn't kiss me. His answer is to put his arms round my skinny shoulders and do so. I believe I cry a little. Henry has never seen me cry. "You *won't* let them give me tuberculin, will you?" "Of course I won't". He is completely calm and confident. A rock as always.

A few days later I'm to go to the Fourth General Hospital to be X-rayed. A Harley Street specialist came there for the war. I like him. Somehow I feel he is on my side. He says drily—"Well she has a very good expansion of chest". I explain I have sung a great deal. He says (talking to me rather than to the doctors) he knows how anxious I must be to hear the result, and he will send it next day. It comes. There are queer dark smudges and marks which should not be there apparently and pepper from a pepper-pot seems to have been sprinkled over the whole thing. The very detailed written description says surprisingly enough I suffer from "chronic bronchitis". How very odd! Bad scars are described, but the final sentence reads, "It is not certain however that these are of tubercular origin".

I am cheered. Nevertheless I have to lie in bed very still and not turn on my side without help. I must be weighed night and morning daily, and drink milk, and milk, and milk again. Any sudden exertion may bring on a haemorrhage. (Now why should turning in bed bring on a haemorrhage, when getting out of bed to be weighed twice daily, and being rolled up and taken to the hospital did not do so?). Having no cough they cannot test my sputum . . . for I have none. But then Major X had none either . . .

Somebody else gives a talk to the Tommies, and John and John's wife run the Y.M.C.A. and Y.W.C.A. party, and how very well they do it! Lying on my bed on the upstair verandah I could hear the voices, and the band, and see through the wooden railings the girls in their white frocks, and the Tommies moving about amongst the clumps of bright cannas on the lovely lawns, playing croquet and other games. It was like being dead and looking down on the earth.

An urgent message comes from some friends in upper Sind. Can we put them up for a night? I have always liked her. She looks ill and harassed. She shows me a hard, dreadful lump on her breast; she is to see a doctor this afternoon.

She is to have an operation here in this house tomorrow morning.

It is over. She is out of her anaesthetic. She is very sick. They have taken off her breast. We were both married the same year. We were both so happy . . . and here she is maimed with a shadow darkening her future, and me motionless in bed with a shadow darkening mine.

The weeks drag by. I don't put on, but that steady loss of weight has been arrested. My temperature is rarely above 99.4°. The night sweats are infinitely less prostrating. I feel worlds better. I declare if I could get to Ziarat I should be perfectly well.

Unfortunately it is bad hot weather. No rain has fallen in the desert. There has been a shocking "Troop train disaster". When the train reached Sukkur, in one carriage alone there were no fewer than twenty-one men dead from heat stroke. It is said they had been careless over putting on their topis at a previous station, and also they had had some beer . . . still . . .

ZIARAT.

Well, we are going to Ziarat. That means crossing the Sind desert in the hot weather though no rain has fallen.

We agree not to mention the temperature till we reach Quetta. The only thing to do. The Mail starts about 9 a.m. The saloon is dim, even dark and looks cool. The close black wire shutters are over each window and behind them the tinted glass, and behind them again the wooden shutters. White coverings glimmer from the chairs and sofas. The various electric fans tilted at correct angles will start when the train does, playing on a wet sheet draped across the top of the carriage, and in the middle of the saloon, awkwardly in the way, is a large zinc tub filled with ice.

We should do.

The moment we start Henry gets into pyjamas, sleeves cut to the shoulder. He settled in his Roorkee chair with the *Pioneer,* whose pages Hyder Khan has seen are stitched together. I lie down in a nightie on the couch which will be my bed to-night. I open the Hindustani grammar which for some reason or other is my invariable companion on a long journey. Owen and Nanny have the bedroom next door. The dogs are in the bath room beyond with its tiled floor and big bath. Beyond that the servants compartment and the kitchen. We are off.

Periodically Hyder Khan or Ibrahim comes in with iced lemon squash. The bath tub has to be emptied as the ice blocks melt into muddy water which the jolting of the train slops over the floor. The hours crawl! You can't look out, but you are aware of the incandescent sky and sand. I loathe the sight of my war knitting and the Hindustani grammar! At sundown the bath is full of muddy water again. Henry calls for more ice and iced drinks. Hyder Khan appears looking strangely perturbed. For once bandobast has broken down. There is no more ice. I rush in seeing the ominous look on Henry's brow. "Never mind. It's evening. The worst over", I say.

My ignorance.

All day the "hot weather" Sind sun had beaten on the arid rocks of the Lakhi Pass. Now the rocks breathe out that infernal heat. It is like opening an oven door. I am amazed. Is it really *possible* such heat can be? The train jolts. We stagger into Nanny and Owen. Both asleep. We go to the dogs. They are very restless. Henry gives them water but it runs from the tap too hot to drink. Henry wets their heads. They are very distressed. One of them is Owen's puppy called ironically enough Lakhi (pronounced lucky).

We lie down again. The black hood is pulled over the light overhead. We go lurching and jolting through the unbelievable heat and half darkness. I can just see Henry fallen uneasily asleep on his stomach. I switch on the little blue light by my side to see the time. Just midnight. In doing so the grass matting on which I lie slips from the woodwork, which burns my hand. This is the hair trigger that sets me off. That woodwork at midnight should be too hot to bear!

"Henry! Henry! The top of my head is blowing off". (Is that my voice?).

He is up. He is in the bath room. Bringing back water. He drenches me. My head, my bed. The water is very hot. Still it saves the situation. The moment is past.

The following morning at dawn pale pupils look from eyes like pits of blood. A horrible thing to see the eyes of a little child like Owen thus.

But we have all escaped heat-stroke.

Ziarat, 1918

We spend the following night at the Residency in Quetta. Early next morning we pack into a big car which will run us up to Ziarat to save that long tonga drive. We are driven by a cheery scallywag in rags, who chatters to us looking back over his shoulder, one hand on the wheel. Delicious climbing into coolness, the assembled hills so uncompromisingly naked at first gradually clothed with a little juniper here and there, and some sharp smelling herb. (Poor Henry, too busy to snatch a few days' leave, instantly obliged to recross that terrible heat of the Sind desert!).

We are putting on woollies. Owen is entranced watching the backward and forward zig-zags of the road as we leave them far below our wheels, but suddenly he lies back in Nanny's arms. "Ba-ba sick?" enquires our scallywag looking back, our near wheels almost over the precipice.

"No, no, just tired".

"But *all* Ba-bas sick just this place here", he insists, and grinned delightedly as Owen was.

The air is sharp and filled with the remembered fragrance of juniper, sweet-briar, thyme, mint and khush-bu. The hills as always ugly at mid-day looking with their yellow rock and black juniper like that horrid spotted thing called "cabinet pudding" . . . but now new ranges of hills come into sight, the valley is carpeted with khush-bu . . . there are the little bungalows . . . the peach trees along the road . . . the streams . . . We are here.

Just before leaving Karachi I had heard of a tragedy. A woman in one of the big business firms had two little boys. These children had been repeatedly and unsuccessfully vaccinated, just as Owen had been. She at last came to the conclusion, as I had, it was no use any more trying to get the vaccine to take. Their ayah went to "her country" on holiday, came back, and gave both little boys confluent small-pox. Both had all but lost their lives, and it was feared that one must lose his sight. Henry had insisted we must try Owen again.

So here at Ziarat I send for the Civil Surgeon. He was a young Indian. Poor Owen bled very freely which I in my ignorance hoped was a good sign. (He did not take!). The young Indian asked me about myself. He was exceedingly sceptical at my having anything wrong with my lungs at all. I showed him my X-rays at which he was still more sceptical. Harley Street specialist or no he declared, X-rays can prove anything or nothing. What was wrong with me was "fever" and the need of change of climate. Now I only write this down to show how strange is the human mind. Here was I frankly appalled at the idea of getting a haemorrhage, yet now feeling a little indignant at this young Indian pooh-poohing the very idea of such a thing!

But any thought of pique was soon forgotten, for almost immediately I did begin to feel perfectly well! Sweats a thing of the past. Always hungry, always full of energy. I got the "politicals" to let me hire a horse from the Escort. Every morning when it was still misty and dewy I was out and away on the hills, along precipitous paths. And then some interfering busy-body wrote to Henry that I was doing too much. I got back a letter . . . a really scorching letter! . . . But here I am, perfectly well, putting on weight steadily, sleeping all night, full of well-being, running full-tilt down the stony paths, rope soles secure on twisted root or rolling stone, impelled to run from exuberance of health. Of what use to rest and take my temperature twice a day? The Indian doctor had not succeeded in making Owen's vaccine take, but he was right enough about me!

Elsie Martin, wife of the Collector in Karachi shares this tiny bungalow with me. She is charming, and highly intelligent. We are entirely different, but become much attached to each other. She tolerates all the bull-terriers, and really they do take up a lot of our very confined space! Her husband, down in Karachi, has the same sense of duty and moral obligation as Henry himself. Little Jean and Owen become fast friends. Owen has a donkey this year, and rides with the other children. We call it Pitcher, Little Pitcher with long ears.

One day an aeroplane comes over the valley and drops a Verey light. Owen is enthralled.

Elsie and I had asked my friend up here to convalesce after her operation. Gone all her fun. She is a haunted woman. The wound is healed, but boil after boil crops up round it causing not only great pain but apprehension. I try not to notice when I see her hand clutch at her breast. She and I had shared illness and fear last June, and now I am riding, climbing, exhilarated and with an immense appetite. And she is a melancholy ghost. How heartless to be cheerful, to savour these glorious blue days like crystal, the leaves splashed with colour, the little streams locked each night in ice. Yet will it help her if Elsie and I go about gloomily, and repress little Owen, and Jean's *joie de vivre*?

Very difficult.

The nights get colder and colder. Last thing I build up the wood fire in my bedroom. The juniper smells delicious. The flames dance over the ceiling cloth which bulges here and there as a civet cat moves about behind it. I have two hot water bottles in my bed, and two bull-terriers on it. They take up all the room and when I shift, growl lazily. I sleep in woolly gloves. As for little Nanny she is so chapped by the edgy wind and sun her hands and legs are bound with rag and cold cream.

Owen's little face is burned a honeyed-rose. The child's great eyes shine dark in his face, though his flyaway hair is almost incandescent in its silveriness. He looks unearthly . . . in no sense delicate, but like some fairy child belonging to those hills which now glitter like blue glass cliffs through the autumn days, and gleam a terrifying gilt in the after-glow.

To-day I rode down the valley with a Pathan. He bestrode, on its hind quarters, a pattering donkey, so small he had to tuck up his feet so that they should not touch the ground. He spoke as these men so often speak of the beauties of his country. And then with a faraway look in his eyes he went on to tell me that once he had gone to Bombay for three years, for many of his people were there. But the longing and yearning for his own country was such that he fell sick and was like to die. But that as soon as he returned to his mountains God gave him back his health. Now by his words I recognised him to be that most villainous of ruffians, a Muhammadan money lender. But it seemed to me that some of his villainy was purged away by the passionate love of the clean silences, the sweet smells of his mountains.

Even as I write this diary, a letter is brought to me from a boy in a Baluchi Regiment. "They are a funny crush", he writes. "Their weak point is home-sickness. If they are refused leave they generally clear out without it. God knows what they see in their country. Stones and rocks and juniper trees, varied by juniper trees and rocks and stones. What on earth can they see in it?"

I think I know.

I was riding this morning down the misty sunny valley. I overtook a Pathan woman and her daughter trudging down the valley road. Little Saman was nine or so, handsome and golden as some little hawk. Hers was a hard little face with its ready smile and sad eyes. I greeted them, and the woman handed up to me a head of Indian corn, green and very tender. To prove to her I had no money I turned out the pockets of my riding coat. In spite of evident disappointment the woman laughed, signing to me to keep the Indian corn. She strode on holding her coarse black yarn with one uplifted hand, whilst from the other rhymically dangled and swung the little chip of juniper wood on which it was being wound.

But little Saman lingered.

We regarded each other gravely.

She was a bare-legged slip in a wide-sleeved dusky scarlet and indigo chola, embroidered on the breast with innumerable white china buttons. Beneath the ashen white of her chadder which she held in one small hand I could see that her hair was very neatly parted and plaited into innumerable tiny plaits hanging on each side of that broad little face, and each plait was fastened off with bootlaces and china buttons. Her glossy brows were bent, her lips set hard. She was thinking deeply. Now she spoke Pushtu and I Urdu. I am ashamed to confess I thought she was loitering in the hope of baksheesh, and to convince her I again turned out my empty pockets. She shook her head. She was clearly perplexed. Then her brow cleared. Darting to the roadside she broke off a large and almost leafless branch which was studded with waxy pink berries. Still regarding me under those straight glossy brows, she bit off the thorns with her square little teeth. Then approaching my rearing and backing horse she handed up the branch with that smile which left her eyes so sad.

Then without waiting for thanks the little girl padded swiftly after her mother.

There were very few berries on my wand, and still a great many thorns. I was riding a hot little Baluchi chestnut from the Escort. Hitherto his rider had been a sowar who had waved such *kuch nahin* ("nothing at all") as Saman and her mother aside with bared sword. The dignity of the chestnut was outraged. He gave me endless trouble all the way home. I longed to throw away my thorny and top-heavy branch . . . but how was that possible when little Saman with such rare delicacy had plucked and given the second gift to show that she bore no resentment for empty pockets?

Curious thing Fear. I should much dislike to go alone into a smart London restaurant and order myself dinner, yet I suppose many people would think it astonishing that Mrs. Martin and I are remaining here on these desolate hills, the two white people amongst the Pathans, who themselves are beginning to "go down the Hill" to winter quarters. Elsie does not care to go out far alone, but I wander for miles completely happy. Indeed it is only when I am quite alone I feel that friendly companionship with all things, part of the pattern, like the gods and the animals, and trees in Hindu carving, the animals and the flowers in a Persian picture, or French tapestry. One is reinforced as it were by their presence.

To-night, sunset found me far from home toiling up a lonely unexplored tangi. Narrow it was and gloomy, with here and there pools of stagnant water. A couple of ravens winged over my head, the beat of their wings very heavy. I passed a dead tortoise. Even with my rope soles my "road was a speediless one", as old Thomas McCrystal would have said, for not only were there the usual stones of the torrent bed, but here and there immense boulders had completely blocked the gorge and had to be climbed over. High overhead a strip of primrose sky wound, the clinging junipers looking like toys etched blackly against it. Gloomy and dreadful it was.

I had thought to be quite alone, but suddenly the sound of a

Pathan song was trolled out in a bold tenor not thirty yards away. The final sustained note went wailing and echoing all down the narrow gorge till the echoes rang. It was startling. The typical pause. Then another voice broke in with another fragment, and the long sustained note. A brief interval for talk and laughter, and yet another voice, loud as the other two, burst out ending too in that long sustained note.

As the tangi turned I came upon the little group of Pathans . . . lads all of them, blue-black locks bobbed to the naked shoulder, beardless chins and merry black eyes. They had hollowed out for themselves little shallow forms in the gravel much as a hare does, and were lying beneath an overhanging rock. A fire of dead juniper branches crackled, and from a pot half seen in the blue smoke came a savoury smell. It is impossible to convey the merriness, the jolliness, the lark of it all.

"You have a good place here", said I.

"Han", retorted a young fellow pointing to the overhanging rock. *"Bahut acchha Bangla, bahut umda Bangla, Khuda ka Bangla.* Yes a fine house, an excellent house, God's House". They burst out into happy laughter amongst themselves, and as I turned to go I carried away the impression of firelight on black ringlets, on bright eyes, and short square teeth.

"Salaam memsahib, Salaam", they all called out together like a crowd of starlings, and once again the bold loud tenor trolled forth and the long sustained note went echoing down the tangi.

I feel a certain guiltiness in writing this down. Pathans are not angels. It was stupid and wrong of me to wander alone as I did, not fair to Owen and not fair to Henry. It all sounds very sentimental and gushy, and "lady-novelisty", but every word is true.

I had heard that some Baluchi shepherds have magnificent and enormous sheep-dogs, white with fur like wool. Very savage. I met one this evening, and confess to being a little scared. He advanced to Rainey on tip toes, and paid the usual respects in a perfectly gentleman-like way, but she, always on the lookout for insults, whipped round and sprang up at his throat.

But those punishing jaws of hers merely sank into layer after layer of wool.

So surprised was she that she instantly let go, fell backwards on the road and lay there, eyes shut, paws in the air.

I never saw anything more ludicrous. The shrew punished for once . . .

There was a thunderstorm this afternoon, and for a short time the torrent bed was completely hidden in a roar of angry waters. Now there were only a few pools left to catch the dying light, and the valley lay dark and wet and silent beneath the still bright sky. For though the sun had set, great clouds like fireships came sailing over the black hill tops, and from their apricot billows lightning still slipped, to be lost in the clear ice-green sky overhead. Up the darkening valley a North wind blew very fresh and free. Already it had begun to freeze, so when a fire danced out beneath an old juniper amongst the mummied khush-bu it looked so welcome I instinctively turned towards it.

There came the sound of voices loud and echoing. A Pathan can never talk; he only calls, whether it be across the valley or to one crouched on the other side of the fire. There were explosive laughs, a baby crowing, and the inarticulate cries of mother-love so alike all the world over. I came upon a wonderfully pleasant little picture picked out from the gathering darkness by dancing flames. Under the juniper squatted a hill man, his arms folded on his knees, his teeth gleaming in the firelight as he watched his woman alternately tossing and hugging an entirely naked baby. A girl with a tousled head was laughing too, but she played with a little sheep. One moment the little creature charged and butted, the next it was cuddling all golden in her arms. And scattered around in the darkness, some in the firelight, was a tiny flock of goats and sheep.

Seldom have I seen more desperate poverty. The mother a laughing, and for once handsome creature, was in rags which gaped and showed her flesh. I asked her man why she did not mend them.

"Memsahib", he replied in his halting Urdu, "How could sufficient thread be paid for?"

He himself had no shirt. The felt coat with its sleeves sewn up which is worn cape wise, he held decently across his chest with one hand, but his splendid shoulders had thrust through great rents and gleamed like dark old copper.

The girl drew nearer. Tangled hair fell over her face, her bright eyes peeping and dancing through. I could see her visibly shivering, yet when I asked if they were not very cold, she and her mother laughed at each other, their long eyes nearly shut by reason of their lashes.

"The season of ice has hardly begun", explained the man stirring the fire with a juniper branch.

"What have you there in the pot? Kid?" (for the feast of Bak-ri-id had been the day before).

That amused my friends. "Meat? How should folks such as we eat meat? Flour is our food, and water is now boiling in the pot".

"You have no blankets, no shelter?"

"We have the juniper".

"And the baby, when it gets very cold?".

The Pathan translated to the woman behind him without turning his head.

She burst out laughing over the baby's topknot.

"See", she cried with beautiful pride; and steadying the baby with one hand she groped behind her with the other, and produced a little scarlet shirt—only cotton, but it was covered with stitches and many white china buttons. In each tiny sleeve was a triangular opening outlined with more stitchery and white buttons.

"When the ice comes we shall sleep with the little sheep in our arms", concluded the Pathan.

The evenings . . . In the darkness outside, the hills watchful and suspicious, and every bush stiffening slowly in frost. Inside, friendliness and warmth. Our tiny sitting-room is alive with lamp-light and firelight. Elsie and I, the salt cellar between us, munching very fresh walnuts, our fingers stained from picking off the crinkly damp golden skin, while the bull-terriers prop themselves against our legs staring into the blazing logs with half-shut eyes. We talk and talk. We read and read . . . often aloud one to the other.

I know far more about Sir Charles Napier than I did that time when the Sirdar came to pay his respects from Napierabad. Just as from the letters of some people you actually hear the tone of their voice, so now I actually hear the voice of my kinsman from his journals, and his letters. Indeed I feel a warmth of affection for him as though he were still living. Whether he be lashing himself into fury over the directors of the East India Company[1], or poking fun at himself, or making vain resolutions to give up using bad language, or vehemently declaring "Protestants and Catholics and Greek by their nonsense delay the progress of their creed, but Jesus Christ is too strong for all their foolery. His words, His deeds His life are known and will overthrow all their absurdities in time", he seems to be actually speaking.

"Have you no conscience at all?" demands Sir George Arthur goaded by those incessant demands for improvement. "What a question to ask a Governor. No to be sure I have not. Did you ever know a Governor who had? He would if discovered be stuffed and sent to the Museum. However as far as I am concerned drying would be unnecessary. Scinde has done that".

Carlyle in his praise had added, "A singular veracity one finds in him, not in his words alone which however I like much for their fine rough naiveté".

His very inconsistencies intrigue me!

The man who wrote "The feeling that when battle comes on like a storm, thousands of brave men are rushing to meet it, confident in your skill to direct, is indescribable; it is greater than the feeling of gladness after victory . . . there is no feeling to equal that exultation . . . " is the same man who wrote of himself and his brothers "We are

1 The Government of India, whether Civil or Military, was under the East India Company at this time.

all a hot violent crew . . . fond of hunting, fishing and shooting, yet gave them all up when young, because we had no pleasure in killing little animals".

When dying he said "I may have to reproach myself for some things but not my regard for the soldier's welfare". But he had written "Rogues always play upon mildness. How the devil can I make soldiers attend by sending a civil message to a rascal a thousand miles off with 'Pray Sir, do me the favour not to get drunk at mid-day. Do think how wrong it is, at least if not wrong at least it is not right'. By the Lord Harry it won't do! Oak trees cannot be cut down with penknives, and so I must and do use the hatchet now and then".

He was long before his time in his dislike of pomp and show. "Old Indians", he writes, "say 'there is no respect for you in India without magnificence and show'. A greater fallacy does not exist. Trumpery and humbug are the enemies in India, as they were and are the enemies of the Indian Princes". (How very like Henry!) One can imagine the contempt with which Charles regarded Lord Dalhousie's pomp when travelling:

"Elephants 135
Camels 1,960
Bullocks 700
Carts 135
Tents 488

Exclusive of the escort the establishment amounts to 6000, but this I apprehend does not include private servants and followers. This camp in motion must cover nearly six miles of ground, and with the baggage of the escort, etc., which would probably cover 8 miles, but in this calculation I reckon an addition of one third of the actual distance to meet the interval caused by the lagging of over-loaded animals".

As Commander-in-Chief he did his best to set an example of moderation, cutting down his elephants, camels and baggage when on inspection to the minimum, thereby saving the Treasury £750 a month. Hitherto officers had done their campaigning in comfort with many servants and the best of wine and food! It enraged Charles. He declared that "two towels and a piece of soap are all that an officer needs in the field besides his ordinary clothes".

Listen to a sample of his day. He is writing from Peshawar to his sister, and is now sixty-nine years old.

"Got up at four o'clock, and rode my elephant till daylight: then mounted my beautiful white Arab Mosaic, and galloped him fourteen miles to the disparagement of some of my retinue half my age who were knocked up: a hearty breakfast after at seven, and from that time to five o'clock write! write! write! and my horse is now waiting for me to review two regiments".

"Write! write! write!" Did not this extraordinary man in the midst of his Sind campaign have his little daughter's lessons sent out to him so that he could correct them and mark their progress?

Susan and Emily were to learn only useful things at first. "My object is to give them means to work, and then they can become as *blue* as burning brandy. So:

1 Religion as the foundation.

2 Accounts to teach the value of money, and how to regulate a a house. To be a good accountant at twelve.

3 Work, that spare hours may not be lost if rich, and if poor they may make their own things.

4 Cooking to a certain extent.

5 French that they may not be dumb in a foreign land. These things I can teach them till they are fourteen. Then they shall learn anything to which their tastes incline".

No. We are not dull, Elsie and I, up in our eyrie. Hours of sparkling sunshine and long evenings in the company of half-forgotten heroes . . . Too soon we must go down into the arena again.

That little glade on the pipe-line where the forget-me-nots and the little white Scotch roses grow had always been a favourite place for the English children. You can still see traces of their picnic fires, but no longer do you come on the nurses, the ayahs and pattawallas, the donkeys with their ring saddles, and the canvas palanquin for the baby! For politicals and Quetta officials of all kinds have gone down the hill, some time ago. Bungalows are shut up and boarded for seven months. The convolvulus climbing up the slanting strings by the Post Office is withered, and the mountain side is splashed with carmine and lemon leaves on the little shrubs. The flocks too have moved down a thousand feet or more to their winter quarters, and no longer can we hear, when the valley is swimming in light, the rattle and slide of shale as the goats and sheep trickle down from the hills on the east, and the hills on the west; no longer do we hear the incessant baaing, and the calls of the little shepherd boys crossing and recrossing from hill to hill, weaving lovely arabesques of sound over our heads. Indeed the valley is oddly silent in the evenings, for the streams begin to freeze by sundown. The tribesmen themselves will be going down next month, for Ziarat will be lying under snow all the winter months.

For some time now Elsie Martin and I have been the only white people within many many miles. We ought to pack up . . . we keep saying we must, yet we linger. There is something so stimulating, so exciting, so exquisite about these brilliant lonely days following one another like glass beads. The children have wild-rose cheeks, and transparent eyes. Their hair and their clothes crackle with electricity.

Elsie's forehead above that intelligent eager face of hers is always lovely with its pencilled brows. Now it seems to gleam like pearl. We are filled with joy, intoxicated with the isolation, the beauty around us. We are like beings translated to another sphere.

Wandering down the valley road after tea I heard a familiar sound, the inconsequent piping of one of the little shepherd boys . . . He was down by the dry torrent bed, sitting on his hunkers, and piping. In spite of the wind whistling up the valley, he was naked to the hip and the thinness of his body gleamed like new copper in the horizontal rays of the setting sun. Between a shock of matted black curls his face was just a wedge with high pointed ears. By now I can manage a few words of Pushtu, but he would not speak, just playing on, his mouth twisted to the scarlet pipe, his eyes so deeply set, that their glossy brows hid the upper line of lashes as he stared back at me.

Rocks and stones sunlit a few moments before were now lifeless. It was freezing cold; the wind seemed to flay one. I turned to go. The mocking notes tripped after me. I turned my head. The little piper had vanished.

I told Elsie about him as we sat over the crackling juniper fire. She stared: "But all the flocks and shepherds have gone!"

So they had. I'd forgotten. How strange.

In the succeeding dazzling blue days there was a kind of suppressed excitement. The feeling is hard to convey, but it was as though something were urging, almost compelling us to go down the hill. I kept looking over my shoulder expecting to see something I did not want to see. Silent little birds hidden in the shrubs flew out with whirr of wings that startled me. The very hills, shining like cliffs, made of blue glass through blue water, seemed to my excited fancy to be crying:

"Ah. You too must go now. The English have long gone. The camels. The flocks and the shepherds. Many of the tribesmen. The magpies will go soon. And the ravens with their voracious beaks. All have to go. Nobody knows what we are going to do when they are gone. Nobody knows".

Still we lingered. There had appeared a strange outbreak of illness in Karachi. In fact all over Sind. Henry was very anxious I should not come back into it. They called it influenza, but people were actually dying. Elsie Martin's husband wrote their cook had died and his mate. Then our husbands wrote they would shortly come and fetch us down. In the meantime we had better stay on. There on our mountain top we seemed to be enclosed in a blue glass bead like a fly in amber secure from all trouble . . .

Then one morning at dawn, as I lay too cold to sleep, I heard a little sound, sweet and twisting. I thought it was a little shepherd far far away on the hills. I remembered the little lad I had seen with the pointed ears thrusting through his curls.

But the little shepherds had gone down the hill!

The following morning as the stars were paling in my window I heard it again. It must be some tiny migrant bird, I told myself.

But the third morning when the tiny pipe awoke me, suddenly I was afraid. The blood seemed to creep icily down my thighs, for with the piping came the scrambling of hoofs, and the fall of scree. Something whispered to me "Pan is not dead".

Then I knew the hills had won. I said to Elsie, "Really we must go". We wired to our husbands. Henry wired back he was sending up Ibrahim, a treasure only second to Hyder Khan, and another pattawalla to help us to pack up beds and furniture and shut up the bungalow. He himself had to go to Sukkur, but he would come on to Quetta and we could travel back together. Mr. Martin was also sending up a boy to help Elsie, and we must take great care of ourselves and the children, as the epidemic was getting very serious indeed.

That morning I went for my last ride. As we clattered along, my little Baluchi pony's half-moon ears cocked so that their tips met, it seemed to me as though something or other were triumphing, as though the hills and the junipers were crying exultantly. "Nobody knows what we are going to do now. Nobody knows what we are going to do now".

Ibrahim, and the Martin's second boy arrived. Full of alarming tales. According to them people are dying everywhere from this influenza. It has spread up to Quetta and men and women are dropping dead in the streets. Only last night a case was reported up here at Ziarat. We are to start day after tomorrow. Camels will be loaded at dawn with all furniture including the very beds we sleep on. We, with the children and servants, will leave here at nine, in tongas, changing ponies twice, and catching the mail train at Kacch to Quetta at noon. Henry will be at Quetta and we shall all sleep at the Residency, then go on to Sukkur.

Later

Elsie's ayah has gone down with high fever. Of course this is the usual month for malaria, but if she thinks it is this Spanish influenza she will probably die. Our invaluable sweeper Fakira reports sick, and also the pattawalla up from Karachi. I hand out the usual aspirin and quinine. Ibrahim has a very heavy cold. He is magnificent. Directing operations like some general, yet not above cording boxes and travelling bookcases himself. Anything to save me. He looks shockingly ill. I dare not take his temperature. Elsie worried to death over Jean. Nannie calm and sensible as always.

Next day

Hideously cold getting out of bed, and dressing in the dark. The children cross. Hurried breakfast. Ibrahim folding up this table and that chair even while we eat. Presently there is not even a wicker mohra left to sit on. The bull-terriers trying to clamber on to one's lap to get warm. Pushing, shoving, immoveably in the way when you want to pass. We safety-pin rugs over the children's coats and they watch the camels being loaded up. There is straw blowing everywhere in that edgy wind. The camel-men shout, the camels snarl and blow bubbles. At last the long file, top-heavy with wooden cases and travelling chests-of-drawers and almiras and bundles, goes lurching down the little path to the valley road. The bungalow has been nailed up, doors and windows, for the cold weather.

We sit outside.

The tongas have not turned up. The sun is climbing the sky. The children swaddled in coats and rugs are complaining they are too hot. No sign of the tongas. Ibrahim coughs and coughs. Elsie's ayah is weeping. Still no sign of a tonga.

Anything to keep the children quiet. Carrying our small stuff we clamber down the little path to the road. What can have happened? We sit there in the sun and the dust and the dead khush-bu, and then at last comes news. The "Head" of the tonga wallahs died last night of influenza and is even now being buried. Indeed we can hear sounds coming from the little Qabristan I have so often ridden by.

Between the rude posts at head and foot of the graves a white tape is suspended weighted in the middle by a stone . . . the soul of man betwixt heaven and hell. Where the grave is a man's you see locks of dark hair, tied to the post rotting in the sun and wind. I can see it all, as I hear the noise of the tonga wallas lamenting . . .

But what is to be done? Thirty-two miles of stony desolate mountains lie between us and Kacch, and the train leaves at noon. Our bungalow is nailed and boarded up. There is no furniture, no food, and here are two small children, several sick servants, and four ramping bull terriers.

Now the children are far too hot. Their cheeks are like crimson silk. They are hungry. They are thirsty. They are cross. We open the sandwiches that should have been eaten at the second post for changing ponies . . . and wait again in the sun and the dust.

An hour before the train is due to leave Kacch, there is a great jingling of bells and all the tongas arrive from the graveyard.

We have thirty-two miles of switch-back deplorable road, and to change ponies twice in that time. Elsie and Jean rattle off in the first tonga. Then comes Nannie and Owen, then me trying vainly to hold the struggling Blanco. He tramples on me till my thighs must be black and blue, his stern knocks my topi continually sideways. Follows the sick Fakira with the other dogs, and more tongas with servants and small luggage. As we rattle and gallop headlong down the road covered with loose stones with a great ringing ching of bells, as we grind and lurch over dry torrent beds, one wheel right up in the air, as the hills rise higher and higher behind us, they seem to me to be pushing us down in triumph. I seem to hear them saying, almost screaming, "You are gone now. You are gone. Nobody knows what we are going to do now . . . go . . . ing . . . to . . . do . . . now . . .".

Sukkur.

Heat, heat, heat. Sizzling heat! At night we try to sleep on the roof. Tortured by sand flies. (I had not met them before. They penetrate any mosquito net. They set one's blood on fire).

All day we are shuttered in dark rooms where one cannot see to read or work and the burning wind howls and raves outside like a wild beast trying to get in, and the sand comes seeping under the doors; everything you touch is gritty, and if you smile the corners of your mouth will split, so dry is your skin.

But in the evening the wind drops and Sukkur is as beautiful to me as ever. The mud buildings of Rohri rise like golden cliffs into the sky. We look from the Circuit House down onto the river, a broad golden flood with the island of Bukkha, and the island of Sath Bela with its Sikh monastery. And up through the quivering swimmy golden air rises the sound of the monastery bells *Tata-Tata*! *Tata-Tata*! and the harsh knocking reminding one of Tenebrae in a Roman Catholic church at home.

So much has happened since last week. When we arrived at Kacch at sunset it was to find the train which had been due at noon had not yet come in! We camped in an icy little room, and the bull-terriers squeezed and pressed into one to try and get warm. (If only they would not stand on one's foot and be impossible to push off). It was two in the morning before we reached Quetta. Henry had been waiting hours at the station. Oh the comfort to see him! We drove to the Residency, and tumbled into bed with hot bottles and hot drinks. Influenza was raging, it appeared, and the death-roll shocking. The following morning I saw carts of dead going through the streets. One is used to seeing uncovered dead in India, but it was dreadful to see these bundles of bodies in carts like bundles of asparagus—a dreadful simile! I kept on thinking of that. I remembered too that letter of Sir Charles, when eight hundred of his men had died of cholera in a few days; the carts carrying away the dead "their legs sticking stiffly out", and "a dying Belooch said to me 'O General, if we were dying in battle with you we should be happy, but to die like this!' And how lightly it would have been to me in comparison if my dear boy[1] had been smashed by a cannonshot. The mind and heart and nerve are sick under these perpetual slaughters".

[1] His much loved nephew.

The following day we came on to Sukkur. Ibrahim had seemed better. Indeed in the Residency garden I had seen him teaching Owen to wrestle Sindi fashion. When the train passed near his village he asked leave to go and see his people for a night. He found them all down with influenza. He waited on them, and the following morning he himself was dead. Dear Ibrahim. I cannot say how I shall miss him.

In Sukkur the epidemic is very bad. All the dhobis have fled from the town . Consequently the dhobi ghat has been locked up and none of the Europeans can get at their washing. Mrs. Barlee, the Judge's wife, has pluckily been down to-day with one or two helpers, and in this sizzling heat sorted out everybody's sheets and clothing. This is the sort of thing the white woman takes in her stride out here, contrary to the notions of some of our politicians and novelists at home! It reminds me somehow of the Indian in the I.C.S. who objected to being posted to Sukkur, declaring the climate was too bad for any one but an Englishman: reminds me too it is an Englishman who usually has to translate Sindi to the Mahratta, Mahratti to the Gujerati, and so on!

But to return to the influenza. The extraordinary thing is that some of the most devasted villages are away in the desert where you would suppose no infection could come. Henry and I rode out to one of these. A week or so ago there were seventy-seven souls, and now there are two. An aged grand-mother or great-grand-mother, and a newly born baby. Here in Sukkur the ryots cannot afford to go on buying wood for burning even if the wood were there, which it is not, so bodies are thrown into the Indus as they are.

Note from *British Rule in India,* by Thompson and Garratt:

"The influenza epidemic attacking a third of the population and resulting in some twelve or thirteen million deaths. It caused more havoc in a few months than bubonic plague during the previous twenty years".

The Armistice. Sukkur, 1918

Thankfulness. Deep thankfulness. But neither Henry nor I are inclined for the little Club, or wild rejoicing. I sit up in my eyrie and paint the strange minaret of Mir Masum Shah rising up into the Western sky. Right below me is a tawny dusty blur of palm trees, flat topped buildings, and the faintly seen road with a raggle-taggle procession of Indians with banners, and the squeak and bang and rattle of Indian music . . . and over all the voice, so beautiful, of the muezzin.

In the evening we look down on Sukkur all sprinkled with lights. And the great cantilever bridge spanning the Indus is outlined with the fairy lights, prepared by the P.W.D. for some time. Every little window in the cliff-like houses of Rohri has its little lamp. The fireworks are magnificent; we go down on the steamer to watch them. The rockets soar and climb to the zenith and burst in showers of stars reflected in the water. All down the river float hundreds and hundreds of little lights racing down on the mighty current. Little lamps fashioned like red white and golden lotus flowers with flaming wicks for sepals. First they came in a long thin line stringing two miles across from bank to bank, so that in the fresh blowy darkness, as we watched that steady advance, the thought came that these were the souls of the dead whose victories we were celebrating. Then as the brightness drew nearer, black gaps of water showed. And now the current whirled some into a backwater where they glowed and clustered awhile before following their fellows, racing swiftly down in little companies of twos and threes. A few came bumping into the steamer's side and looking down we could see into their very hearts where the wicks burned so bravely, before they sped on once again. Far as the eye could reach up stream, hundreds and thousands of little hurrying lamps with their quivering reflections on that night of Armistice, 1918.

SIND, 1918

It had always been a pet scheme of Henry's to introduce olive-growing into Sind. But like so many other things it could not be done during the war. Now we get a wild olive and an Italian one as a symbol of peace and plant them in the grounds of Government House. I feel there should be some suitable inscription, and plague Henry to think of something classical. For once he is unable. He refers me to Mr. Calthrop Kennedy, the Judge, who in a few hours sends me across the following:

"Cedant Arma Togae.
November 11th, 1918
Teutonibus victis posuit Laurentia signum".

Later this was engraved on marble and placed by the two trees.

Strenuous work and nerve strain for everybody preparing for the victory celebrations in Karachi. Henry has to be in Bombay, so I am acting for him. There is so much sickness still, I dare not let Owen watch the sports and games and feastings of thousands which will take place on the great maidan in front of Government House.

The evening of November 26th was most moving. Thousands upon thousands were assembled under a sky which was more lovely than any I have ever seen. On a little platform below the Union Jack I stood to take the salute of twelve thousand marching school-children, European, Eurasian, Muslim and Hindu. They were all carrying flags and bright tinsel favours. They marched eight abreast, escorted by the military bands and officers of the Bedfordshire Regiment. I had my back to the West, so as these children passed before me their uplifted rapturous faces were painted in golden light as though they saw some glorious vision. They cheered and cheered again, and all the multitudes around were cheering too. It was a wonderful sight. Those illumined faces, the brilliant satins and silks of saris, the white dresses of the Eurasians and Europeans, the flags and favours, the brass instruments of the band all glittering through the clouds of rising burnished dust . . . all beneath that strange flamingo sky.

The sight, the sound, the thought of what it meant. I trembled and shook.

Separation of Sind, 1918

There has been much talk lately on the separation of Sind. Sind, when conquered by Sir Charles, was ruled by him from his Government House. When he retired it was handed over to the Bombay Government, though a large measure of independence (jealously prized) was left to the officer in charge, known as the Commissioner-in-Sind, who issued his own regulations, had his headquarters in Government House, Karachi, and had the comfortable steamer *Jhelum* for travelling up and down the river Indus on his tours of inspection.

My diary will have shown how dissimilar are the two provinces. The population of Bombay is chiefly Hindu, the population of Sind Muhammadan. Instead of "men like monkeys" (as Hyder Khan had disdainfully described the men, at all events of the Konkan) here are bearded upstanding Sindis and Baluchis looking as though they had stepped out of the Bible. The very goats are big as calves. The Province of Bombay depends on its heavy monsoon rains for its agriculture. Sind may go for five years without any rain at all. Much of it is desert. Camels are universal, and the crops grow bountifully, though they only can be grown on water drawn from the canals cut from the Indus.

The great Sukkur Barrage will make Sind one of the granaries of the world. The inundation season in the hot weather, when the snows melt in the Himalayas, brings huge and majestic floods of water sweeping precious fertile silt through the Punjab, through Sind, uselessly out to sea. The Barrage will allow this water to flow into the canals, but some Sindis fear that in the cold weather when the river runs low, the Punjabis with their systems of barrages higher up will take the water before it reaches Sind. Henry and others feel this danger would be removed if one single Government were responsible for the prosperity of both the Punjab and Sind. Therefore why not unite Sind to the Punjab rather than to the Bombay Presidency, with which it has nothing in common, in people, in climate, in religion?

But we have a new Governor, determined that such a jewel as Sind shall not be picked out of his crown. What is more, he is suspicious that Henry might be advocating this change for personal reasons. (I could laugh if it did not make me so angry). "I mean to grapple Sind to myself with hoops of steel!" he told Henry bitterly at their very first interview. Both men respected each other's brains and capacity for hard work, but they were not "sympathetic". Sir George lays much value on the pomp and ceremony to which his estate entitles him.[1] Henry cares less than nothing at all for it. Sir George, perhaps because he was, as he was for ever proclaiming himself, "a business man" would prefer the astute Hindu. Henry championed the Muhammadan, who by reason of being generally less educated, got pushed and shouldered aside from any appointment carrying responsibility.

I forsee rocks ahead.

Camp, Sujawal, December, 1918

This is the extraordinary coincidence which has probably saved the lives of Henry, Kalu and myself.

In this district there is much salt in the sand, and when rain falls, which may be only once in five years, it has the peculiar effect of binding the sand into a slimy impacted mass, so that camels slither and spreadeagle and may split themselves, and human beings will find each foot as large as a meat dish after one or two steps.

Henry was making a circular tour of inspection of some eighty miles, revisiting scenes of his earliest schemes in agriculture. Starting early as always, it was decidedly parky. Heavy dew on the tamarisk, fingers and nose chilly, a rug round one's legs acceptable. But after

[1] Later on the Prince of Wales wrote home disgruntledly that there was far more state kept up at Government House, Bombay, than in Buckingham Palace.

leaving Maghilbhin and its babul trees it soon warmed up. Kalu drove a bit carelessly over a culvert. There was an ominous bump and grinding noise. The Fiat has low clearance and we had loosened the exhaust pipe. Kalu tightened it with a length of cord. Now the day was getting hot. As we came to the desert it lay glittering before us like mica, every tiny pebble casting its sharp blue shadow as on snow.

It had been arranged for mounted police to be posted along a camel track at intervals of two miles to show us the way. Each sowar was to deliver us to the next waiting sowar who would be waiting in profile, looking just like a lead soldier with his short sharp noon-day shadow just beneath him like a tin stand! As the car drew level, the tin soldier came suddenly to life. Saluting he would wheel round his flea-bitten Arab. The animal would pivot, rear with arched neck and flying mane and tail to gallop alongside the car for the following two miles. And all the while his long tail would flash and brandish over his hindquarters, Arab fashion, like a flag.

Lovely. I was sorry when the last of the sowars had wheeled and galloped off, leaving us to follow a faint track patterned by the pads of camels.

For some time there had been ominous rattlings and bumps. No longer could they be denied. The exhaust pipe fell off altogether. Whilst we ate our tiffin Kalu fastened it on again with the fraying cord, adding his braces to strengthen it. Shortly it was off again. This time I surrendered my white petticoat. Ten minutes later this too had worn through, and the pipe lay in the sand.

"Very well. We'll go on without it", announced Henry calmly.

So the clumsy hot pipe was put in at the back of the car with Kalu, and Henry drove deeper into the desert, me sitting beside him.

Long before this, coats had been discarded, the rug pushed away, and black glasses worn to mitigate the glare, for Henry and I never have the top on the car when he is inspecting. The desert itself seemed only another part of that radiant light which was the sky.

I grew restless.

"It's hot", I said.

"Well what do you expect in the desert at noon?" asked Henry not unreasonably.

"It *is* hot!"

Henry merely grunted.

"My feet do burn", I remarked presently.

"Aren't you rather fussy to-day?"

Surreptitiously I reached down to feel the sole of my shoe.

"My shoes feel scorching. I s'pose the car couldn't be on fire?"

And the next moment I am falling out of my side, and Henry bundling from his. For the car is indeed on fire, and all three of us are frantically grabbing up handfuls of sand to throw on the flames and smoke bursting out from where my feet had rested a moment before.

The fire was soon out, and all of us laughing, if a little grimly. What to do? We were still forty miles from home. We had finished our curry puffs and egg sandwiches, whilst Kalu was tying on the pipe. Worse. We had finished the last drop of soda water, and remembering this I instantly became thirsty! Now, though it was so hot you could not bear your hand on the woodwork of the car, it would become most bitterly cold at night with a raving wind blowing stinging sand over you.

I could see Henry was uneasy, though he said nothing.

Then on the far horizon we spied a tiny speck. Kalu screwing up his eyes announced it was a camel—three camels. Slowly they advanced, undulating nearer and nearer till we could make out that three men were riding them seated behind the hump, Sindi-fashion. As they drew up before the stationary car Henry addressed them as one always does greet the passer-by in this part of the world.

"*Salaam*! *Khush ayo*? *Chang a balla*? *Mille khair*?" (Salaam. Are you well? Are you happy? Is your belly comfortable?).

The three men looking down from the height of their great beasts, silhouetted up against the sky replied in like manner.

Then I heard Henry observe in a faintly sarcastic voice:

"I suppose you are not blacksmiths?"

"Han, Sahib".

"And you have your tools with you?"

"Han, Sahib".

"So you could fix this exhaust pipe?"

"Han, Sahib".

So the three bearded Sindis gravely unstrapped their tools, the camels burbling and grunting and sighing knelt down, and from bags and bundles the men produced a blow-pipe, and as if it were the most natural thing in the world, there in the blinding empty desert proceeded to solder on our exhaust pipe. Then with thanks and gratitude for payment given, courtesies exchanged, the three blacksmiths proceeded on their way, melting into the horizon.

Now the point of the story is this. That night heavy rain fell. All round the country became impassable. Even the bull-terriers dared not venture off the plinth of the verandah after the first attempt, their paws immediately becoming as large as soup plates.

Certainly we should have perished but for the advent of the blacksmiths in the desert, for help could not have reached us for at least a week.

The following day Henry had been expecting a meeting of mullas coming from the villages for many miles. These are Muhammadan priests who have a local reputation as experts in the Koran and Muhammadan law. Many will have made the pilgrimage to Mecca and have added the title of Haji to their names, and are privileged to wear green turbans. Henry had made friends with them in an unorthodox way when spending his early years in this district. When cases concerning women had come before him as District Magistrate he had recommended both parties to accept the decision of a Moslem priest. These gentlemen were grateful for the dignity and prestige thus acquired, and Henry himself was freed of intricate problems for which he had no experience nor aptitude. For example, one woman had asked his protection against a distasteful marriage, and had prayed that he would find her a good husband. The more important

Mullas were termed Kazis; and under Moslem laws a Kazi dealt with matrimonial cases, and acted as a marriage bureau. In Henry's opinion these matters concerned the Church rather than the State.

So a week or so later when all was dry again I watched the arrival of these dignified-looking old fellows, most of whom came on camels. They were in dazzling white with immense and complicated turbans, sometimes green, signifying they had made their pilgrimage to Mecca.

A Zemindar has sent in from the hills a dumba (fat-tailed sheep), for Christmas. He is woolly and big as a very large ram. Some of these dumbas have tails so large the Zemindars attach little carts on wheels to support them. The tail itself makes delicious eating. As Owen strolls about, his arm half-round the dumbas's neck, the eyes of the Muhammadan pattawallas follow their slow progress with interest. The tail in little cubes on toast for the Sahib-log's breakfast, and much much mutton for *them*!

But what shall I tell Owen?

Christmas Camp, Sujawal

Christmas Camps are notoriously delightful, but sometimes they may be more fun for the guests than the hostess, who is probably a bit tired anyhow with the constant move of camp, and periodical goes of fever. Nanny is down in Goa for her annual six weeks' holiday, and Owen has a heavy cold. He keeps hitting out at me and Ayah and his beloved Hassan Shah, and yelling with passion. The latter in their endeavours to soothe him spoil him. How strange the way small children suddenly become complete changelings for the time being! Sorry our visitors should see him thus.

Yet we had fun. Our guests were General and Mrs. Money and Mrs. Arthur Money and Mr. Pope, now Assistant-Commissioner. Mrs. Arthur had just learned that all her extremely good furniture, her wedding presents, silver, linen, had been torpedoed and sunk on the way home. Incredible to think anyone could be so foolish as not to have insured them. Still she never complained. Never grumbled, never whined. I think not to permit your own worries to spoil others' pleasures is one of the rarest things.

Christmas night General Money, always capital company, was skinning his first crocodile under the stars. The shivering pattawallas in the big coats Henry had supplied them with, and their heads all tied up in shawls, bent round him with hurricane lanterns, and the shikari stood aside, huffed at the idea anyone could cut out the belly piece to better advantage than himself. I, appearing on the verandah under the hanging lamp, "Henry, do see the waghus (crocodiles) are taken right away and buried, or we shall have the jackals yowling round all night . . . *That's not a table knife General Money is using*?!".

But it was.

The pale tents round the bungalow, the jetty date-palms and tamarisks, the unseen camels snarling and grunting, the red carcases of the crocodiles even more loathesome in death than in life, the camp fires, the shawled beblanketed figures squatting and eating wild duck! What fun it all was in spite of Owen's refusal to even glance at his Christmas Tree.

S.S. Jhelum, December 29th, 1918

Owen better, but still peevish. Guests dispersed, and here we are, horses, dogs, goats and chickens and all back on the *Jhelum* again, bound for Argamani, famed for crocodiles. Henry had got two at Christmas, but that was not enough for the suit-cases we were to have made up in Cawnpore, as only the soft under-belly can be used.

We arrived at Argamani at sunset. The gangway was thrown across the cliff-like bank and we went ashore at once . . . Sky very bright, but the great river sliding gently by was the colour of skim-milk, though the shore had darkened to slate. Climbed down the steep bank crowned with its tamarisk on to a wide stretch of sand. Though it was getting dark we could still see that the whole surface had been patterned all over by the bellies of hundreds of crocodiles who had basked there during the day. That patterned sand and the little sharp holes pierced by their claws seemed somehow hateful and loathsome. I had been told we might see hundreds of waghus at Argamani, but I had not believed it. Now I did.

December 30th

A real "cold weather morning". Wind and the turquoise sky whitened with blown sand which flicked and stung us like whips. With bent heads, and topis well down, we made our way to the spot where we had been the evening before. Not a waghu to be seen! I was cruelly disappointed. The Shikari told us that they disliked a cold wind. It might drop and then they would come forth. Accordingly Henry and I went down stream, sheltered in warm sand beneath a tamarisk, and waited, Henry's rifle lying between us. Here the river was blown into waves slapping smartly up just beneath us. The sand-banks in mid-stream, and the opposite bank perhaps a mile distant seemed to be smoking silver-bright, from the blown sand.

The wind did drop. Then with our eyes popping out of our heads we watched hundreds of waghus swimming across. They were almost entirely submerged. Just their nose-holes showing, and occasionally a wave of black behind. They looked like submarines. As they approached nearer you saw the jagged comb to their tails. Then they submerged again, and only the stub end of snout and tip of tail was visible. It was horrible seeing this army of evil steadily approaching our shore.

A little baby one was rocking in the waves immediately below us. We looked down on to its back.

Very few climbed out onto that reach of sand, as the cold wind still blew; and when they did they lay on the extreme edge of the water. At the crack of Henry's rifle they flopped in, including the one shot. (You are always apt to lose more than you secure, for dead or alive the extreme swiftness of the current bears them away). After each shot we had to wait motionless for them to crawl out again. Henry secured sixteen. I hate shooting myself, but this morning I did go up to one which had been hauled out on to the shore, and though staining the sand with its blood, was still alive. From a bare two yards away I discharged a *coup-de-grace* with Henry's elephant gun, which all but knocked me over. Nevertheless some hours later, when the carcase had been roped and dragged through the water and finally hauled on deck and they came to skin it, its tail lashed out so furiously that Narayan, John Shillidy's "boy", was thrown violently to the ground, spraining his wrist.

The crocodiles here had done much damage lately, killing cattle, and not long ago had dragged a woman in. She had never been seen again. So there was much rejoicing at the kill. Ropes were slipped round their bodies by the klassis, and one by one they were hauled in. Two -and-a-half-year-old Owen tugged at the rope too, and his shrill pipe could be heard joining in with their chant.

"*Allah! Allah!*
Shabash Juwan!
Waghu ko pukkaro.
Zor . . . se Juwan!
Musti Khencho
Tu-le-la".

"Allah! Allah!
Bravo young fellow!
Catch hold of the crocodile,
Put your back into it young fellow,
Make an effort.
Tu-le-la".

Baghiar Canal, December 30th, 1918

Along these canals are bands or embankments shaded by babul trees. These bands are used as roads by the country people. You see banias ambling along on their small country-bred ponies, their shoes all but touching the ground. These little long-tailed rats have a peculiar gait, both legs on the same side moving forward at the same time like a camel's. It is called the Sindi *pand* and is very comfortable and smooth. You see bullock carts with their solid wheels crawling along, a string of stalking camels, or perhaps a whole drove of little pattering donkeys half hidden by the sacks on their backs. All these pass along the band, taking advantage of the shade of the babul trees. When Henry has to go any distance to inspect the canals or crops, rice straw is laid down on the top of the band as as to enable the car, or dogcart, to travel without sinking in sand. This morning we had left the car some way back, and were walking, accompanied by Mahomed, the shikari pattawalla. Just here there were no babuls, only scrubby grey tamarisk with its pink bloom. The thick yellow waters of the canal slid slowly and sullenly by at the foot of the high scarped bank.

Mahomed, carrying Henry's rifle, which he usually took along with him, pointed out an unusually large waghu lying at the brink of the water. We were a good many miles from the Indus, but at this time of the year they may travel miles across country.

Lying on my tummy at the top of the bank I watched Henry and Mahomed creeping forward, bent double, and almost indistinguishable from the tamarisk in their grey-green. Henry fired; instantaneously the waghu flopped into the water which closed over him. Two ryots passing by were greatly excited. They were naked but for a loin cloth, and were very dark. One was a handsome bearded youth who had combed up his hair at the front and sides and fixed them thus with wooden combs *à la Pompadour*. This young man volunteered to Henry they would retrieve the waghu for him. They began cutting down young tamarisk, and then getting down the sticky pasty bank, coolly walked into the water in spite of Henry's protestations. Laughing and joking they waded about for some twenty minutes stirring up the mud with their branches. In the meantime I had seen something dark pass me in the sliding turgid water. It might have been the trunk of the tree, but I thought it was the corpse. Henry told the men to come out. The Memsahib had seen it carried past, but at that moment the young man with the wooden comb shouted out, "But Sahib I feel him!" Then the other shouted, "And I, I am standing on his back. He is alive!" And both began dancing up and down in the water and bubbles were rising to the surface.

By this time I was in a state of apprehension, and Henry was ordering them to come out. The men cared not a jot. Shouting to Mahomed for a rope they splashed about and poked and prodded with their branches, and in some unexplained way got the rope round the crocodile who was lying on the bottom. Yelling, shouting and chanting they dragged him out still alive. I took a photograph of them hauling him backwards up the bank, Mahomed holding on to his tail, and Henry gingerly grasping one of those hands I find so repellent.

Followed a horrid scene. The men had their axes, and as the waghu was still alive Henry told them to despatch him. This they delighted in, and they went on hacking and hacking till the poor brute's head was all but severed from its body. *"Bas! Bas!"* shouted Henry . . . and then to our amazement and horror, with its head almost off, the waghu began snapping furiously at the men's legs. Reflex action? I don't know. But hot sun, excitement, and bloody axes and the sight of the unfortunate animal combined, nearly did for me . . . and I rather think for Henry too.

Government House, January, 1919

We had not been able to get back from Camp to welcome the very first batch of our prisoners from Kut. But a few days later came the second ship, and we were down at Keamari by noon, awaiting it, the sun beating down on our topis. The whole scene was blinded with light, fluttering with flags and pennants, blazing with red carpets and bunting. Sky, sea, buildings and quay fused in a white glare causing one to screw up one's face. Words of command, troops, crowds, winking of brass instruments of the band, boat sirens, all making up a jig-saw puzzle of brilliant sight and sound.

Out thundered the salute, and *H.M.S. Britomart* rounded the corner escorting *H.M.S. Elephanta,* both fluttering with flags and pennants in the stiff breeze and incandescent sunshine. Owen, seeing the *Elephanta,* immediately waved and waved his little Union Jack, screaming at the top of his voice "Hip Hip Hooray!" The cheering! The cheering! The bands crashing out into "See the Conquering Hero Comes". We cheered. How we cheered. We shouted, and even as we cheered I heard my voice quaver and break. One can never forget. Such things lift the soul, remembering what these men had endured.

General Fowler read out the message from the Commander-in-Chief in Urdu. Then Henry made a speech, also in Urdu. I'll copy it out, so that if ever any future generations shall read this diary they will realise the courage of these men. This speech was printed on mauve and scarlet double folding cards at our Government House Printing Press, both in Urdu and in English characters. Each man received a copy. Then I garlanded the officers with roses. They were cinematographed, and stood there stiffly to attention. When urged to move and "be natural", one, with a super-human effort did manage to scratch his thigh with two fingers while still keeping his arm glued to his side, but no other move would he make. After all kinds of food, gifts and entertaining of various kinds, they went off in a decorated train, with garlands round the engine's neck, and the coal whitewashed, to the Rest Camp where they will spend some days. There each man receives a large card designed by me and printed. On a jet black background, surrounded by a wreath of bright red roses and bright green leaves, two white horses. On one an Indian woman in a sari, on the other Britannia. Both hold spears which are united over their heads by a banner on which is printed in English and in Urdu "India proudly welcomes her returning heroes". The colouring was suggested to me by memories of the first page of Struwelpeter of nursery days.

Henry's Speech.

Officers and men of the garrison of Kut, welcome back to India. On behalf of India, this great motherland of brave races, the citizens of the harbour and city of Karachi where you first arrive, offer you their greeting and their gratitude.

You have experienced the greatest changes of fortune that can befall men. Many of your garrison opened the war with the capture of Basra, and the brilliant victory of Shahiba. With scanty numbers and meagre equipment you conquered a great country and pressed forward even to the gates of Baghdad. Overwhelmed by superior forces you retreated to Kut-el-Amara, and there sustained with undaunted courage and tenacity a siege of 150 days, until starvation compelled your surrender. That siege occupied the attention of important forces of the enemy, and your self-sacrifice enabled the British Empire to prepare fresh armies and put them in the field for the protection of India. Since then you have suffered two and a half years of captivity in circumstances of hardship which have roused deepest sympathies of all parts of the British Empire.

We have heard to our sorrow that large numbers of your comrades are dead, unable to survive the hardships of your marches and your captivity. We think of them with reverence. In this greatest of all wars in history our soldiers have fought for the highest ideals of humanity, and human nature has risen to a pitch of devotion and self-sacrifice seldom seen before. To you, the survivors, we pay our homage in this ceremony, which however slight in itself, is an indication of the gratitude of India; and we venture to offer our heartiest congratulations on the imperishable glory that you have earned.

You are returning home with the complete triumph of a holy cause; and we all unite in the hope and prayer that you may be fully restored to health and strength, and that a full measure of happiness may await you in your homes".

1948. Anyone reading this should now read the account of what these men had suffered as recorded in Lloyd George's *War Memoirs* and the evidence given by Colonel Markham Carter, I.M.S., in the House of Commons.

The Handley Page arrives, January 15th, 1919

For the past three days the big Handley Page biplane, the very first to attempt to fly to India, has been expected here. The landing place is prepared in the desert on the Magar Pir Road. It is all marked out with white stones. There is a hut and shamiana erected for addresses and welcomes and so forth, from the Army and the Municipality. But after three days of alternate expectation and disappointment the news comes through that the arrival is indefinitely postponed. One of the four cylinders had blown off and the machine was forced to land at Ormara on the Persian Gulf. General MacEwan decided she would have to be dismantled. Dreadfully disappointed, as ever since a little girl, balloons and aeroplanes have had an uncanny fascination for me.

At the Gymkhana an A.D.C. hurried past me, and muttered between his closed teeth, not looking at me, "Don't let it out. But she's coming. *Now.* You may just get there in time".

What a temptation to leap into the car, and go straight away to the landing place! . . . but I overcome it and hurry off to look for Henry. Find him in his office, still in his tussore suit. No time to change into anything warmer. We dash into the Fiat and tear away in clouds of dust down the Magar Pir Road.

Sunset when we arrive. She has not yet come! Just General Fowler, and Henry and a few officers and myself waiting. We get out and stand there on the sand, shivering with cold and excitement. The sand was a curious dark purple. A full moon was rising at our backs swimming into a violet East, whilst in the West a daffodil band of sky shone behind the black craggy line of low hills over which the "Old Carthusian", as she is called, must come. A tiny hum. One didn't know whether it was a loud sound a long way off, or a tiny sound inside one's own ears . . . but now it was getting louder, and louder . . . *it was she*! A tiny speck against that still faintly bright West . . . and here she came flying terribly, oh! so terribly low over those cruel peaks, the engines thumping hard. Our hearts were in our mouths. The merest novice could tell she was in great distress. It was moonlight now. Rockets soared into the zenith. They dropped a Verey light, green as *crême de menthe.* Another. She was looming enormous up there, the noise tremendous. She dropped down a light before her as she alighted. The moon cast her gigantic shadow across the desert as she feebly taxied a very few yards, and then abruptly came to a standstill. Out of her tottered Major Maclaren, Captain Halley, Sergeant Smith, and a very small fox terrier, and stood there in the moonlight motionless. All were dead beat, and frozen stiff. They were in their shirt sleeves. To get over those jagged peaks they had been forced to throw out maps, instruments, glasses, even their clothing as ballast. They were almost speechless with cold and fatigue.

We got them into the car with little Tiny, the dog, and hurried them off to Government House. They were too exhausted to eat. We opened the treasured last remaining bottle of champagne which was to be drunk on Victory day . . . to find it corked!

This machine was built for bombing Berlin, with Captain Halley as pilot, had the Armistice not been declared. She had been dogged by atrocious weather and ill luck of every kind since she had left Ipswich on December 13th. Here is an official description of her.

"She weighs 14 tons when fully loaded, and actually weighed well over 13 tons during the flight. She has four engines of 350 horse power, that is 1,400 horse power in all. The machine, however, is underpowered in proportion to its great weight and size, and it has been necessary during the whole voyage to run the engines at a far greater number of revolutions than normally, with the result that engine trouble has been experienced owing to the heavy strains put upon them".

On January 13th Brigadier-General MacEwan had come to the reluctant conclusion she must be dismantled at Ormara. But finally it was decided to lighten her as much as was possible, taking off all kit, all spare parts, all fixtures such as wireless, reducing the crew and petrol to a minimum, and tuning the three remaining engines to the very highest pitch and to make an attempt to get to Karachi! The next day was spent in making these alterations and preparations.

I now quote from a subsequent press interview with Brigadier-General MacEwan. "On January 15th the engines were run up, and as they gave satisfaction a start was made. The low tide gave the advantage of a hard beach, and after a run of about a mile, the machine left the ground about 5 p.m. About 20 minutes after leaving Ormara, when over a rocky portion of the coast, with no chance of landing safely for 50 miles, two engines momentarily gave out, owing to all the wind-vanes coming off the petrol pumps. This was rectified by hand pumping, and the engines picked up again, and all went well till about 35 miles from Karachi, when the starboard rear engine showed signs of distress, and finally gave out altogether, owing to the fracture of one of the oil leads, which had come adrift, so that the engine was not receiving any oil. The final thirty miles to Karachi was therefore completed on two engines by dint of just not stalling.

Our three guests, Major MacClaren, Captain Halley and Sergeant Smith were delightfully modest. Their one concern was to assure us there was nothing wrong with the engines, that indeed they had responded most nobly to the demand made on them. When actual engine trouble occurred it was due to the very heavy strain which was put upon them. During the whole voyage they had had to run the engines at a far greater number of revolutions than normally. No hint of their own determination and courage in completing the trip (for General MacEwan after declared, "That the voyage is completed is due to the skilful piloting of Major A. S. Maclaren, and the physical energy of Captain Halley and Sergeant Smith in keeping up the flow of petrol after the wind vanes had broken")—no hint of this, only a great enxiety that the public should recognise that the engines had played up wonderfully, and that the rumour prevalent in India that the intention had been to complete the flight in five or six days was quite incorrect; (actually it had taken thirty-one). The organisation en route is not yet sufficiently complete for supplying spare parts such as propellers and so on at different landing stages, only oil and petrol.

Unfortunately we were bound to go into district the following day, but before we left Henry and Owen and I went all over her. Owen asked most intelligent questions, they said.

The very first aerial letter to India came to Henry. Lord Willingdon had handed it to Major Maclaren to give. He did so on arrival, when he could hardly speak. I stuck it in Owen's diary, with their signatures on the envelope.

Some day when we are all flying it may be of interest to read of this first flight to India.

Government House, Karachi, February, 1919

Karachi at its best. Scintillating sunshine. Wind blowing off the desert instead of from the sea. The railway station very gay. Bunting everywhere. Banks of flowers in pots. Red carpets and hundreds of flags and pennons flapping noisily in a cool north breeze. Henry and John Shillidy in full uniform, cocked hat, sword and all. The G.O.C. with all his staff. A large Guard of Honour. The Municipality assembled, and every chink on the platform filled up with the élite of Karachi to welcome the new Governor of Bombay and his wife to Sind.

The train draws in. The Guard of Honour more ram-rod than ever. God Save The King strikes up . . . but the stationary train remains obstinately closed, looking like a child's tin train whose doors are not made to open!

It turns out that the dust of the Sind desert has so increased Lady Lloyd's hay-fever, that paroxysms of sneezing make appearance impossible for some minutes.

This is going to be far worse than the Viceregal visit. That was merely three days in Karachi itself. Now their Excellencies are to be our guests for ten days, staying first at Karachi, accompanying us up to Northern Sind, then back to Hyderabad and Karachi again. And here let me say to his eternal credit that Sir George Lloyd has announced beforehand his intention of paying his way. Hitherto visits of Viceroys and Governors and their retinues have imposed a crushing financial burden on those on whom they descended. Sir George Lloyd has been the first Governor to recognise this, and to take appropriate steps.

Misteri, the cook, and I have made out the menus for ten breakfast parties, ten luncheon parties, and ten dinner parties. He of course accompanies us on the train with his mates and all his cooking pots. I have the certainty of food well cooked, and that there will be no fear of him getting drunk as many otherwise excellent Goanese cooks are apt to do at critical times. Like Hyder Khan, he is a treasure.

What are my labours in making up menus, and thinking out suitable clothes compared to the labours of John Shillidy, Mr. Birch, and dozens of clerks? For the past three weeks they have toiled into the night. They are done in. Even John has scarcely a twinkle left. Few realise the preparation demanded by the visit of a Governor. To begin with innumerable cars must be borrowed or somehow got hold of. The seating in each to be arranged, and printed in neat little booklets in the Government House Printing Press, together with all the name cards, menus, and so on. Then the exact time at which each of these cars sets out from Government House to visit the hospital, institution, or what you will. Moreover the correct order in which they go. The time spent there, the time at which they depart, and the route which they will follow to the next school or whatever it may be. Then all invitations to be issued for breakfasts, private and important interviews, luncheon parties, receptions and dinners, the correct precedence of Army and Civilian seniority being carefully worked out from the Army and Civil list . . .

The first three days is to be spent in Karachi. Henry, uncomfortably dressed up, will be taking H.E. round the port and the harbour, which is being dredged. The dredger has unfortunately blown up owing to the inexperience of the Indian mechanic in charge! Work will be held up for months. Henry tactfully suggests to H.E. the same calamity may be likely to occur in Bombay, where Sir George Lloyd is pressing on with fierce energy the Back Bay Reclamation Scheme. Would it not be wise to get a second dredger? The proposal is not at all well received. (But it did happen, and was one of the chief contributary causes to the heavy financial loss on the scheme). Henry takes him over the five great war hospitals, the gaol, and round the Lyari where development is bound to follow.

Meanwhile I am escorting Lady Lloyd round the Dufferin Hospital and the "Louise Lawrence", and the "Sind Women", the Y.W.C.A., the Soldiers' Home and various missions, and European and Indian charities, presenting endless people, European and Indian. A let-off at 7-30 p.m., and Tulsi, her face full of concern at Memsahib's fatigue, exclaiming "*Are*! *Are*!", and brushing out her hair with smooth regular strokes, and malishing her aching ankles. (One thing, Lady Lloyd having been a lady-in-waiting so long, knows well what standing means, and saves us all she can!). Dinner at 9-45 and reception after.

Three days of this and then we all entrain for Northern Sind. Can it be that only three months ago I was scrambling about the stony hills of Baluchistan on my rope-soled shoes?

What Lady Lloyd thinks of the night journey and the days at Sukkur I shudder to think. The fatigue, the sun and dust aggravating her hay fever, the inevitable discomfort, the clasping of innumerable moist hands, the bewildering effect on one new to India of those presented to her. One moment a bleached but vigorous lady doctor from the Mission, the next an Indian barrister speaking perfect English, the next an enormous corpulent Sindi zemindar made more enormous still by his white draperies, and huge turban, unable to speak a word except Sindi . . . and then to return exhausted to the Circuit House to the complainings of a sick and incompetent English lady's maid. But she bore up bravely, and made charming little speeches here and there and looked the part.

Etiquette demanded I should be seated at the Governor's right hand for every meal during those ten days. Tired as I was, and aware in every fibre that he was critical of my husband, I doubt whether I can have been a very exhilarating companion! But H.E. likes Sind, if he doesn't like Henry. Its sun and dust and palms are familiar enough, for was he not the friend of T. E. Lawrence in Arabia? Certainly he is the easiest person to talk to, and full of interesting experiences. We get on to Russia, and dancers, and tribesmen dancing. I tell him of a wonderful Sindi dancer Henry has seen, thinking him unique. H.E. is clearly sceptical; but Henry tells Hyder Khan, Syed Jaffar Shah must somehow be found in Sind. Hyder Khan, as always says, "*Accha, Sahib* (very good, Sahib)." Sind is rather larger than England and Wales, but Jaffar Shah is found.

Jaffar Shah does not dance to the tabla, nor to the tinny rattle of the tasha played with two sticks, nor to the timki. Jaffar Shah dances to the dhol, whose rich sonorous note I had first heard beating, night and day, as we sailed down the Malabar Coast, in memory of the deaths of Hassan and Husayn. Those round full notes keep time to the intricate flying steps, yet lose nothing of their sombre majesty. The dhol seems the perfect accompaniment to such manly grace. For about Syed's dancing there is something grand and noble. This magnificently built Sindi, with the Christ-like face and loose white garments, swoops and stoops, and flies with outstretched arms. A faint smile is on his bearded lips, and his eyes are half closed as though he saw a vision. And though the dhol waxes faster, faster, never does it lose its richness of tone; and though Syed whirls and swirls faster and faster, clapping his long-fingered hands now high above his head, now close to his spinning feet, never is he aught but noble inspiration.

Sir George Lloyd is moved to the utmost enthusiasm.

This dapper, olive-skinned, and rather bitter-tongued little man cannot say enough. Never has be seen such dancing . . . and in my pleasure I give him all the little flying sketches I had made of Jaffar Shah as he danced . . . and have regretted it ever since!

On our return to Karachi, Henry took H.E. out into the desert to show him where the city must inevitably develop. There a rough circular track of about five miles had been made in the sand, and along it sowars were posted at intervals.

Now one of Henry's pet schemes had been the reinforcing of the Sind Mounted Police. There are far too few sowars, and police on foot are of little use in this land of desert and dacoity.

He had urged for some time past that it was not necessary to have expensive uniforms, nor the Arabs on which the regular sowars were mounted. He suggested supplementing the force something after the fashion of the Baluchistan Levy with its rough country-bred animals, the sort of horse I had been riding at Ziarat.

Now seemed a good moment to put the scheme before H.E.

Indicating the sowars motionless like tin soldiers on either side of the desert track, he expatiated on the excellence of their riding, their invaluable aid in dacoity. He gave as an example of their spirit the case of Mir Khan, who was sent by train to fetch the official post. Returning with the "mailbag" at night he was carried past his station. The train thundered on. Mir Khan leaped out into the darkness, delivered his bag, and said no word of his misadventure.

"Let me see them gallop", said H.E. briefly, looking at the sowars.

The order was given. The horses moved off . . . but what was this? Riders clutching at manes and bridles, losing stirrups, and even rolling off into the sand . . . !

They were dummies. They had never been on a horse before. After, Henry was to learn all the regular sowars had been kept back for the great display of tent pegging, jumping, etc., which was to take place on the maidan in front of Government House when Sir George returned from his drive!

No. I don't think Henry will get his levy!

They're gone!

No war-dance of triumph this time.

Prostration complete.

In Camp at Jherruk, Februry, 1919

What a strange passionate-looking district. Rocks and stones too hot to handle, ochre-coloured, chestnut, red and black, with here and there candelabra cactus sprouting from them, glaucous green. The pale waters of the Indus spreading out, and from the plain these little flat-topped hills rising with extreme abruptness; and over their summits in the thin air, the chils swinging in smooth circles. I watched one this evening at the level of my eyes. In the light of the westering sun he glittered chestnut too, and hanging between his outstretched wings seemed crucified.

It was not far from here that Sir Charles Napier all but lost his charger Red Rover from drowning. Had I not read in his journal "I was in a great fright for my dear horse Red Rover"?

So sitting on my hill top, sky all round me, the Indus spread below, I fall now to thinking of those "dear horses" of whom my kinsman was almost foolishly fond. When we first came to Government House it had pleased me to think of Leviathan and the others stamping and whisking their tails in the very stalls built for Sir Charles's chargers. Indeed it had pleased me to fancy the phantoms of Red Rover, and Mosaic and others of "My dear horses" had come sidling back into the stalls at night to commune with ours. Hurricane lanterns burn all night to ward off snakes, and the shadows of our Walers must loom enormous on the white-washed walls. But the two old chargers would cast no shadow!

Leviathan at seventeen hands must have towered beside "my beautiful white Arab Mosaic", as Sir Charles described him . . . yet I feel Leviathan and the others would be as shy and awkward as any newly joined young officer at mess listening to talks of battle he had never known! As for the sowars' white Arab ponies in their stalls lower down, they would stand as though on parade, for though I hate to say it, animals are shocking snobs.

Red Rover with the consciousness of being supreme favourite with Sir Charles grunts and shakes his head. "I never felt so much as the prick of his spur though how often he exclaimed, 'Man, thou art a beast in whose side the spurs should ever be plunged' ".

But Mosaic, "such a playful coaxing animal", was a little bored by such sententiousness. He fidgeted, pawed, flourished his tail around as all good Arabs do, interrupting, "Tell them about that time you were nearly drowned. Allah! What an escape!"

Not unwillingly Red Rover shook himself so violently that his skin rattled as though again he were shaking off the water of the Indus, and holding his head high, his eyeballs glinting, he began:

"The d . . . d rascals were drunk, and "He" told the boatswain to give the Christians twelve strokes with a ratan over their clothes, and the others six. The steamer ran aground, and our horse-boat came bumping along into it, and immediately began to sink with us seven horses all fast by the collar and head ropes!"

"Three of the blacks jumped off the steamer with knives (d . . . d brave fellers . . .) and cut us loose. At once the whole seven of us began the very devil of a rumpus and fight, kicking, biting, squealing in the water . . . till suddenly we found ourselves swimming for our lives. I took the farthest bank, and landed about a mile down, and then two of the others clambered out, and instantly we set to again 'like good soldiers' as 'He' said afterwards. I was bitten and kicked all over, but the doctor's little grey pony had kicked and bitten us while we were fighting, and now when we turned on him he ran off . . . cunnin' little rascal."

Red Rover was clearly enjoying himself. He stamped, and shook himself from side to side with a rattle of hide. "Our horseman could swim like a fish, but he had jumped overboard and never stopped to cut our ropes . . . d . . . d rascally coward . . . He climbed on to the Master's steamer from where 'He' instantly kicked him into the river. And serve him right. God's truth! We might all have been drowned. We'd been all through the campaign, and Flibbety still had a large sabre wound . . . ".

But enough of this nonsense of mine. Let Mosaic, flea-bitten no longer, white with age, yet still with gaily carried tail, and Red Rover, faithful old campaigner, "always steady under fire", steal back to the Elysian Fields, leaving Leviathan, Larrikin and Lot and the two humble police ponies dozing in their stalls, with the crickets going "sing-sing-sing" all through the hot night.

As for me, I must get back before dark. The Indus is burnished below me, the varied plain bright as nasturtium, the air suddenly cool, though the rocks still hold the noonday heat.

Clambering and sliding down to get back to camp I pass a little mosque set lonely on a hillock and walled round with cactus. Its white-washed dome and pinnacles are dimmed to violet against the sunset. It looks serene in this harsh landscape. A refuge.

Through the still air sound little hooves on stones, and a Sindi, naked except for his full trousers, leads a very little ass towards the mosque. On its back is a shrouded figure I guess to be a woman. At the bottom of the almost perpendicular stones which had been whitewashed and are meant to serve as steps, the man helps the woman off, and leaving the little ass, the two climb very slowly and laboriously up to the door, disappearing inside.

Are they about to pray for a son?

Government House, Karachi, 1919

Among the victorias, packed with Parsi ladies and their children, in white frocks and little black embroidered pill-box hats, and the rich merchants lolling back in their cars, which travel across the three miles of flats every evening to Clifton, to get the sea breeze, and watch the sun setting in the long line of tumbling waves, we always met a high dog cart spanking along, driven by a very upright and smart-looking young man in an astrachan fez. This was a nobleman of a royal family across the border. He is a young barrister who had been made a good deal of in London society when reading for the bar, singing Persian songs in drawing rooms and so forth. He lives now with his mother in a house near the Botanical Gardens, and is a member of the Municipality. Now his mother had been on very friendly terms with Louise years before, and on our arrival in Karachi Henry had told me I must get in touch with her. But my letters remained unanswered. The Khan often dined at Government House, and when I suggested coming to call on her if she preferred that, he was full of smiling apologies and evasions. "You know how it is with us. How old fashioned our women are. They will *not* come out. My mother will not even see Europeans, she keeps such strict purdah". "But she was so fond of my sister", I objected. It was of no use. But this year the hot weather had told on the old lady and she is not at all well, I hear. "Does she ever drive down to Clifton to get the evening breeze?" I asked, for one did occasionally see victorias, muffled in sheets, on the sandhills which one knew contained Muslim ladies.

"She would never go", declared the Khan.

"If I came myself one night when there is *no* moon, at midnight when everyone has gone to bed, would she drive with me to Clifton?"

This at last has been agreed upon. On a pitch black night at twelve o'clock I set out to fetch her. It is stifling hot, for the servants had arranged sheets over the windows, and between Kalu's back and the car. Between the porch and the car a tunnel of sheets had been arranged, and through this the old lady was bundled on her tiny slippered feet, shrouded in a white cotton burka with lattice work for the eyes. A manservant of hers climbs into the seat beside Kalu and we drive away in the stifling darkness. Gasps, giggles, squeezing of jewelled hands, and many bracelets catching on to scarves and draperies, and suffocating heat. The sweat trickles down me, for the windows are closed, and there are sheets and wrappings everywhere. I can see nothing. But the old lady is transported with joy. She keeps telling me how much she loved Louise, her Bai, her Sister, and how she longed to see me, for she knew she would love me too . . . "But why would you never come to see me or answer my letters, or let me come to see you?" I reproached. And then hotly and ticklingly she whispered right into my ear that her son had become so strict about purdah he would allow her no liberty at all. He refused to let her see anyone. He had taken away her embroidery, saying it was not fitting that she should sew, he had forbidden her to sing and play her vina. She was forbidden to even go into their little garden in the cool of the evening . . . I listened amazed. The sophisticated Khan dining with us at Government House, driving his high-stepping horse in the dog-cart. It seemed incredible . . . yet here was this dear, soft, affectionate old lady clinging to me, saying how happy she was to be out of prison, how much she loved Louise, how much she would love me, I was now her *Bai* also.

Clifton at midnight not unnaturally was completely deserted, the sandhills hidden in pitch darkness. Kalu got down, and the manservant, both standing there unseen in the soft sand. Boldly I let down the windows, and the strong tepid sea wind came charging round the edges of the cotton sheets and fanned our dripping faces. But after a few minutes I had to shut the windows!

We drove home.

Kohinoor

Henry came back from Bombay this evening. A lovely top-of-the-bubble feeling. I did go to the station to meet him . . . but it was rather official and I did not really get him back to myself till we were wandering about the compound amongst the pink oleanders in the westering sunlight, and the bull-terriers, all pink, were careering about, leaping over the three-foot hedges for pure light-heartedness, pink one moment in the sunlight, blue the next in the shadow. Henry had his hand under my elbow. We were so happy I really did not pay much attention to what we were actually saying, but for some reason or other he was asking me if I liked sapphires. Now he has taught me to have a disregard of jewelry. When we first became engaged he had laughingly declared "You know I shall never give you jewelry. It's a barbarous custom in my opinion". And he never had, except for my engagement ring.

He had told me of his grandfather's brother, John, and his experience with the Kohinoor. This was handed over by the Sikhs, and was entrusted to John. He put it in his pocket, and promptly forgot all about it. Queen Victoria decided she would have it as "the brightest jewel in the Crown Jewels". Dalhousie consulted John. "By all means, send it at once", wrote John to Lord Dalhousie the Viceroy. Back came the reply. *"But you have it"*.

Inward panic succeeded to John's indifference; but how characteristic of him; instead of yielding to it, he first finished his business, then sent for his bearer. Characteristically also, his bearer, always accepting the strange whims of the Bara Sahib, had kept the box with the bit of glass in it which had been knocking about in his master's pocket, and now produced it. Substitute Henry for John, and Hyder Khan for the bearer, and it might have happened yesterday . . . so knowing Henry's complete indifference to jewels, I paid small heed to this talk of sapphires, answering at random, thinking what fun it was to have him back, and how the leaping bull-terriers looked like animated anatomical casts, pink-washed in the light of the setting sun. "Sapphires?" I rattled on. No, I can't imagine what anyone sees in them. The good ones are so dark it looks just as though a stone has dropped out of its setting . . . "

"That's a pity", said Henry at last, "for I went to the races, backed an outsider, and a brooch is being made for you. I asked Lady Lloyd's advice. She said all women liked sapphires. We had Tarachand up to Government House, and she herself picked out the best sapphires she could find, and her own favourite brooch of diamonds and sapphires is being copied for you". . .

For some months past the whole of the maidan in front of Government House has been covered with enormous dumps of ammunition which should have been dumped into the sea, but for some reason or other were not. Arriving from Mespot they were enclosed in barbed wire, and guarded by native sentries. Henry was not too happy about it, and half jokingly used to say to me "Not only Government House, but the whole of Karachi will some day be blown up into the sea".

One evening after sunset we prowled around, and found the sentry to the entrance, absent. There was nothing to prevent any coolie wandering in, smoking his eternal bidi!

When Lord Jellicoe was with us, Henry spoke seriously of the danger to Captain Dreyer, Chief of the Staff. He was appalled. Wired immediately to Delhi. An expert on explosives was sent down—Colonel Musprat Williams ("Musk-rat Bill").

It appears it is only by the mercy of God we have not all been blown sky high. This ammunition was considered to be safe for three months at the outside, owing to the dampness of the climate. It has lain at our gates for many months.

A relief to see the end of it.

An amusing incident has occurred. The Convent has a very good swimming bath. The water is always changed on Saturday evenings, and on Sunday morning the delightful Mother Superior allows us to go and bathe. Henry asked Lord Jellicoe and the others to come along. They had no bathing suits. "That doesn't matter", said Henry. "We have it to ourselves". Off they went, I of course having to stay behind. They larked about like so many schoolboys, and were just thinking of coming out when in sails a little nun carrying coffee and biscuits held on a tray before her. Shouts, shrieks, yells. All frantically dive to the bottom of the bath . . . not that that is of any use, for the bath is lined with white tiles, and the water is limpid Nile green!

Unperturbed, looking neither to right nor left, the little nun marches up to the top of the bath, and there on the table by the diving board deposits her tray of biscuits and coffee and marches out again . . .

Lord Jellicoe was hoping to get some big game shooting later on but had no rifle. Henry offered to lend him his elephant gun with which he had brought down tiger, panther, ibex, and so on. The little man climbed up a ladder on the *New Zealand* to practise; but as he laughingly told Henry after, each time he fired it, he fell off, such was its impact; so regretfully he returned it.

Owen presented Lord Jellicoe with a sucking pig, a pink and delightful little creature, clean as a pin. He came from the model pig farm in the desert, from where the Sind Club get their famous pork. The eyes of Captain Dreyer literally bulged at the thought of sucking pig for dinner, but to his dismay Lord Jellicoe was horrified at the idea of eating the little chap, and the decree went forth he was to be the ship's mascot.

We took him on board ourselves—had luncheon; Owen of course blissfully happy, and made a great fuss of.

Government House, Karachi, March, 1919

I am to have tea with the mother of the Khan!

Henry needs the car, so Kalu will drop me there for a long, a very, very long visit, and then come back to pick me up. As we drive up, the door opens immediately. Someone must have been watching for us. It slams so smartly behind me I am startled. After the glare outside I can see nothing, but a tall dim figure beside me in softest white muslin and bare feet. Then to my amazement I recognise this is the Khan himself. I confess panic seizes me. The door opened and shut with such unexpected swiftness. Kalu had driven away for hours. And why was the Khan hitherto always dressed in European clothes except for his fez, like this? Ridiculous sheik-like stories go helter-skelter through my head, as I follow him down dark and crooked passages. It is indeed a relief to be brought into the presence of my old gentlewoman. The Khan converses for a little, and then goes off to change for the inevitable evening drive to Clifton. I feel foolish.

The room is poor, mean and closely shuttered. It is also very hot. I peer out through the lattice at the dusty little garden with its few dead plants in pots. The garden my hostess so grieves she is no longer allowed to enter! We have tea. It is all I can do to swallow the nauseous decoction which has been made for me, but the sweetmeats on the silver tray are delicious, though there are rather too many flies on the halwa. We go over and over again every detail of the midnight drive to Clifton. What an adventure! No trifle too small to dwell upon . . . but at last even the drive gets exhausted. In spite of those hours I spend on railway journeys with my little crimson Hindustani book, my honorific Urdu is still limited, and I am not really fluent. I wonder how the hot hours will be spent before Kalu comes back for me! And then my old hostess leans to me, her voluminous draperies half smothering me. Very hot and ticklingly, just like a child whispering right close into one's ear, she confides to me she is going to show me a great surprise, for I am her Bai.

I follow the shuffling old dear down a dark passage. Suddenly, surprisingly comes the parrot sound of many women's voices, and children's and babies crying. We enter an unexpectedly large room. An astonishing sight. Instantly I am a child again in "The Turkish Harem" of "Constantinople", at Olympia. The word "Odalisque" rises to mind. For all round the walls reclining . . . yes reclining is the word . . . on divans and gorgeous cushions are black-eyed women in the most brilliant brocades and spangled gauzes. Children are everywhere, babies crawling round one's feet, and silver trays piled with fruit, and slaves, and graceful silver vessels with long curved spouts. The air is heavy with perfume and the smell of fruit. The women are chattering in a tongue I do not recognise. They are laughing and their teeth are big and white, and their black eyes bold. Their physique is infinitely better than the average Indian woman's and rich dark blood . . . or perhaps rouge . . . shows beneath cheeks far more swarthy than any I had ever seen in India! Now they crowd round me. It is indeed a parrot house. My old lady implores silence. She is clearly terrified. They pay no heed. They thrust slaves with fruit on trays at me, they push their children forward. They display their own glittering jewels, and are amazed at my single ring. They make so much noise the terrified old hostess gets me out of the room long before I am ready to go. Back from that scintillating scene of green and gold and crimson and silver and silks and satins, and laughing ladies with long-lashed kohled eyes, back to the hot dusty little room and its chairs with the broken springs.

"But who *are* they?"

Scared yet excited, the old lady like a mischievous child who has stolen a march on the grown-ups, confesses, "They are Afghan ladies".

They had arrived in secret only the day before. They were the ladies from the Court of King Amanulla, and were being sent down here for safety. Trouble was going to start in Afghanistan very shortly.

I'm unpleasantly startled! I shall *have* to tell Henry this! And sure enough, very shortly after, Afghanistan *did* invade the Punjab!

Our Misteri is ill.

Goanese relatives and friends have been crowding into his quarters all day. Dark-faced priests with blue chins coming and going.

And forty-eight hours later Misteri is dead.

Three men are making his coffin down there, just outside his quarters. "Knock! Knock! Knock!" There are unceasing lamentations and cries from the little window and the long family, ranging from a twenty year old son to one of five. And now there rises to me the terrified screams of this little boy as he is held up to watch the coffin shut down on his father . . .

Amritsar

A vague uneasiness is troubling everything, an underground unrest, a communal tension. Talk of the Rowlatt Bill still haunts the Club, the Gymkhana; it is on everybody's tongue, whether they have the first idea about it or not. The Rowlatt Bill is in the air. It appears to be quite innocuous, but Indians have suddenly discovered the value of propaganda. They are spreading abroad that meetings of more than two or three people are forbidden by Government, and other things like that, equally untrue. Henry calls meetings, makes speeches, and pamphlets are issued from the printing press in our grounds . . . but there is general uneasiness, unrest; and in spite of the increasing communal tension there is no doubt that some Moslems and Hindus are making common cause. I am always hearing the names of Mahomed Ali and Shaukat Ali now for instance, coupled with Gandhi's. In the papers one reads of hartals, the ceasing of all work and fasting. We hear too of Gandhi's "satyagraha" for the first time. All this is mixed up with violent racial bitterness, and economic as well as political discontent.

April 10th

Gandhi has been arrested on his way up to the Punjab. This, Henry says, will certainly mean trouble with the mill-hands at Ahmedabad. Crowds are rioting in Amritsar. Banks attacked. Two bank managers murdered and burned. The station set alight, a European guard killed, and Miss Sherwood the teacher, bicycling to the homes of her Indian girl students in Amritsar warning them not to come to school, is pulled off her bicycle, beaten and left for dead in the street.

April 11th

General Dyer arrives, and forbids all public meetings.

April 13th

The day of the big Horse Fair when thousands of outsiders come in. They attend a prohibited meeting in the Jallianwalla Bagh. They refuse to disperse. General Dyer orders fifty-six of his men to fire on the crowd.

April 15th

Martial Law.

To-night there is a dinner at the Judge's Bungalow. Just as I was finishing dressing Henry came to my room looking grave.

"Hyder Khan is going to sit outside the nursery whilst we are away at dinner. You had better tell Nanny".

Now Hyder Khan despises Nanny for being a half-caste and a Christian, and Nanny with the dreadful inferiority complex of her kind, thinks of the majestic Hyder Khan as just kala log ("black people"), and he knows it. It is always difficult to keep the peace. There must be some unusual reason for Henry to suggest he should not only approach, but sit outside the nursery.

"I'm not happy altogether at leaving Owen to-night", Henry admits.

"I *can't* go, I'll stay at home. Say I've got fever . . . anything . . . ".

But Henry says it is essential we should carry on as usual; that Owen will be safe there with Hyder Khan and the pattawallas, and the sentry down below. So all dressed up, and with my heart thumping, we go off to our dinner party.

We had not got farther than the soup before the Judge's chobdar, all in scarlet, holding his mace, comes in and hands Henry a note. Pretending to talk to the Judge I'm watching him reading it. He gets up abruptly and excusing himself leaves, taking with him John Shillidy. I am left for the dinner, and the long evening afterwards, playing foolish card games, and with a knocking heart wondering what is happening. Why has Henry been called out? And John Shillidy? Where have they gone. Is Owen all right? Are Nanny and Hyder Khan disputing?

By and by I leave. Henry is not at Government House. Owen is safe. Asleep. Hyder Khan lying outside the nursery door.

April 16th

As I went into the kitchen this morning I surprised a naked fakir daubed with ochre and ashes, his hair matted, his eyes wild from bhang. He was in the servants' quarters. "What is that fakir doing here?" I demanded sharply. The second and third mate fell back guiltily, and one or two pattawallas tried to hide in doorways. Hyder Khan met me on my return from the go-down. I told him of the fakir, and looking troubled he declared the Bara Sahib must be informed immediately. I write a note which he himself takes to Henry in his office. From the coded telegrams constantly pouring in we know these holy men are going from place to place, worming their way into households, spreading rumours and disaffection.

These are horrible days. For the past week Henry has ordered that Owen is not to leave the compound. Indeed he has to play immediately in front of the sentry under the palms and the amaltas. It is difficult to explain to Nanny, as the civil population knows nothing and is to be kept unsuspecting. We are on the edge of a volcano. There is dissatisfaction amongst the British troops also, as leave is cancelled.

Henry tells me he thinks it possible that the Commissioner may be struck at through Owen. I am terrified. When we first came up here had I not seen how, in spite of every precaution, the head mali Mahomed, dismissed for gross dishonesty, had yet contrived to poison the whole litter of bull-terrier pups? They were kept in the marble bath room opening out of our bedroom . . . but poisoned they were.

So Nanny and Owen no longer sleep in the nursery, for it has a little outside staircase to it. No. Nanny and Owen's beds stand on the wide verandah that runs the length of the top story. Their beds touch Henry's and mine. The last thing Henry and I do before getting into bed ourselves is to bolt each door which leads into the rooms behind us, and bolt too the windows in the criss-cross jaffery work enclosing the verandah from the night skies. Henry lays a revolver on the charpoy between our two beds, and Lucy, one of the bull-terriers, is brought upstairs. She is not chained to her cot but wanders about, her nails tinkling on the bare boards between the dhurries.

We try to sleep . . . at least Henry does sleep worn out by the day. He has the capacity of the "big man" of sleeping at will. I alas! have not. The more worn out I am the more staringly wide-awake. And anyhow that noise from the bazaar! Incessant tom-toming from the deep voiced dhols, interrupted by bursts of frantic cries and shouts of multitudes. It reminds one of rolling thunder torn across by lightning.

This evening Henry had purposely driven through the Cutchi quarter after tea. (Gandhi's birthplace was Porbander in Cutch). The streets were thronged with Cutchis all flowing in one direction occupying the entire width of the street so that it looked like a torrent in spate. They stared at our crawling car suspiciously. Their numbers appalled me. Why had they poured like this into Karachi? What were they up to? All round the National Bank were piles and piles of stones ready to hand. Building and road making is going on. The temptation is too great. Immediately Henry resolves to have these stone heaps removed. The Cutchis and Marwaris stream on past and round the car, shoulder to shoulder. How strange to feel these Indians with whom one has always been on such friendly terms are suddenly changed into hostile beings ready to stone, to beat, to burn alive? I can't believe it somehow. The car creeps on through the dense crowds. What does Kalu think? We pass the Civil Hospital which, like the Y.W.C.A. and the various banks, is picketed with tommies. Lonely little handfuls of white men they seem in that pouring multitude.

At dinner to-night a cipher telegram is brought in. John Shillidy goes out to decipher it. I didn't like to glance at Henry, for the Hamid Alis are staying here and the Sahib-zada, and Mr. Crump, the judge, have come in to dinner. Mr. Hamid Ali silent and correct in fez, buttoned to the throat in mouse-grey, fine facecloth, his wife very short and plump gurgling with laughter, diamonds in her ears and on her fingers, her Benares sari stiff with gold. The Sahib-zada of Tonk in spotless white with an immense turban, breaking out into ludicrous and indecorous swear-words taught to him by mischievous subalterns in the Hyderabad Mess. (At times I wonder if he does not blunder purposely, seeing what amusement it causes).

John's place remains empty all dinner. After dinner I take Mrs. Hamid Ali into the drawing room. How pretty and peaceful it looks! The chandelier overhead, the parquet floor, and old Persian rugs gleaming like dark jewels beneath, and all the water colours of Sind and Deccan low on the ledges which run round the square pillars that form the archways opening onto the verandah; and beyond that the outer verandah, and beyond that again the moonlit grounds. If only the noise from the bazaar would stop for one moment . . . That new cry becoming so familiar "*Gandhi ki jai!*" and the full-throated wild beast roar that follows, the threatening sound of the tom-toms. It all sounds louder than ever for the wind is blowing from that quarter.

Mrs. Hamid Ali and I both pretend to ignore it. I hang desperately on to the conversation.

We talk of Rohina, Mrs. Hamid Ali's sister, and her glorious voice. Perhaps not a happy choice, for Rohina and her father are devoted admirers of Mr. Gandhi, and have been in slight trouble with the Government. Awkward for Mrs. Hamid Ali whose husband, still sitting in the dining room with Sahib-zada, is in the Indian Civil service . . . a judge! Still talking at random, I look curiously at Mrs. Hamid Ali. Very fat, very dainty and feminine, with a witty tongue and infectious laugh, a diamond winking from one delicate nostril. How feminine to look at . . . yet a strong feminist! What does she think of it all? Is she listening to those wild beast noises from the bazaar?

Suddenly there is such a frenzied outburst, shouting, screaming, and the hurried throbbing of tom-toms, waxing louder and louder, I lose my thread . . . our eyes meet.

"Perhaps I had better speak to my husband . . . ".

I go swiftly to the dining room. Henry is not there. Mr. Hamid Ali and the Sahib-zada are sitting alone.

Both Henry and Mr. Crump have been called out, they tell me.

Where to? Are they down in the bazaar from whence come that tom-toming and those bestial noises, I ask myself wildly? But we all three go decorously into the drawing room, and the two men ask us to sing. Mrs. Hamid Ali has a raucous voice quite unlike Rohina's. She accompanies herself on the vina. My turn now. The air is never free for one moment from the heavy notes of the dhol, or bursts of shouting.

I sing Schubert's *Peace*.

"Don't hurry", I tell myself, but I have to sing too fast or I should have to take a breath in the middle of a line, so nervous I feel. My fingers stick to the keys. I play a wrong note. Ought I to run up to Owen? or do I sing another song?

Ah! Henry returns. White. Fagged. Still in his dress clothes. Nothing is said. Good-night to everybody. We come upstairs. Bolt the doors. Nanny lies asleep there, her fuzzy black head dimly discernible through the curtain nets. Owen asleep, chubby arms flung above his head, silver as thistle-down.

Henry lays a second revolver on the little table between our beds. "Loaded. For you".

It is arranged that if anything happens, and the sentry below is overpowered, and someone gets up here, I must try and get Owen down the little staircase into the servants' quarters. I remember the fakir I had seen there.

"I'm expecting trouble. There may be shooting. Wake me up the moment you hear anything unusual", says Henry.

He gives me a few more directions, and almost in a minute falls asleep.

It is a full moon and windy. The shadows of the palm and the other trees curtsey and sway across our beds and the boarded floor.

I pull up my nets, and stare out at the rattling fronds of the palms through the jaffery work. Incessant threatening tom-toming, now very loud as the wind blew strong, so that the words *Gandhi ki jai* could be distinctly heard, now dying away again so that the sound of the sentry's boots as he passed below came up to me. The night itself was full of noises and creakings. I lay there on my stomach staring out through the jaffery work, glancing over my shoulder one moment at Henry on my right, and at Nanny and the sleeping Owen on my left, then at the revolvers glinting on the little charpoy beside me. The shouting seemed to get nearer. But how much nearer? Do I wake Henry up? It may be just that the wind is blowing more that way. The shadows of the palms move up and down on the walls, and across my bed. The walls glare in the moonlight. Why do I get such a pain in my heart when I'm scared? I feel too as though I am going to be sick.

Suddenly the tom-toming takes on a much quicker, more frenzied note. It starts a dreadful measure in three time, that goes on and on and on, punctuated by bursts of full-throated voices. I think of hounds baying round a stag at bay in some deep Exmoor coombe. I think of that book I had lately read *Indiscreet Letters From Pekin.* I remember my own kinsman the ninth Lord Napier, the ambassador, drummed to death by the Chinese as he lay on board his ship.

"*Dom*-dom-dom. *Dom*-dom-dom. *Dom*-dom-dom".

I glance at Henry again. "Wake me at once at any out of the way noise", he had said. Is this out of the way? I don't know. But listen! A shot. A cry and then the sound of swiftly running feet.

"HENRY!"

But he is out of bed already. Pattawallas come rushing up to the rooms behind us . . .

A tommy had got the jumps and fired. Exactly what Henry has been fearing for days. Enough to start anything . . .

After some time Henry returns. We whisper. Nanny sits up behind her net. "What is it, Madam?"

"Nothing Nanny. Go to sleep".

Henry too falls asleep. I stare out again. I can see the office of the *Daily Gazette* from my bed. If they attack, Henry thinks they will go there first, then to the *Bijli Khana* (the Power House). I remember those little groups of Tommies in the bazaar with their fixed bayonets.

How small and isolated they seemed . . .

Nothing happens. I fall asleep.

All home-going troops are held up. Ships stopped. Troops are disaffected thereby. There has been looting in the bazaar. An unpleasant situation with Calcutta, Amritsar, Ahmedabad, Lahore, Multan, Bombay in uproar. Horrible, most horrible murders. Police beaten, kerosene poured over them and set light to while they are still alive. What a fearful thing a mob! One remembers Balzac's saying "how terrible is the vengeance of a sheep". I think how brave English women were, with their children, in the Afghan war, in the Mutiny; but I am afraid, though Henry does not guess it. The strain of being the only woman but one who knows of the situation. Elsie Martin knows, and she shares my nervousness and apprehensions. She has Jean to think of just as I have Owen. We suffer tortures when our husbands are called out and are away for hours, and that devilish shouting and tom-toming never ceases day or night. She comes to sleep at Government House, and that helps us both. If only there were something to *do*. I suggest to Henry I might take on the job of deciphering the codes. He agrees. I did my first this morning. The code book is kept locked in a safe in Henry's office, and while I am deciphering I am locked in there too. It is a slow but perfectly easy job. My first telegram was full of bloodshed, riots and burning, but with something to do one felt perfectly calm. In fact there is rather a fascination in wondering what is coming out. It reminds me of the transfers one did as a child. I used to like the dipping of the plain white paper in a tooth glass full of water. The laying it on a bit of paper, the careful pulling off, and then the gaudy little picture appearing beneath.. This afternoon there were three very long telegrams. I was locked in for over four hours. Disquieting, horrible incidents . . . trivialities too. How annoying to take some ten minutes spelling out the fact that five muskets and three bags of cartridges had been stolen and subsequently recovered. The Commissioner of the Northern Division has scarcely a sense of proportion.

Mrs. Tuke has had a terrifying time in Ahmedabad. I learned of it first de-coding, and since, I have had a letter from her. She was alone in the bungalow. She heard a great tumult, the servants fled, and the mob armed with sticks and carrying lighted torches came streaming into the compound. Setting fire to the Kutcherry they came rushing on to the bungalow. Colonel Tuke was at the Civil Hospital. Thinking all was up she seized her revolver and came out on to the verandah where the mob were shouting for the doctor . . . Someone shouted that the Colonel Sahib was at the Civil Hospital . . . so the great stream of shouting excited people turned and swept like some horrible muddy flood, sweeping out of the compound on up to the hospital. But Colonel Tuke had received friendly warning, and had managed to escape at the back. This of course she did not know. Impossible to imagine this happening to the quiet Mrs. Tuke I had known in Belgaum!

We were supposed to be sailing for home on May 1st, but I fear no chance of Henry getting off. I have "compassionate leave" because of my lungs, but when I realised Henry would be delayed I elected to stay with him. Now I'm beginning to wonder whether it is right to keep Owen here with the country so unsettled. On the other hand how can I send little inexperienced Nanny all alone to England? She has never left India. I wonder whether I ought to go too. But apart from the personal dislike of being separated from Henry at such a time I do know that I am a help to him. There is the usual strain between the Civil and Military administration. He can talk over things with me. He knows I am safe . . . As I was writing this morning a sealed note is brought up to me from the office. I open it to find this cutting from *Punch,* initialed by Henry:

To the Wife Silent in War-time.

Far as the Empire's bounds are flung
She shall be honoured, she shall be sung
Who keeps safe locked within her breast
Unboasted, unbetrayed, unguessed,
Bound as with triple chains of gold,
What things her soldier lord hath told.

O woman, in our hours of ease
Careless in chatter as the seas,
When pain and anguish wring the brow
(In point of fact precisely now),
Accept the homage of a bard
Who knows it more than common hard
To hear unmoved from age and youth,
Rumours when you must know the truth!

To hear them ever seeking why
And smiling put the question by,
But when the Dawn shall break at last
And the long vigilance be past

Be yours this recompense sublime
To say "I knew it all the time".

I was never more proud of anything in all my life.

Henry feels if only Government would let him do what he wishes he could crush the Karachi trouble in a week. I wonder? The mob is so thoroughly roused. High prices and hunger adding to the persuasions of the political few, and all this coming on the top of the war, and the ravages of influenza. Of course I don't know much, but just what Henry calls the novelist in me, tells me the politicians have purposely raised the mob to such a pitch, as an answer to our assertion that it is THEY who oppress the poor whereas We are their friends!

Good Friday

No tom-toming to speak of for two nights. Probably because the villains of the piece are away at the moment. Be that as it may, things are much quieter. Henry said Nanny could go to her church, Owen was left in charge of Ayah and pattawallas, and he and I went to the Parade service. There I was perturbed, for presently a soldier came up and fetched Major Tobin out as he sat beside the General, and then the C.I.D. man was also called out. Immediately after came the sound of heavy motor traffic, machine guns and armoured cars thundering past. The mournful Good Friday hymn was unheard amid that thundering and vibration.

Henry is calling a meeting of all citizens by order. He intends speaking his mind. He will tell them that even as they sit listening to him, arrests of influential people are being made. Mr. Bhurgri is the arch villain, and there will be amazement and consternation when they learn so influential a person is for it, and this will have a salutory effect. (I don't know whether Henry intends giving out his name at this meeting). It will be intensely exciting.

Of course one cannot help feeling apprehensive for Henry whilst he is actually speaking, but I am sure the plan is good. There will be machine guns and police, tommies and armoured cars surrounding the building. Henry will have his automatic in his pocket. (Unfortunately he has very little ammunition).

I want to go with him. He says "Out of the question". I appeal to John. John says he thinks it might be a very good thing if I do go. He argues. Henry does listen. It is one of the very rare occasions in my life I have seen him persuaded. It is decided I go.

April 27th

Henry is making internments and arrests even as I write. The great Mr. B is at the point of arrest. Roy Horniman, Editor of the *Bombay Chronicle,* is being deported to-day. Everything is quieting down. No tom-toms. Hyderabad and Karachi are alarmed at the machine-guns and armoured cars in their midst. But the Punjab is still disturbed. There they have soaked the clothes of living Europeans with kerosene and set light to them. In their madness they have even set fire to the grain set aside for famine relief. The staunchness of the native police is amazing, magnificent. These men face horrible death from their own people for the paltry sum of fourteen annas a day.

The meeting is over and was a great success. The Hall was packed and packed again. "Citizens by order". It was intensely exciting for me as I watched Henry mounting the dais, I alone knowing what he was about to announce. I was, of course, the only woman present. The tension was tremendous. Henry spoke in a clear ringing voice . . . but suddenly all was blotted out for me by appalling pain in my heart and all down my left arm. Exactly the same as attacked me that night eighteen months before on the *Jhelum* after that wild headlong gallop from Larkhana. I defy anyone to be conscious of anything but their own pain in a spasm such as this . . .

The whole affair has been mismanaged, and Henry will have to pay the price. When Mr. Bhurgri's house was raided by the police, it was found he had been warned. He had gone, and all incriminating documents had been destroyed.

Anxious days. Conferences behind closed doors in Henry's office. The General shut in there with his staff; the District Magistrates from Hyderabad and Karachi, the Police Superintendent. Many cars parked outside. I see little of Henry, and at night he looks so tired I forbear to question. He says little.

Bhurgri had been the mainspring of the agitation. He was the Secretary of the Congress and in close touch with Gandhi. An energetic and clever man, Bhurgi; a barrister-at-law, and a rich landlord. He lived at Hyderabad, and when he saw trouble imminent, skipped to one of his many country estates. As Henry remarked a little drily to me, the Hyderabad officials were singularly innocent to expect him to leave incriminating evidence in his Hyderabad house!

Henry must pay for this innocence . . .

Like all strong men he has his enemies, and now the jackals are yapping. Soon they will be in full cry. Hitherto criticised for his forward policy towards the Indian, that he should now be condemned as a reactionary tyrant! Very piquant.

For he has been marked out for savage attack by the Hindu political press of Sind, supported by the extreme press of Bombay, and the home-rule organ of Madras, for the reason that since coming here, he has been indefatigable in transferring much official power from the Hindu clique that oppress Sind, though they only number one quarter of the Mahomedan population. Also during those troublous days in April he had stirred up the resentment of wealthy influential members of Kathiawar and Cutch by deporting three of them as undesirables.

Now they mean to break my Henry. And I am not sure they won't. When open rebellion started in the Punjab the Viceroy had declared he would support all officers who kept the peace anywhere . . . but how many men in past history have been "broken" in spite of official promises?

One Harchandrai, an Amil, has fled with Mr. Bhurgri to Bombay, beseeching the Governor to protect them from the "tyranny of the Honourable Mr. H. S. Lawrence, Commissioner-in-Sind". Now the Governor had from the first regarded Henry with suspicion, if not dislike. So he promptly sends up the Advocate-General from Bombay to investigate this case. There are more endless conferences. I have to sit next the Advocate-General at meals and talk prettily to him, though I feel him to be an enemy, as indeed the poor man has to be in making out the case for Bhurgri and Harchandrai.

All this time there is serious trouble with Afghanistan. My old lady was right. The British troops kept from sailing are giving the G.O.C. much anxiety. They are disaffected. Daily there are endless consultations and difficulties in solving Civil and Military Administration. Henry has all this on the top of the other. Our sailing is so long delayed that our temporary successors the future "Acting-Commissioner-in-Sind" and his wife have already taken up residence in Government House. This does not make for comfort. Our servants bitterly resent them, and one day little Nanny comes to me blazing. She has learned that the "New Commissioner Memsahib" has already given orders to the P.W.D. that the day we leave the house "Moushie! Moushie!" is to be painted off the nursery walls. Ah! well! There will certainly be the new and pretty chintzes in the drawing room which Henry has not allowed me to buy, and champagne will be given at all dinner parties, and the Y.M.C.A. will not be encouraged to share their "Socials" with the Y.W.C.A. and the Railway staff, and the Matron of the Dufferin will have to acknowledge the flowers from Government House . . . but all this is little enough. What of my Henry's labour? Hindus reinstated in the posts the Mahomedans should have. His incessant teaching of Sindis to grow better qualities of wheat and cotton, the pressing forward of the Sukkur Barrage allowed to lapse . . .

"Then I looked on all the works that my hands had wrought and on labours that I had laboured to do; and behold all was vanity, and vexation of spirit, and there was no profit under the sun.

Yea, I hated all my labours which I had taken under the sun; because I should leave unto the man that shall be after me. And who knoweth whether he shall be a wise man or a fool? Yet shall he have rule over all my labour wherein I have laboured and wherein I have showed myself wise under the sun. This is also vanity".

L'ENVOI.

Henry's last official act before leaving Sind was to write to Sir George Lloyd a detailed account of the turmoil and the action he had taken. This letter never reached him, as Henry learned twelve months later. It had probably been intercepted. In the meantime Bhurgri and Harchandrai, known to be implicated in stirring up riots, and now thoroughly frightened, had fled to England to interview Edwin Montagu, the Secretary of State. He was much impressed by their plausible tale, and at once wrote out to the Governor of Bombay that he had managed the trouble in the Presidency proper very well, "but that Sind was a black spot on the record".

At that time Henry and I were in London. Lunching one day at the Piccadilly Restaurant who should we see sitting a few tables away but Bhurgri and Harchandrai. Henry had no notion they were in England, but instantly guessed they had come to vilify him, and capture the sympathy of the Secretary of State . . . Now this is just the sort of situation in which Henry's particular brand of humour delights.

Up he saunters, and with perfect composure gossips to the two about Sind while they show ever increasing discomfiture.

But they had won the first trick all the same. For six months later, at the end of Henry's furlough, when we were looking forward to our return to Sind, Montagu, through Sir George Lloyd, informed him he was "dissatisfied with his conduct in Sind". He was not to return. He would be posted to one of the Presidency Divisions, which meant not only loss of pay, but position.

It was clear that Montagu meant Henry to plead for pardon, and Sir George Lloyd meant him to resign from the service.

But Henry did not mean to do either.

Shortly after he noticed that the Secretary of State was billed to take the chair at a Royal Arts lecture on Indian ports. Now Henry had been in charge of the important port of Karachi during the war, so he informed the secretary that he himself would speak.

It was after this that the Secretary of State sent for Henry, and subsequently told a mutual friend that he had been completely misinformed about him. He cabled to the Governor of Bombay, Sir George Lloyd, that Henry would be doing special duty at Whitehall Treasury on special pay, and would after return to the Bombay Government as Chief Secretary. This meant no loss of pay, or promotion . . . though, alas, no more wandering through village, jungle or desert for me . . . In April, 1921, Montagu appointed Henry as Finance Member of Council, and he finally became Acting-Governor of the Province.

It was twelve years later that Lord Lloyd very generously said to Henry one day at dinner: "You must have known long since that I recognised in the Sind affair you were right and I was wrong". But in the interval the hatchet had been buried. Both had recognised the good qualities of the other. Indeed Henry was to stick up stoutly for the Back Bay Reclamation Scheme for which Lloyd had been criticised, when the enormous profits that were at one time anticipated failed to materialise . . . "I am one of those who believe that the work is well worth doing for the country as a whole", declared Henry.

In lighter vein, I remember a speech at a farewell dinner party given to Henry by three Indian Ministers. "Lord Lloyd", said Henry, "burst upon this Presidency like a brilliant comet, emerging from the lurid background of the clouds of war. A comet is, I believe, the fastest thing known to science and is commonly regarded as carrying death and destruction to all that comes in its track. This comparison is therefore singularly inept, and I should explain at once that it is my privilege through the irony of fate to stand up and say this particular comet was different. It was a good kind comet, and its beneficent work will redound to the benefit and glory of Bombay in the future".

Now Indians, contrary to the usual idea, have a keen sense of humour. They had been well aware of the uproar in Whitehall over Sind, and the idea of Sir George Lloyd having been "good and kind" to Sir Henry Lawrence at that time, tickled them beyond measure.

ERRATA

On page 86, line 1, *for* Belgaum *read* Bombay Presidency.

The reference to Roy Horniman on line 7 of page 392 is entirely mistaken, an error which the author and publisher deeply regret and for which they have already apologized to the press.